The Skeptic's Guide
to American History

Mark A. Stoler, Ph.D.

THE
GREAT
COURSES

PUBLISHED BY:

THE GREAT COURSES
Corporate Headquarters
4840 Westfields Boulevard, Suite 500
Chantilly, Virginia 20151-2299
Phone: 1-800-832-2412
Fax: 703-378-3819
www.thegreatcourses.com

Mark A. Stoler, Ph.D.
Professor Emeritus of History
The University of Vermont

Professor Mark A. Stoler is Professor Emeritus of History at The University of Vermont, where he specialized for almost 40 years in U.S. diplomatic and military history. He received his B.A. from The City College of New York and his M.A. and Ph.D. from the University of Wisconsin–Madison.

Professor Stoler is the author of *The Politics of the Second Front: American Military Planning and Diplomacy in Coalition Warfare, 1941–1943*; *Explorations in American History: A Skills Approach*, with Marshall True; *George C. Marshall: Soldier-Statesman of the American Century*; *Allies and Adversaries: The Joint Chiefs of Staff, the Grand Alliance, and U.S. Strategy in World War II*; *Debating Franklin D. Roosevelt's Foreign Policies, 1933–1945*, with Justus D. Doenecke; and *Allies in War: Britain and America Against the Axis Powers, 1940–1945*. In addition, he has written numerous articles and book chapters on U.S. diplomatic and military history. Professor Stoler is the editor of *The Origins of the Cold War* and *Major Problems in the History of World War II: Documents and Essays*, with Melanie S. Gustafson and Thomas Paterson.

Professor Stoler has been a visiting professor at the U.S. Naval War College, a Fulbright Lecturer at the University of Haifa in Israel, a visiting professor at the U.S. Military Academy at West Point, the Harold K. Johnson Visiting Professor at the U.S. Army Military History Institute, the Stanley Kaplan Visiting Professor of American Foreign Policy at Williams College, and a visiting professor and the Robert S. Griffith, Jr. '52 Visiting Scholar at Washington and Lee University.

Professor Stoler's multiple awards include the Distinguished Book Award of the Society for Military History for *Allies and Adversaries*; inclusion in *Who's Who Among America's Teachers*; The University of Vermont's George

V. Kidder Outstanding Faculty Award, University Scholar Award, Dean's Lecture Award, and Kroepsch-Maurice Excellence in Teaching Award; honorary membership in the university's chapter of Phi Beta Kappa; and two public service awards from the U.S. Army.

Professor Stoler was a member of the Board of Trustees of the Society for Military History and a Presidential Counselor to the National World War II Museum; he has also served on the U.S. Army Historical Advisory Committee and the Board of Directors of the World War Two Studies Association. He was a member and the 2004 president of the Council of the Society for Historians of American Foreign Relations. Since 2008, he has been the editor of *The Papers of George Catlett Marshall*, with volume 6 scheduled to appear in fall 2012 and volume 7 scheduled for 2014.

Professor Stoler has previously taught *America and the World: A Diplomatic History* for The Great Courses. ■

Table of Contents

Table of Contents

Table of Contents

SUPPLEMENTAL MATERIAL

The Skeptic's Guide to American History

Scope:

Everyone recognizes as myths the idea that Columbus was the first to discover America or the story that George Washington admitted cutting down a cherry tree. But very few people realize how much of what we think we know about American history is also mythical and mistaken. As historians often emphasize, many popular beliefs about history in general—and about U.S. history in particular—are myths, either totally false or, at best, only half true.

In this course, we will examine some of these myths, such as those concerning the origins of religious tolerance in America, the American Revolution, George Washington, the causes of the Civil War, the causes and conduct of World War II and the Cold War, and America's supposed history of isolationism and anti-imperialism, as well as our government's laissez-faire policies regarding business. But the course is far from limited to challenging these and other myths. It will also examine how and why these myths arose and what historians now say about what really happened—as opposed to what most Americans believe happened.

In the process, we will also explore the complexities of history and just what historians do. In that exploration, we will again challenge popular misconceptions—this time about the study of history itself. For example, it is often said that those who cannot remember the past are condemned to repeat it, but the idea that history repeats itself is a myth. It does not. World War II was not a replay of World War I in this regard, and the Cold War was not a replay of World War II; the belief that they were led to disastrous consequences.

Beyond challenging such misconceptions, we will explore some of the important but little known realities of historical study, most notably the law of unintended consequences and the need to separate results of actions from their causes and the motivations of those who acted. We will also examine the pitfalls of projecting contemporary values onto the past and other forms of anachronistic thinking, the changing meaning of key words over time, how and why people and events in history are lost and then rediscovered, and the differences between history and memory.

Below are just a few examples of the questions this course will consequently raise and attempt to answer:

- Did religious toleration truly begin in America's colonial history? And if not, when did it arise?

- Was the American Revolution less revolutionary (and less American) than we commonly believe?

- What were George Washington's numerous failures and most important contributions to American history, and why are they commonly overlooked?

- What is the difference between separation of church and state and separation of religion and politics?

- Why is empire-building a surprisingly constant feature of U.S. history?

- Was slavery truly the major cause of the Civil War? And if so, how?

- Has the United States ever had a truly laissez-faire approach to economics?

- When and why did states' rights become a rallying cry not only in the South but also in New England?

- Is Woodrow Wilson overrated? Is Herbert Hoover underrated?

- Who have been America's greatest presidents and according to what standards?

- How have such important concepts as "progressive" and "populism" changed drastically from what they originally meant?

- Just what did Franklin Roosevelt's New Deal do and not do?

- How does our collective memory and commemoration of World War II differ from the actual history of that conflict?

- Was the Cold War inevitable, and why did it occur and last so long?

- What were America's true blunders during the Vietnam War?

- Who are some of the most notable but often forgotten figures in American history, and why have they been forgotten in comparison to their contemporaries?

- How dramatic and consequential are contemporary changes in American life compared to previous changes in U.S. history?

In this skeptical journey through American history, we will consider anew key people, events, periods, and legacies and gain a much deeper understanding of the extraordinary history of the United States. ∎

Religious Toleration in Colonial America?
Lecture 1

T wo well-known historical myths about Christopher Columbus are that he discovered America and that he proved the earth was round rather than flat. Of course, in reality, educated people had for centuries believed the world was round. A great deal of what we think we know and believe about American history is just as wrong as these myths about Columbus. In this course, we will identify some of those myths and examine how and why they arose.

Myths and Realities of Historical Study

- These lectures are devoted to identifying myths of American history and learning what historians now say about the true course of events in our past. In the process of this exploration, we will also challenge popular misconceptions about the study of history itself.

- As we will see throughout these lectures, history does not consist of rote memorization of facts about the past, and those facts do not "speak for themselves." Further, history does not repeat itself, nor can we draw lessons from these supposed repetitions. It's also not true that history and memory are synonymous; they are, in fact, separate and often antithetical to each other.

- Among the important realities of historical study is what historians sometimes call the law of unintended consequences—the fact that consequences of human actions often differ sharply from the motivations of those who acted. Columbus, for example, wanted to find a western water route to the Indies, not "discover" America.

- Further, we often select facts to study in history on the basis of those unintended consequences. For example, even though Columbus was not the first European to "discover" the Americas, his explorations are far more important historically than those of Leif Eriksson because of their enormous consequences.

The Myth of Religious Toleration in America

- Many people believe that toleration arrived in North America with English colonists who were seeking religious freedom, beginning with the Pilgrims in 1620 and proceeding through the establishment of all 13 colonies. That is not the case.

- Many colonies, including Virginia and New York, were founded for non-religious reasons, and even in colonies that were religiously founded, many colonists came for non-religious reasons.

- Moreover, religious toleration was not considered a virtue at the time. Even a desire to escape from religious persecution in Europe usually did not lead to a belief in tolerance for others. As a result, colonial history is filled with religious conflict and persecution. Puritans, for example, persecuted and banned virtually anyone who disagreed with them.

Much of what we believe about American history is as untrue as the myth that Columbus discovered America.

- Toleration did begin to develop during the colonial era but only gradually—and largely accidentally.
    - For those who came to North America seeking religious freedom and an end to their persecution, religion was central to their entire belief system and worldview. Almost by definition, then, they could not conceive of another belief system as valid.

    - Indeed, the Pilgrims who arrived in Plymouth in 1620 were not escaping religious persecution in England but toleration in the Netherlands, where they had moved and where they feared their youth would be led astray.

    - The Puritans who arrived in Massachusetts Bay a decade later banished dissenters in their own Congregationalist denomination, such as Roger Williams and Anne Hutchinson, as well as those from other denominations or religions, and executed those who violated such banishment.

    - Furthermore, religious warfare broke out in colonies that did allow other denominations and religions. Maryland, for example, was founded by George Calvert (Lord Baltimore) as a haven for persecuted Catholics but soon had a Protestant majority—and a virtual civil war between the two.

The Development of Toleration

- Religious toleration was partially established by Puritan dissenters, most notably Roger Williams. After he was banished from Massachusetts Bay, Williams founded Rhode Island and is known to us for his insistence on the separation of church and state, as well as his opposition to forced worship.
    - Not well known is the fact that Williams wanted separation of church and state in hopes of maintaining the purity of the Puritan church against a corrupt state, not vice versa! Unlike the Puritans, who sought to reform the corrupt Anglican Church, Williams also wanted total separation from the Church of England.

o Equally unknown is the fact that in his continuing efforts to create a pure church and retain his own purity, Williams's separatism accelerated in Rhode Island until "he could not conscientiously have communion with anyone but his wife." At that point, he realized the error of his ways and admitted sinners into his church and all denominations to his colony.

o Williams, in short, was a religious absolutist and purist who came to toleration only gradually and only by a series of what we would consider backdoors.

• Toleration also resulted from settlers more interested in profits than religion, particularly the Dutch in New Amsterdam. In the mid-1650s, these settlers even allowed the first Jewish community in what would eventually become New York.

• Another partial explanation for the development of toleration can be found in the negative example of the English Civil Wars during the 1640s, followed by the execution of the English king and the establishment of a Puritan dictatorship under Oliver Cromwell. This experience illustrated where both religious and political conflict could lead. Greater tolerance arose in England after the restoration of the monarchy in 1660.

• It's also true that no one Christian denomination was dominant in all 13 colonies, which led many groups who feared persecution by others to support toleration as a means of protecting themselves. Maryland's famous 1649 Act of Religious Toleration, for example, was approved by Calvert's son, Cecilius, to protect Catholics against a Protestant majority, but it was passed by a Protestant legislature to protect them against Calvert's Catholics!

• Finally, toleration was partially the result of the founding of a new colony in the 1640s, Pennsylvania, by a new and more tolerant denomination, William Penn's Quakers.

Why Do We Believe the Myth?

- Our belief in the myth of toleration may be the result of a tendency to confuse colonial practice with the First Amendment to the Constitution, which banned any state-established religion and established legal toleration of all religions. But that amendment passed in 1791 and should not be confused with events that occurred more than a century and a half earlier.
  - Furthermore, the First Amendment banned only Congress from establishing a state religion (i.e., the federal government), not the individual states.

  - Only with the Fourteenth Amendment in 1868 and 20th-century Supreme Court rulings was state-established religion completely prohibited.

- Even more anachronistic and incorrect than this projection of events from 1791–1833 onto the 1600s is a tendency to project our contemporary values onto the past in the process of attempting to discover the roots of those values. The praise of Roger Williams serves as a classic example in this regard. He did indeed call for tolerance and the separation of church and state but in the interests of protecting what he considered his true church from the corruption of the state.

- Further, the passage of the First Amendment and the later disestablishment of Congregationalism in New England by no means resulted in religious tolerance as we understand the term today. Toleration did not translate into social acceptance, and plenty of religious prejudice existed in 19th- and 20th-century U.S. history, as well as in 17th- and 18th-century colonial history.
  - Anti-Catholicism, a deep prejudice in much of U.S. history, reached a peak of sorts with the anti-immigrant and anti-Catholic Know-Nothing party of the 1850s, which fused religious and racial intolerance and almost eclipsed the newly founded Republican Party as the successor to the Whigs and the second major political party.

- Anti-Catholicism reemerged in the 20th century with the rise of the Ku Klux Klan and played a role in the defeat of the Catholic Al Smith in the presidential election of 1928. The 1920s also witnessed a major wave of anti-Semitism.

The Real Emergence of Religious Toleration

- Religious tolerance has historical roots in early colonial history, but it didn't emerge in its modern form until the second half of the 20th century, primarily as a result of World War II.

- Hitler's racist ideas came from more than a century of European and American thinking and practice. However, in witnessing the hideous consequences of the literal implementation of those ideas, Americans finally began to question their religious and racial prejudices.

- Simultaneously, defeating Hitler required placing more than 15 million Americans in uniform—many of whom saw and interacted with other Americans of different religions and races for the first time.

- The impact of this awakening on many Americans was profound and nearly immediate. In just a few years after the war, Major League Baseball was integrated, a film about anti-Semitism in America won the Oscar for Best Picture, Truman ordered the integration of the armed forces and supported recognition of the state of Israel, and the Supreme Court ordered integration of the public schools.

A Skeptical Approach

- What we've said in this lecture exemplifies the broader approach that we will take throughout this course. Specifically, our skeptical approach will involve paying attention to the law of unintended consequences—the fact that the consequences of human actions often differ quite sharply from the motivations of those who acted.

- We must also be wary of anachronistic thinking, that is, distorting the past by dealing with events and ideas out of their proper chronological order and context. As we saw in this lecture, such thinking often takes the form of projecting contemporary values onto the past.

- We will further see how key words change meaning and significance over time. Religious toleration once meant not killing one another and accepting that others might live in the same colony. Today, toleration tends to have a much broader meaning than it did in previous centuries.

- Finally, we see that history and memory are not the same. Our memory and ensuing commemoration of the origins of events and ideas often differ quite dramatically from historical reality.

Suggested Reading

Morgan, *The Puritan Dilemma*.

Questions to Consider

1. Why do we tend to equate the desire to escape religious persecution with a desire for religious freedom and tolerance?

2. Why do we assume that 17th-century Europeans thought the same way about religion that we do today?

Religious Toleration in Colonial America?
Lecture 1—Transcript

Two well-known historical myths about Christopher Columbus are that he discovered America, and that he proved the earth was round rather than flat.

In reality, educated people had for centuries believed that the world was round; the disagreement was over its circumference. In this debate Columbus was wrong: He substantially underestimated that circumference; and had North and South America not existed, he and his men probably would have starved long before they could reach the Far East. In addition, Leif Erikson and other Norsemen had long before Columbus—nearly 500 years earlier—become the first Europeans to discover, explore, and colonize the North American coast, down to Newfoundland. Of course, millennia before Erikson—about 20,000 years ago—numerous people had walked from Siberia to Alaska across the land bridge that had previously existed across what is now the Bering Sea and had migrated south.

These two myths about Columbus are well-known; but a great deal of what we think we know about American history, and subsequently believe, is equally mythical and wrong. This course is "A Skeptic's Guide to American History," and a key aspect of the course will be identifying these myths.

What is a skeptic? A skeptic is an individual who frequently asks questions about widely accepted ideas and facts. Almost by definition, the serious student of history must be a skeptic; for as historians know and often emphasize in their classes, many popular beliefs about history in general—and about U.S. history in particular—are myths, either totally false or, at best, only half true. I often quip that my two introductory courses in U.S. history should really be entitled "Iconoclasm I" and "Iconoclasm II."

In this course, we will examine these myths of U.S. history, but not only the myths. We will also examine how and why they arose and what historians now say about what really happened, as opposed to what most Americans believe happened. In the case of these Columbus myths, two causes were probably: Washington Irving, who in a bestselling work first published in 1828 disseminated this mythology about proving the earth was round; and the ignorance of that time, as well as lack of physical evidence about both Erikson and the land bridge to Asia.

In process of examining these myths, their origins and their historical realities, we will also explore the complexities of history and just what historians do. In that exploration, the course will once again challenge popular misconceptions, this time about the study of history itself.

Specifically, history does not consist of rote memorization of facts about the past, and those facts do not "speak for themselves." I often tell my introductory courses that I have never seen a talking fact; and I ask my students, "Have you?" Facts do not speak, human beings do; and human beings both select and organize facts about the past so as to make sense out of it.

In addition, history does not repeat itself, and the incorrect belief that it does often leads to faulty analogies between past and present with tragic, often disastrous consequences. Two examples of this are the French construction of the Maginot Line during the 1930s in the incorrect belief that any new war would be a repeat of the First World War and, as we will see in a future lecture, Cold War thinking that Joseph Stalin was a reincarnation of Adolf Hitler.

Along with this incorrect belief that history repeats itself often goes the equally incorrect belief that one can draw clear lessons from these supposed repetitions. But as the political scientist Bernard Brodie accurately noted more than 45 years ago, "The phrase 'history teaches,' when encountered in argument, usually portends bad history and worse logic."

Another fallacy is the belief that history and memory are synonymous, or nearly so. In truth, they are separate, and they are often antithetical to each other.

Beyond challenging such misconceptions, this course will explore some of the important realities of historical study. For example, what historians often call the law of unintended consequences; the fact that consequences of human actions often differ quite sharply from the motivations of those who acted. Columbus, for example, wanted to find a western water route to the Indies, not "discover" America (and he incorrectly thought he had found that route, which is why he called the native inhabitants he met "Indians"). In addition, we select facts to study in history on the basis of those often unintended consequences. Even though Columbus was not the first European to "discover" the Americas, his explorations in this regard are far more important historically than those of Leif Erikson because of their enormous consequences. Nothing permanent and important came of Erikson's explorations, but 500 years later, Europe was ready to exploit Columbus's discovery and colonize the Americas; which it did, and which eventually led to the creation of the United States and numerous other nations.

The Columbus myths concerned world history. Now let's examine a myth more specific to American history. To begin our exploration of the complexities of U.S. history, let us take a close look at the origins of religious toleration in America.

The common belief is that toleration arrived with the English colonists who were seeking religious freedom, beginning with the Pilgrims in 1620 and proceeding through the establishment of all 13 colonies. That is not the case. First of all, many colonies—Virginia, New York, for example—were founded for non-religious reasons; and even in colonies that were religiously founded, many colonists came for non-religious reasons. Secondly, religious toleration was not considered a virtue at this time. Even a desire to escape from religious persecution in Europe usually did not lead to a belief in tolerance for others. As a result, Colonial history is filled with religious conflict and persecution. Puritans, for example, persecuted and banned virtually anyone who disagreed with them. Toleration did begin to develop during the Colonial Era, but only gradually and largely accidentally.

For those who did come to North America seeking religious freedom and an end to their persecution, religion was central to their entire belief system and worldview. That being the case, almost by definition they could not conceive of another belief system being valid. Indeed, if they admitted that, they would have to question the validity of their own belief system. It may be difficult for us to understand this today. One way to do so is to view 17th-century religion as we view democracy today in the 21st century. Given our belief in democracy, and the centrality of that belief to our worldview, we cannot and we do not view alternative political beliefs as in any way valid. Nor have we in the past: Fascism, Nazism, Communism, and Islamic Fundamentalism are all considered antithetical to democracy and have been labeled as enemies to be fought.

Similarly, 17th-century religious believers viewed alternative religious views as enemies to be fought, or to be escaped if they were too powerful to be fought. Religious conflicts and wars had thus wracked Europe throughout much of its history: Christian against Moslem, Protestant against Catholic, Protestant against Protestant.

The dissenters who came to the New World to escape persecution did not come to tolerate others who were also escaping persecution. Indeed, the Pilgrims who arrived in Plymouth in 1620 were by that time escaping not religious persecution in England, but actually toleration in the Netherlands where they had moved; that toleration, they feared, would lead their youth astray. Even more telling was the attitude of the Puritans under John Winthrop who arrived in Massachusetts Bay a decade later. They banished dissenters from their own Congregationalist denomination, such as Roger Williams and Anne Hutchinson, as well as those from other denominations and they executed those who violated such banishment. In addition, religious warfare broke out in colonies that did allow other denominations and religions. Maryland, for example, was founded by George Calvert (Lord Baltimore) as a haven for persecuted Catholics, but it soon had a Protestant majority and a virtual civil war between the two.

How, then, and why did religious toleration develop in America? It had numerous sources. Partially it was established by Puritan dissenters, most notably Roger Williams, who, when he was banished, founded Rhode Island and is known to us for his insistence on separation of church and state as well as his opposition to forced worship, which he said "stinks in the nostrils of God." But in this case, religious toleration came as an almost accidental byproduct of his other concerns.

Not well known is the fact that Williams wanted separation of church and state in hopes of maintaining the purity of the church against the corrupt state, not vice versa. The state as a human institution was corrupt by definition. Williams wanted to maintain the purity of the Puritan Church by totally separating from the state. He also wanted to maintain that purity—as had the Pilgrims previously—by separating from the corrupted Church of England. Puritans in Massachusetts Bay, on the other hand, wanted to reform that corrupted Anglican Church via the example of their model Christian community in Massachusetts Bay. Williams's insistence on total separation from the Church of England was one of the key factors that led to his banishment from Massachusetts Bay and founding of Rhode Island.

Equally unknown is the fact that in his continuing efforts to create a pure church and retain his own purity, Williams separatism accelerated in Rhode Island until "he could not conscientiously have communion with anyone" except his wife, at which point he did realize the error of his ways and admitted sinners into his church and all denominations into his colony. As Winthrop wrote—in obvious disagreement and amusement, if not total disgust—"Having, a little before, refused communion with all, save his own wife, now he would preach to and pray with all comers." Williams, in short, was a religious absolutist and purist who came to toleration only gradually and by a series of what we would consider back doors.

Toleration also resulted from settlers more interested in profits than religion, most notably the Dutch in New Amsterdam, who in the mid-1650s even allowed the first Jewish community in what would eventually become New York and part of the U.S. Partially toleration developed because of the negative example of the English Civil War during the 1640s between Parliament and the King—a war at least partially religious in nature—followed by the execution of the king and the establishment of a Puritan dictatorship under Oliver Cromwell. That illustrated where religious as well as political conflict could lead, and it led to greater tolerance in England after the restoration of the monarchy in 1660. Partially toleration resulted from the fact that no one Christian denomination was dominant in all 13 colonies, or even within many colonies, and this led many groups who feared persecution by others to support toleration as a means of protecting themselves. Maryland's famous 1649 Act of Religious Toleration, for example, was approved by Calvert's son Cecilius to protect Catholics against a Protestant majority but it was passed by a Protestant legislature to protect them against Calvert's Catholics. Furthermore, it applied only to Trinitarian Christians, and actually sentenced to death anyone who denied the divinity of Jesus Christ.

In addition to all these reasons, toleration was also the result of a new and more tolerant denomination that founded a new colony in the 1680s: William Penn's Quakers in Pennsylvania. Nevertheless, religious conflicts continued to divide the colonists and led to serious conflicts throughout Colonial history.

Given these facts, why do we believe that the early colonists brought toleration to North America with them? It may be the result of a tendency to confuse Colonial practice with the First Amendment to the Constitution: That First Amendment banned any state-established religion and it established legal toleration of all religions, as well as the right of free speech, free press, peaceful assembly, and petition. But that First Amendment passed in 1791, and should not be confused with what had occurred more than a century and a half earlier. To do so is a classic example of anachronistic thinking; of projecting the document and values of one time period onto an earlier time period where it does not belong or fit.

In addition, the 1st Amendment banned only Congress—and thus the Federal Government—from establishing a state religion, not the individual states. The Anglican Church—which had sided with the king and been disestablished in the southern colonies where previously it had been the official religion— when that disestablishment took place, a similar disestablishment did not take place for Congregationalism in New England. Congregationalism remained the established religion in Vermont, New Hampshire, Connecticut, and Massachusetts until the first few decades of the 19th century. Indeed, Massachusetts did not disestablish Congregationalism until 1833; and only with the 14th Amendment to the Constitution in 1868 and 20th-century Supreme Court rulings was state-established religion completely prohibited.

Even more anachronistic and incorrect than this projection of events from 1791–1833 on to the 1600s is a tendency to project our contemporary values onto the past in the process of attempting to discover the roots of those values. The praise of Roger Williams today serves as a classic example in this regard. He did indeed call for tolerance and for the separation of church and state, but in the interests of protecting what he considered his true and pure church from the corruption of the state, not vice versa. Furthermore, the passage of the First Amendment to the Constitution as part of the Bill of Rights in 1791 and the later disestablishment of Congregationalism in New England by no means established or resulted in religious tolerance as we understand that word today. Toleration did not translate in any way into social acceptance, and plenty of religious prejudice existed in 19th- and 20th-century U.S. history as well as 17th- and 18th-century Colonial history.

Anti-Catholicism, a deep but now almost forgotten prejudice, existed throughout much of American history and reached a peak of sorts with the anti-immigrant and anti-Catholic national party known as the Know Nothing Party of the 1850s. That party fused religious intolerance with racial intolerance, and it almost eclipsed the newly-founded Republican Party as the successor to the Whigs as the second major political party in the country. This anti-Catholicism also reemerged in the 20th century with the rise of the new Ku Klux Klan, which during that time period expanded its messages of hate from race to religion in the North as well as the South. Anti-Catholicism also appeared in the defeat of Catholic Al Smith in the presidential election of 1928. No Catholic would be elected or even nominated again for the presidency until 1960.

Interestingly, the 1920s also witnessed a major wave of anti-Semitism, one fanned and illustrated by the following quote from the 1921–1922 publication *The International Jew: the World's Foremost Problem*:

> The immigration problem is Jewish. The money question is Jewish. The tie-up of world politics is Jewish. The terms of the peace treaty [that had ended World War I] are Jewish. The diplomacy of the world is Jewish. The moral question in movies and theaters is Jewish. The mystery of the illicit liquor business is Jewish.

That statement comes not from Adolf Hitler, but from the writings and publications of Henry Ford; writings that preceded Hitler's and were known to him.

Religious tolerance as we understand the two words is thus a recent phenomenon. It does have historical roots in early Colonial history, but not roots as direct or as strong as we tend to believe.

If that's the case, just when and why did religious toleration as we know it today emerge? Primarily, I would argue, in the second half of the 20th century, and largely as a result of World War II. At the risk of sounding flippant, Hitler gave intolerance and racism a bad name in this country. His racist ideas—and really all of his ideas—came from over a century of European and American thinking and practice; the only original thing about him was that he was a literalist in implementing those ideas. Only in witnessing the hideous consequences of the literal implementation of those ideas did Americans truly begin to question their old religious prejudices as well as their old racial prejudices.

Simultaneously, defeating Hitler required placing more than 15 million Americans in uniform, many of whom saw and interacted with other Americans of different religions for the first time. In many parts of the country, Protestants and Catholics seldom had contact with each other. A Jewish World War II chaplain once told me that two white southerners came into his tent one night just to see that, in fact, he did not have horns. World War II army chaplains were taught to deliver death rites of all religions practiced by Americans, and no one was asking questions about what religion the chaplain himself belonged to in such battlefield situations.

The impact of all of this on many, if not most, Americans was profound and nearly immediate. Major League Baseball was integrated in 1947, only two years after the war ended, and by a black serviceman, Jackie Robinson, at that. *Gentlemen's Agreement*, a film about anti-Semitism in the United States, won the Oscar for best film in the same year. Harry Truman, a president from a southern border state (Missouri) who often uttered racist and anti-Semitic comments, in 1948 ordered the integration of the armed forces and also overruled his own State Department in order to support the establishment and then the diplomatic recognition of the state of Israel. The Supreme Court, less than a decade after the war's end in 1954, reversed a previous ruling in order to declare segregation unconstitutional and to order integration of southern schools "with all deliberate speed"; and the push for integration was spearheaded by black veterans who during the war had talked about the "Double V": victory over the Axis Powers and victory over racism at home. Equally telling is the fact that only 15 years after the war ended the country elected its first Catholic president, who also happened to be a war veteran.

Religious and racial tolerance as Americans understand it now is thus a relatively recent phenomenon. It clearly had some roots in the Colonial period, but the links to that distant past are neither as strong nor as direct as we believe. Recent history was just as, if not more important, in its development.

What we've said so far exemplifies the broader approach that will be taken throughout this course to the study of history. Specifically, a skeptical approach involves paying attention to the law of unintended consequences: the fact that consequences of human actions often differ quite sharply from the motivations of those who acted. Roger Williams's call for separation of church and state in order to maintain the purity of the church offers a classic example in this regard. We also select facts to study in history on the basis of their consequences, choosing Columbus over Leif Erikson. In addition, historical myths—such as these about Columbus as well as those about religious toleration—often develop because of anachronistic thinking; that is, distorting the past by dealing with events and ideas out of their proper chronological order and context. We confuse events and ideas from the 1630s, for example, with religious toleration in the First Constitutional Amendment of 1791, or the New England disestablishment of state religion in the early 19th century. Anachronistic thinking often takes the form of projecting our contemporary values onto the past, such as projecting our present definition and practice of religious toleration on those of the 17th, 18th, and 19th, as well as early 20th centuries.

That said, events 100, 200, and even 300 years old do continue to influence our lives and thoughts today. The very fact that we consider Williams important and study him, for example, reflects our contemporary values and illustrates his influence on us today. In addition, people and parts of history, such as Leif Erikson, get lost quite frequently, and are also quite frequently later rediscovered. We further see how key words change meaning and significance over time. Religious toleration once meant simply not killing each other, or perhaps minimal toleration for living in the same colony, nothing else. Toleration tends to have a much broader meaning today than it did in previous centuries.

Finally, we see that history and memory are not the same. Our memory and our ensuing commemoration of the origins of religious tolerance, for example, differ quite dramatically from the historical reality that we have just analyzed. Consider in this regard how we remember Thanksgiving, which we credit to the Pilgrims in 1621. That holiday actually had its origins in a traditional English harvest celebration. Given that fact, it conceivably might have first been celebrated in the future United States not by the Pilgrims at Plymouth, but in the colony of Virginia that had been founded 14 years before the Pilgrims arrived. Canadians sometimes claim an even earlier instance of Thanksgiving in the New World, dating from a 1578 expedition led by Martin Frobisher. Thanksgiving did not become a national holiday in this country until 1863. That is nearly 250 years after the Pilgrims's first Thanksgiving. It was not set at the fourth Thursday of November—rather than the third as some wanted, or the fifth as others wanted—until 1941.

In short, what we commemorate and remember can thus be very different from historical reality. Of course, what we've discussed in this lecture are not the only myths about American history in the 17th century and the 18th century. Let's move on to myths about the American Revolution and War for Independence.

Neither American nor Revolutionary?
Lecture 2

The American Revolution is generally portrayed in terms of a unified "American people" rising up to defeat a great empire and establishing a democratic republic. As with all myths in history, this one contains an element of truth, but it also ignores some inconvenient facts: The colonists didn't view themselves as Americans or as undertaking a revolution, and they could never have defeated the British alone. Indeed, it was almost despite themselves that the colonists created a revolution and a unique American ideology.

American Perceptions in 1763

- A key to understanding the very nonrevolutionary origins of the American Revolution lies in the perceptions Americans held in 1763.

- The colonists saw themselves not as Americans but as proud members of the British Empire, which had just achieved a stunning victory in the Seven Years' War—one that eliminated the French from the North American continent.

- Unlike the French or Spanish empires, the British Empire was not a monarchial tyranny. Parliament had asserted its supremacy over the monarchy in the so-called Glorious Revolution of 1688.

- This action was justified by John Locke and others with the "social contract" theory of government, whereby government exists through the consent of the governed to protect certain "natural rights," and a government that did not protect them should be overthrown.

Changing Perceptions

- Colonists were proud to be part of this liberty-loving British Empire, but that perception would change dramatically over the next decade in response to acts by Parliament.

- o To put an end to continued warfare with Indians in the west—and the rising costs associated with it—Parliament declared the Proclamation line in 1763, prohibiting colonists from crossing the Appalachian Mountains into Indian territories, with troops to enforce the prohibition.

- o Parliament also levied taxes on the colonies to pay off some of the debt incurred during the Seven Years' War, from which the colonists had benefited most.

- o This taxation would take place through three measures: (1) the enforcement of existing navigation acts to raise revenue, (2) the requirement of partial payment for troops needed to enforce the navigation acts and the Proclamation line, and (3) new taxes, most notably the Stamp Act of 1765.

- The colonists saw the Proclamation line as denying them the fruits of their military victory and the land they needed to survive economically. They also realized that enforcement of the navigation acts would interfere with smuggling, without which the colonial economies could not survive.

- The colonists further complained that the enforcement mechanisms for these new taxes violated their "rights as Englishmen" by allowing for the issuance of search warrants without evidence and trial by Admiralty courts without juries.

- The new direct taxes from Parliament were seen as invalidating the powers of the colonial assemblies to tax—thus the cry of "no taxation without representation."

Revolutionary Ironies
- These economic problems and political differences between the colonies and the mother country had existed for nearly 100 years but had never been raised because they were meaningless in practice.

- What made them meaningful were the new British policies resulting from the victory in the Seven Years' War and the ensuing need to reorganize the empire and pay off the war debt. Britain's problems thus stemmed from its military successes.

- The colonial response would eventually create an American identity that had never existed before. The idea that citizens of the colonies and the mother country were all English was beginning to unravel.

Colonial Resentment

- Colonial resentment built from 1761 to 1765, then exploded over the Stamp Act. The Stamp Act Congress was formed, at which representatives from nine colonies agreed to boycott British goods until the law was repealed.

- Parliament agreed to repeal the Stamp Act, but in the Declaratory Act, it asserted its power to make laws "in all cases whatsoever." Parliament then passed the Townshend Acts in 1767 to tax colonial imports from England, with a new Board of Customs Commissioners established to enforce these acts.

© Getty Images/Photos.com/Thinkstock.

The Tea Act of 1773 created a monopoly for the British East India Company and imposed "taxation without representation" on the American colonists, sparking the Boston Tea Party.

- The colonists responded with more nonimportation agreements and mob violence against customs officials. Troops were called in, leading to the Boston Massacre and the intensification of the so-called "country ideology," with its attendant fears of parliamentary corruption and a royal plot to establish despotism.

- In 1773, the Tea Act allowed the bankrupt British East India Company to sell tea in the colonies, paying a tea tax of only one penny. The colonists, already sensitive because of the events of the 1760s, exploded, demonstrating their indignation with the Boston Tea Party.

- Parliament retaliated with the Coercive or Intolerable Acts of 1774, closing the port of Boston, revoking the Massachusetts charter, appointing General Thomas Gage as governor, and sending troops to be quartered in the colony. Simultaneously, the Quebec Act extended Quebec into the Ohio valley, making the Proclamation line permanent.

The First Continental Congress

- These actions fed colonial conspiracy theories and prompted more intercolonial cooperation. The First Continental Congress was convened in September of 1774.

- Radicals at the Congress argued that Parliament had no rights in the colonies, but moderates disagreed. By now, four distinct groups had emerged in each colony: loyalists, neutrals, moderates, and radicals. This last group wanted a break with England; some members, angered by the undemocratic nature of colonial assemblies, even sought a revolution at home.

- The moderates controlled the Continental Congress and most colonial assemblies, but their position could hold only if the king and Parliament agreed with it, which they did not. Instead, London ordered General Gage to arrest John Adams and John Hancock and to seize guns and ammunition being collected at Concord.

The Second Continental Congress
- Moderates remained in charge of the Second Continental Congress, yet the opening of hostilities at Lexington and Concord forced them to agree to fight. The Continental Army was established under George Washington to maintain the siege of the British in Boston.

- The king rejected the moderates' Olive Branch Petition, and Parliament ordered all colonial ports closed; arrangements were made to send Hessian mercenaries to the colonies.

- As the fighting continued, colonial assemblies seized power from royal governors and became de facto revolutionary (and illegal) governments. Loyalists objected, and civil wars broke out in many colonies.

- In early 1776, Thomas Paine's *Common Sense* was published, offering a radical position on the logic of independence phrased in simple and inflammatory rhetoric.

- Gradually, the moderates in the Second Continental Congress were forced—against their will—into independence. The decision for independence was finally announced in July 1776.

The Declaration of Independence
- The reason the Declaration of Independence was directed against the king, despite the fact that the colonies' struggle had been against Parliament, was twofold: (1) The Continental Congress had already declared its independence from Parliament via previous acts, and (2) the colonists believed that Parliament was being manipulated by the despotic king.

- The famous Preamble is based on John Locke's social contract, and three-quarters of the document is a bill of indictment against the king to justify the revolt on the grounds that he had broken the social contract.

- In effect, Jefferson used British theories regarding liberty from Locke and the Glorious Revolution to declare American independence. In that sense, the Revolution and the Declaration were not very revolutionary at all. The entire movement was an attempt to maintain traditional British rights against new and tyrannical British policies.

Redefining Liberty
- In revolting, the colonists implicitly and explicitly expanded and changed the definition of liberty—and of themselves.

- With the perceived failure of the British constitutional monarchy to protect liberty, the colonists turned to an alternative form of representative government, personified in elected legislatures: republicanism. This was a new and radical ideology.

- With the overthrow of the authority of the king and his governors, as well as Parliament, the traditional "rights of Englishmen" came to exist only in the former colonies. They thus became, in Paine's words, "the rights of man." This new nation was to be the haven of liberty and the source from which it would eventually spread throughout the world.

- In the process of reaching this conclusion, the people in what had been 13 separate British colonies came to see themselves for the first time as Americans.

- The revolt had begun with the questioning of parliamentary and royal authority. But once one begins to question authority as antithetical to liberty instead of defensive of it, where does the process end? The question of home rule leads logically to the question of who should rule at home, and the answer will inexorably lead to government that is more representative and more democratic.

The True Course of the Revolution

- The colonists quickly learned that declaring independence and achieving it are two very different things. They would be fighting against the largest and most powerful empire in the world and against fellow colonists who remained loyal to the king.

- Washington was able to stave off total defeat with successful raids at Trenton and Princeton, but the only way to force the British to accept American independence was to obtain foreign aid, most notably from the despotic French monarchy. Indeed, American victory over the British would have been impossible without French money, equipment, and forces.

- The American revolutionaries thus wound up creating a new nation and "cradle of liberty" only with the help of tyrannical European powers and against the wishes of their neighbors who remained loyal to England.

- It's safe to say that the American Revolution was far less American and far less revolutionary than we might think. A variety of reasons explains the emergence—and persistence—of myths to the contrary: the tendency of nations to overemphasize their own role versus that of their allies in war; the admiration of the French general Lafayette for the American ideology, perhaps leading to a larger myth of aid from the "liberty-loving French"; the migration of many loyalists to Canada; and the tendency to look at the end result of a series of events rather than its origins.

- What remains true is that the Americans rose up against a tyrannical British Parliament and king, in a coalition that ultimately involved all the other major powers of Europe—uniting against the greatest empire in the world and making it possible for a group of rebellious colonies to form a new nation.

Suggested Reading

Bailyn, *The Ideological Origins of the American Revolution.*

Chernow, *Washington: A Life.*

Middlekauff, *The Glorious Cause.*

Wood, *The Creation of the American Republic, 1776–1787.*

Questions to Consider

1. Why do we tend to look at results of events rather than their origins and causes?

2. What other events in U.S. history have results that differ from their causes and origins?

Neither American nor Revolutionary?
Lecture 2—Transcript

We are used to seeing the American Revolution in terms of a unified American people rising up against the tyrannical British king, militarily defeating the greatest empire in the world, and establishing a democratic republic. As with all myths in history, this one contains an element—indeed much more than an element—of truth. But it also distorts the past by ignoring some very inconvenient facts.

As we will see: The English colonists did not view themselves as Americans, or as undertaking a revolution, prior to 1776; indeed, they considered themselves and asserted again and again that they were loyal British subjects merely defending their "rights as Englishmen." In addition, their struggle was primarily with the British Parliament, not the British king. In all likelihood, a majority of them never supported independence from England, even after 1776; indeed, in most colonies a civil war took place between those who did and those who did not. Furthermore, the English colonists did not—indeed they militarily could not—defeat the British Empire by themselves once hostilities began. They succeeded only because of aid from other countries, most notably the previously hated and feared absolute monarchy of France, which was anything but liberty-loving at this time. As we will see in the next lecture, they never intended to establish a democracy either.

Yet they did wind up creating a revolution almost despite themselves, as well as a unique American identity and ideology. How and why that happened are the subjects of this lecture.

A key to understanding the very non-revolutionary origins of this American Revolution lies in the perceptions that Americans held in 1763; perceptions far different from those they would hold just a few years later. For a start, they did not see themselves as Americans. In 1763, they saw themselves as proud members of a triumphant and liberty-loving British Empire that had just completed a stunning victory in the Seven Years', or French and Indian, War. That war had eliminated the powerful and dangerous French from the North American continent. Quebec had become a British colony; Louisiana had gone to a weak Spain.

Unlike the French or Spanish Empires, the British Empire was not a monarchial tyranny. To the contrary, Parliament had asserted its supremacy over the monarchy in the so-called Glorious Revolution of 1688, during which it threw out King James II and invited William and Mary of Orange to assume the throne instead. This revolution had been justified by John Locke and others via the social contract theory of government, whereby government existed via consent of the governed to protect certain "natural rights"—which Locke listed as life, liberty and property—and a government that did not protect them can and should be overthrown.

The colonists were proud to be part of this liberty-loving British Empire; indeed "American" was a term with little if any meaning for them. They saw themselves as English and as members of their specific colony (e.g., Virginians), with their colonial assemblies as mini-Parliaments, some of which had participated in Glorious Revolution by overthrowing tyrannical royal governors; and those colonial assemblies, they believed, governed them while the Parliament in London governed the entire empire.

Such perceptions would change dramatically over the next decade in response to acts by a British Parliament faced with a staggering debt as a result of the French and Indian War. That debt could have been as high as 146 million pounds in 1763. The total budget had never been more than 8 million pounds. The interest alone on this new debt was 5 million pounds; and that debt was only increasing as a result of continued warfare in the west with a powerful coalition of Indian tribes under Ottawa Chief Pontiac.

To stop this Indian warfare, England in the Proclamation Line of 1763 prohibited the colonists from crossing the crest of Appalachian Mountains into Indian territories, with troops to enforce this. To help pay the debt, a party in Parliament led by George Grenville known as Friends of the New and Young British King George III (who was in his 20s) decided that since the colonists had gained the most from the war via the destruction of French and Indian power in North America, they should be taxed to help pay the debt in three ways: first, via enforcement of the existing 17th-century Navigation Acts that had originally been designed to control trade but that would now be used to raise revenue as well in order to pay off the debt (and along with this would be a massive naval and bureaucratic presence in the colonies to enforce these measures); second, via partial payment for troops needed for enforcement of these acts and the Proclamation Line; and third, via new taxes specifically designed to raise revenue, most notably the Stamp Act of 1765 that required colonists to purchase stamps for all published documents.

The colonial perspective on all this is quite different from Parliament's. The colonists saw the Proclamation Line of 1763 as denying them the fruits of their military victory and the land they needed to survive economically. Tobacco, the cash crop of the South, wears out the soil; furthermore, there was a major balance of payments problem that got partially resolved by land speculation and sales. The colonists also saw enforcement of the Navigation Acts as further destroying their economy. The imperial economic system had worked before only via a policy of what was known as "salutary neglect"; that is, toleration of wholesale smuggling. The colonial economies could not survive if the Navigation Acts were strictly enforced.

The colonists complained that the enforcement mechanisms for these new taxes violated their "rights as Englishmen"—note: not as "Americans"—and they violated their rights as Englishmen by allowing for the issuing of search warrants without evidence and trial by Admiralty Courts that did not have juries. These were violations of British law and custom, and there were early objections to this by, amongst others, James Otis. The colonists also saw the new direct taxes from Parliament as invalidating the powers of their colonial assemblies to tax; and thus you got the cry of "no taxation without representation"

London claimed the colonists were represented in Parliament via the theory of virtual representation whereby each Member of Parliament represented the entire empire. But colonial experience in their colonial assemblies had been with direct representation instead whereby each representative represented his own district. The difference was meaningless in practice before 1763, but it was not meaningless now. In addition, if colonial assemblies did not have the sole power to tax the colonists, the assemblies' "power of the purse" to control the royal governors by paying their salaries would be destroyed, and thus their political liberties supposedly guaranteed via the Glorious Revolution of 1688. Consequently, conspiracy theories began to grow of a royal despotism manipulating Parliament and trying to destroy liberty everywhere.

Please note the ironies here: These economic problems and political differences between colonies and mother country had existed for nearly 100 years but had never been brought up because they were meaningless in practice. What made them meaningful were the new British policies resulting from their great victory in the Seven Years' War and the ensuing need to reorganize their empire and pay off their debt. British problems thus stemmed from their great military successes; and the Colonial response would eventually create an American identity that never even existed before. What we see here is the beginning of the unfraying of the concept that "we are all English" along with a Colonial perception that "we are not changing but you are."

Colonial resentment accumulated from 1761–1765 and then exploded over the Stamp Act, which led to the Stamp Act Congress where representatives from nine colonies met and agreed to boycott British goods until the law was repealed. This was the first real example of intercolonial cooperation. Parliament agreed to repeal the Stamp Act and lower other taxes, but in the Declaratory Act it asserted that it nevertheless had the power to make all laws "in all cases whatsoever"—in other words, Parliament gave in on the specific act but not on the principle—and it then passed the Townshend Acts in 1767 to raise money via taxes on colonial imports from England, with a new Board of Customs Commissioners established to enforce these acts.

The colonial response: More non-importation agreements and mob violence against the customs officials, at which point troops were called in; and that led to the Boston Massacre. It also led to greater and greater acceptance in the colonies of the so-called "Country Ideology": fears of Parliamentary corruption and a royal plot to establish despotism.

In 1770, a new British ministry under Lord North repealed all the taxes except the one penny tax on tea as a symbol. Then, in the Tea Act of 1773, it allowed the bankrupt British East India Company to sell tea in the colonies without paying any of its old taxes except the one penny Tea Tax that was left over from the Townshend Duties. Eliminating the other taxes would make

British Tea cheaper than smuggled Dutch tea; but the colonists exploded. Everyone was super sensitive by now because of the events of the 1760s; the tea tax became a symbol, and it was a symbol for both sides and for everything else. It led to the Boston Tea Party.

Parliament then retaliated with the Coercive or Intolerable Acts of 1774. It closed the port of Boston until restitution was made for the dumped tea; it revoked the Massachusetts Charter; it put appointments to the Massachusetts Council in the hands of the king; and it appointed a general, Thomas Gage, as governor with troops sent back in and quartered in colonial barns and empty houses. At the same time, it passed the Quebec Act that extended Quebec into the Ohio Valley. That, in effect, made the Proclamation Line of 1763 permanent. Furthermore, Quebec was to have no assembly, and the Catholic Church would have a protected position.

All of this provided further evidence for the conspiracy theories and led to more intercolonial activity. The First Continental Congress would meet in September, 1774. The radicals at this congress argued that Parliament had no rights in the colonies; that the colonial assemblies were the complete equals of Parliament. The moderates disagreed, and they controlled this congress. They thus petitioned the king and admitted that Parliament had the right to regulate the trade of the empire. They were still talking about their "rights as Englishmen."

If you break it down, there were by this point four distinct groups within each colony: Loyalists, who remained loyal to the king and Parliament; Neutrals; Moderates, who demanded only their "rights as Englishmen," which might have translated into Commonwealth status had that existed at this time; and Radicals, who now wanted a break with Parliament and, for many of them, a revolution at home. For there also existed at this time a conflict inside each colony and inside the colonial assemblies. That conflict would be grafted onto the conflict with England. It's important to realize that the colonial assemblies were not democratic at this time—there were property qualifications for voting; there were oligarchies running them—and there were cries by the lower classes and the West that "we are not represented here and we should be." One historian, Carl Becker, concluded that there was a dual conflict going on: a conflict over home rule and a conflict over who shall rule at home.

The radicals were not a majority or in charge. The moderates controlled the Continental Congress—they also controlled most of the colonial assemblies—but their position could hold only if the king and Parliament agreed with it, and they did not. Instead, London decided on a showdown. General Gage in Boston was ordered to arrest Sam Adams and John Hancock, two colonial leaders; and he also decided to seize guns and ammunition that were being collected at Concord. The result would be Lexington and Concord, and the "shot heard 'round the world." Hostilities had begun.

Lexington and Concord were followed by a colonial siege of Boston, as well as the Battle of Bunker Hill and the taking of Fort Ticonderoga by the colonists. When the Second Continental Congress opened on May 10, all of this had taken place. The moderates were still in charge, and they would come up with the Olive Branch Petition to the king. But the logic of events was simultaneously forcing them to agree to fight. Not only had hostilities begun, but Ethan Allen had taken Fort Ticonderoga from British troops in "the name of the great Jehovah and the Continental Congress." One historian quipped that while we will never know if Allen had authority from the former, we do know that he did not have authority to do this from the latter. A Continental Army was thus established under George Washington to maintain the siege of the British in Boston. Washington was chosen because he was a Virginian; and when he walked in with his Virginia militia officer's uniform on, he was in effect saying that Virginia was willing to fight for Massachusetts.

But King George rejected the moderates' Olive Branch Petition, and Parliament ordered all colonial ports closed and then hired Hessian mercenaries to suppress this uprising. Furthermore, as fighting took place, the colonial assemblies seized power from the royal governors and they became de facto revolutionary governments. The Loyalists said this was illegal; they objected; and civil war broke out in many colonies. Then, in early 1776, Tom Paine's "Common Sense" was published. "Common Sense" presented the radical position on the logic of independence, and it is phrased in very simple and inflammatory terms that convince many. As a result of all this, the moderates in the Second Continental Congress were gradually forced, against their will, into independence. It was a very gradual process.

In January, 1776, the Continental Congress threw open all colonial ports to the world. That was the Declaration of Independence from Parliament. Parliament would not even be allowed to regulate the trade of the empire. But the tie to the king remained: In effect, what was declared was commonwealth status. In March, privateers were authorized to attack British shipping. A month later, a secret committee was established to obtain foreign aid. The French made clear that they were quite willing to give it if independence was the goal. France had no interest in reconciliation between England and its colonies; it wished to weaken England after its humiliating defeat by the English in the Seven Years' War, and the way to weaken England was to have the colonies break away. Only in June/July did the Continental Congress decide for independence. The motion was passed on July 2 and it was publicly announced on July 4.

The Declaration of Independence is an extraordinary document in many ways: First, it was directed against the king, despite fact that the struggle had been against Parliament. Why? Because the Continental Congress had already declared independence from Parliament via its previous acts; and furthermore, there was a view common then that the despotic king was behind all of this and a total break now needed to be justified. The famous Preamble to the Declaration of Independence is based on Locke's social contract: that government exists by consent of the governed to protect the natural rights of life, liberty, and with property now becoming happiness.

> We hold these truths to be self-evident, that all men are created equal, that they are endowed, by their Creator, with certain unalienable Rights, that among these are Life, Liberty, and the pursuit of Happiness.

> That to secure these rights, Governments are instituted among Men, deriving their just powers from the consent of the governed, That whenever any Form of Government becomes destructive of these ends, it is the Right of the People to alter or abolish it.

But that's just the Preamble. Three-quarters of the document is a bill of indictment against the king to justify this revolt and independence on the grounds that the king has broken the social contract. In effect, Thomas Jefferson used British theories regarding liberty and the social contract from John Locke and the Glorious Revolution of 1688, a contract he claimed has been subverted and broken in England by a despotic king and his corrupt Parliament.

In that sense, the Revolution and the Declaration of Independence are not very revolutionary at all; the entire movement had been and remained an attempt to maintain traditional British rights against new and tyrannical British policies with revolt as a last resort. But in revolting, the colonists implicitly and explicitly expanded and changed the very definition of liberty and of themselves. How?

With the perceived failure of the British constitutional monarchy to protect liberty, the colonists turned to an alternative form of representative government as personified in their elected legislatures; a form of government that they (and we) called "republicanism" rather than any inherited/constitutional monarchy, and these legislators were to be the guarantors of liberty. You had here a new, radical ideology. With the overthrow of the authority of the king and his governors as well as his Parliament, you in effect said that the traditional "rights of Englishmen" now existed only in the former colonies and they thus became, in Tom Paine's words, "the rights of man." This new nation was to be the haven of liberty, and the source from liberty would eventually spread throughout the entire world.

In the process of reaching this conclusion, the people in what had been 13 very separate British colonies came to see themselves for the first time as Americans. But, again, not all the people, or even a majority: John Adams figured that one-third of the people supported the revolution, one-third opposed it, and one-third were neutral. Furthermore, those who did support the revolution saw themselves first as citizens of their state.

The revolution did not end there. This revolt had begun as a questioning of parliamentary authority and royal authority; but once you begin to question any authority as antithetical and threatening to liberty instead of defending it, where does the process end? Are your own assemblies truly representative? If not, how can they possibly defend and promote liberty? Indeed, if you reject Parliament's concept of "virtual representation," then how can you deny representation to westerners and the lower classes within each new state? Going further, how can you continue to hold slaves? If they are not to be slaves, how can you deny them representation; or women for that matter?

An ideological chain reaction thus began, one that continues throughout American history and right down to this very day. The question of home rule leads logically to the question of who should rule at home, and the answer— admittedly over a long period of time—will inexorably lead to government that is more representative and more democratic. Ensuing American history can thus be seen as an ongoing, evolving revolution stemming from these very conservative beginnings.

Declaring independence and achieving it are two very different things. The colonists would be fighting against the largest and most powerful empire in the world; one that now had decided to mobilize its power to crush this revolt. They would simultaneously be fighting against their own fellow colonists who remained loyal to the king.

In the summer of 1776, they experienced the extent of London's power. The British invaded New York with 32,000 troops—that's larger than the entire population of New York City—and they defeated Washington's Continental Army again, and again, and again. Loyalists in New York City welcomed the British, who made the city their headquarters for the duration of the war. Washington was able to stave off total defeat and surrender with his end of the year successful raids at Trenton and Princeton, but the only way to force the British to accept American independence was to obtain foreign aid, most notably from Britain's chief enemy: the detested and despotic French monarchy.

Despite the American ideology of liberty, that monarchy proved willing to provide such aid as a means of weakening its mortal enemy Britain once the Americans declared their independence and once they showed at Saratoga in 1777 that they could defeat and capture a British army. The result in early 1778 was a formal alliance with France and French armies and navies as well as money, guns, and ammunition. Military victory over the British was impossible without all of this; indeed, there were probably more French naval and ground forces at Yorktown, perhaps twice as many: 24,000 compared to 11,000. In addition, the successful blockade at Yorktown depended on a prior engagement between French and British navies just outside the Chesapeake Bay—a battle sometimes called the Battle of the Virginia Capes—and it was fought during early September, 1781. Here, the French repelled the British with essentially no Americans involved at all.

France was not alone. Spain joined the war in 1779 as an ally of France—though not of the U.S.—and Spain wreaked havoc on the British in Florida. Britain also went to war with the Netherlands, and in effect with the European League of Armed Neutrals. At the same time, French diplomacy kept Britain isolated without allies; Britain was at war with all of Europe. It was also internally divided, and it had been for quite awhile, as dissenters such as Edmund Burke and Adam Smith opposed the war.

The American revolutionaries thus wound up creating this new nation and "cradle of liberty" only with the help of these tyrannical European powers and against the wishes of their neighbors who wished to remain loyal to England. The American Revolution and War for Independence were thus far less American, as well as far less revolutionary, than one would think.

Where did myths to the contrary come from? For a start, all nations tend to overemphasize their own role versus that of their allies in war. Some French officers, in addition—most notably Lafayette—did fall in love with the U.S. and its new ideology. In addition, the French Revolution occurred just a few years later, and that perhaps led to a larger myth of aid from the "liberty-loving French"; but they were not liberty-loving when they provided that aid. In addition to those two factors, many Loyalists left for Canada, and with their departure went their side of the story.

There is also a natural tendency to look at the end result of a series of historical events; in this case, the Declaration of Independence and the fact of independence rather than the very conservative and very English origins of the Revolution. Also we tend to forget the reluctance with which many

Americans came to accept that revolution and the critical role of other European powers in making victory possible.

But what remains true is that the Americans did rise up against a tyrannical British Parliament and king in a coalition that ultimately involved all the other major powers of Europe uniting against the greatest empire in the world and making it possible for a group of rebellious colonies to form a new nation.

In the next lecture, we will see what kind of a nation they had in mind.

The Constitution Did Not Create a Democracy
Lecture 3

W e often hear talk about the "original intent" of the writers of the Constitution, but the Founding Fathers did not plan to create the political system we have today: a democratic republic based on two national and permanent political parties. Indeed, "democracy" and "political parties" were dirty words to them. They did realize, however, that the world was likely to change, which is one reason they included an amendment process in the Constitution that has allowed this document to survive as our frame of government for so long.

Historical Views of the Constitution
- The Constitution was not the original frame of government of the newly independent United States. The states were originally governed by the Second Continental Congress and then, from 1781–1789, by the Articles of Confederation.

- Late-19th-century historians saw these Articles as a disastrous failure, engendering the "critical period" concept, in which the infant and endangered United States was saved by the godlike Founding Fathers.

- That interpretation was questioned by early-20th-century historians, who argued that the Constitution was the response of moderates protecting their own economic and class interests. In this view, the Constitution was an antidemocratic, counterrevolutionary document.

- In turn, that interpretation came under attack in the mid- and late 20th century. Many historians today view the Constitution as a continuation, not an antithesis, of the Revolution.

The Articles of Confederation

- The process of creating governments began in the 1770s as the colonial assemblies transformed themselves into state legislatures and governments. This process would involve a rejection of the British concept of "balanced" government in favor of overwhelming legislative power and a move from unwritten to written constitutions.

- At first, the central government was the Second Continental Congress. The Articles of Confederation, meant to serve as a bridge between the Congress and a federal government, were presented to the states in 1777 but not ratified by all until 1781, largely because the states retained their distrust of both centralized power and one another.

- The Articles set up a central government of sorts but a weak one, with no executive or judiciary, no power to tax or enact any important measures without a two-thirds vote, and no power to change the structure without unanimity. Each state had one vote and, thus, a virtual veto power.

- This organization was established very consciously. The states saw themselves as independent republics retaining sovereignty and joining into a loose confederation, something like the United Nations. They feared centralized power and sought to guarantee their liberty through decentralization and state legislatures.

Successes of the Articles

- Despite the inherent weaknesses of this frame of government, much was accomplished under the Articles, including the winning of independence and a favorable peace treaty in 1783, with a western boundary for the United States all the way to the Mississippi River.

- State governments were also established under the Articles, with many social and political reforms, including the extension of the franchise, frequent elections, and the separation of church and state.

- The pattern for western expansion and settlement was established with the Northwest Ordinances of 1784, 1785, and 1787.

- Internationally, the Articles opened trade with European powers and Asia.

Problems with the Articles
- By 1787, problems under the Articles appeared to outweigh successes.

- The Confederate Congress had no power to tax and, thus, to pay for a military force or pay its debts. The nation's military power rested, essentially, with untrained and unreliable state militias. This translated into a lack of power in foreign affairs and a lack of respect from European nations.

- A postwar economic depression was also blamed on the Articles. To halt land foreclosures, states began to repudiate debts and print paper money, causing inflation; such measures were easy to enact

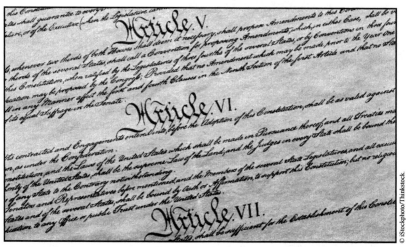

The Constitution was written to address the need to create a government strong enough to preserve liberty without giving it enough power to become tyrannical itself.

because there was little or no check on legislative powers in the states. Some states established their own currencies and trading systems, causing a breakdown in interstate relations and presenting the danger that states would turn to European allies for intervention.

- With Shays's Rebellion—a march of 1,200 men on the Supreme Court in Massachusetts and on an arsenal—fear of anarchy spread. No national army was available to halt the rebellion, and although the state militia did, it could just have easily failed from lack of training or even joined the revolt.

- These problems convinced many that the national government was incapable of defending the liberty won during the Revolution and that a new frame of government was necessary. Note that the definition of "liberty" here was not democracy but individual freedom from tyranny, either from above or below.
  - The Revolution had fought successfully for liberty and against tyranny from above, but the threat now seemed to be tyranny from below—mob rule as in Shays's Rebellion.

  - With the danger of European intervention and the possible destruction of the republican experiment, tyranny from above had not been eliminated either.

The Constitutional Convention
- In 1787, a special convention was called to revise and strengthen the Articles of Confederation. Revolutionary leaders Benjamin Franklin and George Washington were present, but aside from these two, most of the delegates were quite young. Many were veterans of Washington's Continental Army or the Continental Congress, which gave them a national, as opposed to a state, outlook.

- The representatives were simultaneously conservative and revolutionary. They were men of property who feared democracy and mob rule as destructive of liberty, but they were also revolutionaries who desired to create something new—a republic with centralized power to preserve rather than destroy liberty.

- Their basic dilemma was this: How to create a government strong enough to preserve liberty from the tyranny of the mob or European monarchs without giving it enough power to be tyrannical itself?

- In the 51st Federalist paper, James Madison noted, "A dependence on the people is, no doubt, the primary control on the government." Thus, the Constitution begins, "We the People." Sovereignty rests with the people.

Checks and Balances

- The Constitution separates sovereignty from rule via a series of intermediaries and divides power among those intermediaries to avoid tyranny. We know this system as "checks and balances," and it exists on two levels: separation of powers among the three branches of the national government and division of powers between the national government and the state governments.

- The Founders returned to the concept of "balanced" government because of the perceived excesses and weaknesses of existing legislative governments. They sought to combine elements of a monarchy, an aristocracy, and a democracy within the new national government.
  o The president would be a monarch indirectly elected via the electoral college by elite electors (the aristocracy), with a four-year term and powers limited to those enumerated in Article II.

  o The Senate would be an aristocratic branch indirectly elected by the people through the state legislatures, with a six-year term and the powers listed in Article I. The national judiciary would also be aristocratic.

  o The House of Representatives would be the democratic branch, with short terms, albeit still with property qualifications for voting.

- As we know, each branch has the power to "check" the others. For example, the president is the commander-in-chief of the armed forces, but Congress appropriates funds for the military and declares war.

- The new national government had enormous powers, but it did not have a monopoly on power. The Tenth Amendment explicitly reaffirmed that all powers not delegated to the new national government or prohibited by it to the states would be reserved to the states, each capable of checking the other.

A Large Republic

- The Constitution set up a large republic, something that, according to political theory of the day, could not survive. In the 10th Federalist paper, Madison turned this theory on its head, claiming that a republic in a large area had a better chance of preserving liberty than one in a small area.

- For Madison, factions were the key problem in sustaining a republic. In a democracy, a majority faction—a group willing to ride roughshod over the rights of others to ensure its own interests—could easily gain control and destroy liberty.

- Such factions cannot be abolished without abolishing liberty, but they must be controlled via checks and balances. A large republic can do this better than small ones because the greater population and area resulted in more factions and a reduced chance that one would dominate.

Disagreement at the Convention

- Despite agreement on certain essentials, disagreements among the delegates almost wrecked the Convention. Major disputes pitted large states against small ones over the issue of representation and northern states against southern on some issues related to slavery. Delegates also split over just how much power to give the national government at the expense of the states.

- Some delegates feared that despite the checks and balances, the new national government had too much power. Only 39 of 55 delegates signed the final document.

- The Constitution called for special state ratifying conventions, with ratification by nine states required to put the document into effect. Intense opposition emerged in virtually every state, primarily from established groups who controlled state governments and feared centralized power.

- The pro-Constitution forces won the struggle for a number of reasons. They were better organized, were on the offensive, and had the advantage of defining themselves as Federalists, while their opponents were labeled Anti-Federalists.
  - o The ratification process also bypassed state legislatures that had a vested interested in the failure of the new system.

  - o Further, the Federalists also agreed to address a key Anti-Federalist objection: the lack of a specific Bill of Rights. Creating one would be the first order of business under the new government.

The Truth about the Founders
- The final version of the Constitution and the Federalist papers show the Founders as Hobbesian realists who distrusted human nature and sought to stop what they considered the excesses of revolution. In that sense, they can be viewed as conservative, even counterrevolutionary.

- Simultaneously, however, they were still Lockeans and revolutionaries who wanted to preserve their republican experiment against what they considered clear and present dangers and were willing to try a radical and unprecedented experiment to do so.

- The Founders succeeded in establishing a new frame of government, but in the process, they left a series of unanswered questions that would cause a split among them within a few years and would be bequeathed to their successors.

Suggested Reading

Chernow, *Washington: A Life*.

Hamilton, Madison, and Jay, *The Federalist Papers*.

Middlekauff, *The Glorious Cause*.

Wood, *The Creation of the American Republic, 1776–1787*.

Questions to Consider

1. Why do we equate liberty with democracy when the writers of the Constitution did not do so?

2. Why do we tend to project our contemporary values onto the past?

The Constitution Did Not Create a Democracy
Lecture 3—Transcript

There is a great deal of talk today about the "original intent" of writers of the Constitution. No matter where one stands on that issue, it is important to realize that the writers of the Constitution did not foresee or plan to create the political system that we have today; that is, a democratic republic based upon two national and permanent political parties. Indeed, "democracy" and "political parties" were dirty words to them. Nor did the writers anticipate the economic system we have today, or our social values. In many if not most ways, the world they lived in was very different from the one we live in. They realized their world was likely to change; that is one of the reasons they put into the Constitution the amendment process, which in turn is one of the major reasons this document has survived as our frame of government for so long and despite all the changes in all aspects of American life.

To understand the world of the Founders, we must first understand who they were, the problems they faced, and why they created this new frame of government. We also need to understand the historical controversies that have swirled around them, and exactly what is in the document that they created. The public lack of knowledge of those contents is frightening. A survey conducted during the 1987 Bicentennial showed 46 percent not knowing the original purpose of the Constitution (26 percent thought it was to declare independence from England); 59 percent did not know what the Bill of Rights is (only 41 percent correctly identified it as the first 10 amendments, 27 percent thought it was the Preamble to the Constitution); and a frightening 49 percent erroneously thought the president could suspend the Constitution.

Let's begin with the world of 1787 and the ensuing historical controversies. The Constitution was not the original frame of government of the newly independent United States. The states originally were governed by the Second Continental Congress, and then from 1781–1789 by the Articles of Confederation. Late-19th-century historians saw these Articles as a disastrous failure, and indeed called this time period the "critical period," where an infant and endangered United States was saved by the godlike Founding Fathers.

That interpretation was stood on its head in the early 20th century by historians such as Charles Beard, who argued that it was not a critical period but that its democratic thrust alienated the moderates of the previous decade—the revolutionary decade—who had become reluctant revolutionaries. Motivated by economic and class interests, they responded with the Constitution as an antidemocratic, counterrevolutionary document in an effort to protect those interests.

That interpretation itself then came under attack in the mid and late 20th century. This, as we will see in later lectures, is part of the ongoing process of historical interpretation and reinterpretation. For now, let me just note that many historians today view the Constitution as a continuation of the Revolution, not the antithesis of the Revolution. Also the issue is far from settled, and it is unlikely ever to be settled; for historical interpretations—again, as we will explore in later lectures—are constantly being affected and revised by present-day concerns. My interpretation that follows will thus reflect contemporary scholarship and contemporary issues and values.

The process of creating governments began in the 1770s as the colonial assemblies transformed themselves into state legislatures and governments. This process would involve a series of major departures from British practice, reflecting colonial experiences. For example, the colonists rejected the British concept of "balanced" government in favor of overwhelming legislative power. The colonial governors and judges had been royal appointees and had been perceived as tyrannical. In the Articles of Confederation period, their powers were extremely limited within each state. You also had a move to written constitutions within each state instead of unwritten constitutions. This was due to the perceived failure of the unwritten British constitution to protect liberty. You also had an old tradition in colonial history of written charters in the founding of many colonies.

State assemblies became more representative due to the logic of the Revolution as I explained in the last lecture, with the franchise extended and frequent elections. The central government at first was the Second Continental Congress—which was obviously makeshift—and it was replaced by Articles of Confederation, which were presented to the states in 1777 but not ratified by all the states until 1781. Why?

The states retained their distrust of any centralized power—that was what they were fighting against—and they also retained their distrust of each other. There has been no history of cooperation before the Revolution, and the cooperation that existed during the Revolutionary period had been quite limited and broke down once the Revolution ended. Smaller states feared larger ones—especially those with western land claims—for fear that they (the small states) would lose their population to larger states that could avoid taxing by simply using land sales to run the government. Maryland, for example, refused to ratify the Articles of Confederation unless state western land claims were given to the national government. Virginia and other states agreed in order to get a central government, and because they believed that a republican form of government could not work in large areas (this is something I'll get to later).

The Articles did set up a central government of sorts, but a very weak one. There was no executive, no judiciary, only a congress with no power to tax or to do anything important without a vote of 9 out of the 13 states; nor could they change the structure without a unanimous vote in favor of changing it. Each state had one vote, and thus a virtual veto power.

This had all been done very consciously. The states saw themselves as independent republics retaining sovereignty and joining into a loose confederation similar to today's United Nations. This came from their colonial past in addition to their fear of centralized power from the Revolutionary era. Liberty was now to be guaranteed by decentralization and by state legislatures.

Despite the inherent weaknesses obvious of this frame of government, much was actually accomplished under the Articles: the winning of independence and the obtaining of a favorable peace treaty in 1783, with a western boundary all the way to the Mississippi River; the establishment of state governments with many social and political reforms; the lowering of property qualifications for voting to extend the franchise; frequent elections; separation of church and state; the beginning of the abolition of slavery in northern states; expansion of education and literacy; and the creation of state Bills of Rights. You also established the pattern for western expansion and settlement with the Northwest Ordinances of 1784, '85 and '87. All western land north of the Ohio River that had been given up by the states to the national government was to be surveyed, divided, and sold in 640 acre lots for $1 per acre. Eventually there would be self-rule and admission to the union as anywhere from three to five new states on an equal basis when the population had reached 60,000. There were also guarantees of freedom of worship, trial by jury, and there was to be no slavery in this entire territory. Internationally, trade was opened with the European powers under the Articles of Confederation and with Asia; and loans were extended to the United States.

But the problems under the Articles appeared to many to outweigh these successes by 1787, and those problems were both external and domestic. The confederation congress had no power to tax, and thus no power to pay for an armed force or to pay its debts. After the Revolution, the navy was sold; at one point the army was down to 80 men. Rather than a national army, reliance was placed on untrained and unreliable state militia. This lack of military power, lack of power to tax, translated into no power in foreign affairs and no respect from the European powers. The British locked the United States out of their mercantilist trading system. They also violated the peace treaty by refusing to leave their posts in the northwest, and they supported—in fact, incited—Indian resistance from those posts to American settlers. Nor was that the end of it. Spain refused to agree to the southern United States boundary with Florida and denied the United States the right to navigate the Mississippi River and the right of deposit at New Orleans. It also incited secessionist movements in the southwest.

Internally, there was a postwar economic depression blamed on the Articles. People in each state demanded relief. The easiest ways to obtain relief were to stop foreclosures on land for nonpayment of debts, to repudiate debts, and/or to print paper money so as to create inflation, which would make repayment of debts much easier. That was easy to do since there was little or no check on legislative powers in each state; and creditors and men of property complained that the state governments were breaking the social contract by doing this and that this was, as we would say today, "democracy run amuck."

States were establishing their own currencies and trading systems. There was a breakdown in interstate relations, with the looming danger of states turning to European allies and thus opening door to European intervention, manipulation, and control. By 1786–1787, there was fear of anarchy with Shays's Rebellion in western Massachusetts. Daniels Shays, a Revolutionary War hero, led a march of 1,200 on the courts to stop foreclosures and then on the Springfield arsenal to obtain weapons. There was no national army to stop this. The state militia did; but they could just as easily have failed due to lack of training, or even joined Shays's men. After Shays's defeat, his followers were elected to office and stopped foreclosures anyway. What all of this illustrated was the weakness of both the state governments and the national government.

All of this convinced many that the present national government was incapable of defending the liberty won during the Revolution and that a new frame of government was necessary. What you had here, one needs to realize, was an elite definition of liberty; it was not democracy at all. It was individual freedom from tyranny or from any form of external control or interference. But, by the political thought of the day, such tyranny or control could come from above or from below; from mob rule that broke the social contract. John Randolph of Virginia I think summed this up best in his famous quote: "I am an aristocrat. I love liberty; I hate equality."

While the Revolution had fought successfully for liberty and against tyranny from above, liberty to those men was now threatened by tyranny from below. Simultaneously, it was once again threatened by tyranny from above as well: the danger of European intervention and the destruction of the entire republican experiment. More centralized power was thus perceived as necessary to fend off the Europeans and their tyranny from above and the tyranny from below that would come from democratic mob rule.

By 1786, those who thought this way found support amongst the middle and lower classes as well as the upper classes: creditors, of course; merchants and shippers who wanted a national commercial policy and power to break into the European mercantilist trading systems; artisans who wanted a high national tariff; westerners who wanted defense against the Indians, the British, and the Spanish; land speculators wanting the same as well as protection from squatters. In 1786, representatives from five states met in Annapolis and asked Congress to call a special convention to revise and strengthen the Articles of Confederation. That would lead to the Constitutional Convention: 55 men from 12 states gathered in Philadelphia from May–September, 1787.

Who were they? It is interesting to note who was not in Philadelphia: such revolutionary radicals as Patrick Henry, Sam Adams, Thomas Jefferson; they were not there. The Revolutionary leaders Franklin and Washington were present; but aside from these two venerable figures, most of the delegates were quite young: James Madison and Gouverneur Morris were only 35; Rufus King and Alexander Hamilton were only 32; Charles Pinckney was only 29. Almost all had continental, as opposed to state, experiences during the Revolutionary War. Many were veterans of Washington's Continental Army or the Continental Congress, and that experience gave them a national, as opposed to a state, outlook. At least one historian has labeled them the first true Americans.

Were they conservative or revolutionary? They were simultaneously both. They were conservative as men of property who feared democracy and mob rule as destructive of liberty. They were elitist republicans, if you will, rather than democratic republicans. But simultaneously, they were revolutionary in their desire to create something new: a large republic with centralized power that preserved liberty rather than destroying it. One needs to understand that this contradicted established political thought and experience. That established political thought and experience held that republics only worked in small areas, and that large centralized nations were best ruled by absolute monarchs. The founders would turn this on its head; and what you get here, one might argue, is a concept of creating an "empire of liberty."

The men who gathered in Philadelphia were also willing to ignore their instructions to revise and amend the Articles of Confederation, and instead they decided to come up with an entirely new frame of government; one that they devised in secret sessions with locked doors and windows despite the summer heat. One can argue that in some ways what you had here was a coup.

The basic dilemma: How do you create a government strong enough to preserve liberty from tyranny of the mob and/or from the European monarchs without giving it enough power to be tyrannical itself? This dilemma was best expressed by the father of the Constitution, James Madison, later, when he wrote the 51st Federalist Paper:

> If men were angels, no government would be necessary. If angels were to govern men, neither external nor internal controls would be necessary. In framing a government which is to be administered by men over men, the great difficulty lies in this: you must first enable the government to control the governed; and in the next place oblige it to control itself.

> A dependence on the people is [Madison continued] no doubt, the primary control on the government; but experience has taught mankind the necessity of auxiliary precautions.

The Constitution thus began with "We the people"; sovereignty rests with the people. But the document then separates sovereignty from rule via a series of intermediaries and it divides power between those intermediaries so as to avoid tyranny. We know this system as checks and balances, and it exists on two levels: the separation of powers between the three branches of the new national government; and the division of powers between that new national government and the existing state governments.

Let's look at the separation of powers first: The founders returned to the concept of balanced government due to perceived excesses and weaknesses of the existing legislative governments. What they decided to do was to combine elements of monarchy, aristocracy, and democracy within the new national government.

Let's look at the president: The president is a monarch, the executive power, but one indirectly elected via the Electoral College. It was perceived at that time that the electors in the Electoral College would be the aristocrats. Furthermore, the president's term is limited to four years and the powers of the presidency are limited to those enumerated in Article II of the Constitution.

The Senate is an aristocratic branch of government. It is not directly elected by the people—not in the original Constitution; you needed a Constitutional amendment to change that—it is done via the state legislatures. One might argue that the people elect senators indirectly: They vote for their betters in the state legislatures, and the state legislatures determine who will be the senators. The term is lengthy (six years) with the powers listed in Article 1 of the Constitution. The national judiciary is also aristocratic.

The democratic branch is to be the House of Representatives, with short terms, frequent elections, but still you have property qualifications for voting. The theory at the time was you had to have a stake in society in order to be able to vote.

Each branch has the power to check the other branches. For example, the president is the Commander in Chief, but Congress appropriates funds for the armed forces and declares war. The president makes judicial and diplomatic appointments and negotiates treaties, but with the "advice and consent" of the Senate and appropriations approved by both houses; Congress makes the laws, but the president can veto them, and the Congress can override the veto with a two-thirds vote.

So much for the separation of powers; what about the division of powers? The new national government has enormous power but does not have a monopoly on power, it is to be shared with the existing state governments; and that is explicitly reaffirmed in the 10th Amendment, which states that all powers not delegated to the new national government or prohibited by it to the states are reserved to the states so that the states can be capable of checking the national government, as the national government can be capable of checking the excesses of the state. Some powers are very clearly shared: State militias are controlled by the state governments unless called into active service for the national government by the president.

The document sets up a very large republic; and as I pointed out before, in theory—by political theory of the day—it cannot survive. Madison, in the 10th Federalist Paper, turns this established political theory on its head. He claims that a republic in a large area has a better chance of preserving liberty than a republic in a small area; and in the process, he explains the logic behind the entire system.

Madison defines factions as the key problem, and factions as a minority or a majority willing to ride roughshod over the rights of others to insure its own interests. In democracies, a majority faction can easily gain control and destroy liberty. Madison insists that such factions cannot be abolished without abolishing liberty; they are inherent in human nature. The key is to control them, and that is to be done via checks and balances. Madison then argues that a large republic can do this better than small republics because the greater the population and area, the more factions will exist and thus the less chance of one faction dominating over the others. As Madison noted in this regard, a major difference between a republic and a democracy was the greater number of citizens and the extent of territory that could exist under a republican government.

> The smaller the society [Madison wrote], the fewer probably will be the distinct parties and interests composing it; the fewer the distinct parties and interests, the more frequently will a majority be found of the same party; and the smaller the number of individuals composing a majority, and the smaller the compass within which they are placed, the more easily will they concert and execute their plans of oppression.

That's for small, democratic society; as for republics:

> Extend the sphere, and you take in a greater variety of parties and interests; you make it less probable that a majority of the whole will have a common motive to invade the rights of other citizens; or if such a common motive exists, it will be more difficult for all who feel it to discover their own strength, and to act in unison with each other.

Despite agreement on such essentials, disagreements among the delegates almost wrecked the convention. Major disputes pitted large against small states; northern against southern states. Delegates also split over just how much power to give to the national government at the expense of the states.

The large versus small state dispute focused on representation in Congress. Madison's Virginia Plan had called for representation in both houses to be based on population. Small states like New Jersey refused to agree. The result was the so-called "Great Compromise": The House of Representatives would be based on population, but there would be equal representation for all states in the Senate.

There was also a split between the commercial and urban North as opposed to the agrarian and slaveholding South. That split was already apparent and it led to a series of compromises: There would never be an export tax, because the South produced a cash crop; there would be no ban on the slave trade for 20 years; a two-thirds vote would be needed in the Senate on all treaties; and a slave was to count as three-fifths of a person for purposes of representation and taxation.

Some delegates feared that despite the checks and balances, this new national government had too much power; only 39 of the 55 who were in attendance signed the final document. But the majority believed they had come up with something superior and unique: a large, centralized republic capable of acting strongly while still preserving liberty.

But would their fellow citizens agree? The document called for special state ratifying conventions in each state, with nine states needed to put the document into effect. Intense opposition emerged in virtually every state, primarily from established groups who controlled state governments and feared such centralized power. The result would be a major struggle in each state; it was very close, especially in the critical states of Virginia and New York. The *Federalist Papers* that I quoted were written not only by Madison, but also by Alexander Hamilton and John Jay in an effort to convince New York voters to accept the Constitution.

The pro-Constitution forces won for a host of reasons: They were better organized; they were on the offensive; and they had the advantage of defining themselves as "federalists." Really, they were nationalists; but by taking the title "federalists," what could their opponents call themselves? "Anti-federalists?" That was quite a negative connotation. Also, the call for ratification via special state conventions meant that the state legislatures, which had a vested interest in the failure of the new system, would be bypassed. Furthermore, the Federalists agreed to a key anti-Federalist objection: the lack of any specific Bill of Rights. They agreed to create one as their first order of business under the new government. The result would be the first 10 amendments to the Constitution. North Carolina and Rhode Island did not agree until 1790–1791, but the rest did agree early enough for the new government to begin functioning in 1789.

What do we have here? The final document and the *Federalist Papers* show the Founders as Hobbesian realists who distrusted human nature and who sought to stop what they considered the excesses of the Revolution. In that sense, they could be considered conservative and even counterrevolutionary. Simultaneously, however, they were still Lockeans and revolutionaries who wished to preserve their republican experiment against what they considered clear and present dangers; and they were willing to try a radical, unprecedented experiment to do so. The only analogy they had for a large republic was Rome, and that was not a very reassuring one. They saw their Constitution as fulfilling, not negating, the ideas of the Declaration of Independence; a way to make republicanism work, and thereby allow liberty to thrive.

They succeeded in establishing a new frame of government, but in the process they left a series of unanswered questions for the future: Is this a union of the people (as the House shows) or of the states (as the Senate shows)? What is proper balance between state and national power? How can you have a republican "empire of liberty" when that liberty is based on the enslavement of others? (Counting slaves as three-fifths of a human being does not really answer that question.) Can you really have an "empire of liberty"—a large, expanding nation run by a central government powerful enough to retain domestic order and military security—without creating a tyranny from above?

Within a few years, the writers of this document would split on their answers to these questions; they would fail to resolve them in their lifetimes; they would change the system they created in trying to solve them; and they would bequeath those problems to their successors. While some of those problems would be resolved in the 19th century—be it by compromise or by civil war—others remain central to our political discourse throughout the 20ᵗʰ century and still today, most notably the proper balance between state and national power; and some would argue whether it is indeed possible to have an "empire of liberty."

Washington—Failures and Real Accomplishments
Lecture 4

W e know that the cherry tree story about George Washington is a myth, but we still accept as fact what is at least partially mythical about the father of our country: that he was a great military and political leader. He was not perceived that way by some of his peers, and many historians agree with some of their criticisms. This lecture will look at Washington's failings and analyze his accomplishments, including some little-known ones that may be his most important contributions to American history.

Washington as General

- George Washington was originally selected by the Continental Congress to head the Continental Army not because of his previous military record, but because he was a well-established and respected figure in Virginia and had affirmed that the southern colonies would fight for Massachusetts in the wake of Lexington and Concord.

- Washington admitted that he did not think himself "equal to the command I am honored with," and he wasn't.

- He succeeded in maintaining a siege of Boston during 1775 and forced a British withdrawal from Boston in March of 1776. But he also ordered Benedict Arnold's ill-advised effort to take Quebec in 1775, which ended disastrously.

- In the summer of 1776, the British invaded New York, defeated Washington at the Battle of Brooklyn Heights, and took over New York City as their headquarters for the rest of the war. They went on to defeat Washington again at White Plains, capture Fort Washington, and force the abandonment of Fort Lee in New Jersey. Washington was chased all the way through New Jersey and across the Delaware River into Pennsylvania.

- All that prevented the pitiful remnants of Washington's army (now fewer than 3,000) from evaporating at the end of 1776—and the Revolution from ending in failure—was his desperate and successful raid on the Hessian garrison at Trenton on Christmas Day, followed by his successful raid on the British garrison at Princeton.

- In the following year, the British defeated Washington again in the battles of Brandywine Creek and Germantown and took the American capital of Philadelphia. Washington went into winter quarters at Valley Forge.

- At that point, a movement known as Conway Cabal emerged in both the officer corps and the Continental Congress to replace Washington with General Horatio Gates. Conway Cabal was squelched, but the attacks on Washington's competence continued.

- From 1778–1780, Washington's forces under subordinate commanders also suffered a series of disastrous defeats in Georgia and the Carolinas. Indeed, with the exception of the 1777 Saratoga victory, in which Washington was not directly involved, the general had only one major victory after Trenton and Princeton in the entire war, at Yorktown.
  - But Washington realized that he did not need a large number of battlefield victories to win the war and achieve independence; he had only to avoid the capture or destruction of the Continental Army to keep the Revolution alive until the British tired of the effort or were distracted by other concerns.

  - And that is exactly what happened. By the time of Yorktown, the British found themselves formally at war with France, Spain, and Holland, as well as unofficially at war with the rest of Europe. The British government also faced major dissent against the war at home. After the defeat at Yorktown, it was thus willing to make peace and recognize American independence.

The Newburgh Conspiracy

- At least as important as the Yorktown victory was Washington's recognition of the appropriate strategy, along with what he did after Yorktown but before completion of the formal peace treaty: his squelching of the Newburgh Conspiracy, one of the most dangerous events in U.S. history.

- While the Continental Army was encamped at Newburgh, New York, during the winter of 1782–1783, officers upset over Congress's refusal to fulfill past promises regarding pay circulated documents denouncing Congress, threatening its supremacy over the military, and calling for a meeting to discuss how to proceed.

- These officers had been encouraged by some political figures who wanted to use the threat of a possible coup to force Congress to agree to an import tax that would have strengthened national power and who turned to the anti-Washington group around General Gates to help foment the threat.

- Washington quickly squelched what could have easily become a real attempted coup, denouncing the documents and countering the threat by reminding his officers in a special meeting of what they had fought for and how perilous their behavior was to liberty.

- He followed that up later in the year with his own resignation as commander of the army. This formal renunciation of military power, as well as the refusal to seize power earlier when he easily could have, made him the American Cincinnatus—the ancient hero who had been granted absolute power, had saved the Roman Republic in a military crisis, and had then given up his power voluntarily.

- This move endeared Washington to his countrymen. In effect, he became the embodiment, as well as the defender, of the American concepts of liberty and civic virtue. He was asked to preside at the Constitutional Convention in Philadelphia in 1787 and thereby lend his prestige to the document the convention produced to replace the Articles of Confederation.

- Given that prestige, it was also apparent that Washington would be elected as the first president under this new frame of government, and he was, unanimously in the electoral college.

Washington as President

- As the first president, Washington set critical precedents in just about everything he did, many of which continue to this day. He also had many specific policy accomplishments, including creating a sound currency and fiscal structure to pay off the national debt, crushing the Whiskey Rebellion, and securing the western frontier by various treaties.

Neither a great general nor a great president, Washington's actions during the Revolution and his two terms in office were nonetheless vital to solidifying the American ideology of republican liberty.

- In 1793, Washington managed to avoid war with Britain and maintain American neutrality during the European war that erupted in the wake of France's declaration of a republic and execution of its king.

- In one area, however, Washington failed miserably: avoiding a major split between his key advisers, Alexander Hamilton and Thomas Jefferson, and among the American people over his policies. That split resulted, during his second term, in the formation of two national political parties and, by century's end, almost a civil war.

The Neutrality Compromise

- Washington had appointed the northerner Hamilton and the southerner Jefferson to the two most important cabinet posts, Treasury and State, to avoid division. But the two quickly came into sharp disagreement over fiscal policies, foreign policy, and their interpretation of the Constitution.

- In general terms, the key differences between the two were as follows: (1) In fiscal policy, Jefferson opposed Hamilton's idea of a national bank and his entire fiscal program; (2) in foreign policy, Hamilton leaned toward neutrality favoring Britain, while Jefferson advocated neutrality favoring France; and (3) in constitutional interpretation, Hamilton maintained a broad view of the powers of the federal government as opposed to the state governments, while Jefferson held a narrow one. Their followers soon referred to themselves as Federalists (for Hamilton) and Democratic-Republicans (for Jefferson).

- Some have seen Hamilton and Jefferson as Washington's surrogate sons and what followed—the neutrality compromise of 1793—as a desperate and failed attempt by Washington to steer a middle course between the two and avoid a "family" crisis.

- Hamilton recommended an immediate proclamation of neutrality in the conflict between Britain and France and no recognition of the new French government or its minister, Genêt. Jefferson recommended the opposite, and Washington's compromise was to issue a Neutrality Proclamation but also to recognize the new French government and receive Genêt.

- Gradually, Washington came to favor Hamilton's positions, and indeed, Hamilton used Washington's prestige to obtain congressional approval of both his fiscal program and the Jay Treaty guaranteeing continued peace with England. The unpopularity of the Jay Treaty—which smacked of surrender on neutral rights issues to the hated British—led to both public and private denunciations of Washington.

The Farewell Address
- Washington announced his retirement after two terms in a document known as the Farewell Address. Contrary to popular belief, that

document was not a call for isolation from European or world affairs. It was a warning against emotionalism in foreign affairs and against future permanent alliances given the grief the wartime alliance with France had cost Washington.

- But the basis of that warning is Washington's preceding warning against political parties based on geography. For Washington, such parties weakened the United States and invited European powers to exploit the split in order to increase their own power in the New World.

- The importance of Washington's advice in foreign affairs has tended to bury what may be the most important part of the address: his decision to leave the presidency voluntarily and after only two terms. It established a precedent for the two-term limit that lasted for more than 140 years and is now enshrined in a constitutional amendment.

- As he had done in his military career, Washington once again voluntarily gave up power and, in doing so, reinforced the constitutional emphasis on limiting the power of government offices as a way of preserving republicanism and liberty.

A Negative Legacy

- Washington was far from perfect as either a general or a president, yet his accomplishments were extraordinary in both fields: He virtually created the Continental Army and developed the appropriate strategy for using it to attain victory. He renounced absolute power when it could have been his and voluntarily gave up power at war's end. As president, he made the new frame of government work and established countless precedents, including the two-term limit when he once again voluntarily renounced power.

- Washington's most important contributions were, thus, negative, that is, critical for what did not happen: creation of a dictatorship. But they were nonetheless vital to the success of the nation.

Suggested Reading

Chernow, *Washington: A Life.*

Clausewitz, *On War.*

Ellis, *His Excellency: George Washington.*

Wills, *Cincinnatus.*

Questions to Consider

1. Why do we tend to ignore negative as opposed to positive accomplishments in history?

2. What personal characteristics and values made Washington so vital to the United States during the War of Independence and his presidency?

Washington—Failures and Real Accomplishments
Lecture 4—Transcript

George Washington is known, of course, as the father of our country, and there are countless memorials in the country honoring him. To cite but a few: the name of our capital city, Washington, D.C.; the monument within that city with his name; the name of the west coast state, Washington; numerous counties in other states; and, of course, his portrait on the one dollar bill.

In some ways, we are long past the late 18th and early 19th century hagiography of Washington; a hagiography epitomized by the story of him as a young boy unable to lie about chopping down the cherry tree. This myth was started by Parson Weems in his 1800 biography of Washington, and historians now treat that biography as part of a general effort in the early 19th century to create a national identity with Washington as its personification. But while the cherry tree myth is well-known, we still accept as fact what is at least partially myth about George Washington.

We do have deep respect and admiration for him for good reason. He was a great military and political leader. But he was not perceived that way by some of his peers, and many historians agree with some of the criticisms leveled by those peers. During the War for Independence, he was attacked as a military incompetent; and in retrospect, his military record was far from stellar. As president, he failed in his efforts to prevent the formation of national political parties. Indeed, however unwittingly, he became a de facto member of one of those parties, and according to some, an unwitting tool of that party.

In this lecture, will analyze his numerous failures and failings as both a military commander and as a president; but we will also look at his numerous accomplishments, including some that are little-known today. In retrospect, those little-known ones may be his most important contributions to American history.

Let's look first at Washington as a general. He was not a professional soldier; he was a Virginia planter, slave owner, and an aristocrat. He had originally been selected by the Continental Congress to head the new Continental

Army not because of his previous military record—which, as we will see, was far from stellar—but because he was a well-established and respected Virginia figure. Others—notably Charles Lee, Horatio Gates—had more military experience and better military records. Indeed, Washington's very questionable behavior in 1754 had led to what some label a massacre of French soldiers who had been on a diplomatic mission in what is today the western part of Pennsylvania. That in turn led to Washington's forced surrender to the French, who counterattacked. He had to surrender his men and a fort he had built near present-day Pittsburgh; and that in turn led to the French and Indian War, the result of all of this.

But with Lexington and Concord in 1775, the fighting during the Revolution was taking place around Boston, and it was unclear in 1775 if the southern colonies would fight for Massachusetts. Washington showing up at the Continental Congress in his Virginia militia uniform said that they would; and it's important to note here that Virginia; and it's important to note here that Virginia was the most populous and important of the 13 colonies at this time. It included present-day Virginia, West Virginia, and Kentucky.

Washington admitted that he did not think himself "equal to the command I am honored with," and he wasn't. He did succeed in maintaining a siege of Boston for the remainder of 1775; and thanks to his orders to Henry Knox, and Knox's ensuing extraordinary movement of cannon from Fort Ticonderoga to Boston—that's 300 miles overland during the winter—Washington was also able to force a British withdrawal from Boston in March, 1776.

But George Washington also ordered Benedict Arnold's ill-advised and unsuccessful effort to take Quebec in 1775; that ended disastrously. So did the entire second half of 1776, with the British invasion of New York City that summer. First, General Howe defeated Washington at the Battle of Brooklyn Heights and forced Washington to abandon the entire city, which became British headquarters for the rest of the war. Then the British defeated him again at White Plains; they captured Fort Washington; they forced the abandonment of Fort Lee in New Jersey; and then they chased Washington all the way through New Jersey all the way across the Delaware River into Pennsylvania.

All that prevented the pitiful remnants of his army—now fewer than 3,000 men—from evaporating at year's end and the Revolution from ending in failure was Washington's desperate and successful raid on the Hessian garrison at Trenton on Christmas Day. That was followed by his successful raid on the British garrison at Princeton. But these were just that: raids that precluded his immediate and total defeat and that led many to reenlist in his army; but they in no way dislodged the British Army from its New York City base or forced the British to accede to the American goal of independence. In the following year, 1777, the British defeated him again in the Battles of Brandywine Creek and Germantown, and took the American capital city of Philadelphia. Washington then went into winter quarters at Valley Forge.

At that moment, a movement known as the "Conway Cabal" emerged in both the officer corps and the Continental Congress to replace Washington with General Gates. Gates had falsely received credit for the great American victory and surrender of an entire British Army at Saratoga in the fall of 1777; that credit properly belonged to two other officers: Gates's predecessor Philip Schuyler and Benedict Arnold, who was at this point Washington's best general. The Conway Cabal was squelched, but not the attacks on Washington's competence. Those attacks continued with the military stalemate that ensured in the North, mutinies in his army in early 1780, Benedict Arnold's treason, and a series of major American defeats in the South.

Arnold's treason not only endangered Washington's major defenses at West Point, but it also deprived him of his best general; the real hero, as previously noted, of the critical victory at Saratoga, and the officer who had made possible that victory the previous year by a little known but vitally important delaying action in the naval battle of Valcour Island on Lake Champlain. Arnold built a fleet at Whitehall, New York to meet the British on the lake. He lost the battle, but what he wound up doing was delaying a planned British movement down the Champlain Valley along with a movement from New York City up the Hudson Valley to split the colonies; to split New England off from the rest of the colonies. The movement from Montreal did not begin until 1777. Had Arnold not done what he did at Valcour Island, the British might have been in Albany by the winter of 1776. Starting from that point, it would have been a lot easier to complete the split. Instead, General

Burgoyne's army was surrounded at Saratoga just north of Albany. In building his ships at Whitehall for this battle, Arnold thus ironically became the founder of the U.S. Navy.

From 1778–1780, Washington's forces under a series of subordinate commanders also suffered a series of disastrous defeats in Georgia and the Carolinas: Savannah was lost, Charleston was lost, and the nightmarish Battle of Camden. Indeed, with the exception of the 1777 Saratoga victory, in which Washington was not directly involved, in the entire war he had only one major victory after Trenton and Princeton; but it was a decisive one: Yorktown, where a combined American and French land force, along with the French Navy, trapped and forced the surrender of another entire British Army, a second entire British Army, this time under General Cornwallis.

But Washington did not need a large number of battlefield victories to win the war and achieve independence. As he came to realize, all he had to do was maintain the Continental Army that he had created and avoid its capture or destruction in order to keep the Revolution alive until the British tired of the war effort or until they were distracted by other concerns; and that is exactly what happened. By the time of Yorktown, 1781, they found themselves formally at war with France, Spain, and Holland, as well as unofficially at war with the rest of Europe in the form of the League of Armed Neutrals. They were also diplomatically isolated. At home, the government faced major dissent against the war. London was thus willing after Yorktown to make peace and to recognize American independence.

But at least as important as the Yorktown victory was Washington's recognition of the appropriate strategy to use, and what he did after Yorktown but before completion of the formal peace treaty. Yorktown took place in 1781, the formal peace treaty was not signed and ratified until 1783, and in the interim, he squelched of one of the most dangerous, and what the historian Richard Kohn has labeled "one of the most bizarre and little understood events in the history of the United States": the Newburgh Conspiracy.

What happened here? While the army was encamped at Newburgh, New York during the winter of 1782–1783, officers upset over the Continental

Congress's refusal to fulfill past promises regarding pay circulated documents that denounced Congress, that threatened its supremacy over the military, and that called for a meeting to discuss how to proceed. These officers in Newburgh had been encouraged by some political figures in Philadelphia and elsewhere who wanted to use the threat of a possible military coup in order to force the Congress to agree to a tax on imports in order to be able to pay these officers; that tax would have strengthened the national government and national power. These politicians turned to the anti-Washington group in the officer corps around General Gates to help foment this threat.

Washington quickly squelched what could have easily become a real attempted coup rather than simply the threat of a coup. He denounced the documents, and he countered the threat by reminding his officers in a special meeting of what they had fought for, what this war had been all about, and how perilous to liberty their behavior was. He also stunned the officers at that meeting by putting on for the first time a pair of reading glasses, spectacles, in order to read a document to them. Noticing just how shocked they were—this was the first time he had worn glasses—he commented, "Yes gentlemen, you will see that I have grown not only gray but almost blind in the service of my country." That ended it, right then and there.

Washington followed that up at year's end with his own resignation as commander of the army. This formal renunciation of military power, as well as the refusal to seize power earlier when he easily could have, made him the American Cincinnatus, the ancient hero who had abandoned his farm to save the republic of Rome when it was in a military crisis. Cincinnatus had been granted absolute power; he had defeated the enemy, but he had then given up the power voluntarily and returned to his farm.

Washington's behavior also endeared him to his countrymen as much as his overall military success did during the war. In effect, he became the embodiment as well as the defender of the American concepts of liberty and civic virtue. For that reason, he was asked to preside at the Constitutional Convention in Philadelphia in 1787. He thereby lent his enormous prestige to the document that convention produced to replace the Articles of Confederation.

Given that prestige, it was also apparent that he would be elected as first president of the United States under this new frame of government; and he was, unanimously in the Electoral College. He remains the only president ever to receive a unanimous vote in the Electoral College.

As the first president, Washington would set critical precedents in just about everything that he did, many of which continue down to this very day. He also had many specific policy accomplishments, most notably: the creation of a sound currency and fiscal structure to pay off the national debt; the crushing of an incipient rebellion in Pennsylvania, the Whiskey Rebellion; the securing of the western frontier by treaties with the Spanish and the Indian tribes in the southwest, and in the northwest by treaty with Britain and war with the Indian tribes there. The treaty with Britain avoided war and maintained American neutrality in the European war that broke out in 1793; this despite the fact that the United States still had its wartime alliance with France. In 1793, France declared itself a republic, it executed its king, and it went to war with virtually all of the crowned heads of Europe.

In one area, Washington failed miserably: avoiding a major split between his two key advisers, Alexander Hamilton and Thomas Jefferson, and also in avoiding a split amongst the American people over his policies. The split resulted during his second term in the formation of two national political parties and almost a civil war by century's end. What happened here?

Washington had appointed the northerner Alexander Hamilton and the southerner Thomas Jefferson to the two most important cabinet posts, Secretary of the Treasury and Secretary of State. He had done so, ironically, to avoid a split; but the two men quickly came into sharp disagreement over fiscal policy, foreign policy, and their interpretation of the Constitution. All of this will be explained in greater detail in the next lecture. For our purposes in this lecture, the key differences in general terms were in the following areas: Fiscal. Jefferson opposed Hamilton's National Bank and his entire financial program. In foreign policy, Hamilton wanted neutrality favoring Britain; Jefferson wanted neutrality favoring France. In terms of interpretation of the Constitution: Hamilton wanted to interpret it broadly, Jefferson wanted to interpret it narrowly regarding the powers that the new federal government had as opposed to the powers that the states still had. Their followers on either side were soon referring to themselves as Federalists (for the followers of Hamilton) and Democratic-Republicans (for Jefferson).

George Washington had no children of his own, and some have seen Hamilton and Jefferson as his surrogate sons and what followed here as a desperate and failed attempt by Washington to steer a middle course between the two and avoid a family crisis. These efforts are best seen in his compromise over neutrality in 1793.

Hamilton had recommended an immediate proclamation of neutrality when war broke out in Europe and no recognition of the new French government or the minister it was sending over, Edmund Genêt. Jefferson had recommended no Neutrality Proclamation at this time, but immediate recognition of the new French government and Edmund Genêt. Washington's compromise on this issue was to proclaim the neutrality of the United States as Hamilton wanted, but also to recognize the new French government and receive its minister, Genêt. Jefferson and Washington, by the way, thereby established the American policy of recognizing any government in power, no matter how much it agreed or disagreed with it; a policy that would hold until Woodrow Wilson reversed it in the early 20th century.

Despite this effort, gradually Washington came to favor Hamilton's positions; and, indeed, Hamilton used Washington's prestige to obtain congressional approval of both his fiscal program and the Jay Treaty guaranteeing continued peace with England. But the Jay Treaty was extremely unpopular. It smacked of surrender on neutral rights issues to the hated British, and it led to both public and private denunciations of Washington. Indeed, by inference if nothing else, Washington was now one of those "apostates" who Jefferson described in a letter as men who were "Samsons in the field & Solomons in the council, but who have had their heads shorn by the harlot England."

Whether attacks like this played a role in Washington's decision to retire after two terms as president is uncertain. Washington had wanted to retire after only one term, but both sides had urged him to stay on at that time. Now, however, only one urged him to stay, and he was unwilling to do so. Consequently, he wrote and had published in a newspaper his decision to retire, a document we know as the "Farewell Address."

Contrary to popular belief, the "Farewell Address" is not a call for isolation from European or from world affairs. Rather, it is a warning against emotionalism in foreign affairs and against any future permanent alliances given the grief that the wartime alliance with France, which was still in effect, had recently cost Washington. But what was the basis of the warning against permanent alliances and emotionalism in foreign affairs? Washington had preceded this, using it as a lead in to the foreign policy section: a warning against political parties based on geography. Such parties, he argued, weakened the United States and invited European powers to exploit the internal split and support one side or the other in order to increase their own power within the New World. Within that warning was an implied attack on Jefferson and his Democratic-Republican Party for being tools of France and being emotionally committed to France in this regard.

The advice to avoid emotionalism in foreign affairs was sound, but the implied attack on Jefferson was a bit unfair, as we will see in the next lecture. The importance of the advice in foreign affairs has tended to bury what may be the single most important part of the address: the decision to leave the presidency voluntarily and after only two terms. What Washington did was establish a precedent for the two-term limit; a limit that lasted for over 140 years—until Franklin Roosevelt ran and succeeded to a third term in 1940— and is now enshrined in a Constitutional amendment that limits the president to two terms.

As in his military career, Washington once again gave up power voluntarily; and in doing so, he reinforced enormously the Constitution's emphasis on limiting the power of government offices as a way of preserving republicanism and liberty.

Washington was far from perfect, either as a general or as a president, and he was severely criticized by his fellow countrymen, both as a general and as a president. Yet his accomplishments were extraordinary in both fields: During the War for Independence, he virtually created the Continental Army and a national consciousness within that army. He also maintained and trained the army under incredibly trying circumstances and developed the appropriate strategy for its use in order to attain victory. He won critical, if not many, battlefield victories. He also squashed what could easily have become an attempted military coup. He renounced absolute power when it could have been his, and he voluntarily gave up power at war's end. Through all of this, he became the personification of the Revolution and its values. Washington then lent his prestige to the Constitutional Convention; and by doing so he helped to assure the ratification of that document and he became our first president. As president, he established the nation's finances on a sound basis; he crushed a rebellion; he avoided war with England; and he secured the western frontier by both treaty and war. He made the new frame of government work, and in the process he established countless precedents. The most important of these may well have been the two-term limit, where once again he voluntarily renounced power and thus further solidified the American ideology of republican liberty.

As a private citizen, by the way, he also renounced slavery by including in his will a provision that his slaves be freed after his death and his wife's death. That was something that Thomas Jefferson, the great apostle of liberty, would not do.

Washington's most important contributions were thus negative, and as such they are easily forgotten, but they were vital to the success of this nation; and his reputation as the father of the country is fully warranted, though not for the reasons we think. Why have these negative contributions been so often ignored? Essentially, because they were not only negative, but also because they were critical to what did not happen—a non-event: the creation of a dictatorship, military or otherwise—and it is very easy to overlook and ignore an event that prevented something from happening.

Yet such a negative consequence is often at least as important in history as positive consequences. Try to remember that as we proceed through this course.

Confusions about Jefferson and Hamilton
Lecture 5

D uring the 1790s, Thomas Jefferson and Alexander Hamilton held sharply conflicting views on foreign and domestic policies and on constitutional interpretation. Today, many label Hamilton's views as conservative and Jefferson's as liberal and see their conflict as a harbinger of contemporary battles. Yet the specific issues over which they argued are not relevant to modern Americans, and their views have little to do with current definitions of "conservative" and "liberal." Still, their conflicts are relevant to us, albeit not in the ways we might think.

The Split over Fiscal Policy

- Washington had selected Thomas Jefferson and Alexander Hamilton for his two most important cabinet positions as part of a general effort to maintain sectional balance—not political/ideological balance—within the new national government.

- The split that developed between the two was primarily over two issues: government fiscal policies and definitions of neutrality as a result of the war between England and France.

- As Treasury secretary, Hamilton believed that the most pressing problems of the United States were financial. The country needed to establish credit at home and abroad if the new government was to work.
  - Hamilton thus proposed that the new national government assume all state Revolutionary War debts, combine them with the national debt, and fund both at par value via a new bond issue.

  - He also proposed new taxes on imports and some domestically produced items to pay government debts and the establishment of a combined private and government-controlled national bank to serve as a depository for treasury notes and fiscal agent for the government, with its own bank notes to be considered legal tender.

- o These actions would tie the wealthy merchant and financial class to the success of the new government, while providing a new circulating medium, establishing the credit of the government, and increasing its power and prestige.

- The opposition to Hamilton was at first led by James Madison, not Jefferson. Later, Jefferson opposed the establishment of the national bank on the grounds that the power to do so was not specifically enumerated in Article I of the Constitution. Hamilton argued that the power was constitutional via the "necessary and proper" clause in Article I. Washington sided with Hamilton, but a serious split had emerged.

The Split over Foreign Affairs

- The division over foreign affairs became apparent in 1793, when the French Revolution turned radical with the creation of the French Republic, the execution of the king, and the institution of the Reign of Terror. This resulted in the outbreak of general war in Europe, pitting republican France against Britain and all the other major monarchies of Europe.

- Everyone in the cabinet agreed that the United States should remain neutral, but a treaty of alliance was in effect with France dating back to the Revolutionary War. Further, the question arose of which country U.S. neutrality should favor. Hamilton argued for neutrality favoring Britain, while Jefferson advocated neutrality favoring the "sister republic" of France.

- At first, Washington took a middle-of-the-road position, but by 1794–1795, he sided with Hamilton by agreeing to the Jay Treaty with England. In an effort to avoid war, the treaty acceded to the British definition of "neutral rights" in return for British evacuation of posts on U.S. territory and peace.

- The Jay Treaty led to a public uproar against it and formation of the first two national political parties: the Federalists under Hamilton and the Democratic-Republicans under Jefferson and Madison.

The Split Widens

- In the presidential election of 1796, Federalist John Adams narrowly defeated Jefferson, who became the vice president.
  - During Adams's presidency, the dispute between the two political parties became white-hot as the United States engaged in an undeclared naval war with France as a result of the Jay Treaty.

  - The Federalists passed the Alien and Sedition Acts, directed against the Democratic-Republicans, while Jefferson and Madison responded with the Virginia and Kentucky Resolutions, threatening nullification of the acts and other "unconstitutional" laws.

  - The specific issues addressed by these laws and resolutions are of little or no relevance to us today, but many argue that the conflicting beliefs behind the issues are significant, though not in the ways we might think.

- As we've noted, Jefferson argued for a narrow interpretation of the Constitution with regard to national power versus state power, while Hamilton argued for a broad interpretation via the necessary and proper clause.
  - This argument over state versus national power is a constant in U.S. history, right down to this day. It pitted Federalists against Democratic-Republicans throughout this era, then Democrats against Whigs in the 1830s and 1840s, then Democrats against Republicans in the modern era.

  - In this case, however, the positions in the 1790s were reversed from what they would later be and still are today. At the time, the supposedly aristocratic Hamilton argued for more national power and the supposedly democratic Jefferson argued for less, whereas since the 1930s, Jefferson's liberal disciples have argued for more and their conservative opponents for less!

- Also relevant in this regard was Jefferson's welcoming of the French Revolution while Hamilton and his followers abhorred it and favored the British.
  - Hamilton favored the British because British trade was essential to provide revenues for the government via import taxes and because British credit and manufactured goods were necessary for his vision of U.S. development.

  Although Jefferson argued for less national power in his clash with Hamilton, as president, he actually expanded the power of the federal government.

  - At the same time, Jefferson's opposition was based not so much on his love for republican France but on the fact that he did not support the Hamiltonian domestic program and, thus, did not believe that the United States needed British trade or credit. He also feared dependency on the powerful British and desired to use a French connection as a counterweight.

- It's also true that, in many ways, Hamilton was not really aristocratic and Jefferson was not really democratic. Both men believed strongly in republicanism (meaning representative government) as opposed to monarchy, but the questions here were: Who would be the representatives, and who would they represent?
  - Despite his reputation, Jefferson was not a democrat who believed in majority rule. He was a slaveholder and aristocrat who believed in property qualifications for voting. He also saw a decentralized, agrarian society of self-sufficient yeoman

farmers as the best way to preserve liberty, and he believed in the "politics of deference"—hardly a democratic notion!

o Hamilton, on the other hand, was no aristocrat. He was an illegitimate child from the West Indies, and he believed that centralized power was necessary to preserve liberty from both internal chaos and external threat. He also believed that self-interest rules human nature and should be used to create such centralized power by a linking of the wealthy commercial and financial interests to those of the national government. Jefferson saw self-interest as evil.

Modern-Day Relevance

• The specific issues facing Jefferson and Hamilton, and their disagreements, have little to do with the issues we as a nation face now, yet their disagreement is still relevant to us on multiple levels.

• First, the disagreement over the interpretation of the Constitution and national versus state power has been a constant throughout U.S. history down to the present day. Here, it is Hamilton's view that contemporary liberals embrace and Jefferson's that contemporary conservatives embrace.

• Second, Jefferson's agrarianism and aristocratic emphasis on property qualifications for voting possessed a strong democratic streak in the agrarian American world of the 1790s. At the time, the United States was overwhelmingly populated by farmers who owned their own land and, thus, possessed sufficient property to vote. Hamilton's commercial/manufacturing and urban vision possesses an unwitting democratic streak in the opportunities for advancement it would provide in the future.

• The conflicting views of Hamilton and Jefferson on human nature and the role of self-interest in government also have continued relevance.
  o Hamilton had a pessimistic view of human nature, which he saw as motivated by self-interest. He sought to harness

that self-interest by tying the wealthy and powerful to the new government.

- o Jefferson saw self-interest and the mutual dependence of government and commercialism as leading to corruption and the destruction of liberty. He also believed strongly in republican virtue and political disinterest (rather than self-interest) as appropriate for politics in a republican society and as the key to preserving liberty.

- o Although Jefferson's words still resonate with our democratic beliefs today, it is Hamilton's vision and views regarding a politics based on self-interest that would become our reality. The concept of republican virtue as central to politics would disappear with the deaths of the Founding Fathers and their replacement by a new generation of political leaders with different ideas.

The Aftermath of the Split
- Hamilton's death did not result in the immediate demise of the Federalist Party, but it left the party leaderless and geographically isolated in New England, while westward expansion brought in more supporters of Jefferson's Democratic-Republicans.

- Jefferson and his successor, James Madison, succeeded in wooing moderate Federalists into the Democratic-Republican Party by agreeing to some Federalist ideas, including a protective tariff for American industry and the chartering of a second national bank.

- During the War of 1812, the remaining extreme Federalists further isolated themselves by opposing the war and, at the Hartford Convention, hypocritically calling for states' rights and virtually threatening secession. News of American military victories and the negotiation of a peace treaty ending the war with Britain led to the party's disgrace and collapse.

- In the election of 1820, the Democratic-Republican candidate James Monroe ran unopposed, and the nation entered an era of one-party rule, during which the Democratic-Republican Party encompassed the views of both Hamilton and Jefferson.

- That, of course, could not and would not continue. The Hamilton-Jefferson disagreements would soon reassert themselves in the creation of the so-called second two-party political system during the 1820s and 1830s.

Suggested Reading

Chernow, *Alexander Hamilton.*

Ellis, *American Sphinx.*

———, *Founding Brothers.*

Questions to Consider

1. How are the conflicts between Hamilton and Jefferson relevant to us today?

2. Where else in U.S. history do we tend to anachronistically project our contemporary values onto the past?

Confusions about Jefferson and Hamilton
Lecture 5—Transcript

During the 1790s, Thomas Jefferson and Alexander Hamilton held sharply conflicting views as to the proper domestic and foreign policies for the new nation and as to how the new Constitution should be interpreted. Today, many label Hamilton's views as conservative and Jefferson's as liberal, and they see their conflict as a harbinger of contemporary conflicts. Yet the specific issues over which Hamilton and Jefferson argued are in no way related or relevant to contemporary issues; and their views have little if anything to do with the terms "conservative" and "liberal" as they are presently defined. To believe that they do is a classic example of anachronistic thinking; of projecting contemporary values and meanings of words onto a past where they do not fit. More accurate might be the terms "aristocratic" for Hamilton and "democratic" for Jefferson; but even here, the terms distort the historical reality more than they enlighten.

Nevertheless, the conflicting views of Hamilton and Jefferson are deeply relevant to us today, but not in the ways we normally think of them. We first need to recognize, as was stated in the last lecture, that Washington had selected Jefferson and Hamilton for the two most important cabinet positions as part of his general effort to maintain sectional balance—not political/ideological balance—within the new national government. This desire for sectional balance is one reason why John Adams of Massachusetts was chosen as Vice President to balance Washington of Virginia as President. Now Washington was trying to create geographic balance within his cabinet by selecting Hamilton from New York City the Secretary of the Treasury and Jefferson from Virginia as the Secretary of State. None of them had any idea of the split that would develop.

That split developed primarily over two issues of no relevance to us today but of great relevance to them, one domestic and one foreign: government fiscal policies and definitions of neutrality when England and France went to war once again in 1793. Hamilton as the Treasury Secretary believed the most pressing problems of the United States were financial; that we needed to establish our credit both at home and abroad if the new government was to work. He therefore proposed that the new national government assume all state Revolutionary War debts, combine them with the national debt, and fund both debts at par value via a new bond issue. He also proposed new taxes on imports and some domestically produced items in order to pay these debts, and the establishment of a combined private and government-controlled National Bank—80 percent private, 20 percent government—to serve as a depository for treasury notes and a fiscal agent for the government. The bank's notes were to be considered legal tender. All of this, Hamilton proposed, would tie the wealthy merchant and financial class to the success of the new government while providing a new circulating medium. It would also establish the credit of the new government and increase its power and prestige. The crack that is usually made is that Hamilton was going to turn the national debt into a national blessing.

Opposition to his plan was at first led not by Jefferson, but by James Madison, with whom Hamilton had collaborated in writing the *Federalist Papers*. Jefferson at first served as a mediator between the two. He arranged a stag dinner during which Madison agreed to support funding and assumption in return for Hamilton's agreement that the permanent capitol—at this time the temporary capitol was New York City—would be in the South on land that Virginia and Maryland would eventually donate on the Potomac River.

But after this mediation, Jefferson, in the Cabinet, opposed Hamilton's proposed National Bank—it should not have been part of the deal; the National Bank was proposed later—on the grounds that since establishing a National Bank was not a specifically enumerated national power within Article I of the Constitution, to establish such a bank would be unconstitutional. Hamilton countered that it was constitutional via the "necessary and proper" clause in Article 1, section 8: that Congress had the power "to make all laws which shall be necessary and proper for carrying into execution" the specific powers previously listed; in this case, the powers to pay debts, borrow money, and coin money. Washington sided with Hamilton on this issue, but a serious split had emerged. Nevertheless, it was only at the highest levels of government, and Washington was unanimously reelected president in 1792.

The split over foreign affairs emerged in following year, 1793, when the French Revolution turned radical with the creation of the French Republic, the execution of the king, and the institution of the Reign of Terror. This resulted in the outbreak of a general war in Europe, pitting Republican France against Britain and all the other major monarchies of Europe. Everyone in Washington's Cabinet agreed that the United States should remain neutral in that war, but the United States still had a treaty of alliance with France dating back to the Revolutionary War; what were you going to do with it? The question also arose as to neutrality favoring whom? Hamilton argued for neutrality favoring Britain; Jefferson argued for neutrality favoring the "sister republic" of France.

As explained in the last lecture, Washington at first took a middle of the road position, agreeing with Hamilton and against Jefferson's advice to immediately issue a neutrality proclamation; but agreeing with Jefferson and against Hamilton's advice to recognize the new French Republic and accept its new minister to the United States, Edmund Genêt. But by 1794–1795, Washington was siding with Hamilton more and more, most importantly by agreeing to the odious Jay Treaty with England. That treaty avoided war with England, which is why Washington agreed to it; but he had to accede to the British definition of neutral rights in return for British evacuation of posts on U.S. territory in the old northwest. When that treaty became public, it led to an uproar against it, and to the formation of the first two national political parties: the Federalists under Hamilton and the Democratic-Republicans under Jefferson and Madison.

In the presidential election of 1796, the Federalist John Adams—the Vice President at that point—narrowly defeated his old friend Thomas Jefferson for the presidency, but Jefferson had the second highest number of electoral votes. Remember, the writers of the Constitution had not imagined permanent political parties. The way they had set the system up, the person with the majority of electoral votes—the highest number of electoral votes—would become President; the second highest would become Vice President. As a result, you had President from one party, Vice President from another party. The 12th amendment of 1804 would separate the electoral vote for President and for Vice President, but obviously that amendment was not in effect in 1796.

During Adams's presidency, the dispute between the two political parties became white-hot as the United States engaged in an undeclared naval war with France as a result of the Jay Treaty, and the two parties—the Federalists and the Democratic-Republicans—came very close to civil war. The Federalists in Congress would pass the Alien and the Sedition Acts, which violated civil liberties and were directed against the Democratic-Republicans. Jefferson and Madison would respond with the Virginia and Kentucky Resolutions, threatening nullification of these laws and any others that violated their civil rights.

These specific issues are of little or no relevance to us today. Both domestically and internationally, they are issues for a young and weak nation, which is exactly what we were at that time vis-à-vis Britain and France, who were the two superpowers of the era. But many argue that the conflicting beliefs behind the specific issues are relevant to us today. They are, but not in the ways you may think.

Most obviously relevant are Jefferson's and Hamilton's conflicting interpretations of the Constitution. Jefferson argued for a narrow interpretation of national power versus state power; i.e., the National Bank was unconstitutional because no such power to establish one was in the Constitution. Hamilton countered with a broad interpretation via the "necessary and proper" clause. This argument over state versus national power is a constant in U.S. history, right down to this very day. It pitted Federalists against Democratic-Republicans throughout this era, then it pitted Democrats against Whigs in the 1830s and 40s, and then Democrats against Republicans. But in this case, the positions in the 1790s were reversed from what they will later be and still are today, with the supposedly aristocratic Hamilton arguing for more national power and the supposedly democratic Jefferson arguing for less. Since the 1930s, Jefferson's liberal disciples—in fact, maybe earlier than the 1930s—have argued for more national power and their conservative opponents for less.

To further complicate matters, after Jefferson became President in 1801 he actually expanded national, especially executive power, as did many of his successors who campaigned against expanded power but nevertheless did expand power. So while this issue is relevant to us today (obviously), the

18th-century hero that each side looks to today actually held the opposite position from the one his supposed followers hold today.

Others see relevance today in Jefferson's welcoming of the French Revolution, while Hamilton and his followers abhorred the French Revolution and thus favored the British. That is also true; but Hamilton had favored the British even before the French Revolution became radical because British trade was essential to his domestic program. Most American imports came from Britain, and in Hamilton's system, import taxes would provide the bulk of the revenue for the federal government. British credit and manufactured goods were also essential for Hamilton's vision of American economic development.

Jefferson's opposition to all this was based not so much on any love of Republican France, but on the fact that he did not support the Hamiltonian domestic program, and thus did not believe that the United States needed British trade or credit. He also feared dependency on the powerful British and desired to use the French connection as a counterweight; in other words, to pit Britain and France against each other in order to preserve American independence from the clutches of both. Let me cite to you in this regard what the French Minister to the United States wrote home at one point:

> Mr. Jefferson loves us [he wrote] because he detests England; he seeks rapprochement with us because he distrusts us less than Great Britain; but he would change perhaps tomorrow from a sentiment favorable to us, if tomorrow Great Britain should cease to inspire him with fears. Although Jefferson is the friend of liberty and science, although he is an admirer of the efforts we have made to cast off our shackles and to clear away the cloud of ignorance which weighs down the human race, Jefferson, I say, is an American, and as such, he cannot sincerely be our friend. An American is the born enemy of all the peoples of Europe.

So while the supposedly democratic Jefferson did support the French Revolution, and the aristocratic Hamilton did oppose it and favor monarchial Britain, both men did so for political reasons having little to do with their feelings regarding any revolutionary ideology. Furthermore, and more importantly, in many ways Hamilton was not really aristocratic and Jefferson was not really democratic. Both men were republicans; they did believe strongly in republicanism as opposed to monarchy. The question would be what kind of republicanism. Republicanism simply means representative government, which the Founders equated with liberty; but who would be the representatives, and who would they represent?

Despite his reputation, Thomas Jefferson was not a democrat who believed simply in majority rule. He and many of his peers considered this mob rule, which is what they equated with democracy. Remember Madison's comments in Federalist 10. Jefferson, like Madison, was a Virginia slave owner and an aristocrat who believed in property qualifications for voting; the stake in society theory: You must have a stake in society in order to participate in government. Jefferson also saw a decentralized, agrarian society of self-sufficient, independent or yeoman farmers as the best way to preserve liberty; and he believed in the politics of deference whereby farmers would be allowed to vote because they had property, but they were to vote for their betters, their economic and their social betters. This was a general belief system in the United States in the late 18th century, and hardly a democratic notion by our standards.

Hamilton, on the other hand, was no aristocrat. He was an illegitimate child from the West Indies, and he believed centralized power was necessary to preserve liberty from both internal chaos and external threat. Hamilton also believed that self-interest ruled human nature, and that self-interest should be used to create such centralized power by linking the wealthy commercial and financial interests of the country to the interests of the national government. Jefferson, on the other hand, saw self-interest as an evil.

As you can see, the specific issues facing Jefferson and Hamilton, and their ensuing disagreements, have little to do with the issues we as a nation now have. Both men had aristocratic as opposed to democratic views by contemporary standards. Yet their disagreement is still relevant to us on multiple levels, albeit not as we think.

First and foremost, as previously noted, was their disagreement over the interpretation of the Constitution and national versus state power. That disagreement will be a constant throughout U.S. history right down to the present day. But here, it is Hamilton's view that contemporary liberals embrace and Jefferson's view that contemporary conservatives embrace. Second, Jefferson's agrarianism and aristocratic emphasis on property qualifications for voting possessed a strong democratic streak not in our contemporary and urban world, but in the agrarian American world of the 1790s. At that time, the United States was overwhelmingly composed of farmers who owned their own land, and who thus possessed sufficient property to vote. Yet for the future, Hamilton's commercial, manufacturing, and urban vision possesses an unwitting democratic streak in the opportunities for advancement that this would provide in the future.

Beyond that, however, was the continued relevance of their conflicting views on human nature and the role of self-interest. Hamilton had a very pessimistic view of human nature. He saw humans as motivated by self-interest, and he sought to harness that by tying the wealthy and the powerful to the new government so that they would be dependent on each other. The government would depend on these upper classes; they would depend on the government.

Jefferson was the opposite: He saw self-interest and dependence as leading to corruption and the destruction of liberty. That's one of the reasons he was so anti-urban and so agrarian. He also believed strongly in republican virtue and political disinterredness of those in office and seeking office rather than self-interest as appropriate for politics in a republican society and as the key to preserving liberty.

While Jefferson's words will resonate with our democratic beliefs today, it was Hamilton's vision and views regarding a politics based on self-interest that would become our reality. The old concept of republican virtue as central to politics—that concept that dominated the late-18th century political world—would disappear with the death of the Founders and their replacement in the early 19th century by a new generation of political leaders with very different ideas.

Ironically, that new view of politics would help to get Jefferson elected president in 1800 via his alliance with Aaron Burr and Burr's early New

York City political machine, Tammany Hall. In a further irony, that is the same Aaron Burr who as Vice President would kill Alexander Hamilton in a duel in 1804, and whose civil liberties Jefferson would then violate after Burr's conspiracy to create a private empire in the southwest is uncovered.

That sounds complicated, and it is. Let me explain. Remember, the 12th Amendment did not come into existence into 1804, so that each elector cast his votes and the person with the highest number of votes became President and the second highest became Vice President. But, because of party discipline in 1800, every Democratic-Republican elector cast one vote for Jefferson and one vote for Burr, so they were tied for the presidency. In that situation, the election went to the House where the Federalists were in the majority, and they would decide who would be the next president. There was a general feeling amongst many Federalists that they could work with Burr; they had come to believe their own propaganda about Jefferson as virtually the antichrist, whereas Burr, they believed, was someone you could work with. Hamilton disagreed; he understood who Jefferson was, he believed that Burr was a total scoundrel. He convinced many Federalists to vote for Jefferson rather than Burr.

In that situation, Burr realized that he was going to be a one-term vice president—no way was Jefferson going to run with him in 1804—so he had to rebuild his political career. He decided to do so by running for the governorship in New York. That, too, was foiled by Hamilton, who denounced Burr, insulted him, and that led Burr to challenged Hamilton to a duel. Dueling was illegal in New York; they rowed across the Hudson River to New Jersey to have the duel, and Burr killed Hamilton. He was still the Vice President of the United States, and he was a fugitive from justice. What he now attempted to do with former Revolutionary War General James Wilkison was to carve out a private empire in the old southwest. The plot was eventually discovered. Jefferson, in a panic, violated Burr's civil liberties on multiple occasions in an attempt to get him jailed. He ordered him arrested, he judged him guilty before there was any evidence; he threw the book at Burr, and he failed. Chief Justice John Marshall presided the case, and Burr was set free.

Burr's killing of Hamilton did not result in the immediate demise of the Federalist Party; but it did leave that party leaderless. It also left it more and more geographically isolated in New England. Westward expansion, both into territory up to the Mississippi River and into the Louisiana Purchase territory that Jefferson had obtained from France in 1803 brought in more and more supporters of Jefferson's Democratic-Republicans. The Federalists had always been strongest in New England; more and more it was becoming a regional party.

Jefferson and his successor James Madison also pursued a policy of wooing moderate Federalists into their party, and they succeeded. Even John Adams's son, John Quincy Adams, joined the Democratic-Republican Party. The way Jefferson and Madison did this was to agree to some Federalist concepts, including by 1816 a protective tariff for infant American industry and the chartering of a second National Bank in 1816, as well as a general expansion of federal power, including executive power. Please note in this regard the expansion of national and executive power: Nowhere in the Constitution does it say that the president or the national government has the power to acquire territory. The Louisiana Purchase resulted from a Hamiltonian interpretation of the Constitution.

During the War of 1812, those still in the Federalist Party further isolated themselves by opposing the war, and at the Hartford Convention they hypocritically called for states' rights and virtually threatened secession from the Union. News of the American military victories at Baltimore, Plattsburg Bay, and New Orleans, and the negotiation of a peace treaty ending the war with Britain, led to the party's disgrace and collapse. In the election of 1820, the Democratic-Republican candidate James Monroe ran unopposed and the nation entered an era of one-party rule, the misnamed "Era of Good Feelings." There were plenty of bad feelings—you had an economic depression; you had the Missouri Crisis—but during this era, the Democratic-Republican Party encompassed the views of both Hamilton and Jefferson.

But given the crises that took place, one-party rule could not and would not continue; and the Hamilton-Jefferson disagreements were basic that they would soon reassert themselves in the creation of the so-called second two-party political system during the 1820s and the 1830s. It is to that new political system, and the individual for whom it is named (Andrew Jackson), that we now turn our attention.

Andrew Jackson—An Odd Symbol of Democracy
Lecture 6

The election of Andrew Jackson to the presidency in 1828 ushered in a new era in U.S. history, one in which property qualifications for voting disappeared and the nation truly became democratic. Yet Jackson was an odd symbol of democratic reform: He was not himself a "common man," and many of the policies he championed would not be considered democratic today. This lecture's careful examination of the age of Jackson reveals much about the nature of American democracy—both in his time and today.

Jackson's Life
- Andrew Jackson was born into poverty on the Carolina frontier in 1767. By the age of 14, he was an orphan. He moved west and prospered, becoming a slaveholding planter and a major political figure in the new state of Tennessee.

- During the War of 1812, Jackson became a national military hero for his victories at the battles of Horseshoe Bend and New Orleans. He also achieved fame for his invasion and conquest of Spanish Florida, which led to the acquisition of Florida.

- Throughout these years, he prospered economically, made a fortune, lost it, and then made another one. In doing so, he became a symbol of the common man, as well as a symbol of his era and its values.
  - He stopped army desertions in the War of 1812 and managed to defeat the British army—the finest in the world—at New Orleans with a ragtag force of farmers, pirates, Indians, and others.

  - He ignored diplomatic protocol and international law by invading Spanish Florida in pursuit of hostile Indians and escaped slaves who had crossed the border. In the process, he took two Spanish forts, executed two British subjects, deposed the Spanish governor of Pensacola, seized the Spanish archives, and appointed his own governor.

o He defeated a superb marksman in a duel in 1806, pretending he was unharmed—even though a bullet had lodged in his chest—then hitting his opponent with a mortal shot.

- The fact that Jackson's success was tempered by personal tragedy only enhanced his appeal as a man of the people. His beloved wife, Rachel, died just a few months before his presidential inauguration.

Jackson in Politics
- Jackson emerged as a major political figure with his 1823 election to the Senate and the 1824 presidential election, which took place during the so-called Era of Good Feelings, when the Federalist Party had disappeared and left only one national party, the Democratic-Republicans.

- In 1824, however, this party split over its presidential candidate, and four candidates ultimately emerged for the race: Secretary of State John Quincy Adams, Senator Henry Clay (Kentucky), Senator John Calhoun (South Carolina), and Jackson.
  o Adams was the son of the former president and a brilliant diplomat. As secretary of state under Monroe, he was responsible for the acquisition of Florida and the Monroe Doctrine.

  o Clay, known as "Harry of the West," was a former speaker of the House, a war hawk, a peace negotiator at Ghent, and a popular voice of the new West.

  o Calhoun was another former war hawk and nationalist, but one who would soon move in the opposite direction to defend slavery in the South. He had a reputation for having a sharp mind, but he dropped out of the race early to run for the vice presidential position, which he won.

- o Jackson ran as a war hero and an alternative to Clay as the voice of the new West.

- • Jackson won a plurality of both the popular and the electoral vote but no majority; thus, the election went to the House of Representatives, where each state casts one vote. The contest came down to Jackson and Adams; Adams won with Clay's support, then appointed Clay secretary of state. Outrage against this "corrupt bargain" poisoned Adams's presidency and ensured Jackson's victory in the 1828 election.

Jackson as President

- • Many historians agree that democracy made Jackson rather than vice versa. Indeed, no one really knew what Jackson stood for in 1829, but as president, he would dominate events and help to define the main political characteristics of this new democracy that had elected him.

- • Key events of Jackson's presidency included Indian removal, the Maysville Road veto, the nullification crisis, and the destruction of the second national bank.

  - o In the 1830s, Jackson refused to enforce the ruling of the Supreme Court that the Cherokee Nation was entitled to federal protection from Georgia state actions to force its removal. Instead, he used federal forces to impel the movement of Cherokees out of Georgia, resulting in the notorious Trail of Tears.

  - o In the Maysville Road event, Jackson vetoed a bill that would have authorized federal funds for internal improvements, insisting this was a state issue and that the bill overstepped the powers granted to Congress.

  - o Although Jackson supported slavery and, thus, the gag rule against abolitionists, he was an intense nationalist who would not tolerate South Carolina's attempt to nullify a new tariff law.

    ○   Jackson also destroyed the second Bank of the United States through his veto of its new charter and removal of federal funds before the old charter expired, moving those funds into state "pet" banks.

A Transformation of the Presidency

- During these and other events, Jackson transformed the office of president in the name of "the people."

- He made massive use of the presidential veto, expanded executive power at the expense of Congress, refused to enforce Supreme Court decisions with which he disagreed, and became known to his enemies as "King Andrew."

- Jackson justified the expansion of presidential power on the grounds that he was the only government official elected by all the people and that this new power was needed to tear down special privilege that had come to dominate Washington.

- Jackson instituted rotation in office and the spoils system for federal appointees, a move he justified as a democratic attack on the entrenched aristocracy of educated bureaucrats. He also instituted the "kitchen cabinet" of special personal advisers not subject to Senate confirmation,

Through his military exploits and business endeavors, Jackson became a symbol of his era: a man able to overcome adversity through an understanding of the natural order and possession of both divine protection and incredible will.

justifying it as a move away from the elitism of the cabinet and necessary given the presence of political appointees in that body whom he did not trust.

- Jackson justified all these moves in the name of democracy, but today, it's clear that many were not democratic and that they resulted in corruption of the American political system, a dangerous expansion and abuse of executive power, a crippling of the American financial system, and a gross denial of rights for opponents of slavery and for Indians.

- Interestingly, many of Jackson's revolutionary moves were also justified via the old Jeffersonian doctrine of limited government and states' rights. The Jacksonian coalition was made up of many contradictory elements that had little in common other than the desire for change. The lowest common denominator able to hold this coalition together was a strict interpretation of the Constitution.

The Bank War

- The contradictions in Jacksonian democracy are best illustrated through analysis of the so-called Bank War.

- Chartered in 1816 for 20 years, the second Bank of the United States stood as a symbol of the Democratic-Republican Party's move to political center after the Jeffersonian opposition to the first national bank. Control of the bank was divided 20/80 between the government and the private sector.

- The bank served many useful functions, both for the government and for the American financial and economic system, but it also had many enemies. It was distrusted by small farmers and eastern workers and opposed by businessmen, western bankers, Wall Street financiers, southern slaveholders, and Jeffersonian Republicans.

- The lowest common denominator among these opponents, which Jackson used to justify his veto of the bank recharter bill in 1832, was strict interpretation of the Constitution to destroy special privilege. But this is also an argument against any government control of the economy and a validation of Adam Smith's economic ideology of laissez-faire.

- Jackson followed up on his veto after his 1832 reelection with a personal vendetta to destroy the bank, despite the fact that its charter still had three years to run. To carry out the destruction of the bank, he had to fire two Treasury secretaries—both of whom feared financial and economic disaster if the bank was shut down—before he found a third who was willing to assist him in removing government deposits from the bank.

- Disaster did indeed follow; Jackson placed federal funds in state "pet" banks, which then used the funds to underwrite more paper money, leading to a vicious cycle of overspeculation in land and inflation.

- Jackson tried to stop the speculation with his Specie Circular in 1836, announcing that henceforth the government would accept only gold and silver for land. The land market collapsed, and overextended banks called in their loans, which led to panic and depression in 1837 under Jackson's successor, Martin Van Buren.

Jackson's Legacy

- Jackson is an apt symbol for a democratic era in which all free white males obtained the right to vote and for an ideological revolution in economics as laissez-faire triumphed over government direction of economic growth. The two were now fused in American ideology by the concept of equality of opportunity and, thus, no special favors from the government for anyone.

- Jackson also helped to re-create a two-party system in the United States. His coalition, now known as Democrats, united around the issues of destruction of special privilege and strict interpretation of the Constitution. His opponents, known as National Republicans, or Whigs, favored continued government control of economic growth and, thus, a broad interpretation of the Constitution.

- Many at the time and still today view Jackson's laissez-faire economics and his political behavior as democratic. But in reality, his economic policies marked the triumph of those who favored a highly speculative economy with rapid growth and its ensuing risks over the traditionalists who favored government supervision and more modest growth.

- In the political realm, the spoils system and other related political reforms wound up enhancing the "special privileges" for some that Jackson sought to destroy. Further, the expansion of rights for free white males during the age of Jackson was paradoxically accompanied by the rise of the "cult of true womanhood" and "scientific racism," almost as if expanded rights for some meant that others must be defined as inferior.

Suggested Reading

Meacham, *American Lion.*

Tocqueville, *Democracy in America.*

Ward, *Andrew Jackson: Symbol for an Age.*

Wilentz, *Andrew Jackson.*

Questions to Consider

1. Why are many of the political reforms considered democratic in the 1830s now considered undemocratic and corrupt?

2. Why do individuals like Andrew Jackson emerge as symbols of their eras despite the facts about their lives and beliefs that run contrary to the symbolism? What other individuals in U.S. history have emerged in this way?

Andrew Jackson—An Odd Symbol of Democracy
Lecture 6—Transcript

The election of Andrew Jackson to the presidency in 1828 ushered in a new era in American history, one named after him: the "Age of Jackson." It's also known as the "age of the common man"; the era in which property qualifications for voting disappeared and the nation truly became democratic (at least in regard to the vote for all adult white males). Jackson became the symbol of this democratic thrust, the "man of the people," elected in 1828 and reelected in 1832 by large majorities, with the people virtually taking over the White House for a wild party on the day he was inaugurated for his first term in 1829 (we'll be talking more about that later).

Yet Jackson was in many ways a very odd symbol of democratic reform. He himself was an anything but a common man; in reality he was a wealthy, slave-owning Tennessee planter and aristocrat. Furthermore, many of the policies he championed would not be considered democratic today; and he opposed most of the major democratic reform movements of his era, most notably abolitionism and rights for women, blacks, and Native Americans. Indeed, the conditions of these people deteriorated during the age of Jackson.

Jackson also supported some very undemocratic behavior: He backed Southern postmasters who had violated federal law by refusing to distribute abolitionist literature within the South, and he also supported the "gag rule" to prevent even the reading of abolitionist petitions that had been submitted to Congress. Yet, simultaneously, Jackson was a very apt symbol for this democratic era, and careful examination reveals much about the nature of American democracy, both then and today.

Let's look at Jackson's background first. He had been born into poverty and travail on the Carolina frontier in 1767. His father died three weeks before he was born; both of his brothers and his mother died during the Revolutionary War. He was left an orphan at age 14. He was largely self-educated; he moved west, where he prospered; he became a major slaveholding planter as well as a major political figure in the new state of Tennessee. During the War of 1812, he became a national military hero for his victory over the Creek Indians at the 1814 Battle of Horseshoe Bend and, of course, for his stupendous victory over the British in the 1815 Battle of New Orleans. He achieved further military fame for his famous 1818 invasion and conquest of Spanish Florida while pursuing Indians and escaped slaves. That eventually led to the acquisition of Florida by a treaty with Spain.

Throughout these years, Jackson also prospered economically. He made a fortune, he lost it, and he made another one. In doing so, he became a symbol of the common man: the poor westerner who went from rags to riches, then to rags again, and then to riches again. He was an aristocrat, but he was a self-made aristocrat. As well, he became a symbol of his era and its values. One historian, John William Ward, has noted that he became known as a man of Nature, a man of Providence, and a man of Will; consistently overcoming adversity and impossible odds through an understanding of the natural order and the possession of both divine protection and incredible willpower.

Let me give you four examples of this. First, how Jackson stopped army desertions in the War of 1812: While campaigning, many in his army at one point decided to go home. As they were walking down the road, they saw in the middle of the road Jackson on horseback with a brace of pistols, one in each hand. You had a very large number of men; clearly they could overcome one man. But Jackson made crystal clear that he would shoot and kill the first two men to try to cross the line. Nobody did; they turned around.

Second, his putting together of a ragtag force of farmers and backwoods militia from Tennessee and Kentucky, along with French-speaking Louisiana militia, Mississippi dragoons (what we would call "cavalry"), pirates from the island of Barataria, Irish regiments, black regiments, and Indian allies to defeat the finest army in the world at New Orleans. It wasn't a battle, it was a massacre: He inflicted 2,000 casualties approximately on that army while suffering only 21 himself.

A third example: Ignoring diplomatic protocol and international law, Jackson invaded Spanish Florida in 1818 in pursuit of hostile Indians and escaped slaves who had crossed the border. In the process, he took two Spanish forts, executed two British subjects whom he found, deposed the Spanish governor at Pensacola (and later asserted that he regretted not hanging him), seized the Spanish archives, and appointed his own governor.

The fourth and final example: Jackson's behavior and survival in a fierce duel in 1806 with man known as a superb and proud marksman, one Charles Dickinson. Jackson came to the duel wearing a big cloak to mask his body size so that Dickinson could not tell where Jackson's body stopped and where the cloak started. Jackson then insisted that his opponent fire first. He did; the bullet lodged in his chest near his heart. Jackson pretended he was not hit. He wanted to make Dickinson think he had missed. Then Jackson carefully fired a mortal shot and left the field without flinching so that his opponent would die thinking he had missed. Ultimate macho, if you will.

But all of Jackson's success was tempered by personal tragedy. That only enhanced his appeal as a "man of the people" who suffered as they did: the death of both parents and his brothers when he was very young; the winning and losing of a fortune; and the death of his beloved wife Rachel just a few months before his presidential inauguration, perhaps as a result of the scandal regarding their marriage. That needs some explanation.

Rachel had been divorced by her husband and had married Jackson in 1791, or so they thought. It turned out that what had occurred in 1791 was not a divorce, but only the granting of a decree authorizing her first husband to sue for divorce; no divorce actually took place until 1793. The marriage to Jackson was thus not legal, and a second marriage took place in 1794. This issue would emerge in the 1828 presidential campaign with charges of adultery that Jackson believed caused Rachel's death at the end of the year.

Jackson emerged as a major political figure in 1823 with his election to the Senate and in the 1824 presidential election. You'll remember, in 1824, we were still in the so-called "Era of Good Feelings." The Federalist Party had disappeared; there was only one national party, the Democratic-Republican Party, which had moved ideologically to the center as it became all-inclusive. But the party split in 1824 over its presidential candidate. The traditional method of nominating a candidate was the party caucus, and the caucus nominated Secretary of the Treasury William Crawford of Georgia. But others refused to accept this because the caucus was under attack as undemocratic. Three other candidates thus emerged to create a four-way race: John Quincy Adams, Henry Clay, and Andrew Jackson. Let me talk a little bit about each of them.

Secretary of State John Quincy Adams of Massachusetts: the son of John Adams; a brilliant diplomat. He had helped to negotiate the peace treaty ending the War of 1812. He had served as minister to Great Britain, and had then become one of the greatest of all American Secretaries of State under President James Monroe. He was responsible for the acquisition of Florida; he was responsible for the Monroe Doctrine; and he was extremely puritanical (more on him in a later lecture).

Next, Senator Henry Clay of Kentucky, nicknamed "Harry of the West": former speaker of the House of Representatives; a war hawk during the War of 1812; also a peace negotiator at the end of the war; and now a senator from Kentucky, the popular voice of the West. A heavy drinker, a heavy gambler; once a woman said to his wife that it was terrible that he gambled so much, and his wife laconically replied, "Oh, I don't know, he usually wins." During the peace negotiations at Ghent, Adams recorded in his diary that as he was getting up in the early morning to say his prayers, Clay was coming in from an all-night card game.

There was another candidate at first: Senator John C. Calhoun of South Carolina; also a war hawk and a nationalist at this time, but an individual who would soon move to states rights in order to defend Southern slavery. Calhoun had the reputation for having a mind like a steel trap, the ultimate logician. The apocryphal story that is told is that once he broke down and wrote a love poem to his wife, but it was a love poem in which each verse began "whereas," except the last verse, which began "therefore." Calhoun dropped out of the race early on to run for the Vice Presidential position, which he won.

The fourth candidate was thus Andrew Jackson of Tennessee, who ran as a war hero and an alternative voice to Clay of the new West. When the votes were counted, Jackson had won a plurality of both the popular and the electoral vote, but no majority; so by the Constitution, the election went to the House of Representatives where each state would cast one vote. Clay had the lowest number of votes, he was out; Crawford had suffered a serious stroke; so really, the contest boiled down to a choice between Adams and Jackson. Clay told his supporters to vote for Adams, whereupon Adams won with the votes of 13 out of 24 states. Soon thereafter, he appointed Henry

Clay Secretary of State; that was the position seen at that time as the key stepping stone to the presidency. Cries quickly erupted of "corrupt bargain." It was not a corrupt bargain, but it poisoned and doomed Adams's presidency. Jackson began running for president in the 1828 election virtually the next day, and he wound up in 1828 defeating Adams with 56 percent of the popular vote and a victory of 178 to 83 in the Electoral College.

His ensuing inauguration was a wild affair, as people came from over 500 miles away and took over the White House during the inaugural party. Jackson himself was forced to leave to avoid being crushed, and in the words of the historian George Dangerfield, people sat and used satin-covered chairs as footstools, tapestries as throwaway napkins, and windows as doors.

Many if not most historians agree that democracy made Jackson rather than Jackson making democracy; in fact, no one really understood what Jackson stood for in 1829. But as president, he would dominate events and would help to define the main political characteristics of this new democracy that had elected him. The key events of his presidency would be the removal of Indians east of the Mississippi River, the Maysville Road veto, the nullification crisis, and the destruction of the Second National Bank.

Very briefly on each of these: Congress in 1830 had given Jackson the money and the authority to get all Indians east of Mississippi to move west of the river (basically to Oklahoma. But Georgia decided to act on its own to remove the so-called five civilized tribes: the Cherokees, who were an agrarian people, who had a written language, and who had a Constitution (as well as slaves). The Cherokees refused to move and, with their white friends and supporters, they took their case to the Supreme Court, which ruled in two cases—*Cherokee Nation v Georgia* and *Worcester v Georgia*—that they could not bring suit but as a "domestic dependent nation" (to use Chief Justice John Marshall's words) they were entitled to Federal protection from any Georgia state action. Jackson simply refused to enforce this ruling, famously stating that Chief Justice John Marshall had made his decision and he could enforce it himself. Instead, Jackson let Georgia do what it wanted to do to the Cherokees and used Federal forces to encourage their movement. The result would be the notorious "Trail of Tears."

In the Maysville Road veto, Jackson vetoed a bill that would have authorized federal funds for internal improvements. He insisted that this was a state issue, and that the bill overstepped the powers granted to Congress.

The nullification crisis: Jackson clearly supported slavery and the gag rule against the abolitionists. He also supported the actions of the South Carolina postmaster who barred abolitionist literature from the mails. But Jackson was an intense nationalist who would not tolerate South Carolina's attempt to nullify a new tariff law.

Jackson also destroyed the Second National Bank of the United States. He did so by vetoing of a new charter for the bank and removing federal funds before the old charter expired. He then moved those funds into state banks, "pet" banks; I'll talk about that more later in this lecture.

During these and other events, Jackson transformed the office of the presidency in the name of "the people." How? First, massive use of the presidential veto: 12, including the first use of the pocket veto. All previous presidents together had only vetoed 9 bills. He also expanded executive power at the expense of Congress; refused, as was pointed out, to enforce Supreme Court decisions with which he disagreed; and became known to his enemies as "King Andrew."

Jackson justified this obvious expansion of presidential power on the grounds that he was the only government official elected by all the people, and that he was using this new power to tear down special privilege that had come to dominate Washington; in other words, stop Congress from acting beyond the Constitution via the Maysville Road bill (Jackson, as you see, had a narrow interpretation of Constitution). He would also act to tear down engines of special privilege when Congress would not act via the Bank veto, and to block the courts when they did not act in interests of "the people."

Jackson also instituted rotation in office and the spoils system for federal appointees. He justified these as democratic moves on the entrenched aristocracy of educated bureaucrats. Education was at that time a luxury of the rich; and since (theoretically) anyone in a democracy was theoretically qualified to hold government office, the best way to choose those who would actually hold office was to reward the party faithful, especially since politics itself was now viewed as a business run by self-interest and reward. This was a major shift from the Founding Fathers and their concept of civic virtue.

Jackson also instituted the "kitchen cabinet" of special personal advisers not subject to Senate confirmation. He justified this as a move away from the elitism of the established Cabinet and necessary given the presence of political appointees in the Cabinet whom he did not trust.

All these moves Jackson justified in the name of "democracy"; but today it is clear that many were not democratic and that they resulted in corruption of the American political system, as well as a dangerous expansion and abuse of executive power, a crippling of the American financial system, a gross denial of rights for opponents of slavery and for Indians; and, by the way, with that denial of rights for Indians, immense profits for land speculators rather than the common people.

Interestingly, many of Jackson's revolutionary moves were justified via the old Jeffersonian doctrine of limited government and states' rights, as well as democracy. Why? There's a psychological point: In an era of drastic change, people will look to a past idea for reassurance; the old concept of Janus-faced, of facing in two opposite directions, of walking backwards into the future. Also, the Jacksonian coalition was made up of contradictory elements. All of them wanted change and were dissatisfied with the way things were, but they otherwise had very little in common. The lowest common denominator able to hold them together was a strict interpretation of the Constitution. This fact, as well as the contradictions in Jacksonian Democracy, are best illustrated via an analysis of the so-called Bank War; the destruction of the Second National Bank of the United States.

Chartered in 1816 for 20 years, that bank stood as symbol of the Democratic-Republican Party's move to political center; Jefferson, you remember, had opposed the First Bank. It was 20 percent government controlled, 80 percent private; and it served many useful functions, both for the government and for the American financial and economic systems as a whole. But it also had many enemies: There was general distrust of the Bank from the Panic of 1819. The Bank had called in its loans, seeing that the Panic was coming, and this was viewed as a cause of the ensuing depression rather than a consequence of it. That reinforced the dislike of the Bank by small farmers and eastern workers who wanted only what was known as "hard money," money backed by gold and silver. They wanted this because they wanted to stop rising prices, and they thus opposed the bank's paper money, which was legal tender.

But it didn't end there: The bank was also opposed by businessmen and western bankers who wanted more paper money for easier loans. The National Bank prevented this by its power to call in notes if local banks had unsound banking practices. The bank was also opposed by financiers on Wall Street in New York City who wanted to emerge from the shadow of the super-bank in Philadelphia that had Federal support. It was also opposed by Southern slave owners who feared it as a dangerous precedent for federal power as well as an institution that built up the power of the Northeast. Finally, it was opposed by old Jeffersonian Republicans who repeated Jefferson's argument that such a bank was unconstitutional.

The lowest common denominator here, which Jackson used to justify his veto of the Bank recharter bill in 1832, was strict interpretation of the Constitution in order to destroy special privilege. But this is also an argument against any government control of economy, and thus part of the new economic ideology of laissez-faire from Adam Smith. Smith had enunciated his ideas in 1776, and they had been gaining public acceptance as the United States began to industrialize. What Smith argued was an end to government control over the economy, something that was dominant in the mercantilist system; to revert instead to the laws of supply and demand, to let the "invisible hand" of the marketplace run things; let business run free. We will get back to that in a later lecture.

Jackson followed up on his veto of the bank bill after he was reelected in 1832 with a personal vendetta to destroy the Bank even though its charter had three years to run. The bank, he asserted, was trying to destroy him but he would destroy by removing all government deposits. To do so, he had to fire two Treasury Secretaries who feared financial and economic disaster if this was done. He finally found a third, Roger Taney, willing to do this.

Disaster did follow. Jackson placed federal funds in certain state banks known as "pet" banks, which then used such funds to underwrite more paper money. That led to inflation and massive overspeculation in land and a vicious cycle: Speculators would borrow bad paper money, give it to the government for land, and the government would give it back to the pet banks, who would then issue more loans. Jackson tried to stop this in 1836 with his Specie Circular, which announced that henceforth the government would accept only gold and silver for land. The land market, which was a bubble, thereupon collapsed. Overextended banks called in their loans; that led to panic and depression in 1837 under Jackson's successor, Martin Van Buren.

What can we conclude from this? Jackson was an apt symbol for the democratic era in which all free white males obtained the right to vote. He was also an apt symbol for the ideological revolution in economics as laissez-faire triumphed over government direction of economic growth. These two—political and economic—were now fused in American ideology by the concept of equality of opportunity, and thus no special favors from government for anyone. Jackson further helped to ensconce laissez-faire and equality of opportunity as major features of American ideology and economic history by appointing Roger Taney, his third Treasury Secretary, who had removed government funds from the Bank, to be Chief Justice of the Supreme Court. In the famous Charles River Bridge case of 1837, Taney's court would rule against state-sponsored monopoly in transportation, and thereby reinforce the ethic of equality of opportunity and no special privileges.

In the process of doing all of this, Jackson also helped to recreate a two-party system in the United States. He and his supporters claimed the Jeffersonian mantle and they called themselves Democratic-Republicans, or Democrats for short. They united around the issues of destruction of special privilege and a strict interpretation of the Constitution. Jackson's opponents would call themselves National Republicans, or Whigs, and they would favor continuation of government control or direction of economic growth and thus a broad interpretation of the Constitution.

Many at that time and still today view Jackson's laissez-faire economics, as well as his political behavior, as democratic. But in reality, his economic policies marked the triumph of those who favored a highly speculative economy with rapid growth and ensuing risks over traditionalists who favored government supervision and more modest growth, and the results were catastrophic in the economic realm for many due to the destruction of the Bank and the ensuing financial chaos and depression of 1837. Furthermore, as we will see in a future lecture, the United States government never truly practiced a total "hands off" laissez-faire policy with the economy, all the rhetoric to the contrary notwithstanding.

What about the political realm? Here, the spoils system and other related political reforms wound up not destroying special privileges but enhancing special privileges some. Indeed, the takeover of the White House and the near-riot on the day of Jackson's inauguration was the work not of the "common people," but a horde of office-seekers. Also, the expansion of rights for free white males during the Age of Jackson was paradoxically accompanied by a deterioration in conditions for those who were not free white males. Women and free blacks lost legal rights that they had previously possessed in some states, while Indians east of the Mississippi River were forcibly removed to Oklahoma. Interestingly, the last full debate in the South over slavery took place during this time period in Virginia, and it ended in defeat for those in the western part of the state who opposed slavery.

Why this deterioration in conditions for all who were not free white males? That's an interesting question. The short answer in regard to women was the market revolution of this time that had led to a new and in many ways more limited role for women via what one historian has aptly labeled the "cult of true womanhood": the belief that women's place was now totally in the home to raise the children and to create a haven for her husband, who spent each day in the competitive and heartless marketplace. For blacks and Indians, it was the creation and rise during this era of "scientific racism" that would claim they were genetically inferior and incapable of improvement.

But why would scientific racism emerge at this time? It is almost as if with the expansion of rights for some human beings (white males) others must be defined as inferior and even nonhuman to justify their exploitation by the privileged group.

The Second Great Awakening—Enduring Impacts
Lecture 7

T he fact that some evangelical groups are politically active has concerned many Americans because we are used to thinking of religion and politics as existing in separate realms. But that is not the case historically. This lecture looks at the Second Great Awakening, focusing on the ways in which it both reflected and affected American politics in the first half of the 19th century. In the process, we will see that this 200-year-old religious movement continues to influence us today.

Romanticism, Transcendentalism, and the Second Great Awakening

- The early 19th century witnessed an intellectual and spiritual upheaval in both the United States and Europe. This movement, known as romanticism, emphasized emotion and intuition, replacing the previous Enlightenment emphasis on reason. In New England intellectual circles, this led to the transcendentalist movement, which was translated into political action by such thinkers as Ralph Waldo Emerson and Henry David Thoreau.

- The mass emotional movement at this time was the Second Great Awakening, a widespread evangelical religious revival that downplayed theological arguments in favor of heartfelt personal experiences.

- Theologically, the Second Great Awakening ended once and for all in the United States the old Puritan concept of predestination, that is, the belief that salvation was available only to a select few chosen by and known to God before they were even born. In its place grew the belief that salvation was available to anyone who admitted his or her sins, accepted Jesus Christ, and chose to lead a good Christian life. Sin thus became voluntary and alterable, and in rejecting it, one could be "born again."

The Impact on Politics

- The Awakening resulted in an explosion of religious commitment, with regular church attendance increasing dramatically. It democratized American religion by making salvation available to all, interestingly, at the same time that American political life was being democratized by the Jacksonian movement. But it also had more specific and direct influences on politics.

- Many Americans at the time held a different interpretation of the Book of Revelation than the one popular today.
  - This interpretation included doctrines of perfectionism and immediatism that emphasized the need for saved Christians to save others and to work to perfect the world as a prerequisite to—and a way to hasten—the Second Coming of Christ.

  - Some thought the Second Coming would occur in their own lifetimes, but many more thought in terms of a millennium that they believed was to precede the Second Coming, a time in which the world would be perfected and one they claimed had begun with the establishment of the United States.

  - Perfectionism led to extraordinary communal experiments as some Americans sought to live on earth as they would in heaven. Extremes ran from the Shakers, who banned sex altogether, to the Oneida Community, in which every male member of the commune was married to every female member.

  - Far more lasting than these communes was the birth and growth at this time of the polygamous Church of Jesus Christ of Latter-day Saints.

- Many other evangelicals became involved in a series of major reform movements that arose during this time.
  - Such famous revivalist preachers as Lyman Beecher and Charles G. Finney rejected predestination and original sin in favor of free will and the idea that salvation was available to all in the here and now. They also preached that one could aid

Christ's work by acting both to save others and to reform or perfect society.

- o One major reform movement was in the field of education, where such figures as Horace Mann emphasized the importance of public education supported by state taxes to strengthen religious and family values and to avoid permanent social classes by providing tools for economic success.

- o Another movement took place in prison reform, with Lewis Dwight and others focusing on the rehabilitation rather than merely the incarceration of lawbreakers.

- o Other reformers, such as Dorothea Dix, focused on care of the mentally ill, establishing the concept of the asylum as a place where sanity could be restored rather than one where insanity was locked away under atrocious conditions.

- o One of the biggest and most important reform movements of the time was temperance. Alcoholism had become a major problem, with consumption per person in 1830 three times what it is today. Calls for temperance soon shifted to those for total abstinence, and by the 1840s–1850s, some states enforced legal prohibition.

Abolitionism

- • Although temperance may have been the most popular of the reform movements, the most controversial and consequential was abolitionism—the movement for the immediate and total abolition of slavery.

- • Abolitionism differed from previous antislavery movements, with their emphasis on gradual emancipation and resettlement in Africa, in its focus on slaveholding as a mortal sin. Thus, for those who truly wished to be saved, slaveholding must be brought to an immediate and total end.

- Contrary to popular belief, most northerners were not abolitionists. Indeed, many abolitionists were denounced and attacked in the North as fanatics, irresponsible agitators, and self-righteous absolutists. Neither the Free Soil Party nor the later Republican Party adopted abolitionism before the middle of the Civil War.

- Nevertheless, abolitionists played a vital role in awakening northerners to the evils of slavery and the need to do something about it.

The Role of Women in Reform
- Women were key figures in the abolitionist movement, as well as the temperance and other reform movements. Their involvement created an uproar and led to the first women's rights movement in the United States.

- According to the "cult of domesticity" then in vogue, women's proper role was in the private sphere, while men were engaged in

© iStockphoto/Thinkstock.

The Second Great Awakening saw the democratization and expansion of religion in America that remain with us to this day.

the public sphere. That private sphere focused on the home, where women were responsible for raising children and creating a retreat from the marketplace for their husbands.

- This, in turn, was part of what one historian has termed the "cult of true womanhood" for middle-class women, based on the four interlocking pillars of domesticity, piety, submissiveness, and purity. Men were considered to be more competitive, dominant, rational, and secular than women by nature, while women were more cooperative, emotional, virtuous, and religious.

- At same time, we see the rise of the family as an institution of affection, dominated by love between husband and wife and between parents and children. This coincided with a declining birthrate as children lost their economic importance and parents practiced extensive birth control.

- Given the fact that women were considered to be more virtuous and religious and were responsible for the moral development of their children, it is far from accidental that they became active in their churches. But with the emphasis on reforming society in the Second Great Awakening, religious women ironically found themselves entering the public sphere in their calls for temperance and other reforms.
  - o Women's benevolent associations began to form to promote moral reforms to control men's "baser instincts," and women began to speak at public meetings for the first time to promote such reforms. This led to major controversies within the churches and within the abolitionist movement.

  - o The reform movements and the strong reactions to their participation also led some women to question the validity of the entire system of domesticity and to launch a reform movement of their own for women's rights.

Disestablishment of Religion

- Disestablishment of religion in the late 18th and early 19th centuries ironically appears to have led to an extraordinary democratization and expansion of American religion in the Second Great Awakening, to the point where Americans became and remain today the most religious people in the industrialized world.

- The Second Great Awakening's emphasis on emotion rather than formal theology and on rejecting sin and accepting Christ continued throughout 19th- and 20th-century U.S. history and continue today with the contemporary evangelical movement.

- The Second Great Awakening also had profound political repercussions. Abolitionism, of course, had the most immediate impact in terms of its role in the coming of Civil War, but not far behind it was the anti-alcohol crusade, leading to nationwide prohibition in the 1920s. Ideologies of many of the other reform movements continue to this day, most notably in the fields of education, prison reform, treatment of mental illness, and women's rights.

- The camp meeting emphasis on renouncing sin publicly that emerged in the Awakening also continues today, a fact illustrated by the call heard on many campuses over the past few decades to "stand up and admit you are a racist." This is incredibly similar to the "stand up and admit you are a sinner" of the evangelical camp meetings.

- Nineteenth-century religious rhetoric has consistently reappeared throughout 20th-century U.S. history, particularly during time of war. The Cold War, for example, was seen as a struggle against "Godless communism."

- Alexis de Tocqueville, who was touring the United States in the midst of the Second Great Awakening, said that the religious atmosphere of the country was the first thing that struck him, and he marveled at the number of sects and their apparently inseparable relationship to American concepts of liberty. Perhaps in this regard, all our politics are—and always have been—evangelical.

Suggested Reading

Howe, *What Hath God Wrought*.

Tyler, *Freedom's Ferment*.

Questions to Consider

1. Why do we tend to view religion and politics as separate realms despite their historical linkage?

2. In what specific ways is the Second Great Awakening still with us?

The Second Great Awakening—Enduring Impacts
Lecture 7—Transcript

Some evangelical groups are very politically active today. That has surprised and worried many other Americans, for we are used to thinking of religion and politics as existing in separate realms. But that is not the case historically; and in incorrectly seeing separate realms, we may be confusing the First Amendment's ban on an established religion and the legal separation of church and state with the very strong links between politics and religion that have always existed in American, and indeed in world, history.

Some historians have argued that the 18th-century religious revival known as the First Great Awakening played a major role in the coming of the American Revolution. How? It was the first major event that took place in all 13 colonies and thus linked them together for the first time; and its successful challenge to existing religious order undermined established habits of deference to constituted authority. That was a prerequisite for the revolution that would follow.

In this lecture, we will be looking at the Second Great Awakening that took place during the first half of the 19th century, and we will focus on the ways in which it both reflected and affected American politics at the time. In the process, we will see that this 200-year-old religious movement continues to have a great influence on us today.

What was the Second Great Awakening? The early 19th century witnessed an intellectual and spiritual upheaval in the United States as well as Europe. The movement known as Romanticism, with its emphasis on emotion and intuition, replaced the previous Enlightenment emphasis on reason. In elite New England intellectual circles, this would lead to the Transcendentalist movement. As verbalized by Ralph Waldo Emerson, whom one historian labeled the "High Priest" of Transcendentalism, the Transcendentalist "believes in miracles, in the perpetual openness of the human mind to the new influx of light and power. He believes in inspiration and ecstasy."

How, you may ask, could this lead to political action? That was best illustrated by the writings and behavior of Emerson's friend Henry David

Thoreau, who refused to pay his taxes because they supported both slavery and the war against Mexico. He was jailed for that; and according to some accounts, Emerson visited Thoreau in jail and asked "Henry, what are you doing in there?" to which Thoreau replied, "Waldo, the question is, what are you doing out there?" Out of this would emerge Thoreau's classic *Essay on Civil Disobedience*, which became and remains today a basic text for those who wish to engage in peaceful, illegal actions as acts of political protest.

Transcendentalism was anything but a mass movement. The mass emotional movement at this time was The Second Great Awakening, a widespread evangelical religious revival that downplayed theological arguments in favor of personal heartfelt experiences. These experiences often took place in huge camp meetings rather than in established churches.

Theologically, the Second Great Awakening largely ended the old Puritan concept of Predestination; so did Unitarianism and Transcendentalism, for that matter. Predestination was the belief that salvation was available only to a select few chosen by God and known to God and only God even before they were born; this was a Puritan belief. In its place grew the belief that salvation was available to anyone who admitted his or her sins, accepted Jesus Christ into his or her life, and chose to lead a good Christian life. Sin thus became voluntary and alterable, and in rejecting it one could be "born again."

The process of being "born again" included public confessions of sin and intensely emotional behavior at these camp meetings; behavior that astounded those who witnessed the meetings. One of the earliest and most notable of these camp meetings took place in 1801 in Cane Ridge, Kentucky. But it was the area along the new Erie Canal between Albany and Buffalo, New York—which became the major route west after the canal was completed in 1825—it was along this corridor that many of these emotional revivals took place; so many that the area became known as the "Burned Over District" for all the fires of religious excitement that swept over it.

The Second Great Awakening resulted in an explosion of religious commitment. Regular church attendance increasing dramatically—by 1850, one out of three Americans was going to church—and it lead to enormous growth for the Baptist and Methodist denominations in particular. Obviously, this Second Great Awakening democratized American religion by making salvation available to all, and interestingly, at the same time that American political life was being democratized by the Jacksonian movement that we discussed in the last lecture. That was not coincidence; there was clearly a cause-and-effect relationship here, though exactly how and in which direction remains unclear. Probably the two movements were mutually reinforcing as they braided and led to greater advances, each for the other.

The Second Great Awakening also had a much more specific and direct impact on politics. Many religious Americans at this time held a very different interpretation of the Book of Revelation than the one popular today. It included doctrines of Perfectionism and Immediatism that emphasized the need for saved Christians to save others and to work to improve and try to perfect the world. That was to be done as a prerequisite to, and as a way to hasten, the Second Coming of Jesus Christ. Some thought this would occur in their own lifetimes. A group known as the Millerites predicted the actual day, first in 1843 and then again in 1844 (needless to say, they were wrong). Many more thought in terms of a millennium that they believed was to precede the Second Coming; a millennium in which the world would be perfected and one they claimed had already begun with the establishment of the United States, if not with the discovery of the New World.

Perfectionism led to some extraordinary communal experiments at this time, as some Americans sought literally to live on Earth as they would in Heaven. Since private property would obviously not exist in Heaven, and since women were still considered property, some of the communes that were established abolished the institution of marriage as it was known, as well as all private property. Extremes ran from the Shakers, who banned sex altogether, to the Oneida Community, in which every male member of the commune was married to every female member and available as a sexual partner if the commune approved.

Far more lasting than these communes, however, was the birth and growth at this time of the polygamous Church of Jesus Christ of Latter Day Saints, better known as the Mormons, under its leader Joseph Smith and—after his murder by an Illinois mob—his successor Brigham Young, who led his followers to present-day Utah.

But many other evangelicals involved themselves deeply in the series of major reform movements that arose in the United States during this time, and with profound political consequences. In this, they were heavily influenced by famous revivalist preachers such as Lyman Beecher and Charles Grandison Finney. These ministers not only rejected predestination and original sin in favor of free will and an emphasis on salvation being available to all here and now, they also preached that one could aid Christ's work by acting both to save others and to reform or perfect society.

They were not alone: Secular reformers were also involved in these reform movements, and in the utopian communal experiments as well (Robert Owen's experiments in communes, for example). But the religious revival brought in a very large number of individuals and underlay much of what followed.

Religious women would play a key role in these reform movements, for reasons I'll explain in a few minutes, and Finney specifically appealed to women. That in turn would have rather unexpected consequences, as we will see.

What were these reform movements of the Second Great Awakening? One was in the field of education, where people like Horace Mann of Massachusetts emphasized the importance of state tax-supported public education to strengthen both religious and family values and to avoid permanent social classes in the United States. How? By giving individuals the tools they needed to succeed in this new economic world coming into existence and to give them the values they needed to succeed, such as competitiveness and punctuality. This movement was highly successful and it created the ideology of public education that we still live with today.

Another was prison reform, with Lewis Dwight and others focusing on the rehabilitation of the lawbreaker rather than merely the incarceration of that individual. That is another ideology that we still live with today; for to rehabilitate the criminal, these reformers constructed new prisons that became known as penitentiaries. That is a religious word at its root, "penitent," and that was far from accidental; for these institutions, along with such innovative methods as solitary confinement, were designed to force the imprisoned criminal to confront himself and his sins and to convert him to a lawful life.

Other reformers such as Dorothea Dix focused on care of the insane with the concept of the asylum as a place where sanity could be restored rather than the old system of merely locking the insane up under utterly atrocious conditions. The origins of the word "bedlam" lie in such an institution in England.

One of the biggest and most important reform movements of the time was temperance. Alcoholism had become a major problem at this time. Some historians have argued that this might have been due to the dislocation caused by early industrialization. Whatever the cause, alcohol consumption per person in 1830 was three times was it is today; and alcohol came to be seen as the evil destroyer of families, of religion, and of the ability of individuals to achieve their full potential. Early calls by preachers such as Lyman Beecher were for temperance in alcohol use, not abolition, with the American Temperance Society being formed in 1826. But this soon shifted to total abstinence, perhaps due to the nature of alcoholism and the addictive component of alcoholism. Revivalist techniques were used to convert alcoholics to abstinence. John Gough, a converted former alcoholic, was a major figure in this field, and his techniques are seen by many as key precursors to the 20th- and 21st-century Alcoholics Anonymous.

The anti-alcohol crusade appealed to all sections of the country and to all classes; but by the 1840s and the 1850s, its emphasis had shifted under such leaders as Neal Dow from moral suasion to state-enforced legal prohibition. In 1851, Maine prohibited the manufacture and sale of alcohol, and so-called "Maine Laws" were soon introduced and implemented in other states. The movement was highly successful: Alcohol consumption fell dramatically by the 1840s.

While temperance may have been the most popular of the reform movements, the most controversial and the most consequential was abolitionism: the movement for the immediate and total abolition of slavery. Abolitionism differed from previous antislavery movements; it was not the first antislavery movement by a long shot, but earlier antislavery movements had emphasized gradual emancipation and some had talked about resettling the slaves back in Africa. Abolitionism at this time, in the 1830s, emphasized slaveholding as a mortal sin—religiously a sin—and thus the need for total and immediate abolition by the slaveholder if he truly wished to be saved. The slaveholder was damned to Hell unless he freed his slaves immediately.

In 1831, William Lloyd Garrison, in the opening issue of *The Liberator*, asserted this new approach in very, very bold language:

> I am aware that many object to the severity of my language; but is there not a cause for severity? I *will* be as harsh as truth, and as uncompromising as justice. On this subject, I do not wish to think, or speak, or write, with moderation. No! no! Tell a man whose house is on fire to give a moderate alarm; tell him to moderately rescue his wife from the hands of the ravisher; tell the mother to gradually extricate her babe from the fire into which it has fallen;— but urge me not to use moderation in a cause like the present. I am in earnest—I will not equivocate—I will not excuse—I will not retreat a single inch—and I will be heard.

Contrary to popular belief, most northerners were not abolitionists; indeed, many abolitionists were denounced and attacked in the North as fanatics and irresponsible agitators, as well as self-righteous absolutists. One of them, Elijah Lovejoy, was murdered by a mob in 1837; Garrison was almost killed by a mob in 1835; and neither the Free Soil Party of the 1840s nor the later Republican Party ever adopted abolitionism, at least not before the middle of the Civil War. Nevertheless, the abolitionists played a vital role in awakening Northerners to the evils of slavery and the need to do something about it; and key figures in the movement included numerous women.

Women also very active in the temperance movement and numerous other reform movements, and that created an uproar. It also led to the first women's rights movement in the United States. By the "cult of domesticity" then in vogue, women's proper role was in the private sphere while men were in the public sphere. That private sphere focused on the home, where they were to be responsible for raising the children as well as creating for their husbands a retreat from the marketplace; what one historian, Christopher Lasch, called "haven in a heartless world." This was in turn part of what another historian, Barbara Welter, has defined as the "cult of true womanhood" at this time for middle class women, and it was based upon four interlocking pillars: domesticity, piety, submissiveness, and purity. These ideas were in turn based upon a belief that men were by nature more competitive, dominant, rational, and secular than women; while women were by nature more cooperative, emotional, submissive, virtuous, and religious.

At same time, we see the rise of the family as an institution of affection, dominated by love between husband and wife and between parents and children. This coincided with a declining birthrate as children lost their economic importance and parents practiced extensive birth control, including abortion, which was not considered a moral or religious issue at the time, probably because a baby was not considered to be alive until it moved in the womb, or "quickened," which was usually in the fifth month.

Given the fact that women were considered to be more virtuous and religious and were responsible for the moral development of their children, it is far from accidental that they became very active in their churches; indeed, two-thirds of all church members were female. But given the emphasis in the Second Great Awakening on reforming society, religious women ironically found themselves entering the public sphere (men's sphere) in their calls for temperance—alcoholism affected them personally—and for other reforms. Women's benevolent associations began to form to promote a host of moral reforms to control what were known as men's "baser instincts," and this was to occur outside as well as inside the home; and women began to speak at public meetings for the first time to promote such reforms. Indeed, the abolitionist Grimke sisters Sarah and Angelina were the first native-born American women to engage in a public lecture tour.

This led to major controversies within the churches and within the abolitionist movement, and these spilled over into the issue whether to engage in politics, as well as moral denunciations of slavery. The abolitionist movement itself was splitting over whether to remain morally pure and thus not involve itself in politics but simply issue these moral denunciations versus those who said, "The only way you are going to accomplish anything is through politics, and politics involves compromise," to which the purists responded, "How can you compromise with sin?" Women became involved in this debate; and there was an uproar in the churches over whether women should be speaking out publicly.

The reform movements in general and the strong reactions to women's participation also led some women to question the validity of the entire idea system of domesticity and to launch a reform movement of their own for women's rights at the 1848 Seneca Falls Convention, with Elizabeth Cady Stanton, Lucretia Mott, and Susan B. Anthony emerging as leaders and emphasizing the obtaining of the right to vote as the key issue.

What can we conclude from this examination? The disestablishment of state-sponsored religion in the late 18th and early 19th centuries ironically appears to have led to this extraordinary democratization and expansion of American religion in the Second Great Awakening, to the point where Americans became and remain today the most religious people in the industrialized world. The Second Great Awakening's emphasis on emotion rather than formal theology, and on rejecting sin and accepting Christ, of course continued throughout the 19th century and the 20th century in U.S. history; and it continues today with the contemporary evangelical movement. Indeed, some have argued that additional "Great Awakenings" have taken place throughout American history, and that we are living through one right now.

But the Second Great Awakening also had profound political repercussions, and those political repercussions also continued throughout the 19th century and the 20th century and still continue to this day. Abolitionism, of course, had the most immediate impact in terms of its role in the coming of Civil War. But not far behind it time-wise was the anti-alcohol crusade. Indeed, as previously noted, Maine prohibited the manufacture and sale of alcohol as early as 1851. Other states followed suit, and in 1919–1920 alcohol was outlawed nationally by Constitutional amendment. That experiment, of course, failed, but the early emphasis on religious conversion continued with the birth and growth of Alcoholics Anonymous and its 12 Steps.

The ideologies of many of the other reform movements also continue to this very day, most notably in fields of education, prison reform, treatment of the insane, and women's rights. Indeed, the modern feminist movement emerged from the civil rights movement of the 1960s, much as the Seneca Falls women's rights movement of 1848 emerged from the abolitionist movement of the 1830s and 1840s.

The camp meeting emphasis on renouncing sin publicly also continues today. That fact can be illustrated in many ways. One way that one of my colleagues liked to illustrate it was to take a close look at the call heard on many campuses over the past few decades to "stand up and admit you are a racist." Isn't that incredibly similar to "stand up and admit you are a sinner," the cry at the evangelical camp meetings? All Western religions do emphasize the need to confess sins, but they and their denominations all do so in different ways; some do it privately with a priest, some do it publicly as part of a congregation, and some do it individually before a public audience.

Whether or not such an individual confession before a public audience is necessary to free one from the evil of racism is not the point here. The fact that people think it is, and that they unconsciously use 19th-century religious rhetoric and forms, speaks volumes regarding the continued impact of the Second Great Awakening on our lives. Indeed, that rhetoric has consistently appeared throughout 20th-century U.S. history, especially in our wars. Throughout the Cold War, we saw ourselves engaged in a life and death struggle not so much against the Soviet Union as against what we labeled "Godless Communism." In both world wars, we saw ourselves engaged in what we labeled "crusades." In World War I, it was "the Great Crusade"; in World War II, Dwight Eisenhower entitled his memoirs *Crusade in Europe*. A similar pattern occurred in the 19th century. As we will see in a future lecture, the Populist movement of the late 19th century consistently employed fiery, evangelical language of holy war. That was also true in the Civil War, as perhaps best exemplified by Julia Ward Howe's "Battle Hymn of the Republic," which she wrote during the war but which has become iconic. Let me quote to you just two of the many verses of that poem:

> Mine eyes have seen the glory of the coming of the Lord:
> He is trampling out the vintage where the grapes of wrath are stored;

He hath loosed the fateful lightning of His terrible swift sword:
His truth is marching on.

In the beauty of the lilies Christ was born across the sea,
With a glory in His bosom that transfigures you and me:
As He died to make men holy, let us die to make men free,
While God is marching on.

The great observer of American life, Alexis de Tocqueville, was touring the United States in the midst of the Second Great Awakening. He said that the religious atmosphere of the country was the first thing that struck him, and he marveled at the number of sects and the apparently inseparable relationship of religion to American concepts of liberty. Perhaps in this regard, all our politics are—and always have been—evangelical.

Did Slavery Really Cause the Civil War?
Lecture 8

O ver the last 150 years, historians have cited numerous causes other than slavery to explain the Civil War: conflict over the extension of slavery into the territories or over states' rights, differences in the cultures and economies of the North and South, and perceptions of conspiracy brought on by a particular American belief system. Nevertheless, as we examine these causes, we'll see that slavery was, in a unique way, indeed the primary cause of the war, and we'll learn much about the nature of historical study.

The Extension of Slavery
- The key issue of the 1850s was not slavery per se but its extension into the western territories. The Kansas-Nebraska Act, passed by Congress in 1854, set off a firestorm by opening to slavery territories previously closed to it by the 1820 Missouri Compromise.

- That firestorm led to the event known as Bleeding Kansas, a small-scale civil war in the Kansas territory, and to the replacement of the Whig Party by the new Republican Party, a sectional party committed to reversal of the act and prohibition of slavery in all the territories.

- The Republican Lincoln was elected in 1860 without a majority of the total vote but with victories in every one of the populous Northern states, thereby giving him a majority in the electoral college. With his election, South Carolina and other states of the Deep South seceded, and with the start of hostilities at Fort Sumter, the states of the Upper South followed suit.

- Lincoln's call for troops in April 1861 was to suppress the rebellion in South Carolina and preserve the Union, not to abolish slavery. Indeed, before hostilities began, Lincoln had been willing to guarantee the preservation of slavery in the states where it existed and had called for barring slavery only in the territories.

- Lincoln's Emancipation Proclamation was issued as a war measure. It did not apply to border slave states that had remained in the Union or to occupied Confederate territories but affected only those areas still in a state of insurrection.

- In light of these facts, historians in the early 20th century began to question the centrality of slavery to the coming of Civil War.

State versus National Power
- One revisionist interpretation of the cause of the Civil War focused on the old conflict between state and national power. Three years after the war ended, for example, Confederate Vice President Alexander H. Stephens maintained that this was the real issue, with the

The abolition of slavery was not a Union war aim in 1861 or the first half of 1862; at the time, Lincoln's objective was preservation of the Union.

South seceding and fighting to support the primacy of states' rights over the federal government.

- As we've seen, this conflict had existed since the days of Hamilton and Jefferson. Was the national government of the Constitution a creation of the states and, therefore, subordinate to them and possessing only limited powers? Or was it a union of the people, possessing strong implied powers over the states?

- Contrary to popular belief, the South has not always defended and the North had not always opposed states' rights over national power.
  o New England had supported states' rights and opposed the federal government before and during the War of 1812 and during the Mexican-American War of 1846–1848.

  o Interestingly, the northeast did not control the federal government during those two wars. Indeed, as historian Arthur Schlesinger Sr. made clear during the 1930s, states' rights had consistently been used throughout U.S. history by whichever section did not control the national government and felt oppressed by national power.

  o It was thus a device to protect specific sectional interests and, in truth, a rationalization for, rather than a cause of, the Civil War.

Economic and Cultural Interests
- Of course, slavery was among the sectional interests that led the South to defend states' rights at the time, but historians during the 1930s saw slavery as just one part of a much larger Southern economic interest. In this view, the Civil War was the defense of an agrarian economy against a diametrically opposed economic system of industrial and commercial capitalism in the North.

- These two economic systems clashed not only over slave versus free labor but also over taxation, tariffs, railroads, monetary policies, and land policies, issues requiring federal action. Given that the three-fifths slavery clause in the Constitution was the basis of

Southern agrarian power in the federal government, disagreements over economic interests became a struggle between competing economic systems for control of that government.

- But economic differences between the North and South had existed since colonial times and had not led to war. In fact, in many ways, the different economies were complementary rather than competitive.

- Some historians answered that the two economic systems were in themselves part of what had become two unique cultures: a Southern agrarian society and a Northern society with different political, economic, social, and intellectual values. Here, too, though, the idea of an aristocratic, agrarian South versus a bustling capitalist North is largely myth. The similarities between the two regions far outweighed their differences.

A Conspiracy against Liberty

- In the 1930s, a group of historians argued that Americans on both sides of the Civil War saw the other as engaged in a conspiracy against liberty.

- Despite the fact that neither Lincoln nor any other major Republican figure proposed abolishing slavery where it existed, many Southerners believed that the hidden aim of what they labeled the "Black Republicans" was to destroy slavery entirely and institute black rule in the South. Similarly, many Northerners believed that Southern slaveholders were engaged in a conspiracy to spread slavery to the North and, thereby, control the entire Union.

- No such conspiracies ever existed, but many people believed they did, and people act on the basis of their beliefs, even if those beliefs are false. Thus, some historians argued that false perceptions led each side to believe it was threatened by an illusionary plot and to go to war to defend its rights.

- Historians also argued that the blame for belief in these conspiracies should be placed on fanatics, agitators, and blundering politicians on both sides. But this leads us to ask why the American people would believe and follow such irresponsible agitators and political incompetents?

The American Belief System

- In the last three or four decades, many historians have concentrated on examining the general beliefs—that is, the ideology—that led Americans to their perceptions of conspiracy. These historians have concluded that the basic problem lay with the belief system itself.

- Americans had come to believe that there should be no barriers to their individual efforts to achieve their own destiny and perfection, and that of their society, in this nation of equal rights, equal opportunity, and individual liberty.

- The problem was that Northerners and Southerners had, by the 1850s, defined their freedom in diametrically opposed terms: The Southerners' fundamental right to property (including slaves) collided with the Northerners' right to compete in a free market of equals, not slaves or slaveholders.

- The Southern idea of property rights also conflicted with the Northerners' concept of the rights all human beings possessed. As historian Avery Craven put it as early as 1950, "right and rights had become the symbols of all those interests and values" that divided North and South.

- Other historians, such as Allan Nevins, saw the slavery issue as inseparable from the "complementary problem of race adjustment." The root of the conflict, Nevins maintained, was that neither side was willing to "face these conjoined problems squarely." For historian David Donald, the cause of this unwillingness was a society "suffering from an excess of liberty" and, consequently, unable to deal rationally with differences.

- By the 1970s, another group of historians argued that a nation so devoted to individual liberty lacked, almost by definition, the strong social and institutional frameworks required to deal with their differences short of war.

- David Brion Davis put all this together in the 1970s and 1980s when he wrote that there had been, in the four decades before the Civil War, an "overleaping of boundaries of every kind" and a growing belief that the American people as a whole, like the American individual, were "free from the burdens of the past and free to shape their own national character."

Multiple Interpretations
- These different interpretations of the causes of the Civil War make abundantly clear that history is a subjective discipline in which disagreements are common. The study of such disagreements is called historiography.

- It's also true that specific interpretations are usually tied in some way to the era in which they were written.
  o It is far from accidental, for example, that the generation that fought the war would come to view it, in the North, as a moral struggle over slavery and, in the South, as a more defensible support of states' rights.

  o Similarly, it's not surprising that an economic interpretation gained popularity during the years of the Great Depression or that the interpretations emphasizing fanatics and incompetent politicians should arise during the ascension of Hitler and Mussolini.

  o Of course, the emphasis on ideology developed during the Cold War, which was both a power conflict and an ideological one.

- It's important to note that if one accepts this ideological approach, all the previous interpretations retain their validity.
  o Even if there were no conspiracies, no differences in economies or cultures, no basic disagreement over the nature of the Union,

and no chance of slavery establishing itself in the territories, Americans North and South believed otherwise because of their ideology—and they acted on the basis of those beliefs.

o   Further, ideology and perceptions are themselves the products of all the general factors previously cited as causes of the war: economics, culture, politics, political theory, and moral values.

o   The common denominator linking all of these previously cited causes is slavery, which is, therefore, the basic cause of the war.

•   Have we simply come back to the earliest interpretation and wasted our time over the last 150 years in false interpretations linked to the values of specific eras? The answer is no. We are far from seeing slavery as the basic cause in the simplistic way originally proposed. Indeed, we now have a much better understanding of the causes of the war than ever before and of the ways in which our interpretations are shaped by the values of our era.

Suggested Reading

McPherson, *Battle Cry of Freedom*.

Perman and Taylor, eds., *Major Problems in the Civil War and Reconstruction*.

Stampp, ed., *Causes of the Civil War*.

Questions to Consider

1.   Are past ideas that historians now consider rationalizations nevertheless causes because people believed and acted upon them?

2.   In what ways does our present synthesis on slavery as the key cause of the Civil War differ from the one enunciated by historian James Ford Rhodes nearly 100 years ago: "there is a risk of referring any historic event to a single cause... of the American Civil War it may be safely asserted that there was a single cause, slavery"?

Did Slavery Really Cause the Civil War?
Lecture 8—Transcript

Today it is commonly accepted that slavery was the primary cause of the Civil War. The North opposed it, the South defended, and the result was, in William Seward's famous words, an "irrepressible conflict," for the United States could not remain half slave and half free. As historian James Ford Rhodes put it in 1913, while there was "a risk of referring any historic event to a single cause ... of the American Civil War it may be safely asserted that there was a single cause, slavery."

Yet the North and South had disagreed over slavery since the inception of the country, and they had consistently been able to compromise their differences before 1861. Moreover, the abolition of slavery was not a stated goal during the 1850s of the new Republican Party of Abraham Lincoln; nor was the abolition of slavery a Union war aim in 1861 or in the first half of 1862. At that time, Lincoln's war aim was merely preservation of the Union. In addition, most Southerners did not own slaves, and many Southern leaders would later claim that they were fighting not for slavery but for states' rights.

Over the last 150 years, historians have cited numerous other causes to explain why the Civil War took place. Nevertheless, slavery was the primary cause of the war, though not in the way Rhodes thought in 1913, and not in the way many Northerners thought in 1865, and not in the way most people still think today. The process of examining the other causes historians have cited in the century since Rhodes can teach us a great deal about the nature of historical study.

The key issue of the 1850s was not slavery per se, but the extension of slavery into the western territories; and when in 1853–1854 Congress passed the Kansas Nebraska Act, which opened slavery into territories previously closed to slavery by the 1820 Missouri Compromise, it set off a firestorm. That firestorm, of course, led to the mini-Civil War in the Kansas territory known as "Bleeding Kansas." But ironically, it is questionable whether slavery could have survived in the Kansas territory anyway given its unsuitability for growing cotton. The Kansas-Nebraska Act also led to the collapse of the Whig Party and its replacement by the new Republican Party, a totally sectional party committed to reversal of the Kansas-Nebraska Act and the prohibition of slavery in all the territories.

Lincoln was elected in 1860 without a majority of the total vote—he only achieved 39.8 percent of the total vote—but he had victories in every one of the populous Northern states; that gave him a majority in the Electoral College, if not in the popular vote. With his election, South Carolina and the other states of the Deep South seceded from the Union: the states of Georgia, Florida, Alabama, Mississippi, Louisiana, and Texas. With the start of hostilities at Fort Sumter in April, 1861, followed by Lincoln's call for troops to suppress the rebellion, Virginia seceded, as did the other states of the Upper South: North Carolina, Tennessee, and Arkansas.

Lincoln's call for troops was to suppress rebellion and preserve the Union, not abolish slavery. Indeed, before hostilities began, Lincoln had been willing to guarantee the preservation of slavery within the states where it existed and had called only for the barring of slavery in the territories. Throughout the first year and a half of the war, that remained his stated aim. As he wrote in the summer of 1862: "If I could save the union without freeing any slave I would do it."

Only on September 22, 1862 did Lincoln announce that he would issue an Emancipation Proclamation, and he did so as a war measure and one that would not even take effect until January 1, 1863. When it did take effect, it did not free a single slave on that date; nor did it ever apply to the border slave states that had remained in the Union, or to Confederate Territory that had already been occupied by Union armies. The Emancipation Proclamation applied only to areas still in a state of insurrection and under Confederate control, and it fit in with previous by the Union army and by Congress to confiscate rebel property, which, of course, included slaves; property that was aiding the Confederate war effort in numerous ways.

In light of these facts, historians in the early 20th century began to question the centrality of slavery to the coming of Civil War. The first of these revisionist interpretations focused on the old conflict between state and national power that dated back to Alexander Hamilton and Thomas Jefferson. Indeed, only three years after the war ended, Confederate Vice President

Alexander H. Stephens maintained that this was the real conflict, with the South seceding and fighting to support the primacy of states' rights over the federal government. In his words, the conflict on the question of slavery:

> from the beginning, was not a contest between the advocates or opponents of that peculiar institution, but a contest ... between the supporters of a strictly Federative Government, on the one side, and a thoroughly National one, on the other. ... It was a strife between the principles of Federation ... and Centralism.

This conflict, of course, was nothing new. As previously stated, it had existed since the days of Hamilton and Jefferson, and it went back to the very nature of the new government that had been established between 1787 and 1789. Was that new government under the Constitution a creation of the states, and therefore subordinate to them and possessing only limited powers? Or was it a union of the people, possessing strong implied powers over the states? The South had long defended the former interpretation, and the North the latter interpretation. To this very day, many Americans, especially in the South, view the Civil War in these terms, even referring to it as the "War Between the States" rather than the "Civil War."

But contrary to popular belief, the South has not always defended states rights and the North had not always opposed them vis-à-vis national power. New England, for example, had supported states' rights and opposed the Federal Government before and during the War of 1812 and during the Mexican-American War of 1846–1848, both of which were exceedingly unpopular in that part of the country. Far from accidentally, the Northeast did not control the Federal Government during those two wars. As historian Arthur Schlesinger, Sr. made clear during the 1930s, states' rights had consistently been used throughout U.S. history by whichever section did not control the national government and felt oppressed by national power. States' rights were thus a device to protect specific sectional interests of different parts of the country, and in truth a rationalization rather than a cause of the Civil War.

But just what were those sectional interests that led the South to defend states' rights at this time? Slavery, of course; but in looking at those interests in broad perspective, many historians during the 1930s saw slavery itself as part of a much larger Southern economic interest: the defense of an agrarian economy against a diametrically opposed economic system of industrial and commercial capitalism in the North. These two economic systems clashed not only over slave versus free labor, but also over taxation, tariffs, railroads, monetary policies, and land policies. These issues all required federal action. Since the three-fifths slavery clause in the Constitution was the basis of Southern agrarian power within the federal government, disagreements over economic interests became a struggle between competing economic systems for control of that government. Historian Louis Hacker put it quite succinctly in 1935 when he stated that the Civil War was:

> a conflict between two different systems of economic production; and with the victory at the Presidential polls in 1860 of the higher order, a counterrevolutionary movement was launched by the defenders of the lower order, the slave lords of the South.

But economic differences between North and South had existed since Colonial times, and had never led to civil war before now; and in many ways, the very different Northern and Southern economies were complementary rather than competitive. Southern cotton fed Northern cotton mills, and the ensuing Northern clothing was then sent back south. Furthermore, the North had substantial agriculture as well as the South.

Some historians answered that the two economic systems were in themselves part of what had become by the 1850s two unique cultures: a Southern agrarian society and a very different Northern society with very different political, economic, social, and intellectual values. The South by this interpretation was rural, deliberate, paternalistic, and hierarchical, with slavery having social as well as economic functions: to maintain the planter class that controlled and set the values for the South, and, of course, to keep the large number of blacks in a subordinate position. The North, on the other hand, did not have large numbers of blacks to deal with, or a planter class for that matter, or old agrarian values. It had developed a bustling, capitalist, and urban value structure that was accepted by its numerous farmers as well as its urban workers and employers. Thus two very different "nations" had come into existence by 1860.

This idea of an aristocratic, agrarian, "Cavalier" Southern society versus a bustling, capitalist, "Yankee" society in the North makes for interesting literature and for interesting movies, but it is largely myth. The South was not settled by rural aristocrats and the North by an urban middle class. In addition, the North was as racist against blacks as the South was, and indeed had racial segregation laws before the Civil War to keep blacks in a separate and inferior status. In point of fact, the similarities between North and South far outweighed their differences. Both sections were dominated by people who considered themselves Americans, and both drew pride from their definition of the United States as a nation devoted to the principles of economic opportunity, representative government, and individual liberty.

Ironically, however, many Americans in each section saw the other engaged in a conspiracy against liberty, particularly against their liberty. A group of historians argued in the 1930s and 1940s that these perceptions were the real cause of the Civil War. Despite the fact that neither Lincoln nor any other Republican figure proposed abolishing slavery where it existed, many Southerners believed that that was the hidden aim of what they labeled the "Black Republicans": to destroy slavery entirely and institute black rule in the South. Similarly, many Northerners believed that Southern slaveholders were engaged in a conspiracy—what they called the "slavepower conspiracy"—to spread slavery to the North and thereby control the entire union.

Historian James G. Randall wrote in 1947 that one could not explain the coming of Civil War:

> If one omits the elements of emotional unreason and overbold leadership. If one word or phrase were selected to account for the war [he said] that word would not be slavery, or economic grievance, or states' rights, or diverse civilizations. It would have to be such a word as fanaticism, misunderstanding, misrepresentation, or perhaps politics.

In reality, no such conspiracies ever existed. But many people believed that they existed, and people act on the basis of their beliefs, even if those beliefs are false; in other words, they act on their perceptions of reality, rather than reality itself. Some historians have therefore argued that false perceptions led each side to believe that it was threatened by an illusionary plot and to go to war to defend its rights. But why did people believe such conspiracies existed? Another group of historians argued that the blame needs to be placed on fanatical, irresponsible agitators on both sides who fanned the flames of such conspiracy theories, as did blundering, incompetent politicians. But then the question arises as to why the Founding Fathers of the late 18th century and their immediate successors of the early 19th century had given way to these irresponsible rabble-rousers and incompetent political fools. Compare the presidents that this nation had from Washington through Andrew Jackson with those who followed, especially those of the 1850s; Franklin Pierce and James Buchanan, for example. Also, why would the American people believe and follow irresponsible agitators and political incompetents?

Another fact to keep in mind is that all societies live by sets of beliefs that appear illusory to later generations who have the advantage of 20-20 historical hindsight; and to label such believers as fools is to use our historical hindsight to distort the realities of the past. Recognizing this fact, many historians over the past three to four decades have concentrated on examining the general beliefs—the ideologies—that led Americans to their perceptions; and they have concluded that the basic problem lay with the American belief system itself, the one that had been largely created during the Age of Andrew Jackson and the Second Great Awakening, the subjects of the two previous lectures in this course.

Americans had come to believe that there should be no barriers to their individual efforts to achieve their own destiny and perfection, and the destiny and perfection of their society; this society, this nation, of equal rights, equal opportunity, and individual liberty. The problem was that Northerners and Southerners had by the 1850s defined their freedom in diametrically opposed terms: The Southerner's fundamental right to his property (including slaves) and the free movement with that property collided with the Northerner's right to compete in a free market of equals, not with slaves or slave owners. Slavery also conflicted with the Northerners' concept of the rights that all human beings possessed, as illustrated by the political slogan "Free Soil, Free Labor, Free Men." As the historian Avery Craven put it as early as 1950, "right and rights had become the symbols of all those interests and values" that divided North and South, and they had an "emotional force and moral power ... far greater than the sum total of all the material issues."

Some historians, such as Arthur Schlesinger, Jr., argued further that these symbols possessed such power because at its root, the conflict over the extension of slavery was a moral conflict; that is what gave it such power. Other historians such as Allan Nevins argued that the slavery issue was inseparable from what he called the "complementary problem of race adjustment." The root of the conflict was that neither side was willing to "face these conjoined problems squarely." Other historians like David Donald saw the cause of this unwillingness to be a society that he labeled "suffering from an excess of liberty" and consequently unable to deal rationally with differences. As he put it:

> The permanent revolution that was America had freed its citizens from the bonds of prescription and custom but had left them leaderless. Never [he wrote in 1960] was there a field so fertile before the propagandist, the agitator, the extremist.

By the 1970s, another group of historians had begun to argue that a nation so devoted to individual liberty lacked almost by definition the strong social and institutional frameworks adequate to deal with differences short of war. By 1860, the few frameworks that did exist and that previously had bound the nation together—from the different Protestant religious denominations to the Democratic Party—had fragmented along sectional lines. David Brion Davis put all of this together in the 1970s and 1980s when he wrote that there had been, in the four decades before the Civil War, an "overleaping of boundaries of every kind" and a growing belief that the American people as a whole, like the American individual, were "free from the burdens of the past and free to shape their own national character."

But:

> The one problem their ingenuity could not resolve [he noted] was Negro slavery.

Paradoxically, the South increasingly came to regard Negro slavery as the necessary base on which freedom must rest [he continued]. From the North a commitment to slavery's ultimate extinction was the test of freedom. Each section detected a fatal change in the other, a betrayal of the principles and mission of the Founding Fathers. Each section feared that the other had become transformed into a despotic and conspiratorial power.

What do we make of all this? First of all, these different interpretations of the causes of the Civil War make abundantly clear that history is a subjective discipline in which such disagreements are common. The study of these disagreements is called "historiography," and historiography is essentially what we have been doing in this lecture.

Secondly, specific interpretations are usually tied in some way to the era in which they were written. It's far from accidental that the generation that fought the war would come to view it in the North as a moral struggle over slavery and in the South as a more defensible support of states' rights. Similarly, it is far from accidental that the economic interpretation gained great popularity during the 1930s, the years of the Great Depression. Nor is it surprising that interpretations emphasizing fanatics and incompetent politicians should arise as people in the 1930 began to see World War I as an avoidable conflict and who were simultaneously witnessing the rise of Adolf Hitler and Benito Mussolini. Nor should we be surprised that all these alternative views to slavery as the cause of the war emerged in decades of intense racism in the United States. Nor should we be surprised by the reemergence of slavery as a moral issue and the question of race relations in the era of Civil Rights and in the years following the end of World War II and the full revelation of Nazi racial atrocities. As I noted in the first lecture on the origins and development of religious toleration with a rather flippant comment, which I will repeat here: Hitler gave racism a bad name.

The emphasis on psychological interpretations in this same time period should not surprise us either. Indeed, David Donald's interpretation is quite similar to David Riesman's concept in the 1950s of "other-directedness" in contemporary American society. Nor should the emphasis on ideology that developed during the many years of the Cold War, which was an ideological conflict between Communist dictatorship and democratic Capitalism as well as a power conflict. Important to realize that if one accepts this ideological approach, then all the previous interpretations retain their validity. For even if there were no conspiracies in reality, no truly irreconcilable differences in economies or cultures, no basic disagreement over the nature of the Union, and no chance of slavery establishing itself in the territories, Americans North and South believed otherwise because of their ideology, and they acted upon the basis of those beliefs.

Furthermore, ideology and perceptions are themselves products of all the general factors previously cited as causes of the war: economics, culture, politics, political theory, moral values. The common denominator linking all of these previously cited causes is slavery. It was the base of the Southern economy, Southern culture, the conspiracy theories North and South, the fanaticism, politics, moral arguments, racism, conflicting Northern and Southern definitions of rights, and ensuing ideological conflicts. It is therefore the basic cause of the war.

Thus, deep down, weren't Southerners correct in seeing abolition as the eventual goal of the North, and the outlawing of slavery in the territories as merely the first stage in this long program? Did not the Southern defense of slavery as a "positive good" instead of the "necessary evil" that defined slavery in the 18th century imply its eventual extension to the entire country? Given all this, was Abraham Lincoln being simplistic and wrong, or in actuality very perceptive and correct, when he said that the nation could not continue to exist half slave and half free? As he wrote to a Southern senator in 1860, "You think slavery is right and ought to be extended, while we think it is wrong and ought to be restricted. That I suppose is the rub. It is certainly the only substantial difference between us."

But if Lincoln was correct, have we simply come back to the earliest interpretation and in reality wasted our time over the last 150 years in false interpretations and indeed sophistry linked to the values of specific eras and the individual hidden agendas of specific historians? Not really. We are far from seeing slavery as the basic cause in the simplistic way originally proposed right after the war. Indeed, we now have a much better understanding of the causes of the war than ever before, and of the ways in which our interpretations are shaped by the values of our era.

I often try to explain and illustrate this in class by asking my students to imagine that the blackboard in front of the classroom is an event and that time is all the space in the room running from the blackboard to the back door and beyond into infinity. An individual who lived through an event, who was part of that event, I illustrate, has his face right up against the blackboard. He sees in incredible detail one small part of the event, but only that small part. As time passes, more and more of the blackboard is seen, though with less detail; a problem historians overcome through the use of primary sources from the time period. But historians do not stand dead-center in the room as time passes. Most, if not all, stand on the left side of the room or on the right side of the room, and higher or lower, depending on the events and values of their particular era; and that gives each of them a new and unique angle in viewing the blackboard. As time passes, they also view where previous historians have stood as well as more and more of the event, and they incorporate those earlier views into their own. Even though James Ford Rhodes and David Brion Davis may seem to stand in the same straight 100-year line regarding slavery as the cause of the Civil War, Davis sees all the other interpretations and he incorporates them into his own.

We thus know far more about the causes of the Civil War than we did when it ended, or than we knew in 1913, even though we use the same word—"slavery"—that many participants and early historians used.

The Civil War's Actual Turning Points
Lecture 9

Most Americans would probably point to Gettysburg as the most important battle of the Civil War, the turning point when Confederate victory ceased to be a possibility. In reality, however, Gettysburg was not all that significant for the outcome of the Civil War. Far more consequential, both militarily and politically, were at least three other events: the Battle of Antietam, the Union capture of Vicksburg, and the Union capture of Atlanta.

The Battle of Antietam

- The Battle of Antietam, fought on September 17, 1862, was not a clear-cut victory for either the North or the South, but in terms of importance, it was one of the most consequential battles of the Civil War.

- Before the battle, Confederate General Robert E. Lee had decided to follow up on his successful summer victories outside Richmond and at the Second Battle of Bull Run with an invasion of the North. If successful, his campaign could result in the capture of Washington and/or British and French intervention on the side of the Confederacy, either of which would mean Confederate victory and independence.

- But Lee's plans were foiled by the accidental Union discovery of his orders. Had the Union commander, General George McClellan, moved quickly, he could have destroyed Lee's army, but his slowness enabled Lee to bring his forces together at Sharpsburg, Maryland, along Antietam Creek. Still, Lee was put on the defensive against a concentrated Union army nearly twice as large as his own.

- Lee was able to counter three uncoordinated Union assaults on his line, but given his heavy casualties and the fact that his location in Maryland was no longer a secret, he was forced to end his campaign and withdraw back into Virginia, with McClellan unable (or unwilling) to pursue.

- The battle itself was thus inconclusive on a tactical level, but it was a strategic defeat for Lee in that he had to end his invasion of the North. And it had decisive political and diplomatic consequences.
    - At the time, both the British and French governments were considering intervention on the side of the South, but Lee's withdrawal from Maryland convinced them to remain out of the conflict.

    - Further, Lee's withdrawal enabled Lincoln to portray the battle as a Union victory, despite McClellan's failures. Lincoln then used the occasion of this "victory" to issue the Emancipation Proclamation, which altered the aim of the war

Despite his failures at Antietam and elsewhere, Union commander George B. McClellan became a viable peace candidate in the North in 1864, threatening Lincoln's reelection.

© iStockphoto/Thinkstock.

from preserving the Union to ending slavery and made the possibility of British intervention in support of the South even less likely.

The Battle of Gettysburg
- Antietam was followed by major Union defeats against Lee at Fredericksburg in December 1862 and Chancellorsville in May 1863. In this latter battle, Lee almost destroyed a Union army twice the size of his own, but the victory did nothing to improve the chances of Confederate success.
    - It did not relieve the Union blockade that was gradually starving the Confederacy, and it did not relieve pressure on

Confederate forces in the west, where Union General Ulysses Grant had isolated and laid siege to the Confederate fortress of Vicksburg.

- o   If Vicksburg fell, Union forces would control the entire Mississippi River and effectively cut the Confederacy in half.

- Lee, therefore, decided to go on the offensive for a second time in June 1863 in an effort to achieve decisive results. This second invasion of the North brought him to Gettysburg in southern Pennsylvania.

- The most important day of that three-day battle is the one least studied—the first one. On that day, Lee's arriving army routed Union forces in the area and captured the town but failed to seize the high ground south of the town, which the Union army, now under General George Meade, immediately reinforced.

- Lee's uncoordinated assaults on Meade's right and left flanks on the second day failed, as did his famous assault on the Union center on the third day, Pickett's Charge. In retrospect, Lee should have broken off the battle after his second-day failures rather than launch the doomed frontal assault that so decimated his forces.

- Even if Lee had succeeded in flanking Meade on the second day and forcing his retreat, the Union commander would have retreated to his prepared position at Pipe Creek, Maryland, or to Washington, which was, by this time, the most heavily fortified city in the world. Lee thus probably could not have destroyed Meade's army or taken Washington, and without one of those results, the British would not have intervened.

- Again, even if Lee had succeeded at Gettysburg, it is doubtful that the British would have intervened at this stage given the slavery issue that Lincoln had introduced with the Emancipation Proclamation and a host of additional factors that had emerged in the 10 months since Antietam.

- On the day after Pickett's Charge failed at Gettysburg, Vicksburg surrendered to Grant's forces, thereby effectively cutting the Confederacy in half. Nevertheless, Lee was far from finished in July of 1863.

Grant's Campaign against Lee

- Grant followed up his victory at Vicksburg by relief of a trapped Union army at Chattanooga and major victories at Lookout Mountain and Missionary Ridge. He was ultimately able to defeat Lee, not by tactical brilliance on the battlefield but by his strategic plan—to bring all Union forces to bear in a simultaneous assault along the entire Confederate periphery—and by his refusal to retreat even when his plan failed miserably.

- Lee defeated Grant at the Battle of the Wilderness on May 5–6, 1864, but instead of retreating, Grant continued to move south in an effort to outflank Lee. Lee was forced to follow him and pin him down so that he could not regain the strategic initiative.

- During the course of the campaign, Lee's casualties were about half of Grant's, but they represented a higher percentage of his total force than Grant's. Grant was draining Lee's army of men while stretching its lines to the limit.

- As a result of military failures and massive Union casualties, peace sentiment in the North grew stronger, threatening Lincoln's reelection. The promise of an end to the war if a peace candidate was elected would mean Union recognition of Confederate independence.

- In July 1864, Confederate General John Bell Hood took command of the defense of Atlanta, but he was forced to abandon the city in September when Sherman threatened to cut his supply lines. That victory, along with Union victories at Mobile Bay and in the Shenandoah Valley, ensured Lincoln's reelection and, with it, a continuation of the war to the bitter end. It also placed Sherman in position to begin his destructive and decisive march through Georgia and South Carolina, the heart of the Confederacy.

Drawing Meaning from Battles

- As these examples clearly show, battles are truly meaningful in the study of history for their consequences, not their size. As we saw in an earlier lecture, Washington lost most of his battles during the Revolutionary War, but the few he won—Trenton, Saratoga, and Yorktown—were incredibly consequential.

- It's also true that the political consequences of battles are especially meaningful. War is, as the Prussian general Carl von Clausewitz famously observed, a political act, and it always has a political goal. Antietam and Atlanta clearly had political consequences for the Union cause far more important than any Gettysburg had or could have had even if Lee had been victorious.

- In terms of military consequences, Grant's simultaneous victory at Vicksburg was more important than what happened at Gettysburg in that it split the Confederacy in half, reopened the Mississippi River to the North, and led to Grant's overall command of all Union armies.

- It's important to note, however, that battles are not the only consequential events in war. Indeed, one could argue that a little-known diplomatic event in late 1861 was at least as consequential, if not more so, than any of these three battles.
  - On November 8, 1861, U.S. Navy Captain Charles Wilkes, in command of the USS *San Jacinto*, intercepted the British mail steamer *Trent* as it left Havana and seized two Confederate emissaries, James Mason and John Slidell, who were on their way to London and Paris to attempt to obtain British and French recognition of the Confederacy.

  - The enraged British government demanded the release of the two emissaries and a formal apology, and Lincoln chose to agree to this humiliation rather than face war with Britain.

Gettysburg: A Turning Point?

- Why is Gettysburg seen by so many as the decisive battle of the Civil War? The explanation lies partially in its sheer size—it was the largest and deadliest battle of the war—and partially in the tendency to look for a single and specific "turning point" in war.

- Such single turning points seldom exist, but Gettysburg appears to be one because it broke Lee's invincibility. Still, that is what we know now with the advantage of historical hindsight; it did not appear that way at the time.

- Gettysburg's fame is probably also a result of what happened there after the battle—specifically, the establishment of a cemetery for the reburial of Union dead, dedicated by Lincoln with his Gettysburg Address.

- In that brief address, Lincoln stated, "The world will little note, nor long remember what we say here," but in commemorating those who had died and imploring his countrymen to "resolve that these dead shall not have died in vain," Lincoln unknowingly immortalized the battle, as well as himself.

Suggested Reading

Clausewitz, *On War.*

McPherson, *Battle Cry of Freedom.*

———, *Tried by War.*

Reardon, *Pickett's Charge in History and Memory.*

Questions to Consider

1. What battles in other wars are more or less important than we think?

2. Why do we have a tendency to look for single "turning point" battles in wars when they seldom exist?

The Civil War's Actual Turning Points
Lecture 9—Transcript

The three-day battle at Gettysburg, Pennsylvania, July 1–3, 1863 was the largest and bloodiest single battle of the entire Civil War. In fact, it was the largest and bloodiest battle ever fought on the North American Continent: approximately 23,000 casualties for Union side, 28,000 for the Confederate side, for a staggering total of 51,000. Probably for that reason, most Americans would name Gettysburg as the most important battle of the Civil War; the key "turning point" when Confederate victory ceased to be a possibility and defeat became inevitable.

But that was not the case. Indeed, Gettysburg was not all that consequential for the outcome of the Civil War. Only in light of what followed Gettysburg—and what was far from predetermined by Gettysburg—does the battle incorrectly appear to be so pivotal. It definitely was not perceived as pivotal at the time, by either side. Far more consequential, both militarily and politically, were at least three other battles: first, the September, 1862 battle of Antietam; second, the Union capture of Vicksburg on July 4, 1863, just one day after Gettysburg; and third, the September 1, 1864 Union capture of Atlanta, Georgia.

In this lecture, we shall examine these three battles as well as Gettysburg. In the process, we will analyze why Gettysburg's importance has been overrated as well as why these three other battles were more important.

Let's turn to Antietam first: Although Gettysburg was the bloodiest battle of the war, September 17, 1862 at Antietam Creek near Sharpsburg, Maryland was the bloodiest single day of combat in the war. Gettysburg took place over three days; Antietam, one day, with 24,000 casualties, including 4,800 dead. Technically, the battle was a draw and was not a clear-cut victory for either side; but in terms of importance, it was one of the most consequential—and in some ways the most consequential—battle of the entire war. How could a battle without a clear winner be so consequential? A little background is needed to answer that question.

Confederate General Robert E. Lee had achieved a series of brilliant summer victories, first over Union General George McClellan outside of Richmond and then over Union General John Pope at the Second Battle of Bull Run, and he decided to follow these victories up with an invasion of the North. If successful, that invasion could have resulted in the capture of Washington and/or British and French intervention on the side of the Confederacy, either of which would mean Confederate victory and independence. But Lee's plans were foiled by the accidental Union discovery of his orders; they were found wrapped around cigars in a Confederate campfire.

At the point that they were discovered, had McClellan moved quickly, he could have destroyed Lee's army, which was divided at that point, and he could have destroyed each component piecemeal. But McClellan's slowness enabled Lee to bring all his forces together at Sharpsburg, Maryland, along Antietam Creek. But Lee was now on the defensive against a concentrated Union army nearly twice as large as his own, 75,000 men to 40,000 men. Lee was able to counter three uncoordinated Union assaults on his line on September 17, assaults that began on the north side of the line and moved gradually south. But given his own heavy casualties and the fact that his location in Maryland was no longer a secret, Lee was forced to end the campaign and withdraw back into Virginia, with McClellan either unable or unwilling to pursue him.

The battle itself was thus inconclusive militarily on a tactical level. But it was a strategic defeat for Lee in that he had to end his invasion of the North; and it had enormous and decisive political and diplomatic consequences. At this time, the British and French governments were considering intervention. Both favored the South, for numerous reasons, and both were seriously considering moves that would recognize the independence of the Confederacy. As French intervention had proven decisive in the American War for Independence, so British-French intervention in the Civil War would have been decisive, had it ever occurred. But the French waited on the British, and the British decided to await the outcome of Lee's campaign before moving. With Lee's withdrawal from Maryland, Britain backed away. British Prime Minister Palmerston concluded that his government should "continue to be lookers on until the war shall have taken a more decided turn." Never again in the war would London, and with it Paris, come so close to intervention.

Lee's withdrawal from Maryland also enabled Lincoln to portray the battle as a Union victory, despite the fact that McClellan had not broken Lee's line and had neither destroyed nor captured Lee's army. Lincoln then used this "victory" to issue on September 22 an Emancipation Proclamation to be effective January 1, 1863. As noted in the last lecture, that Proclamation actually freed no one in September, 1862 or in January, 1863 as it applied only to areas still in a state of rebellion and not under Union control. But it eventually would free a large number of slaves, and it dramatically altered the nature of the war: from one to preserve the Union into one to end slavery.

The British had utterly no interest in the preservation of the American Union; quite the contrary, they would have welcomed the dissolution of the United States. But the British people had very real interest in the abolition of slavery, which they had ended within their empire nearly 30 years earlier. In that sense, the announcement of the Emancipation Proclamation made British intervention, and with it French intervention, much less likely in the future, for it turned the Union effort into a moral cause with which the British sympathized.

Antietam was followed by major Union defeats against Lee at Fredericksburg in December, 1862 and at Chancellorsville in May, 1863. In the Battle of Chancellorsville, often considered Lee's tactical masterpiece, he split his heavily outnumbered army in three and then incredibly enveloped and almost destroyed an army twice the size of his own. It was a masterpiece, but it did nothing to improve the chances of eventual Confederate success. Chancellorsville did not lead to a revival of British interventionist sentiment, nor did it relieve the Union blockade that was gradually starving Lee's army and the entire Confederacy. It did not relieve the pressure on Confederate forces in the West. In the West, Union General Ulysses Grant had, in a brilliant campaign, isolated and laid siege to the Confederate fortress of Vicksburg, despite the fact that he was outnumbered by Confederate forces in the area. If Vicksburg fell, Union forces would control the entire Mississippi River and effectively cut the Confederacy in half.

Lee therefore decided in the summer of 1863 to go on the offensive for a second time in an effort to achieve decisive results. In retrospect, Lee would have probably been better off staying on the defensive in the East and sending part of his army west in an effort to break the siege of Vicksburg. Some of his subordinates suggested this at the time: that what he should do is send part of his army to Tennessee in order to allow the Confederate Army in Tennessee to defeat the Union Army there and thereby threaten Kentucky and Ohio. That threat would force Grant to end the siege of Vicksburg and come to the rescue. But Lee rejected this approach, and instead decided to attempt a second invasion of the North, one that brought him to Gettysburg, a town in southern Pennsylvania.

In retrospect, the most important day of that three-day battle is the one least studied: the first day, during which Lee's arriving forces routed Union forces in the area, captured the town of Gettysburg, but failed to seize the high ground south of the town. The Union Army, now under General George Meade, immediately reinforced that high ground. Lee's uncoordinated assaults on Meade's right and left flanks on the second day failed. So did his famous (but misnamed) assault on the Union center on the third day, Pickett's Charge (Pickett's Charge actually included more than Pickett's division).

In retrospect, Lee should have broken off the battle either after his first day failure to obtain the high ground or after his second day failures to outflank the Union line rather than launch the doomed frontal assault on the third day that so decimated his forces. Even if Lee had succeeded in flanking Meade on the second day and forcing Meade's retreat, the Union commander would have retreated to prepared positions at Pipe Creek, Maryland, or to Washington, DC; and Washington at this time was the most heavily fortified city in the world, with a ring of self-contained forts connected by trenches and garrisoned by an entire army corps. In all likelihood, Lee thus could not have destroyed Meade's army or taken Washington; and if Lee had decided to try for one of the other major Northern cities—let's say Baltimore, Philadelphia, or Pittsburgh—if Lee threatened any of these, there were hastily-constructed fortifications at each of them into which Meade could have poured his army. Without Lee destroying Meade's army or taking Washington, the British would not have intervened.

Indeed, even if Lee had succeeded at Gettysburg, it is doubtful the British would have intervened at this stage—the summer of 1863—given the slavery issue that Lincoln had introduced with the Emancipation Proclamation, and given a host of additional factors that had emerged in the 10 months since Antietam. First, there were problems in Europe that the British had to focus on, including the possibility of war with Russia. Britain had fought a war with Russia in the 1850s, the Crimean War; there was now the possibility of yet another war. There was also the fear of losing Canada in any war with the North and suffering major commercial losses. The British relied on Northern foodstuffs as well as on Southern cotton. Southerners had thought that their cotton crop, King Cotton, on which the British economy depended, would lead to British intervention. But the British also relied on Northern foodstuffs; and by 1863, the British had developed alternative sources of cotton for their numerous textile mills.

Finally, there was very skillful Union diplomacy under Secretary of State William Henry Seward and the American minister to Court of Saint James, Charles Francis Adams, the son of John Quincy Adams and the grandson of John Adams. Furthermore, on the day after Pickett's Charge at Gettysburg, Vicksburg surrendered to Grant's forces, thereby effectively cutting the Confederacy in half. That would have also led the British to second thoughts about intervening.

Nevertheless, Robert E. Lee was far from finished in July of 1863. He had failed to roll up or break the Union line at Gettysburg; he had suffered very heavy casualties; but his opponent, General Meade, had in turn failed to trap, capture, or destroy Lee's Confederate Army of Northern Virginia. Instead, Lee and his army escaped across the Potomac River to fight another day. Not yet had Lincoln found a general to match Robert E. Lee.

But Grant's victory at Vicksburg also led to his expanded command over of the entire Western theater, and that was followed by his successful relief of a trapped Union army at Chattanooga, Tennessee and ensuing major victories at the battles of Lookout Mountain and Missionary Ridge. After those victories, Lincoln promoted to Grant to Lieutenant General—the first Lieutenant General since George Washington—and placed him in command of all Union forces in early March, 1864. Grant would be able to defeat Lee, but not by tactical brilliance on the battlefield. Instead, he would defeat him by a strategic plan to bring to bear all Union forces in a simultaneous assault along the entire Confederate periphery, and by a refusal to retreat even when the original plan failed and when he was defeated tactically by Lee. All of this requires a little bit of explanation.

The assault all along the Confederate line would include: Meade's Army of the Potomac with Grant actually in charge moving against Lee in Northern Virginia; General Benjamin Butler moving up the James River hopefully to Richmond or at the very least cutting Lee's supply lines to Petersburg, south of Richmond; General Franz Sigal moving up the Shenandoah Valley to deny Lee's army the resources of that valley; General Banks to take Mobile, one of the last Southern ports still open; and General William Tecumseh Sherman to take Atlanta and get into the Southern interior.

Good plan; it failed wretchedly: Butler was unsuccessful on the James Rivers; Sigal was unsuccessful in the Shenandoah Valley; and Banks was unsuccessful in Mobile. Sherman was able to advance from Chattanooga on Atlanta, but he did so very slowly given the terrain and the tactics of his opponent, General Joseph Johnston. Furthermore, Lee defeated Grant in the battle known as the Wilderness Battle of May 5–6, 1864. But instead of retreating with his failure, Grant continued to move south in an effort to outflank Lee, eventually all the way down to Petersburg; and in doing so, he forced Lee to follow him and pinned Lee so that he could not regain the strategic initiative.

The problem, though, was that this campaign led to massive Union casualties: 18,000 in just the first two days in the Wilderness Battle, followed by tens of thousands more in the weeks that followed, weeks of continuous fighting, a total of 64,000 casualties for the Union Army at battles such as Spotsylvania Court House, North Anna, Totopotomy Creek, and Cold Harbor, and then Grant's movement of his army across the James River and the siege of Petersburg. Lee's casualties were only about half of Grant's causalities, but they were consistently a higher percentage of his total force than of Grant's total force. What Grant was doing was draining Lee's army of men while stretching Lee's lines to the limit. The two combined, something would have to give.

The casualty rates, however, were appalling, and Grant became known as "the butcher"; and all of this took place during a presidential election year, no less, with few if any visible decisive results by the fall of 1864. Nor were there any major Union victories in other theaters of the war. Especially worrisome were events in the Shenandoah Valley, where Confederate General Early defeated Union forces and in July was actually at the outskirts of Washington, DC. Sherman's army also continued to make very slow progress moving from Chattanooga towards Atlanta, with General Johnston constantly countering his movements and limiting his advance to an average of about a mile a day. As a result of these military failures and the massive casualties, peace sentiment in the North—sentiment that had existed throughout the war—now grew stronger and threatened Lincoln's re-election in 1864. Indeed, the Democrats nominated the popular former Union commander George McClellan as a peace candidate, and peace would mean Union recognition of Confederate independence.

But in July of 1864, Confederate President Jefferson Davis replaced General Johnston in front of Atlanta with General John Bell Hood, a highly aggressive (if not too intelligent) commander who boldly launched attacks against Sherman's army in its entrenched Union positions even though that army was twice the size of his own (the battles of Peach Tree Creek and Ezra Church). Hood suffered 13,000 casualties compared to 6,000 for Sherman, and he was not only defeated but he lost so many men that he was not able to prevent Sherman from swinging totally around him to the south of Atlanta and threatening to cut his supply lines. That forced Hood to abandon Atlanta to Sherman in early September.

That victory, preceded by Admiral Farragut's victory at Mobile Bay and then followed by General Sheridan's victory in the Shenandoah Valley, insured Lincoln's reelection, and with it a continuation of the war to the bitter end. It also placed General Sherman in position to begin his famous destructive and decisive march through Georgia and South Carolina, the heart of the Confederacy.

As these examples clearly show, battles are truly meaningful in the study of history for their consequences, not for their size. As we saw in an earlier lecture, Washington lost most of his battles during the Revolutionary War;

but the few that he won—Trenton, Saratoga, and Yorktown—were incredibly consequential: Trenton, preventing the total collapse of his army and with it the Revolution; Saratoga, leading to French intervention and a world war for Britain; and Yorktown, leading the British to give up on the Americas and make peace with the Americans.

As these examples show, political consequences of battles are especially meaningful. War is, after all, an instrument of policy and a political act, as the Prussian military theorist Carl von Clausewitz famously observed in the early 19th century, and war always has a political goal. Antietam and Atlanta clearly had major political consequences for the Union cause far more important than any that Gettysburg had, or could have had, even if Lee had been victorious. Even in terms of military consequences, Grant's simultaneous victory at Vicksburg was more important than what happened at Gettysburg in that it split the Confederacy in half, reopened the Mississippi River to the North, and led to Grant's overall command of all Union armies. Only Meade's trapping or capture of Lee's army, or Lee's highly unlikely total destruction of Meade's army and an equally unlikely British intervention, could have made Gettysburg more important and consequential than Vicksburg or Antietam.

Battles are not the only consequential events in war. In fact, one could argue that a little-known diplomatic event in late 1861 was just as consequential, if not more consequential, than any of the three battles we have gone through. On November 8, 1861, U.S. Navy Captain Charles Wilkes in command of the *USS San Jacinto* intercepted a British mail steamer, the *Trent*, as it left Havana and Cuban waters and seized two Confederate emissaries—James Mason and John Slidell—who were on their way to London and Paris to attempt to obtain British and French recognition of the Confederacy. The enraged British government demanded the release of the two emissaries and a formal apology. Without one forthcoming, war loomed on the horizon. In a Christmas Day meeting, Lincoln's Cabinet chose to agree to this humiliation rather than face war with Britain. As Lincoln later quipped: "One war at a time." This humiliation, this surrender, was rationalized by stating that the Americans were glad to see that the British had finally accepted American ideas of freedom of the seas that the War of 1812 had been fought over, but it really couldn't cover the fact that the North surrendered on this issue; and it's a good thing that it did.

Why, given what we've gone through, is Gettysburg seen by so many as the decisive battle and the turning point in the Civil War? Partially it is a matter of sheer size: It was the largest and deadliest battle of the Civil War; indeed, it is the largest battle ever fought on the North American continent. Partially the emphasis on Gettysburg is also a result of the tendency to look for a single and specific "turning point" in a war. Such single turning points seldom exist. World War II, for example, had numerous "turning point" battles, depending upon how one defines "turning point." Do you mean the point at which the Axis powers could no longer obtain total victory, or do you mean the point at which they were doomed to total defeat? Those are very, very different ideas of pivotal battles, and they were very, very different battles. Gettysburg appears to be a single turning point because in retrospect Lee had appeared invincible before the battle but was consistently on the defensive after the battle. But that is what we now know with the advantage of historical hindsight. It did not appear that way at the time, and Lee's defeat and retreat did not mean he had to lose and surrender his army. Only the ensuing campaigns of Grant and Sherman led to that result.

Gettysburg's fame was probably also a result of what happened at Gettysburg after the battle: specifically, the establishment of a cemetery there for the reburial of Union dead, a cemetery at whose dedication four-and-a-half months later Lincoln delivered one the briefest but one of the most famous addresses in U.S. history, the Gettysburg Address, which took only a few minutes to deliver. In that brief address, Lincoln stated that "The world will little note, nor long remember what we say here, but it can never forget what they [those who died] did here." That denigration of his own words was, of course, incorrect. But in both commemorating those who had died and in imploring his countrymen to "resolve that these dead shall not have died in vain—that this nation, under God, shall have a new birth of freedom—and that government of the people, by the people, for the people, shall not perish from the earth" Lincoln unknowingly immortalized the battle as well as himself.

But that, too, was unknown at the time. Lincoln was but one of many speakers at the November 19 dedication of the cemetery, and indeed he was not the main speaker at all. The main speaker was the orator Edward Everett, who spoke before Lincoln for nearly two hours, compared to Lincoln's two minutes. In fact, it was Everett's speech that was at first considered "the Gettysburg Address." Furthermore, while Republican supporters praised Lincoln's speech, his Democratic opponents severely criticized it. One Democratic newspaper put it this way: "The cheeks of every American must tingle with shame as he reads the silly, flat, and dishwatery utterances." Only with Lincoln's own death and the passage of time would his words, as well as those of the battle, obtain the iconic status that they possess today.

The Myth of Laissez-Faire
Lecture 10

The years between 1865 and 1900 are known as the age of industrialization, a period in which enormous national and personal wealth were created in the United States and one that also witnessed a huge gap between rich and poor. People have attributed these outcomes—both positive and negative—to a governmental policy of noninterference in the business world. But the truth is that such a policy toward business did not exist then or at any previous time in American history.

The Age of Industrialization

- The era of industrialization brought the United States to a position of leadership among the powers of the world, but it also produced major problems, including significant corruption and an equally significant gap between the rich and poor.

- Both at the time and later, people viewed the positives and negatives of this era to be the result of a governmental policy of noninterference in the business world, a "hands-off" policy that the British economist Adam Smith had most famously proposed in his 1776 classic, *The Wealth of Nations*, and which became known popularly as laissez-faire.

- Smith and other economists had argued against governmental controls over the economy, such as government-chartered monopolies, on the grounds that they hindered economic growth and the accumulation of wealth. If left alone, they argued, the marketplace would produce more wealth and would be self-regulating by the laws of supply and demand. The "invisible hand" of the marketplace would allow for constant competition among individuals and unlimited economic growth and progress.

- This was a revolutionary, liberating thought in 1776, countering the mercantilist idea that wealth is finite and that to get more, one must take it away from someone else. Laissez-faire ideas gained popularity over the ensuing 100 years and, by the late 19th century, dominated economic thought in the industrialized world. Since then, they have been praised by their supporters for the wealth they helped to create and condemned by their opponents for the corruption and income disparities that accompanied them.

- Despite the rhetoric, a hands-off governmental policy toward business did not exist during this era or any previous era in American history.

Government Economic Interventions

- The age of industrialization was a period of very high protective tariffs (taxes on imports). Early U.S. tariffs were designed to raise revenue to run the government, but protective tariffs were much higher and were designed to protect American industries from foreign competition. Such protective tariffs reached a high point in the 1890s with the passage of the McKinley Tariff Act at the same time that the Supreme Court ruled that any income tax was unconstitutional.

- Another form of government aid involved land grants to railroads as construction incentives, along with loans and financial subsidies. In fact, numerous businesses successfully lobbied the federal government for special favors during this era.

- Government aid also took the form of immigration policy. Congress maintained open

Thomas Edison took advantage of the federal government's support of inventions via patents and its encouragement of the growth of large-scale corporations.

immigration policies, which provided surplus workers for industry and kept salaries low.

- Government also encouraged inventions by issuing patents. Inventing itself became a big business, with Thomas Edison developing and patenting more than 1,000 items at his Menlo Park "invention factory."

- The growth of large-scale corporations, such as Edison's General Electric Company, was sanctioned and encouraged by the government, even though such corporations tended to destroy competition. In addition, courts defined corporations as possessing the same constitutionally guaranteed rights as human beings, while labor unions were defined as "combinations in restraint of trade."
  o Monopolistic corporations were thus ironically protected from state regulations via the Fourteenth Amendment's equal protection clause, while unions would be prosecuted under the 1890 Sherman Antitrust Act designed to outlaw monopolies!

  o Court injunctions were issued against numerous labor strikes, and government forces were brought in to break such strikes, including the railroad strike of 1877 and the Pullman strike of 1894.

The Myth of Laissez-Faire in America
- Government in America had always seen its role as promoting business to increase the wealth of the country, an idea with roots in the mercantilist beliefs under which the colonies had originally been founded. Americans broke out of the British mercantilist system as too confining during the Revolution and gradually accepted the laissez-faire ideology, but they certainly did not reject all mercantilist thought.

- Hamilton's proposal of, and Congress's agreement to, the first national bank in the 1790s, for example, can be seen as a continuation of the mercantilist concept of government-sanctioned and -controlled monopolies. The same holds true for the second national bank in 1816 and the first protective tariff, passed in the same year to protect infant American industries from British competition.

- Not all Americans agreed with such government support for business before the Civil War. The Democratic Party—in particular, Andrew Jackson—appeared to oppose government favors to any one group, as well as any federally funded internal improvements. This could be seen in Jackson's veto of the Maysville Road bill and his destruction of the second national bank. But that destruction was, in effect, government action in support of Wall Street and other banks desiring to escape from the national bank's control!

- The Whig Party opposed the Democrats on these points. And the rise of the Republican Party in the Northern states during the 1850s created an alliance of classes in the North who favored government action against slavery and economic competition from slave labor and supported free government land for homesteaders and a high protective tariff for Northern industry. The sectional division of the Democratic Party in 1860, the Republican electoral victory, and the secession of Southern states removed the major political barriers to the passage of the entire Republican platform.

- After the Civil War, the reunited Democratic Party claimed to be laissez-faire via its low tariff policy, but in reality, it too favored continued government support of business.
    - As we will see in later lectures, the reform movements of the late 19th and 20th centuries sought to regulate the perceived excesses of big business but did not halt government promotion of business.

    - Further, some big businesses may have actually wanted this regulation at the time as a way to stifle future competition, by establishing rules that large corporations could easily obey but small newcomers could not.

- Contrary to popular belief, the 1920s did not mark a return to laissez-faire policies. Indeed, the Republican administrations of those years were quite active in promoting business and, in the early 1930s, in promoting major government programs to end the Great Depression.

- Business also has the ability to obtain the types of government actions it desires—and block those it does not desire—via the need of elected government officials to retain business confidence to ensure economic prosperity. As we will see in a future lecture, one reason the New Deal failed to end the Great Depression was the fact that business would not accept its temporary expedient of deficit spending and other measures.

Belief in the Laissez-Faire Myth

- If all this is true, then where, when, and why did the myth of laissez-faire government policy regarding business develop?

- Although the U.S. government has never been completely laissez-faire, different groups throughout U.S. history have favored sharp restrictions on government's role in regulation of the economy. Such restrictions have often been proposed and defended in the name of laissez-faire, even though that was a distortion of what was being proposed and why it was being proposed.
  o In this regard, we're reminded of the use of states' rights arguments by different sections of the country at different times, as discussed in the causes of the Civil War lecture.

  o In a similar fashion, laissez-faire has been used by different groups at different times to lend ideological support to their self-interests.

- Does that make such proponents of laissez-faire hypocrites? Critics say yes, but if so, the same can be said for all the varying advocates of states' rights. Is it hypocrisy to honestly believe in something that is not true?

- Further, if people honestly believed in laissez-faire or states' rights, and if they acted on such beliefs, can we consider the belief to be a real cause of an ensuing historical event, even if it is not true? Many historians would say yes. Human beings create history not on the basis of reality but on their perceptions of reality—perceptions that are often far removed from what actually occurred. And what actually occurred, as we have seen, is often visible only with the hindsight that the study of history provides.

Suggested Reading

Heilbroner, *The Worldly Philosophers*.

Questions to Consider

1. How and why did the myth of laissez-faire develop in this country?

2. As with states' rights, is belief in a myth a valid causal factor in history?

The Myth of Laissez-Faire
Lecture 10—Transcript

In trying to explain the period from 1865–1900, I often play a game with my students that I would like to try with you regarding ability to name past presidents: First, I ask them to name as many presidents as they can before 1865. Most are familiar with at least some, if not many, of those names: George Washington, father of the country; John Adams; Thomas Jefferson, creator of the Declaration of Independence; James Madison, father of the Constitution; James Monroe, the last of the Founding Fathers; John Quincy Adams; Andrew Jackson; Martin Van Buren; William Henry Harrison; John Tyler; James K. Polk; Zachary Taylor; Millard Fillmore; Franklin Pierce; James Buchanan; and Abraham Lincoln.

Then I ask the students to name as many presidents as they can after 1900, and most are familiar with at least some of those names as well: Theodore Roosevelt; William Howard Taft; Woodrow Wilson; Warren G. Harding; Calvin Coolidge; Herbert Hoover; Franklin D. Roosevelt; Harry Truman; Dwight Eisenhower; John F. Kennedy; Lyndon Johnson; Richard Nixon; Gerald Ford; Jimmy Carter; Ronald Reagan; George Bush the first; Bill Clinton; the second George Bush; and Barack Obama.

But then I ask them—and far fewer know—to name any of the presidents in the 35-year period between Abraham Lincoln and Theodore Roosevelt, 1865–1900. I get puzzled looks. They are: Andrew Johnson; Ulysses Grant; Rutherford B. Hayes; James Garfield; Chester Arthur; Grover Cleveland; Benjamin Harrison; Grover Cleveland again; and William McKinley. They do not know, and there is no reason why they should be able to know; these are relative nonentities in the history of the American presidency. But the following non-political figures from that era are very familiar to them: Andrew Carnegie; John D. Rockefeller; J. P. Morgan; Cornelius Vanderbilt; the so-called "captains of industry" to their supporters, or "robber barons" to their detractors. They are the individuals best known at the time, and they remain the best known today.

That fact tells us a great deal about this era and its values. It was the great age of industrialization, and with it the creation of enormous national wealth as well as personal wealth. The United States by 1894 was the greatest industrial power in the world; by 1914, its coal and steel output was greater than that of all the European powers put together. The British historian A.J.P. Taylor once quipped that by 1914, the United States was not a rival country economically, but a rival continent.

This era—from 1865–1900—also witnessed major problems in the United States; two of these were enormous corruption and an equally enormous and growing gap between rich and poor. As Henry George famously noted in his 1879 book *Progress and Poverty*, the expectation that industrialization "would make real poverty a thing of the past" had not been fulfilled. To the contrary, it had become harder to make a living. "The gulf between the employed and the employer is growing wider" George wrote; "social contrasts are becoming sharper; as liveried carriages appear, so do barefooted children."

By 1890, 10 percent of American families owned 73 percent of the national wealth, while less than half of all industrial workers have an annual income above the poverty line (then from $500–$600 annually). As a result of having an annual incoming below that line, their wives and children had to work at even lower wages just to make ends meet. Today, when people complain about the maldistribution of wealth that exists in the country, they often say it is the worst since this particular time period.

Both during this time and later, people viewed both the negatives and the positives of this era to be the result of a governmental policy of noninterference in the business world; a "hands off" policy that the Scottish economist Adam Smith had most famously proposed in his 1776 classic *The Wealth of Nations*. It became popularly known as "laissez-faire," literally meaning "let do" but broadly implying "let it be," or "leave it alone." What was this all about?

Smith and other economists had argued against any governmental controls over the economy, and such governmental controls were part of the value structure during the Mercantilist Era in which he wrote. These controls, such as government-chartered corporations and monopolies, actually hindered economic growth, Smith argued, and the accumulation of wealth. If left alone, the marketplace, according to Smith, would produce more wealth and would be self-regulating by the laws of supply and demand. This "invisible hand" would allow for constant competition between unfettered individuals and unlimited economic growth and progress.

I think it's important to realize that this was revolutionary, liberating thought in 1776 containing the novel idea that wealth was not finite, as was believed at the time; that wealth could actually create more wealth. The old mercantilist idea that wealth is finite and that to get more you had to take it away from someone else. Smith argued that was not the case, and your wealth did not have to be organized and controlled in any way if you wanted wealth to create wealth.

Smith's ideas and those of other economists consequently gained popularity over the next 100 years; and by the late 19th century, they dominated economic thought in the industrialized world. Since then, they have been praised by their supporters for the wealth that they helped to create, and condemned by their opponents for the corruption and the income disparities that accompanied them.

There is one problem here with everything I've said: The problem is that despite the rhetoric, a "hands off" governmental policy towards business did not exist during this era; nor did it exist in any previous era in American history or in any future era in American history. The belief that it did exist in the past is essentially a myth. Rather than laissez-faire, governmental policy at this time was, and previously had been, to intervene in the economy in numerous ways in order to help business. Let us examine how the government did this, first in this particular era and then previously.

Government aid to business in the era of 1865–1900 took numerous forms. One was tax policies. This was an era of very high protective tariffs; very high taxes on imports from other countries. The United States has always had a tariff, since the first administration under George Washington; but it was a tariff designed to raise revenue in order to run the government. There was no income tax at this point; the government relied upon a low tariff, but one that was constant, in order to be able to run. A "protective tariff" is much higher and has a different aim. It is designed to protect American industries from foreign competition. It also enables American industries to maintain high prices without fear of losing business. By the 1880s, over 4,000 items were covered by tariffs. In 1890, the McKinley Tariff raised the rates on imports to nearly 50 percent of the price; some items, such as tin plates, were up to 70 percent. What did this mean?

A woolen blanket or coat that was made in Scotland and that would have cost $10 would now cost an American customer $15. That means an American manufacturer who might normally charge $11 was not only protected from cheap foreign competition and a loss of business, but he could actually raise his price to $14 and not lose any customers. While such protective tariffs reached a high point in the 1890s, the Supreme Court simultaneously ruled that any income tax was unconstitutional, and that remained so until the passage of the 16th Amendment to Constitution in 1913.

Another form of government aid to business was Land Grants to railroads as an incentive for construction of the railroads. Over 180 million acres were granted to the railroads by the federal and state governments; that was about seven percent of the total U.S. land. There were also loans and financial subsidies for the railroads. Furthermore, numerous businesses successfully lobbied the federal government for additional special favors and they received them.

A third form of government aid was immigration policy. Congress maintained open immigration policies, which provided surplus workers for industry. That helped keep workers' salaries very low by the laws of supply and demand; you had an excess supply, so the wages were going to be low. The government also encouraged inventions via patents; and the number of patents exploded after the Civil War. Between 1790 and 1860, the government had granted 36,000 patents total; in 1897 alone, it granted 22,000 patents. By 1910, it had granted 1,000,000 patents, 900,000 of which had been issued since 1870.

Inventing itself became a big business with Thomas Edison developing and patenting not only the lightbulb, but hundreds of other items—over 1,000—at his Menlo Park "invention factory." Edison also developed the first complete system for electric power generation—Consolidated Edison in

New York, better known as Con Ed—and you needed such power generation systems to run many of his inventions. He also founded the General Electric Company, which Elihu Thompson bought in 1892, and which by 1914 was producing 85 percent of the world's lightbulbs. It also contained the first corporate research and development division.

The growth of such large-scale corporations was sanctioned and encouraged by the government, even though many such corporations tended to destroy competition. Indeed, the modern corporation could not even exist without some very important court rulings. Let's start with limited liability: A corporation is only liable—the people who buy stock in a corporation—for the money they have invested. That had not been the case earlier in world history. In addition, the courts defined corporations as possessing the same constitutionally guaranteed rights as human beings; that was done during the 1880s. Labor unions very soon thereafter were defined as combinations in restraint of trade whose strikes could be halted by court injunctions. Monopolistic corporations were thus ironically protected from state regulation via the 14th Amendment's "equal protection" clause, while labor unions would be prosecuted under the 1890 Sherman Antitrust Act designed to outlaw the monopolies. Then, in 1895, the Supreme Court said in the EC Knight that Congress did not have the Constitutional power to regulate manufacturing at all, only commerce. As previously noted, the Supreme Court also ruled at this time that the income tax was unconstitutional.

Along with all of this came court injunctions against numerous labor strikes and government use of armed force to break strikes. This was frequently done by volunteer state militias, who during this era were reorganized largely for this purpose and became known as National Guard. Federal troops were also used on occasion, most notably during the Railroad Strike of 1877 and the Pullman Strike of 1894.

The Railroad Strike of 1877 was caused by the four largest railroads agreeing in the midst of a depression to another wage cut. When workers at one of the four struck in protest, President Rutherford B. Hayes sent in Federal troops to protect railroad property. That led other railroad workers to strike and state National Guard troops and police to be called out as well. In Pittsburgh, they opened fire on the strikers and their families, killing 25. That led to even more strikes nationally and more violence. One hundred would be killed; and what you had was really the first nationwide work stoppage in U.S. history.

The Pullman Strike of 1894 will be covered in greater depth in another lecture. The basic facts, which I'll mention now, are that the wage cut during the Depression of 1893 at the Pullman Railroad sleeping car company and its town outside Chicago took place without any cut in the rent charged for workers' housing. That led to a strike, and a boycott by the American Railway Union of all trains with Pullman cars. The court issued an injunction against the strike that it was affecting interstate commerce. When the Illinois governor refused to send in state troops, federal troops were sent in; and the leader of the railway union, Eugene Debs, was arrested, jailed, and both the strike and the union were broken.

I would argue that all of this was hardly laissez-faire. Rather, it constituted active government encouragement of business on its own initiative and at the request of business; and it was not new. There is a long history of government promotion of business. The government had always seen its role as promoting business in order to increase the wealth of the country. That idea had roots in the old mercantilist series beliefs under which the Colonies had originally been founded. Under mercantilism, the way to do this was to strive for economic self-sufficiency through creation of an empire and imperial trade regulations and incentives, including special corporate grants and special monopolies.

Americans broke out of the British mercantilist system as too confining during the Revolution, and they gradually accepted instead the laissez-faire ideology, at least in theory. But reality is another matter, and the Revolutionary War breakout from the mercantilist system did not mean Americans rejected all mercantilist thought. To the contrary, Hamilton's proposal and Congress's agreement to the First National Bank in the 1790s can be seen as a continuation of the mercantilist concept of government sanctioned and controlled companies, even monopolies. The Bank was not a monopoly, but it was a super-bank with enormous government reserves and enormous powers to keep other banks in line and direct both the fiscal policy of the country and its economic growth. The same holds true for the Second National Bank in 1816, and the first protective tariff in same year to protect from British competition the infant industries that had emerged in the War of 1812. They emerged because during the war commerce was shut off, and the funds that would have been used for commerce were now available for industrial investment. After the War of 1812, both the state and the federal governments provided financial and other support for the building of canals and roads.

Not all Americans agreed with such government support for business before the Civil War. The Democratic Party in particular under Andrew Jackson appeared to oppose government favors to any one group, as well as—as we have previously discussed—any federally-funded internal improvements. This could be seen in Jackson's veto of the Maysville Road bill and his veto of the recharter of the Second National Bank, as well as his ensuing destruction of that Bank as previously discussed. But as previously noted, that destruction was supported by numerous bankers and by Wall Street; it was, in effect, government action in support of other banks, other investors, desirous of escaping from the National Bank's oversight and control.

Furthermore, the Whig Party opposed the Democrats on these points, and the rise of the Republican Party in the Northern states during the 1850s created an alliance of all classes in the North who favored government action; government action not only against slavery, but also against economic competition from slave labor and in favor of free government land for homesteaders, a high protective tariff for Northern industry, something for everybody, which was summed up beautifully in the slogan "free soil, free labor, free men."

The sectional division of the Democratic Party in 1860, the ensuing Republican electoral victory, and the following secession of the Southern states removed the major political barriers to the passage of the entire Republican platform, including a high protective tariff, government support for internal improvements including a transcontinental railroad, and a Homestead Law. All of these had been previously blocked by the South. This was the only time that a total national party platform was completely implemented. While the reunited Democratic Party after the Civil War claimed to be laissez-faire via its low tariff policy, in reality it too favored continued government support of business. That was most clearly seen in

President Cleveland sending of federal troops to break the Pullman Strike of 1894.

As we will see later, the reform movements of the late 19th and early 20th centuries will want to regulate the perceived excesses of big business; but they will not want to halt government promotion of business, for Americans always have seen promotion of economic growth as a major function of government. Furthermore, some big businesses will in the future actually want this regulation. According to at least one historian, they wanted it as a way to stifle future competition by establishing government rules that large corporations could easily obey but small newcomers could not without disastrous consequences.

Contrary to popular belief, the 1920s did not mark any return to laissez-faire. Indeed, and as we will see, the Republican administrations of those years were quite active in the promotion of business, and in the early 1930s in promoting major government programs to end the Great Depression, myths to the contrary about Herbert Hoover notwithstanding.

Business also possesses and uses an ability to obtain the types of government actions it desires—and to block those it does not desire—via the need of elected government officials to retain business confidence to ensure economic prosperity; and without their economic prosperity, they will not ensure their reelection to office. As we will see in this regard in a future lecture, one reason that the New Deal failed to end the Great Depression was the fact that business would not accept its temporary expedient of deficit spending as well as a host of other New Deal measures. Ironically, that in turn forced the Roosevelt administration to return to deficit spending; it had dramatically cut deficit spending, but that, without business confidence, led to the recession of 1937.

If all of this is true, then where, when, and why did the myth of laissez-faire government policy regarding business develop? Whereas the U.S. government has never been completely laissez-faire, different groups throughout U.S. history have favored sharp restrictions on government's role in the regulation of the economy. Such restrictions have often been proposed and defended in the name of laissez-faire, even though that was a distortion of what was really being proposed and why it was being proposed. One is reminded in this regard of the use of states' rights arguments by different sections of the country at different times, as discussed in the lecture on the causes of the Civil War. In a similar manner, laissez-faire has been used by different groups at different times to lend ideological support to their self interests.

Does that make such proponents of laissez-faire hypocrites? Critics say yes. But if so, the same can be said for all the different advocates of states' rights whom we have studied; which raises the fundamental question: Is it hypocrisy to honestly believe in something that is not true? Furthermore, if people honestly believed in laissez-faire or states' rights, and if they acted upon such a belief, can one consider such a belief to be a real cause of an ensuing historical event, even if it is not true?

I have argued this with some colleagues in other departments. Many would say "no"; many historians, though not all of them, would say "yes"; for human beings create history on the basis not of reality, but their perceptions of reality, perceptions that are often far removed from what actually occurred. But what actually occurred, as we have seen and as we will continue to see in this course, is visible only with the hindsight that the study of history provides. In the last lecture, for example, Gettysburg was not perceived at the time in the same way it would later be perceived. The same is true of Lincoln's "Gettysburg Address" and numerous events that we study. It is only with the advantage of historical hindsight that we see what was truly happening and what was truly important.

Misconceptions about the Original Populists
Lecture 11

W e often hear the word "Populist" used today either to praise or to attack political movements and leaders. Obviously, there is disagreement and confusion over whether the term denotes praise or contempt—as well as whether it refers to the Left or the Right. Interestingly, that echoes historical disagreement regarding the original Populist Party of the 1890s and its leaders. This lecture will analyze that original movement and explore what links it may have to later movements and leaders described as Populist.

The Plight of Farmers

- Populism arose in the decades after the Civil War as an agrarian movement of farmers victimized by the industrial revolution then sweeping the United States. Although that revolution created enormous wealth for some, it also impoverished many others, most notably unskilled factory workers and farmers.

- In the last quarter of the 19th century, millions of farmers faced the problem of overproduction, primarily brought on by the mechanization of agriculture and the massive expansion of acreage under cultivation. By the laws of supply and demand, the result of this enormous expansion of supply was falling prices with each bumper crop.

- The problem was compounded by overseas competition. The U.S. farmer was now part of the world market, and the agricultural revolution was taking place worldwide.

- Farmers' economic problems were worsened by a host of additional factors.
  - The general deflation of the time, combined with the fact that farmers were perennially in debt owing to the need to buy land, seed, and equipment, made it more difficult for farmers

to pay off their debts. A 50 percent drop in the prices farmers received for their produce meant that they had to grow twice as much to pay off their debts, but the more they grew, the lower prices dropped.

- o In addition, high tariffs raised prices of manufactured goods farmers bought but not prices for their produce. In effect, farmers were forced to sell on a world market of depressed agricultural prices but buy manufactured goods on a protected market of high prices.

- o Farmers also faced high property taxes; high interest rates from banks, loan companies, and insurance companies; and high railroad rates to ship their produce to market. Moreover, the railroads controlled land and land sales through government land grants and charged high fees for the use of grain elevators they owned.

- Farmers' problems were also a result of the shift from self-sufficiency to specialized commercial farming, which placed farmers at the mercy of market forces beyond their control.

- Finally, farmers faced social isolation and a loss of social status in the newly industrialized and urbanized America.

- Existing political parties were unable or unwilling to help, essentially for two reasons.
  - o What has been labeled the "steel chain of ideas"—a combination of Smith's laissez-faire ideology and the laws of supply and demand with David Ricardo's Iron Law of Wages—led to the conclusion that nothing could be done politically to change conditions for American farmers. Andrew Carnegie asserted that economic inequality in the industrial era was inevitable and that it was useless to criticize the inevitable.

  - o The fact that the two parties were so evenly matched and elections hinged on a very small number of votes in just six states led to marginalization of the real issues in favor of an emphasis on political machines in the cities, corporate contributions, and special favors to swing key states.

Organization

- From the farmers' perspective, both parties were corrupt and there was no real difference between them. As a result, they began to organize, at first on the local level, with the Grange.

- In the 1870s, the Granger laws were passed in the Midwest to regulate rates charged by railroads. The Supreme Court at first upheld such laws but later ruled that they were unconstitutional.

The enormous expansion of farm production brought on by the industrial revolution brought falling prices and poverty to many of the nation's farmers; in response, they created the Populist Party in 1892.

- Those decisions led to the formation of Farmers' Alliances—one in the Midwest and two in the South—to elect both state and national officials. The Alliances were successful in 1890, electing 6 governors, 3 senators, and 50 congressmen.

- In 1892, the Alliances met and created the People's or Populist Party in Omaha, Nebraska. The party attempted to unite farmers, industrial workers, and reformers, but it would be dominated by the three Farmers' Alliances.

- The party platform has been called "one of the most comprehensive reform documents in American history." It called for an end to government subsidies for private corporations, a graduated income tax, political reforms to return power to the people, sympathy for labor unions, and numerous other measures.

- The key plank was one that called for free and unlimited coinage of silver, as well as gold, at a ratio of 16 to 1.
  - o Until this time, the government had printed money as it received gold or silver, but in 1873, it agreed to accept only gold. Populists labeled this the "Crime of '73" and called for the acceptance of silver again, at a higher-than-open-market rate. This would allow the creation of more money and change deflation to inflation, enabling farmers to pay off their debts more easily via the ensuing higher prices for their produce.

  - o Opponents protested that such moves represented unsound economics that would lead to disaster via Gresham's law ("bad money drives out good"). Further, neither England nor the rest of the world would accept the currency.

  - o Congress had agreed to limited silver purchases with the 1878 Bland-Allison Act and the 1890 Sherman Silver Purchase Act, but the Populists wanted free and unlimited coinage at 16 to 1 with more printing of paper money as a result.

- Along with this platform came a revivalist tone of holy war, impending doom, and cataclysmic confrontation—the forces of good versus evil. In the words of Populist orator Mary Lease of Kansas, it was time to raise "less corn and more hell."

The Incredible Election of 1892
- In the run-up to the elections of 1892, opponents in the Midwest characterized Populists as filthy, illiterate idiots who would wreck the country if put in office. In the South, some Populists attempted to unite whites and blacks in a class war against conservatives. Merchants refused credit to farmers who wouldn't disavow Populist candidates, and violence, fraud, and intimidation were seen across the country.

- The Democrat Grover Cleveland won the election, but the Populists scored 1 million votes for president and 22 electoral votes and elected numerous senators, congressmen, governors, and state legislators.

- In the wake of Cleveland's election, the U.S. economy suffered its worst depression to date, with 20 percent of the workforce unemployed and no government relief, as well as massive salary cuts for those who still had jobs. The fallout would include 1,400 strikes in 1894 and violence as the government once again sided with business and sent in troops.

- A rush on the U.S. gold reserve led Cleveland to turn to J. P. Morgan to bail out the U.S. Treasury and to have Congress repeal the Sherman Silver Purchase Act, which only made the economic situation worse and increased the popularity of free silver.

- Populist Ohio businessman Jacob Coxey organized the first march on Washington (labeled Coxey's Army) to support his idea of a government public works program for the unemployed, to be financed with paper money. But he was arrested when he reached the capital, and his marchers were forced into detention camps.

The 1896 Nomination

- In 1896, the Democrats repudiated Cleveland as silverites from the South and West gained control of the convention and placed free silver, as well as many other Populist proposals, in the proposed platform, leading to an intense floor fight. The last to speak was William Jennings Bryan, who delivered the extraordinary Cross of Gold speech.

- Bryan's words ensured the passage of the platform and his nomination for the presidency. Gold Democrats bolted, initiating a major party realignment.

- The fact that the Democrats had taken their most popular issue put the Populists in a quandary. Fusion with the Democrats would mean loss of identity and much of their party platform, but no fusion meant that the anti-silver Republican William McKinley would win. Their solution was to nominate Bryan for president but their own candidate, Tom Watson, for vice president.

The 1896 Election

- The 1896 campaign was one of the most polarized in U.S. history. Bryan was portrayed as a wild-eyed radical. Businesses threatened to close if workers voted for him and contributed massively to McKinley's campaign. His only major resources were his youth and his extraordinary oratorical ability.

- The election was an overwhelming victory for McKinley. Bryan carried only the South, part of the Great Plains, and the Rocky Mountain (silver) states. McKinley swept the industrial Northeast and the old Midwest. Bryan failed to gain votes from the Granger states, some wheat states, labor, and urban areas.
  - o Labor and urban voters feared inflation and were personally affronted by Bryan's and the Populists' evangelical rhetoric, which was seen as anti-Catholic and anti-urban.

  - o Many historians agree with these anti-Bryan voters and have labeled the Populists as reactionaries.

Populism Today

- Although the Populists were defeated in the 1890s, some of the measures they called for in the Omaha Platform were enacted during the Progressive and New Deal eras. Nevertheless, many of the issues that led to the Populist movement lost relevance with the passage of time and with the tremendous decrease in the percentage of the population engaged in farming.

- Still, the word lives on in both our historical and our political controversies, as does the rhetoric of the Populist platform in calls today for action to address the enormous gap between rich and poor and the economic plight of many Americans.

- Historians still debate who and what the Populists were: radical revolutionaries trying to overthrow the existing order, progressive reformers, reactionaries, or just an agrarian interest group out to get its piece of the pie.

- Similarly, the public continues to debate what a Populist is as the term is used today. The word means "for the people," but which people and in what ways? Is Populism forward- or backward-looking? The answer depends on your own politics and your views of the politicians you are describing.

- Descriptions and disagreements related to contemporary Populists echo descriptions and disagreements regarding Populists of more than a century ago, despite what appears to be the lack of relevance to our lives today of the specific problems they faced and their attempted solutions.

Suggested Reading

Goodwyn, *The Populist Moment.*

Hofstadter, *The Age of Reform.*

Woodward, *Tom Watson.*

Questions to Consider

1. How do you reconcile the successful later passage of many Populist proposals in the Omaha Platform with the failure of the movement as a whole in the 1890s?

2. Describe your views of the original Populist movement and its leaders.

Misconceptions about the Original Populists
Lecture 11—Transcript

We often hear the word "Populist" used today either to praise or to attack political movements and leaders on both the Right and the Left. Obviously, there is disagreement and confusion as to whether the term denotes praise or contempt, as well as whether it refers to the Left or to the Right. Interestingly, that echoes historical disagreement regarding the original Populist Party of the 1890s and its leaders. Whatever side one takes in these arguments, contemporary Populism appears to have very little in common with the original movement. In this lecture, we will analyze that original movement, and then explore what links if any it has to later and contemporary movements and leaders that we describe as "Populist."

Populism originally arose in the decades after the Civil War as an agrarian movement of farmers victimized by the industrial revolution then sweeping the United States. While that revolution had created enormous wealth for some as well as for the nation as a whole, it also impoverished many others, most notably unskilled factory workers and farmers. Today, some know about the workers' plight, but far fewer know about the farmers' plight, perhaps because such a small percentage of our population is today engaged in farming. But that was not the case in the last quarter of the 19th century, and the problems those millions of farmers faced were quite serious.

The basic problem was overproduction, due primarily to the mechanization of agriculture and a massive expansion of acreage under cultivation. Between 1860 and 1910, the number of farms in the country tripled. Simultaneously, the quantity of crops one could grow and harvest expanded enormously as the industrial revolution hit agriculture. For example, the number of acres one could harvest in a day increased from 2 using a hand scythe to 12 using a McCormick Reaper. By the laws of supply and demand, the result of this enormous expansion of supply was falling prices with each bumper crop. Between 1881 and 1894, wheat fell from $1.19 a bushel to $0.49 a bushel, and corn from $0.63 to $0.18.

This problem was compounded by overseas competition. The American farmer was now part of a world market, and the agricultural revolution was worldwide. The farmers' economic problems further worsened by a host of additional factors: First, the general deflation of the time, combined with the fact that the farmer was perennially in debt due to his need to buy land, seed, equipment, and now large-scale machinery as well. Deflation made it more difficult to pay off his ensuing debts: a 50 percent drop in the price the farmer receives for his produce means he has to grow twice as much to pay off the original debt; but the more he grows, the lower the price goes, and what you get is a vicious cycle.

Second, high tariffs raised the price of manufactured goods that the farmer had to buy, but not the price of his produce. In effect, he was forced to sell on a world market of depressed agricultural prices but buy manufactured goods on a protected market of high prices. He also faced high taxes on his property—all of his property was very visible—and he faced very high interest rates from banks, loan companies, and insurance companies. Farmers also faced very high railroad rates to ship produce to market. By the laws of supply and demand, the railroads were charging farmers more in the West and South, where there was a lack of competing railroad lines, than they were in the East, where there plenty of competing lines. In addition to that, the farmer was often charged more for a short haul than a long haul; indeed, it often cost a farmer more to ship a bushel of wheat than that bushel of wheat was worth. The railroads also controlled land and land sales due to the government land grants that we discussed in a previous lecture. The railroads also controlled the grain elevators and storage area costs, and middleman fees.

In the South, all of these problems were compounded by tenant farming, sharecropping, and the crop lien system. Many Southern farmers, white as well as black, did not own their own land. Instead they lived and worked on someone else's land as tenants, and they paid the owner (i.e., the landlord) with a percentage of their annual crop. They also pledged a percentage of their crop in order to be able to purchase tools, seeds, and daily necessities. This was all taking place as their crops were worth less and less, and that just drove them further into debt.

The farmer's problems were also a result of the shift from self-sufficiency to specialized commercial farming, which placed him at the mercy of market forces beyond his control. Farmers faced social isolation and a loss of social status in this new industrialized and urbanized America. In Thomas Jefferson's time, Jefferson had described farmers as God's "chosen people"; by this time period, farmers were referred to by such insulting terms as "hayseed" or "hick."

The existing political parties were incapable or unwilling to help the farmers, essentially for two reasons: What one historian, Eric Goldman, labeled the "steel chain of ideas"; combine Adam Smith's laissez-faire ideology and laws of supply and demand with David Ricardo's "Iron Law of Wages," which holds that labor's wages will always go to the subsistence level. You combine both of these with other economic beliefs and you reach the conclusion that nothing can be done politically to change things; that these are economic laws. Andrew Carnegie would comment that economic inequality in the industrial era was inevitable and that it was useless to criticize what was inevitable.

That's the first factor, but there was a second one, a political one: The two parties were so evenly matched at this time that elections would hinge on only six states and a very small number of voters. One would think that it would lead to discussion of the real issues, but the very opposite happened: Given how close the elections were, there was an extraordinary emphasis on political machines in the cities, corporate contributions, and special favors to swing key states. From the farmer's point of view, both parties were thus corrupt, and there was no real difference between them.

As a result of all of this, the farmers began to organize; at first locally, with what began as a social organization, the Patrons of Husbandry, or Grange, in 1867. The Grange then became political, and you had in many states in the Midwest in the late 1870s so-called "Granger laws" passed to regulate the railroads. At first, the Supreme Court had allowed such laws, specifically in the 1877 of *Munn v. Illinois*; but by 1886 in the Wabash Cases, the Court had shifted. It ruled that the state Granger laws were unconstitutional; that the railroads were interstate commerce and thus they were a federal issue rather than a state issue (and, of course, the federal government was not doing anything). That led to the formation of the Farmers Alliances to elect national as well as state officials. There were three Alliances: one in the

Midwest and two in the South—one white and one black—with over five million members. In the election of 1890, they were very successful: They elected six governors, three senators, and 50 congressmen.

In 1892, the Alliances met and created the People's Party, or Populist Party, in Omaha. The Party attempted to unite all farmers, all industrial workers, and all reformers, but it would be dominated by the three farmers' alliances. The Populist Party's platform began with apocalyptic language:

> We meet in the midst of a nation brought to the verge of moral, political, and material ruin. Corruption dominates the ballot-box, the Legislatures, the Congress, and touches even the ermine of the bench. ... The fruits of the toil of millions [it boldly asserted after giving examples of this moral, political and material ruin,] are boldly stolen to build up colossal fortunes for a few, unprecedented in the history of mankind; and the possessors of these, in turn, despise the Republic and endanger liberty. From the same prolific womb of governmental injustice we breed the two great classes— tramps and millionaires.

What then followed was, as one historian has aptly stated, "one of the most comprehensive reform documents in American History." The Populist platform called for government ownership of the railroads, the telegraph lines, and the telephone. It also called for an end to government subsidies to private corporations. It maintained that unused land held by the railroads and other corporations, as well as aliens, was to be expropriated and held for "actual settlers." It called for a graduated income tax. It called for political reforms to give power back to the people. That included: the initiative where legislation could begin by petitions signed by a large number of people rather than simply the state legislature; the referendum whereby the people as a whole rather than the legislative body would vote on a bill; and the recall where an elected official could be recalled before the end of the term of office. The platform also called for direct election of senators instead of through the state legislatures, and one term for the president.

Nor was that the end of it: They called for an end to government subsidies for corporations, and the abolition of the corporate private armies, such as the Pinkerton detectives. It called for a sub-treasury plan for the storage of grain by the government and the ability of farmers to borrow on that grain. It expressed sympathy for labor unions trying to shorten hours and called for rigid enforcement of the eight-hour day for government workers and limited immigration instead of unlimited immigration. But the plank that became the key one was the free and unlimited coinage of silver as well as gold at ratio of 16 ounces of silver to one ounce of gold. That requires some explanation.

The government had printed money as it received gold or silver, but in 1873 it agreed to accept only gold. The Populists would label this the "Crime of '73" and would call for the acceptance of silver again at a higher rate than in the open market rate so that people who had silver would bring it to the government, and the government would then create more paper money and thereby change the deflation that existed to inflation in order to be able to pay off debts more easily via the ensuing higher prices for the farmers' produce.

This was not a new idea. Back in the 1870s, the Greenback movement had called for keeping in circulation "greenbacks," special paper money that the government had printed during the Civil War. In fact, this deflation/inflation thing is still an issue today: There is presently (and always has been) fear of the impact of a deflation.

Opponents of what was called "free silver" screamed that this was unsound economics that would lead to disaster via Gresham's Law; that bad money drives out good money. They also argued that the financial king at that point, England, would never accept this, nor would the rest of the world, and that it would ruin the economy of the United States. Congress in 1878 and in 1890 had agreed to limited silver purchases in the Bland-Allison Act and the Sherman Silver Purchase Act; but what the Populists called for was free and unlimited coinage at the 16:1 ratio with more printing of paper money as a result. This would become Populists' most popular plank, but the party's general aim as stated in its platform was to get an alliance of all farmers, all labor, all races, in all sections of the country.

Along with the platform went a revivalist tone of holy war, impending doom, and cataclysmic confrontation; the forces of good versus the forces of evil. This can be seen in the preamble to the platform that I quoted, and in the nicknames of some of the Populist leaders: "Calamity" Weller of Iowa; "Sockless" Jerry Simpson of Kansas; "Bloody Bridles" Waite of Colorado; "Cyclone" Davis of Texas. But the fury of the Populists was perhaps best summarized by the statement of Mary Lease from Kansas, who said that it was time to raise "less corn and more hell."

The result was the extraordinary election of 1892. In the Midwest, opponents of the Populists pictured them as filthy, illiterate idiots who would wreck the country if they were elected. As Kansas newspaper editor William Allen White would put it a few years later—this is from an 1896 editorial entitled "What's the Matter with Kansas?"—what is, what White said:

> We all know; yet here we are at it again. We have an old mossback Jacksonian who snorts and howls because there is a bathtub in the statehouse; we are running that old jay for Governor. We have another shabby, wild-eyed, rattlebrained fanatic who has said openly in a dozen speeches that "the rights of the user are paramount to the rights of the owner"; we are running him for Chief Justice, so that capital will come tumbling over itself into this state.

> Oh, this is a state to be proud of! We are a people who can hold up their heads! What we need is not more money, but less capital, fewer white shirts and brains, fewer men with business judgment, and more of those fellows who boast that they are "just ordinary clodhoppers, but they know more in a minute about finance than John Sherman"; we need more men who are "posted," who can bellow about the crime of '73, who hate prosperity, and who think, because a man believes in national honor, he is a tool of Wall Street. We have had a few of them—some hundred fifty thousand—but we need more.

In the South, some Populists—not all of them, but some Populists—attempted to unite whites and blacks in a class war against the white conservatives. Tom Watson of Georgia put it this way:

> You are kept apart that you may be separately fleeced of your earnings. You are made to hate each other because upon that hatred

is rested the keystone of the arch of financial despotism which enslaves you both. You are deceived and blinded that you may not see how this race antagonism perpetuates a monetary system which beggars both.

Watson would nominate a black man to the party's state executive committee in Georgia, and would protect that individual's home with armed white Populists when racists threatened. Conservative white Democrats realized that the South at this point was a one-party area; no Republican could be elected within the South. The struggles were all within the Democratic Party, but now the Populist Party was coming forth as an alternative. Conservative white Democrats would respond to Watson by saying that he was threatening anarchy, "negro supremacy," "Mongrelism," and the "destruction of the Saxon womanhood of our wives and daughters." Merchants would refuse credit to farmers who would not disavow the Populists, and there was violence, fraud, and intimidation in both sections of the country, along with some armed state legislatures. By the way, in the South, conservative Democrats now completed the disenfranchisement of blacks out of fear that Watson's rhetoric might work.

When the smoke was cleared, the Democrat Grover Cleveland had won the presidential election of 1892, but the Populists had scored one million votes for president, which translated into 22 electoral votes; they had also elected numerous Senators, Congressmen, governors, and state legislators.

In Grover Cleveland's first year in office, 1893, a massive depression hit. It was the worst one to date: 20 percent of the workforce was unemployed and there was no government relief at all. Those who still had jobs faced massive salary cuts. The results would include 1,400 strikes in 1894 alone and violence as government sided once again with business and sent in troops. There was also a rush on the U.S. gold reserve, and that led Cleveland to turn to J. P. Morgan to bail out the U.S. Treasury and to have Congress repeal the Sherman Silver Purchase Act. Cleveland did not believe in free silver, and he thought even the limited Silver Purchase Act was making things worse. He was dead wrong; and what he did by repealing that act made the economic situation worse and only increased the popularity of free silver.

At the same time, Populist Ohio businessman Jacob Coxey organized the first march on Washington, labeled Coxey's Army, to support his idea of a government public works program for the unemployed to be financed with paper money. He was arrested when he reached Washington with his marchers forced into detention camps. It was also in 1894 that the Supreme Court would declare the income tax unconstitutional.

It all came to a head in the election of 1896. The Democratic Party repudiated Cleveland as "silverites" from the South and the West gained control of the Democratic convention and placed free silver, as well as many other Populist proposals, in their proposed platform. That led to a huge floor fight over whether to accept this. The last individual to speak was a 36-year-old congressman from Nebraska, William Jennings Bryan, who delivered the extraordinary speech known as the "Cross of Gold" speech, which ended with the following statement:

> Having behind us the producing masses of this nation and the world, supported by the commercial interests, the laboring interests, and the toilers everywhere, we will answer their demand for a gold standard by saying to them: You shall not press down upon the brow of labor this crown of thorns, you shall not crucify mankind upon a cross of gold.

That got the platform passed; it also got Bryan nominated for the presidency. Gold Democrats like Cleveland thereupon bolted, and this initiated a major party realignment, as those in favor of the gold standard moved to the Republican Party and any Republicans in favor of free silver moved to the Democratic Party (or the Populist Party, for that matter).

This also put the Populists in quandary: The Democrats had taken their most popular issue. Obvious solution: fusion with the Democrats. But that meant a loss of identity and much of their party platform, whereas no fusion meant that the anti-silver Republican candidate William McKinley would win the election. The Populist solution was to agree to nominate Bryan for the presidency in their party—the Democrats and the Populists nominate Bryan—but to choose their own Vice Presidential candidate, none other than Tom Watson.

The campaign would be one of the most polarized in all of American history. Bryan was portrayed as a wild-eyed radical. Businesses threatened to close if workers voted for him. McKinley's campaign manager Mark Hanna capitalized on this fear to obtain massive contributions from business and brought people to McKinley's home, rather than vice versa. Bryan didn't have such resources. His major resources were his youth and his extraordinary oratorical ability, though critics argued that he was like the Platte River of his home state: six miles wide and six inches deep at the mouth. For or against Bryan, he became the first presidential candidate to barnstorm the country, and he made free silver the issue. One historian, Richard Hofstadter, quipped that Bryan was the only presidential candidate to run on the strength of a monomania.

The conflict, in financial terms, appeared to be David versus Goliath, and Goliath won; McKinley won handily. The election was a huge, overwhelming McKinley victory: 271 to 176 in the Electoral College and 7 million popular votes for McKinley to 6.5 million for Bryan. That may not sound like a landslide, but remember this was the era when presidential elections had often hinged on one state and 10,000 votes. Bryan carried only the South, part of the Great Plains, and the Rocky Mountain silver mining states. McKinley swept the industrial Northeast and the old Midwest. He also took the Granger states, some of the wheat states, and labor and urban areas; these did not vote for Bryan.

Labor and urban voters in particular did not want inflation—that might help farmers; it would not help them—and they were personally affronted by the Bryan-Populist evangelical rhetoric, which they saw as anti-Catholic and anti-urban. Bryan even referred to the Northeast as "enemy country," and in the Cross of Gold speech he countered cries that the cities favored the gold standard by saying:

> The great cities rest upon our fertile prairies. Burn down your cities and leave our farms, and your cities will spring up again as if by magic; but destroy our farms and the grass will grow in the streets of every city in the country.

That didn't go over too well with working men.

Many historians, such as Richard Hofstadter, agree with the anti-Bryan voters, and they label the Populists as counterrevolutionaries, reactionaries who wished to reject modernity. That interpretation is reinforced by what happened to Populism after its collapse as a third party movement. Watson turned racist; he saw that the race card was more effective than the class card. The Populists also showed streaks of anti-Semitism, anti-Catholicism, and conspiracy theories. Bryan became a prohibitionist, and by the 1920s he was defending a Tennessee law outlawing the theory of evolution; we'll talk more about that in a later lecture. Other historians disagree sharply.

What conclusions can we reach from all of this? Although the Populists were defeated in the 1890s, some of the measures they called for in the Omaha Platform were enacted during the Progressive Era and the New Deal Era. Nevertheless, many of the issues that led to the Populist movement lost relevance with the passage of time, and with the tremendous decrease in the percentage of our population engaged in farming. Yet the word lives on in both our historical and our political controversies, as does the rhetoric of the Populist platform in calls today for action to address the enormous contemporary gap between the rich and the poor and the economic plight of many Americans.

Historians still debate who and what the Populists were and whether they were radical revolutionaries trying to overthrow the existing order, or progressive reformers just a few years ahead of their time, or reactionaries rejecting modernity and trying to turn the clock back in time, or just an agrarian interest group out to get its piece of the pie. Similarly, the public continues to debate what a Populist is as the term is used today. Literally, "Populism" means "for the people"; but which people, and how? Is it forward-looking, or backward-looking, hysterical, and dangerous?

The answer to that depends on your own politics, as well as your views of whomever you are describing. In the 20th century, the term "Populist" was used to describe political figures on both the left and the right. That included Eugene Debs, Robert La Follette (the Progressive), Huey Long of Louisiana, and Senator Joseph McCarthy. In 2008, Senator Bernie Sanders of Vermont on the left was described as a Populist; while Alaska Governor Sarah Palin, Vice Presidential nominee of the Republican Party, was also described as a

Populist. People who are labeled "Populists" are described in both positive terms (such as "man or woman of the people") and in negative terms (such as "ignorant demagogue") depending upon whether one is at the same end of the political spectrum, the opposite end, or somewhere in the middle.

Such descriptions and disagreements echo descriptions and disagreements regarding the Populists more than a century ago, despite what appears to be the lack of relevance to our lives today of the specific problems they faced and their attempted solutions. Those descriptions and disagreements over contemporary Populists may also determine how one views the original movement and its leaders, and whether one believes, or not, their problems and their proposed solutions are relevant or irrelevant to our lives today.

Labor in America—A Strange History
Lecture 12

During the early 21st century, a movement gained traction to rescind the collective bargaining rights of unionized teachers and other state employees. Whether in favor or opposed to this action, many Americans perceived it as a dramatic reversal of historic governmental policy toward unions. But as we will see, this 21st-century effort is a continuation of traditional government hostility to labor unions that dates back to at least the last third of the 19th century.

Origins of Organized Labor in America
- The industrial revolution of the 19th century led to the creation of a new class of largely unskilled industrial workers. In response to low wages and dangerous working conditions, these workers attempted to organize into labor unions, using the strike as their key weapon to force employers to bargain.

- As noted in a previous lecture, U.S. government policy in the late 19th century was pro-business rather than truly laissez-faire. That policy included hostility toward labor unions that tried to form during this era and the use of armed force to suppress union strikes.

- Partially as a result, effective unionization of industrial workers in America would take much longer than it did in Europe and would lead to a very different union ideology.

Opposition to Organized Labor
- A number of factors contributed to the hostility toward labor unions and failure to organize during this period.

- First, many industrial workers continued to believe in the traditional American dream and ideology of individualism. Unionization meant recognition that they could not "make it" on their own.

- In addition, this was the era of the so-called "new" immigration from eastern and southern Europe and Asia, as opposed to the older immigration wave from western and northern Europe. Linguistic and cultural differences divided American workers, making union solidarity extremely difficult if not impossible. Compounding this problem was the fact that employers often pitted these groups against each other as strikebreakers.

- As previously noted, the courts defined corporations as individuals possessing the same guaranteed rights as citizens. Consequently, they voided state laws attempting to regulate industries as violations of the equal protection clause in the Fourteenth Amendment.
    o Courts also issued injunctions against union strikes on the grounds that they threatened property rights and constituted restraint of trade.

    o Both state and national governments used armed forces to enforce these injunctions and break strikes.

The 1892 Homestead Strike
- The Carnegie steel plant in Homestead, Pennsylvania, employed 3,000 unskilled workers who were paid 14 cents an hour for a 10-hour day, 6 to 7 days per week. The 800 skilled and unionized workers at the plant did much better, getting paid $50 to $70 per week but only when the mill was in full production.

- In 1889, Andrew Carnegie appointed Henry Frick, who already had a reputation as a union buster, to manage the Homestead plant. Carnegie instructed Frick to sign no new union contract when the old one expired in June 1892. Instead, Homestead was to overproduce steel before that date in order to create surplus, then close the plant to break the union.

- The union called on all Homestead workers to strike, which they did, and to take over the company town. Frick responded by hiring strikebreakers and Pinkerton detectives. On July 6, the opponents exchanged gunfire; seven Pinkertons and nine workers died, and sympathy strikes spread to other Carnegie steel mills.

- The strike and violence continued throughout the summer, but by October, 1,600 workers were on relief rolls, and in November, the union gave up. Only 800 of the original 3,800 workers were rehired. In retrospect, this failure spelled the end of any unionization in the steel industry for 40 years.

The 1894 Pullman Strike

The failure of the strike at Andrew Carnegie's Homestead plant set back the union movement in the steel industry for 40 years.

- The 1894 Pullman Strike took place in the supposedly model company town of Pullman, Illinois. Plant workers there declared a strike after five wage cuts in one year, with no reduction in company rent. Pullman responded by closing the plant.

- The independent American Railway Union, under Eugene Debs, voted to aid the strikers by boycotting Pullman cars nationally. When the railroads began to fire participants in the boycott, Debs called on his 150,000 members to walk off the job, crippling the national rail system.

- U.S. Attorney General Richard Olney sent in 3,400 special deputies, over the protests of the governor of Illinois, on the grounds that the trains must be kept running for the mail and interstate commerce.

- This move led to violence, and Debs was jailed for violating a federal court injunction that had prohibited the strike on the grounds that it violated the Sherman Antitrust Act as a "combination in restraint of trade."

The Socialist Movement

- When Debs emerged from jail, he announced that he was a socialist. He would later run for president as the candidate of the Socialist Party of America (SPA) and, in 1912, would poll nearly 1 million votes. But that was as close as socialism ever came to being accepted in the United States.

- The situation was quite different in Europe, where socialist political parties were forming with union members as their backbone. They demanded not only better working conditions and wages but an end to the capitalist system via a government takeover of the factories. Many of these socialist parties would emerge as the largest parties in their countries.

- It's important to note that not all European socialist parties were communist. Both the SPA and the large socialist parties of Europe were democratic and believed in achieving socialism via the ballot box. Communists, in contrast, believed in the violent overthrow of capitalism and the establishment of what Karl Marx had called "the dictatorship of the proletariat."

- In the late 19th and early 20th centuries, many Americans were attracted to socialism, although the ideology had far less appeal in the United States than it did in Europe. One major reason that socialism didn't take hold in the United States was that Americans as a whole did not possess the class consciousness that Europeans did.

The American Federation of Labor

- Only one national labor union succeeded during this period, and it did so by eschewing any anti-capitalist political goals. This was the American Federation of Labor (AF of L).

- Under Samuel Gompers, the AF of L refused to have anything to do with socialist ideas, socialist political parties, or anti-capitalist radicalism. Gompers emphasized that his organization's only aim was to improve the wages, hours, and working conditions of its members within the capitalist system.

- Gompers was willing to use strikes and boycotts and to back specific candidates from existing political parties but only to obtain his limited goals. In effect, he was willing to use what were perceived in the late 19th century as radical means but only for conservative, limited ends.

- Gompers favored mediation and arbitration of labor disputes when he ran into businesses that were willing to deal with his union. And many big businesses were, on the grounds that Gompers was far better than the radicals and that they could afford to offer the higher wages and shorter hours he demanded, whereas most small businesses could not.

- Socialists opposed the AF of L and, in 1905, founded their own radical industrial union, the Industrial Workers of the World (IWW), declaring, "The working class and the employing class have nothing in common."
  - In direct opposition to the AF of L, the IWW sought to organize all workers, both unskilled and skilled, and to amass sufficient members and power to be able to eventually overthrow the entire capitalist system.

  - But the IWW never achieved the popularity, strength, and acceptance of the AF of L, and both before and during World War I, it was decimated by government repression.

Unions in the 20th Century and Today

- Gompers and the AF of L have been accurately described as "a new generation's capitulation to the corporate revolution." In effect, they constituted a corporation of labor, organized in a corporate manner to obtain profits for their members within a capitalist system.

- Operating in this manner, Gompers was able to obtain, in the 1914 Clayton Antitrust Act, a clear statement that labor was "not a commodity or article of commerce" and that it had a right to organize and use peaceful strikes, picketing, and boycotts. The act also placed restrictions on the use of court injunctions against organized labor.

- The AF of L would become the model for later successful unions, most notably, the Congress of Industrial Organizations (CIO). Although willing to use more radical methods than the AF of L, the CIO similarly accepted the capitalist system and asked simply for its "share of the pie."

- Franklin Roosevelt's New Deal broke with traditional governmental policy in the 1930s by supporting unionization in general. In effect, the AF of L and the CIO replaced, through the activities of their members and their financial donations, the many corporate businesses that broke with the Democratic Party in the 1930s over the New Deal.

- But the New Deal's break with past governmental policy should not be overstated. During and after World War II, Roosevelt and Harry Truman proved more than willing to move against union strikes when they were perceived as endangering the national welfare. In our own time, Ronald Reagan would fire striking air traffic controllers who refused to obey his order to return to work.

- Union membership as a percentage of the workforce declined in the last third of the 20th century as the economic base of the United States moved away from heavy industry. Unionization of some white collar professions, such as teachers and government workers, took place, but with uneven success and with numbers and power that did not make up for the losses by industrial unions.

- We tend to view this decline as a break with history, but the real aberration is the pro-union policies of the New Deal during the 1930s. That this aberration has come to be viewed as what has always existed speaks volumes about the way in which an event in the relatively recent past can distort our perceptions about our entire past—and, with it, our perceptions about the present.

Suggested Reading

Heilbroner, *The Worldly Philosophers*.

Salvatore, *Eugene V. Debs*.

Questions to Consider

1. Why were Wisconsin Governor Scott Walker's actions—proposing the elimination of most collective bargaining rights for state government workers—incorrectly viewed as a dramatic reversal of government policy toward unions?

2. Why has there been so much governmental and public hostility to unions in the United States?

Labor in America—A Strange History
Lecture 12—Transcript

During the early 21st century, a movement gained traction in this country to rescind the collective bargaining rights of unionized teachers and other state employees. Whether in favor or opposed to this action, many Americans perceived it as a dramatic reversal of historic governmental policy towards unions; a governmental policy often described as either pro-union or as trying to be a fair arbiter between business and labor. But in reality, that 21st-century effort is a continuation or reassertion of traditional government hostility to labor unions; a hostility that dates back at least to the last third of the 19th century, if not earlier. This lecture will explore the reasons for that hostility and the ensuing governmental actions. It will also explore the responses of American labor during the late 19th century; responses that separated American workers sharply from their European counterparts.

The Industrial Revolution of the 19th century led to the creation of a new class of largely unskilled industrial workers as traditional artisans were put out of business. Before the Industrial Revolution, a shoemaker would make an entire shoe. He would also own his own shop, set his own hours, and probably live above his own store. Come the Industrial Revolution and the assembly line, which could produce shoes much cheaper than this individual working by hand, he would be closed down; he could not compete. He would become an unskilled worker on a shoe assembly line nailing, for example, heels onto shoes; doing hundreds of them a day rather than producing the entire shoe.

Work in these factories was boring, it was repetitive, and it was often dangerous, with very long hours and very low pay. The average work week in many factories during the late 19th century was 60 hours; pay: approximately 20 cents an hour for the few still-existing skilled jobs and 10 cents an hour for unskilled work. Steelworkers had 12 hour shifts, seven days a week, for such pay. In occupations such as mineworking, laborers were often paid in company scrip that was redeemable only at the company store. In all fields, workers would be laid off or suffer pay cuts during the periodic economic depressions that occurred. As a result of all this, more than half of industrial workers did not make enough to support their families—somewhere between

$500 and $600 annually was needed for that—so as noted in a previous lecture, their wives and their children had to work for even lower wages; and contrary to another myth, women made up approximately 20 percent of the industrial workforce at that time.

Workers responded to all of this with efforts to organize into labor unions in order to fight for better pay and better working conditions. Their key weapon was the strike to force employers to agree to bargain over their demands or face a shutdown of their factories.

As noted in a previous lecture, the U.S. government's policy in the late 19th century was not laissez-faire, it was pro-business; and that pro-business policy included hostility toward labor unions that tried to form during this time period and the use of armed force to suppress numerous union strikes. Partially as a result, effective unionization of industrial workers in this country would take much longer than it did in Europe. It would also lead to a very different union ideology.

One obvious question to arise here is: Why was there such hostility to labor unions, and why was there such failure to organize during this time period? There were numerous reasons: Many industrial workers continued to believe in the traditional American dream and the traditional American ideology of individualism; the belief that they could make it on their own as individuals. Unionization equaled recognition that they no longer could do so. For that very reason, the American middle class also opposed unionization and saw it as an attack on the American dream. That middle class was also alienated by the violence that accompanied many strikes.

In addition, this was the era of the so-called "new" immigration from Eastern and Southern Europe as well as Asia; the older wave of immigration had come from Western and Northern Europe. These new immigrants came from different races, different ethnic, and they possessed different religions, different languages, and different cultures. Those differences divided American workers, making union solidarity extremely difficult, if not impossible. Compounding this problem, employers often pitted these groups against each other as strikebreakers. For example, if Polish workers struck, the employers might hire Italian workers to replace them or black workers. Employers also hired private armies, often of Pinkerton detectives, to violently break strikes. Unions also often collapsed under economic pressure during the periodic depressions that wracked the country during this time period.

In addition—and as previously noted—the courts defined corporations as individuals possessing the same guaranteed rights as citizens. Consequently, the courts voided state laws that attempted to regulate industry as violations of the equal protection clause in the 14th Amendment. The courts also issued injunctions against union strikes on the grounds that they threatened property rights and, in an incredible irony previously noted, that these strikes constituted a restraint of trade in violation of the 1890 Sherman Antitrust Act.

Both state and national governments would use armed force to enforce these injunctions and break strikes. On the state level, again as previously noted, this led to the revival of the largely moribund state militia system through government support of volunteer militia units that came to be known as the National Guard. On the national level, it would lead to the use of the United States army against strikers.

In a previous lecture, we looked at the Railroad Strike of 1877 and very briefly at the 1894 Pullman Strike to illustrate the government's use of military force against unions as one way the government did not have a laissez-faire attitude towards business. In this lecture, we will take a much closer look at the Pullman Strike. We will also examine the 1892 Homestead Strike to explore government-labor relations during this time.

Let's look first at the 1892 Homestead Strike at the Carnegie steel plant in Homestead, Pennsylvania. That plant employed 3,000 unskilled workers. They were paid 14 cents per hour for a 10-hour day, six to seven days a week. There were also 800 skilled and unionized workers at the plant. They did much better: They were getting paid anywhere from $50–$70 per week, but only when the mill was on full production. Only 40 percent of steelworkers worked a full year. The average was 32 weeks per year; the factories would close when demand was not sufficient to keep them open.

In 1889, Carnegie appointed Henry Frick, who already had a reputation as a union buster, to manage the Homestead plant; and he instructed Frick to sign no new union contract with the skilled workers when the old one expired in June, 1892. Instead, Homestead was to overproduce steel before that date in order to create a surplus and then close the plant in what was called a "lockout"; keep the workers out, and that was designed to break the union.

The union responded to this by calling upon all Homestead workers, skilled and unskilled, to strike, which they did. They also took over Homestead, which was a company town. Frick responded by hiring strikebreakers and 300 Pinkerton detectives. On July 6, workers opened fire on those detectives and burned their barges. Seven Pinkertons and nine workers died; sympathy strikes soon spread to other Carnegie steel mills. On July 12, the governor of Pennsylvania sent in 7,000 state militia; and on July 18, seven strike leaders were arrested and charged with murder.

Then, on July 23, an anarchist, Alexander Berkman, attempted to assassinate Frick. He failed. On August 30, the strike committee was arrested on conspiracy charges, and some were denied bail; 185 separate indictments were issued. By October, 1,600 Carnegie workers were on the relief rolls, and in November the union gave up. Of the 3,800 total workers at Homestead, only 800 were ever rehired. In retrospect, this failure spelled the end of any unionization in the steel industry for 40 years.

Let's now turn to the 1894 Pullman Sleeping Car Strike. This took place originally in the supposedly model company town of Pullman, Illinois. Pullman plant workers declared a strike after five wage cuts in the year, totaling anywhere from 25–40 percent of their wages—those wage cuts were due to the Depression of 1893—but while you had these five wage cuts, there was no reduction in company rent. When the workers struck, Pullman responded by closing the plant. No violence took place at this time.

On appeal by the striking plant workers, the independent American Railway Union under Eugene Victor Debs voted to aid the strikers by nationally boycotting Pullman cars; they simply would not deal with Pullman cars. The railroads began to fire union members who did boycott Pullman cars. Debs then called upon his union, 150,000 members strong, to walk off the job.

That crippled the entire national rail system. The Governor of Illinois, John Altgeld, was sympathetic to the union. He refused to send in state troops; at which point the railroad owners went to President Grover Cleveland, whose Attorney General, Richard Olney, sent in 3,400 special deputies over the protests of Governor Altgeld. The grounds: the need to keep the trains running for the mail and the fact that the federal government was responsible for interstate commerce.

That move led to violence, and Debs was jailed for violating a federal court injunction that had prohibited the strike on the grounds that it was a "combination in restraint of trade" that violated the Sherman Antitrust Act. When Debs emerged from jail, he announced that he was now a Socialist; and soon thereafter, the Socialist Party of America would be formed with Debs as its standard bearer. Debs would run for President of the United States five times as the candidate of the Socialist Party; in 1912, he would poll nearly a million votes. But that was as close as socialism ever came to being accepted in the United States, and it really was not close at all.

The situation in Europe was quite different. Indeed, in most European countries, Socialist political parties were forming with union members as their backbone. They demanded not merely better working conditions and wages, but an end to the entire capitalist system via a government takeover of the factories. Many of these Socialist parties would emerge as the largest parties within their countries. In an extraordinary irony, the highly conservative and class-conscious German aristocrat and political leader Otto von Bismarck would make Germany the first country to institute social security. He did this as a means of co-opting and weakening the very large Social Democratic Party, a party that he hated.

This is a good time to explain some very important distinctions within the Socialist movement. First of all, European Socialist parties were not Communist; in fact, Communist parties did not even exist until the Russian Revolution of 1917 and the fragmentation of the international Socialist movement during World War I. Both Debs's Socialist Party of America and the large Socialist parties of Europe were democratic, and they believed in achieving Socialism via the ballot box. They were thus named Social Democrats, or Democratic Socialists. Communists, on the other hand, believed in the violent overthrow of capitalism and the establishment of what Karl Marx had called "the dictatorship of the proletariat," which is what occurred in Russia. In point of fact, Socialism as a whole is an economic system, whereas Communism is a dictatorial political system.

Contrary to common belief, many Americans in the late 19th and the early 20th centuries were attracted to Socialism. The American middle class would be introduced to Socialist ideas through Edward Bellamy's very popular 1888 novel *Looking Backward* and the ensuing formation of "Bellamy Clubs" throughout the country. By 1912, while Debs was polling a million votes for president, 450 socialists had been elected to office; that included more than 50 mayors and one congressman.

But this was not Marxian Socialism as it developed in Europe. Bellamy, for example, placed much more emphasis on nationalism and on a peaceful shift in the United States from Capitalism to Socialism. He did this through a Rip Van Winkle-type character who began the book in a very strike-filled, violence-filled American, only to wake up to find that this violent Capitalist world had been peacefully transformed into a utopian Socialist world, as people simply voted to have the government take over the factories.

Despite the popularity of Bellamy's novel, and the limited success of the Socialist Party of America, Socialist ideology nevertheless had far less appeal in the United States than it did in Europe. In fact, the United States never developed the large social democratic parties that many European nations did; and indeed, those social democratic parties in the 20th century would govern many of these European countries, including England after World War II under the Labor Party.

Why the United States did not develop such a party and such a movement is a question that numerous historians have long asked. There are numerous reasons: One major reason was that Americans as a whole did not possess the class consciousness that Europeans did from their very lengthy history—dating back at least to the Middle Ages—a history of very distinct classes. You had aristocrats; you had a middle class; you had peasants. Americans lacked that history, and the Europeans who came here came here to a large extent to escape that history; and without that history, you would not have that class consciousness that accompanied it.

Indeed, Marxism and many other varieties of Socialism were viewed by many in the United States as European and "un-American." In this environment, only one national labor union succeeded during this time period, and it did so largely by eschewing any anti-capitalist political goals. I am talking about the American Federation of Labor (the AFofL) under its longtime leader, Samuel Gompers.

Under Gompers's leadership, the AFofL refused to have anything to do with Socialist ideas, Socialist political parties, and anti-capitalist radicalism, whether it was democratic or undemocratic. "Plain and simple trade unionism" was Gompers's motto, and he emphasized the fact that the AFofL's only aim was to improve the wages, the hours, and the working conditions of union members within a capitalist system. Furthermore, and unlike other national unions of this era such as the Knights of Labor—the Knights of Labor welcomed all—the AFofL limited its membership to skilled, male, white workers. That was an elite group, constituting only five percent of the total workforce. That elite group was organized in the AFofL along craft lines rather than factory lines. All cigar makers like Gompers would be in the cigar makers union. The alternative in heavy industry was to place all workers—whether they made cigars or anything else—into the same union.

Gompers was willing to use the strike and the boycott. He was also willing to back specific candidates from existing political parties, but only to obtain his limited goals of higher wages, shorter hours, relief from technological unemployment, and pro-labor legislation. In effect, he was willing to use what were perceived in the late 19th century as radical means, but only for limited, conservative ends.

Gompers and the AFofL made clear in this regard that they did not want to overthrow the capitalist system; they just wanted to get their piece of the pie. Indeed, Gompers favored mediation and arbitration of labor disputes rather than strikes when he ran into businessmen who were willing to deal with him and his union; and there were many big businessmen who were willing to do so on the grounds that Gompers and the AFofL were far better than the radicals. These businessmen also figured out that they could afford to give the higher wages and shorter hours that Gompers demanded. Small businessmen, on the other hand, often could not, and they therefore continued to oppose labor unions.

Big businessmen were not the only individuals to see this. Socialists saw it as well, and they opposed the AFofL, founding in 1905 their own radical industrial union, the Industrial Workers of the World (the IWW) or Wobblies; and that union was founded with the ringing declaration that "The working class and the employing class have nothing in common." In direct opposition to the AFofL, the IWW sought to organize all workers, unskilled as well as skilled, along industrial—that is, factory—rather than along craft lines, and to amass sufficient members and power so as to eventually be able to overthrow the entire capitalist system. The IWW never achieved the popularity, strength, and acceptance of the AFofL, and both before and during World War I it was decimated by government repression.

Gompers and the AFofL have been accurately described as "a new generation's capitulation to the corporate revolution." In effect, they constituted a corporation of labor, organized in a corporate manner, to obtain profits for their members within a capitalist system. Operating in this manner, Gompers was able to obtain in the 1914 Clayton Antitrust Act a clear statement that labor was "not a commodity or article of commerce," and that it had a right to organize and use peaceful strikes, picketing, and boycotts and not to be considered a combination in restraint of trade. The Clayton Act also placed restrictions on the use of court injunctions against organized labor.

Furthermore, the AFofL would become the model for later successful unions in this country, most notably the Congress of Industrial Organizations, better known as the CIO. The CIO first developed within the AFofL, but then broke away to organize unskilled factory workers in the 1930s. The CIO was willing to use more radical means than the AFofL. In particular, rather than striking outside the factory, CIO workers would sit down inside the factory, thereby closing down the factory, making it impossible for employers to hire strike breakers. But the CIO similarly accepted the capitalist system and, like the AFofL, simply asked for its piece of the pie as well.

Franklin D. Roosevelt's New Deal, as we will see, broke with traditional governmental policy in the 1930s by supporting this effort and supporting unionization in general, most notably with the 1935 Wagner Labor Relations Act. In effect, the CIO, this new and powerful corporate union, along with the AFofL, replaced through the activities of its members and its financial donations the many corporate businesses that broke with Roosevelt and the Democratic Party in the 1930s over this and over the entire New Deal.

But the New Deal's break with past governmental policy should not be overstated. Indeed, during and after World War II, Roosevelt and his successor Harry Truman proved more than willing to move against union strikes, especially in coal and steel industries, when those strikes were perceived as endangering the national welfare. Furthermore, a Republican Congress would in 1947 pass the Taft-Hartley Act over Truman's veto, and that act placed sharp limits on labor union activities, including strikes. Despite his veto of the bill, which was overridden, Truman would wind up using the act on numerous occasions; so would his successors. In 1981, President Ronald Reagan would fire striking air traffic controllers who had refused to obey his order to end this illegal strike and return to work.

Union membership as a percentage of the workforce also declined in the last third of the 20th century as the economic base of the United States moved away from heavy industry; and with that came a decline in union power. Unionization of such white collar professions as teachers and government workers did take place, but with uneven success and with numbers and power that could not and did not make up for these losses by industrial unions. Whether total union power is now so reduced as to lead to an end to collective bargaining rights for at least some unions remains unclear and to be seen. What is clear is that what is occurring in the 21st century is far from an aberration and a break with past history. Indeed, the real aberration was the pro-union policies of the New Deal during the 1930s. That this aberration has come to be viewed incorrectly as what has always existed speaks volumes about the way in which an event in the relatively recent past can distort our perceptions about our entire past, and with it our perceptions about the present.

Myths about American Isolation and Empire
Lecture 13

G iven that the United States was born in an anti-colonial revolt, we have come to believe that our country has opposed imperialism throughout its history and even sought to encourage anti-colonial republican revolts elsewhere. Along with this anti-imperialism, we have evidenced a desire to remain isolated from the rest of the world. But the United States has never been isolated or anti-imperialist; indeed, it has been a highly expansionist power always involved with the rest of the world.

Early American Expansion

- The 13 original American colonies were founded in the 17th century as part of an expanding British Empire, and in the next century, they rebelled against that empire. But that does not mean they rebelled against the concept of empire.

- One of the first military acts in the Revolution was the attempted conquest of French Canada in 1775 in an effort to make it the 14th state—an effort that ended in failure at Quebec at the end of the year.

- In the 1783 peace treaty with Britain, the United States acquired not only what had been the 13 colonies east of the Appalachian Mountains but also the huge territory between those mountains and the Mississippi River.

- Nor did the Founding Fathers see the Mississippi as the final boundary of the United States. They often referred to the United States as "our rising empire." The Fathers envisioned an expanding entity, but not one that would acquire formal colonies that might eventually rebel. Instead, acquired land would gradually be incorporated into the Union on an equal political basis, first as organized territories, then as states.

- This pattern was first established in the Northwest Ordinances of the 1780s, and it would serve as the model for American expansion across the entire North American continent over the next 50 years— by both war and treaty.
  - Americans did not consider these activities imperialism because of the political equality granted settlers in the new areas, as opposed to colonial status.

  - Further, they saw the entire continent as theirs by divine right, as evidenced by the expression "Manifest Destiny" in the 1840s. Of course, others—Native Americans, Spanish, Mexicans, Canadians—saw it as aggression, subversion, and imperialism.

The Reality of Isolationism

- The American expansion across the North American continent was hardly isolationism. Neither was the 1823 Monroe Doctrine, which asserted that the entire Western Hemisphere was "off limits" to European colonialism but open to continued American expansion. The expansion of American commerce throughout the world in the late 18th and 19th centuries was not isolationism either.

- American isolation was limited to nonparticipation in Europe's numerous military alliances and wars, which was made possible by two factors: (1) the geographical separation of America from what Jefferson called "the exterminating havoc of one quarter of the globe" and (2) the American belief that expanded commerce was a way to avoid war and, indeed, a rational alternative to war.

- In reality, of course, commerce was often a cause of war.
  - A clear example was the American declaration of war against Britain in 1812, prompted by British violations of American commercial "neutral rights" via seizures of American ships and goods on the high seas.

  - Commerce as a cause of conflict was also obvious in the declaration of war against Germany in 1917, again for violation of commercial neutral rights, but this time, via submarine warfare.

o   In retrospect, the major reason we did not go to war with a European or world power in the 105 years between the end of the War of 1812 and our entry into World War I was the fact that British balance-of-power politics maintained overall European peace.

Expansion in the 19th Century

- Sectionalism and the Civil War brought a temporary end to American territorial expansion during the 1850s and 1860s, but throughout the 1850s, numerous adventurers—known as filibusters and supported by the U.S. government—attempted to conquer Cuba and portions of Central America.

- Within two years of the end of the Civil War, the United States purchased the enormous Russian colony of Alaska.

- In 1898 came the war with Spain and the acquisition of the Philippines, Guam, and Puerto Rico, as well as the annexation of Hawaii.

Informal Empire in Central America and the Caribbean

- Much more extensive than any formal colonial empire of the United States was the informal empire it created in Central America and the Caribbean in the aftermath of the war with Spain. That empire included protectorates over five nations: Cuba, Nicaragua, Panama, the Dominican Republic, and Haiti.

- Although these countries were nominally independent, the United States controlled their economies, finances, and foreign policies and reserved the right to intervene militarily in each of them.

- In 1901, Cuba was forced incorporate the Platt Amendment into its constitution. Provisions of this bill included agreement not to incur indebtedness beyond Cuba's means or take any other actions that might endanger its independence, to grant the United States a naval base on the island (Guantánamo), and to allow U.S. military intervention in the country.

- In 1903, the United States helped to organize and supported a successful revolt in the Colombian province of Panama in order to obtain the right to build and fortify a canal through that now independent country.

- Over the next decade, the United States would foist treaties similar to the Platt Amendment on Nicaragua, Haiti, and the Dominican Republic, as well as Panama, and would intervene militarily in each of them.

- Careful examination of the map explains why these nations became part of the American Empire: Panama and Nicaragua held the two key potential routes for an interoceanic canal, while Cuba, Haiti, and the Dominican Republic, along with Puerto Rico, controlled the Caribbean approaches to such a canal.

Commercial Expansion and Domination

- The American policy of free trade, most clearly enunciated in the 1899 and 1900 Open Door notes regarding China, also promised, and often led to, further commercial expansion and domination of other areas.

- Given the enormous size and power of the American economy by this time, free trade (free of tariff barriers) would almost inevitably mean that U.S. goods were cheaper than those of other powers.

- Continuation of commercial expansion during the years between the two world wars has led many historians to question the supposed "isolation" of the United States during this period.
  - Although the Senate rejected membership in the League of Nations, the United States remained actively involved in the world

during the 1920s, signing numerous treaties and expanding its economy globally.

   o   Indeed, the American economy undergirded the entire global economy of the 1920s and, with it, the peace structure of that decade.

•   The American economy, the global economy, and the peace structure collapsed during the 1930s. Admittedly, what both preceded and followed that collapse is what one historian has accurately labeled a "mood of isolation" in the United States, but once again, it was limited to a desire to stay out of another European war.

•   That mood would change dramatically in 1940–1941 under the impact of the Nazi conquest of Europe, and it would result in the permanent demise of isolationism in this country. Indeed, the United States would emerge after World War II as the most powerful and influential nation in the world.

Belief in the Myth of Isolationism
•   Belief in the myth that America was once isolationist and almost always anti-imperialist stems partially from our belief in an anti-empire history. It also stems from the fact that our Founders defined our nation as an "empire of liberty," not tyranny, and we tend to equate empire with tyranny.

•   The 19th-century idea that the North American continent was ours by divine right meant that our claims to land were superior to any contrary claims by Native Americans, Europeans, or Latin Americans and could not be considered imperialistic.

•   Along with that went the belief that the entire Western Hemisphere was separated from Europe by a republican form of government, as well as geography. Consequently, the 1823 Monroe Doctrine was (and still is) perceived as a defensive document against European encroachment—and, thus, isolationist and anti-imperialist, rather than expansionist and aggressive.

- Similarly, we believed that we were liberating the Cubans in 1898 and that we were both defending and spreading freedom against mortal threats in World War I, World War II, and the Cold War.

- Our belief that we were anti-imperialist also partially stems from the fact that we equated imperialism with formal colonialism, rather than viewing the latter as but one form of the former. Further, we have always viewed trade as a rational alternative to empire and war, which it often is not.

Is America an Empire?

- A debate about whether or not America was an empire—and if so,

Many Americans believe that our nation's expansionism has resulted at least partially from the need to counter Soviet threats.

what kind—began during the Cold War and accelerated after the collapse of the Soviet Union in 1991.

- To most Americans, the answer definitely remains no. Our political leaders tell us that our major foreign policies are and always have been to protect our own security and to promote democracy around the world—not to create an empire.

- But in the name of protecting our security and promoting democracy, we have created and consistently use the largest military force in the world. If this is not imperialistic, then what is? Further, isn't promotion of American-style democracy imperialistic to cultures that do not share or want our democratic values?

- On the other hand, isn't much of our previous expansion the unplanned, defensive result of our need to counter mortal threats to our security, such as Nazi Germany or the communist Soviet Union?

- Perhaps so, but that does not negate the domination we have been able to exercise over others in the process of defending ourselves and ensuring our security—a domination those others clearly define as imperialistic.

- Indeed, in a world of nation-states all claiming sovereignty—including the right to make war—the only absolute security is expansion designed to preclude the emergence of any other centers of power that could pose a threat. In that regard, one nation's defense is another's aggression. And that will be the case as long as we live in an anarchic international system in which every nation maintains its right to make war on any other nation.

Suggested Reading

Beisner, *From the Old Diplomacy to the New, 1865–1900.*

Stephanson, *Manifest Destiny.*

Williams, *The Tragedy of American Diplomacy.*

Questions to Consider

1. Is the United States today an empire? If not, why? If so, how and why, and is its empire of a unique form?

2. Is free trade "the imperialism of the strong"? Why or why not?

Myths about American Isolation and Empire
Lecture 13—Transcript

In 1898, the United States went to war with Spain for stated purpose of freeing the Cuban people from the tyrannical Spanish colonial empire and to establish an independent Cuban republic. Yet the ironic result of that war was the creation of an overseas American colonial empire, with the acquisition from Spain of the Philippines, Guam, and Puerto Rico, as well as the annexation during the war of Hawaii.

By the standard interpretation, this was our first and our last American experiment with overseas imperialism; what one prominent diplomatic historian, Samuel Flagg Bemis, labeled the "Great Aberration." By this interpretation, the United States, being born in an anti-colonial revolt, opposed imperialism throughout its history, and in such statements as the Monroe Doctrine sought to encourage anti-colonial republican revolts elsewhere. Along with this anti-imperialism went a desire, as enunciated most clearly in Washington's 1796 "Farewell Address," to remain isolated from the rest of the world and to sign "no entangling alliances."

As with most historical myths, these contain elements of truth. But in reality, the United States was never as isolated and anti-imperialist as is commonly believed. Indeed, it has been a highly expansionist power always involved with the rest of the world. Illustrative of the difference between the myth and the reality here is the fact that Washington, in the "Farewell Address," never proposed isolationism and as president he never practiced it; he never even used the word "isolationism," or the expression "no entangling alliances," in his "Farewell Address." The common belief that he did so is yet another myth. In this lecture, we will explore the realities as opposed to the myths of American isolationism and American imperialism.

We do have a problem here, a semantic one: Both "isolationism" and "imperialism" have multiple meanings, and we will need to clarify in this lecture what those different definitions are, which definitions Americans in the past used, and which ones we are using in this lecture.

Clearly, the original 13 colonies that became the United States were founded in the 17th century as part of an expanding British Empire, and in the next century they rebelled against that empire and its monarchial form of government. But that does not mean that they rebelled against the concept of empire. Interestingly, one of our first military acts in the Revolutionary War was the attempted conquest of French Canada in 1775 in an effort to make that the 14th state. That was an effort that ended in failure at Quebec at the end of the year.

In the 1783 Peace Treaty ending the war with England, the United States acquired not only what had been the 13 colonies east of the Appalachian Mountains, but also the huge territory between those mountains and the Mississippi River. The Founding Fathers did not see the Mississippi as the final boundary of the United States. They often referred to the nation as "our rising empire." Thomas Jefferson talked about this "empire of liberty." What they had in mind was an expanding entity, but one that would not acquire formal colonies; colonies that might eventually rebel against them as they had rebelled against England. Instead, land that was acquired would gradually be incorporated into the union on an equal political basis, first as an organized territory, then as a state, once an area had enough white settlers.

This pattern was first established under the Articles of Confederation in the Northwest Ordinances of the 1780s. Those Ordinances would serve as the model for American expansion across the entire North American continent over the next 50 years, and that expansion took place by both war and treaty: treaty, the Louisiana Purchase of 1803; Florida, Andrew Jackson's invasion, followed by a treaty, during the years 1819–1821; Texas, rebellion by settlers against Mexico in 1836 and annexation in 1845; California and the Southwest via war with Mexico from 1846–1848; Oregon, by treaty (albeit with the threat of war) in 1846; and the southwest Gadsden Purchase by treaty in 1853. There were also continued and consistent attempts to conquer and annex Canada, from the War of 1812 onwards; and, of course all this expansion was accompanied by dispossession of the Native American tribes who had inhabited the land.

Americans did not call any of this imperialism because of the political equality granted to settlers in the new areas as opposed to colonial status.

In addition, Americans saw the entire continent as theirs by divine right, as can be seen in the expression "Manifest Destiny" in the 1840s. But others— Native Americans, the Spanish, Mexicans, Canadians—did not see it that way; they saw it as aggression, subversion, and imperialism.

It's important to note that colonialism is not the only form of imperialism. There are other, more informal forms of domination of one area over another and one people over another. In this regard, I think it's interesting to note that both the Southern secessionists before and during the Civil War, and the Populists of the Midwest and Great Plains as well as the South in the 1880s and 90s, defined their sections as economic colonies of the Northeast despite the supposed political equality within the entire Union.

This expansion across the entire North American continent was hardly isolation. Nor was the 1823 Monroe Doctrine asserting that the entire Western Hemisphere was henceforth to be considered "off limits" to European colonialism while it remained open to continued American expansion. Is that isolationism? Not unless one again uses the American belief in "Manifest Destiny," this time to expand across Central and South America as well as North America. Nor was the expansion of American commerce throughout the world in the late 18th and 19th centuries isolationism. Commercial expansion with Europe, with Latin America, and with Asia—this would include the opening of Japan in 1854 and other Asian areas throughout the 19th century—were hardly moves of isolationism.

Was there an American isolationism? Yes; but it was limited to nonparticipation in Europe's numerous military alliances and wars, something many Americans had come to the United States to escape and something they saw as being made possible by two factors: The first was what Jefferson had referred to in his first Inaugural Address; the fact that geographically the United States was separated by thousands of miles of ocean from what he labeled "the exterminating havoc of one quarter of the globe." The second factor was the American belief that their expanded commerce was a way to avoid war, and that indeed it was a rational alternative to war.

In reality, however, commerce could be and often was a cause of war. We can clearly see that in the American declaration of war against Britain in

1812 because of British violations of America's commercial "neutral rights" via seizures of American ships and goods, as well as the seizure of American citizens via impressments of sailors on the high seas. In point of fact, Americans viewed both this throttling of their commerce and simultaneous British support for Indian tribes in the old Northwest as a conscious effort to halt the expansion of the United States, both landed and commercial, to throttle this new American Empire and to destroy it.

Commerce as a cause of war was also obvious in the declaration of war against Germany in 1917 for violation again of our commercial "neutral rights" on the high seas, this time via submarine warfare. In retrospect, the major reason we did not go to war with a European world power in the 105 years between the end of the War of 1812 and our entry into World War I— Spain was hardly a major power in 1898—was the fact that British balance of power politics maintained overall European peace and that precluded the emergence of any hegemonic continental power that could threaten us or lead to the outbreak of a general European war.

What about the war with Spain? Before we even get to the war with Spain, what happened to this expansionism? Sectionalism and the Civil War brought it to a temporary end during the 1850s and the 1860s. But throughout the 1850s, numerous adventurers—known as filibusters and supported by the U.S. Government—attempted to conquer Cuba and portions of Central America. They failed, but the efforts were there. Within two years of the end of the Civil War, the United States had purchased the enormous Russian colony that we know as Alaska. Interestingly, that was the first territorial acquisition by treaty that did not include a provision for eventual incorporation into the Union as a state. Alaska would be officially known as a possession; in reality, a colony. Then came the war with Spain I 1898 and the acquisition of the Philippines, Guam, and Puerto Rico, as well as the annexation of Hawaii; Hawaii, where American settlers had a few years earlier overthrown the native Hawaiian monarchy.

But much more extensive than this formal colonial empire was the informal empire that the United States created in Central America and the Caribbean in the aftermath of the war with Spain. That empire included protectorates over five nations in the Caribbean and Central America: Cuba, Nicaragua,

Panama, the Dominican Republic, and Haiti. All five were nominally independent, but the United States controlled the economies, the finances, and the foreign policies of these countries, and it reserved the right to intervene militarily in each of them; and it did so.

The pattern was first established in Cuba with the 1901 Platt Amendment; it was an amendment to a U.S. military appropriations bill. The Cubans had to agree to this amendment by treaty and add it to their constitution in order to get the U.S. Army off the island; the army that had helped to defeat the Spanish. The Cubans within the Platt Amendment had to agree not to incur indebtedness beyond their means, and not to do anything else that might endanger their independence. They also had to agree to grant the United States a naval base (which became Guantanamo Naval Base), and to allow U.S. military intervention in the country. A year later, Cuba and the United States signed a commercial reciprocity treaty that linked the Cuban economy to the American economy in a dependent role. The way this was done was by granting Cuban sugar a lower tariff rate than the tariffs on sugar from other countries. What that did, of course, was it allowed the Cuban sugar industry to prosper, but it reinforced the island's single crop economy and in effect made the entire Cuban economy dependent not only on sugar but on a continuation of this lower American tariff, thereby giving the United States, in effect, control over anything it wanted in Cuba.

Also, in 1903, the United States helped to organize and then supported a successful revolt in the Colombian province of Panama in order to obtain the right to build and fortify a canal through what was now an independent country. As Theodore Roosevelt famously stated, "I took Panama, and let Congress debate it." Over the next decade, the United States would foist treaties similar to the Platt Amendment on Nicaragua, Haiti, and the Dominican Republic, as well as Panama, and it would intervene militarily in each of them: The Cuban military inventions occurred from 1906–1909, 1912, and 1917–1922; Nicaragua, it was 1909–1910, 1912–1925, and then 1926–1933; Haiti, 1915–1934; the Dominican Republic, 1916–1924. The United States would also exercise financial supervision over the Dominican Republic, Haiti, and Nicaragua, which did not end until 1941 for some of these countries.

Careful examination of the map explains why these nations, as well as Puerto Rico, the Philippines, Guam, and Hawaii, became part of the formal and the informal American Empire. Panama and Nicaragua held the two key potential routes for an inter-oceanic canal; what would eventually become the Panama Canal. Cuba, Haiti, the Dominican Republic, and Puerto Rico controlled the Caribbean approaches to such a canal. They were also vulnerable to a feared European military intervention because of their chronic indebtedness and instability. What about Hawaii, Guam, and the Philippines? They were all stopping points for both commercial and naval vessels needing to resupply; ships at that point ran on coal, and you needed to resupply your coal. They were coaling stations and stops for other provisions on the route across the Pacific to the fabled "China market" of the late 19th and early 20th centuries.

The American policy of free trade, most clearly enunciated in the "Open Door Notes" of 1899 and 1900 regarding China also promised and often led to further commercial expansion and domination of other areas. Given the enormous size and power of the American economy by this time, free trade (meaning free of tariff barriers) would almost inevitably mean that American goods were cheaper than those of any other power—the United States could simply produce those goods more efficiently given its awesome economic size—and if the United States controlled trade with certain areas, it would give the United States control of nations in Asia and Latin America that had much smaller economies. As a famous late-20th-century history doctoral examination question in Great Britain posed the issue, "'Free trade is the imperialism of the strong.' Discuss."

Continuation of this commercial expansion during the years between the two world wars has led many historians to question the supposed "isolation" of the United States during this time period. The United States Senate did reject membership in the League of Nations; but, as we will see in a later lecture, it remained very actively involved in the world during the 1920s, signing numerous treaties and expanding its economy globally. Indeed, the American economy undergirded the entire global economy of the 1920s and with it the entire peace structure of that decade.

Both the American economy and the global economy collapsed during the 1930s, and with them went the peace structure; and admittedly, what both preceded and what followed that economic collapse is what one historian has accurately labeled a "mood of isolation." But once again, it was a mood limited to a desire to stay out of another European war; and the closer Europe came to war, the stronger that mood became. It would change dramatically in 1940 and 1941 when Nazi Germany conquered virtually all of Europe, and it would result in the permanent demise of any isolationism whatsoever in this country. Indeed, after World War II, the United States would emerge as the most powerful and influential nation in the world, and indeed in world history.

But as this lecture has hopefully shown, the shift was not nearly as dramatic as our national mythology would have us believe. Our past isolation has been grossly overstated, as has our anti-imperialism. Given this history, why have most Americans continued to maintain that we were once isolationist and almost always anti-imperialist? Partially it stems from the fact that we successfully rebelled against the greatest empire in the world, and thus believe we have an anti-empire tradition and history. Partially it stems from the fact that our Founders defined our empire, in Jefferson's words, as an "empire of liberty," not an empire tyranny; and we tend to equate the word "empire" with tyranny. Partially it stems from the 19th-century belief, via the ideology of "Manifest Destiny," that the North American continent was ours by divine right, and thus our claims were superior to any contrary claims by Native Americans, Europeans, or Latin Americans. Our expansion, by this mode of thinking, across the North American continent could not be considered imperialistic.

Along with that mode of thought went the belief that the entire Western Hemisphere was separated from Europe not only by an ocean but by the republican form of government. The 1823 Monroe Doctrine was and still is consequently perceived as a defensive document against European encroachment, and thus isolationist and anti-imperialist, rather than expansionist and aggressive as others have interpreted it. Similarly, we believed we were liberating the Cubans in 1898. We also believed we were both defending and spreading freedom and democracy against mortal threats in World War I, in World War II, and in the Cold War. Partially our belief that we were anti-imperialist stemmed from the fact that we equated imperialism with formal colonialism rather than viewing formal colonialism as but one form of imperialism. In addition, we have always viewed trade as a rational alternative to empire and war; which it can be, but which it often, as we have seen, is not.

A debate did begin during the Cold War as to whether we were indeed an empire; and if we were, then what kind of empire? That debate accelerated after the Cold War ended and the Soviet Union collapsed in 1991. It was clear from that point on that the United States was the hegemonic power of the world. So were we an empire if we were the hegemonic power. To most Americans, the answer remained definitely "no." We are not an empire. Our major foreign policies, we are told consistently, are and always have been protection of our own security and promotion of democracy around the world, not the creation of an empire. But in the name of protecting our own security and promoting democracy, numerous critics point out that we have created and we consistently use the largest military force in the world. It is a military force whose total cost is greater than that of the armed forces of all other major nations combined. If that is not imperialistic, the critics ask, what is? There's another fact to consider: Isn't promotion of American-style democracy imperialistic to cultures that do not share or want our democratic values? On the other hand, isn't much of our previous expansion really the unplanned, defensive result of our need to counter mortal threats to our security; mortal threats that appeared first in the shape of aggressive European monarchies, and then in the shape of Nazi Germany and the Communist Soviet Union? Perhaps so, but that does not negate the domination we have been able to exercise over others in the process of defending ourselves and ensuring our own security; and others clearly define that domination as imperialistic.

In truth be told, in a world of nation states that all claim sovereignty—and keep in mind that sovereignty includes the right to make war—the only absolute security is expansion designed to preclude the emergence of any other center of power that could threaten you. Clearly, during the Cold War, that is the way we interpreted Soviet behavior, and, in fact, all of Russian history. Realize that in this regard, one nation's defense is another nation's aggression; and that will be the case as long as we live in this anarchic international system in which every nation maintains that it is sovereign and maintains the right to make war on any other nation.

Perhaps relevant here is what the ancient Athenians asserted to the Spartans 2,500 years ago about their empire—that is, the Athenian Empire—at least according to Thucydides in his classic *The Peloponnesian War*. The Athenians said to the Spartans that their "principal motive" in acquiring an empire was fear. Then Thucydides added, "though honour and interest afterwards came in."

Are we all that different from the Athenians? Or, indeed, are we all that different from ancient Rome, to which we are often compared by others and, indeed, to which throughout our history we have often compared ourselves?

Early Progressives Were Not Liberals
Lecture 14

Many Americans, whether liberal or conservative, trace contemporary liberalism back to the late-19th- and early-20th-century reform movement known as Progressivism. As with other historical myths, there is a kernel of truth in the supposed connection between Progressivism and contemporary liberalism, but it has been grossly overstated. It also distorts the history and meaning of Progressivism, as well as the meaning of contemporary liberalism and conservatism.

A Contradictory and Confusing Movement

- Confusion over Progressivism is understandable because the movement was never unified. It contained many different groups with many different goals, a fact clearly illustrated by the incongruous legislation and constitutional amendments passed during the Progressive era.

  o Amendments Sixteen through Nineteen to the Constitution established the income tax, direct election of senators, alcohol prohibition, and the vote for women.

  o Major Progressive legislation included railroad and antitrust regulations, the Pure Food and Drug Act, creation of the Federal Reserve System, major attacks on civil liberties during and after World War I, and immigration restriction.

- The Progressive era would also see the creation of numerous professional organizations with enforced standards, the rise of social work and settlement houses, the beginnings of a national birth control movement, a further deterioration in the condition of African Americans, the Social Gospel movement in churches, and a racist eugenics movement that sought to sterilize those it labeled "inferior."

- The movement elected two of our best-known presidents—Theodore Roosevelt and Woodrow Wilson—who ran against each other in 1912 on two Progressive but diametrically opposed platforms and who hated each other.

- The Progressive movement included people famous in other areas of American life but with little if anything in common: philosophers, such as William James and John Dewey; ministers, such as Walter Rauschenbusch and Washington Gladden; jurists, such as Oliver Wendell Holmes and Louis Brandeis; journalists; novelists; and others.

- Progressive programs included many ideas from the 1892 Populist platform, but most Progressive leaders had been anti-Populist in the 1890s.

- Most Progressives wanted to regulate big business, but numerous business leaders were part of the movement. Other opposing groups among the Progressives included

The New Nationalism reform program of Theodore Roosevelt emphasized regulation of big business and economic and social welfare legislation.

immigrants and those who were anti-immigrant, African Americans and racists, and women and those who sought legislation to "protect" women because of their alleged inferiority.

- The movement was perhaps best described by the historian Robert Wiebe as a "search for order"—an attempt to redefine American politics and society in light of the radical changes created by the industrial revolution and the ensuing urbanization of the country.

- In this regard, a new class of urban, white-collar professionals created by the industrial revolution would join with the older urban middle class to be two of the driving forces in the movement.

General Goals of Progressivism

- In general, the Progressive movement sought to end the abuses of power and corruption that had come to dominate American economic and political life. Corrupted institutions would be replaced with reformed ones that would restore power to the people.

- Another general goal of the movement was to restore morality to American politics and life, that is, honesty in business, government, and production.

- Progressives sought to help the victims of industrialization— children and women who were forced to work, new immigrants, and others.

- The movement aimed to use scientific and efficiency principles and expertise from the academic and business worlds to minimize disorder and establish cooperation. A related goal was to professionalize and regularize certain aspects of American life by establishing clear standards for doctors, lawyers, and other professionals.

- Finally, the Progressives wanted to restore a sense of discipline, virtue, and service to the nation by encouraging people to look beyond their narrow self-interests to the good of others and the good of the country as a whole.

Progressivism versus Liberalism

- For Progressives, the key tool to accomplish these goals was positive government action. This is the key shift in what we might call the "liberal perspective" and the one clear link between the Progressives and contemporary liberals: a belief that government is not the problem but the solution to the problems that plagued American life at this time.

- Traditional 18th- and 19th-century liberalism feared government power as the source of tyranny throughout history and had sought to limit that power in whatever ways it could.

- But Progressives turned traditional liberalism on its head by arguing that the large monopolistic corporations and corrupt urban political machines had become the problems and that positive government action was imperative to control big business, reform the political and economic systems, and thereby restore and save the American dream.

- One of the most important Progressive thinkers was Herbert Croly, who attacked the notion of laissez-faire and Adam Smith's "invisible hand." The marketplace was no longer self-regulating and did not lead automatically to better things in the economic or in any other sphere. What was needed to restore the "promise of American life" was greater government power—nationalization and centralization.

Competing Progressive Platforms

- Although Progressives tended to agree on these general goals and the positive use of government, they disagreed over just how government should be used, for example, how it should be used to regulate business. That fact is most clearly seen in the competing platforms of Roosevelt and Wilson in the 1912 presidential election.

- Wilson's New Freedom sought to use government to break up big business in order to restore competition.

- Roosevelt's New Nationalism argued that this was both impossible and counterproductive. Instead, government should seek to control and legitimize big business and play a key role in arbitrating differences between business and labor. Far from accidentally, this indirect attack on laissez-faire also led the New Nationalists to propose legislation to help the victims of industrialization.

Progressivism and Contemporary Politics

- Those who opposed the Progressive call for positive government action would henceforth be considered conservatives. But in actuality, they were retaining one of the major principles of 18th- and 19th-century liberalism: fear of government power. American conservatives were, thus, diametrically opposed to traditional European conservatives, who favored strong government power.

- In this regard, American conservatives and liberals both base their belief systems on John Locke's concept of the social contract, not the concepts of Thomas Hobbes and other European conservative thinkers that underlay the very different European definition of conservatism.

- Hobbes maintained that the natural, original state of human life was "solitary, poor, nasty, brutish, and short" and that the only way to organize a society to overcome this condition was to give total power and obedience to a monarch or small group empowered to decide every issue.

- Although some American conservatives might agree with Hobbes's pessimistic view of human nature, they do not agree with his proposed solution of absolute obedience to a powerful, centralized, and authoritarian government. Instead, they argue that strong centralized government—not big business—remains the greatest threat to freedom.

- It's also important to note that while the logic of Progressive thought leads to many programs contemporary liberals might support, it also led to many programs that are anathema to contemporary liberalism.

- For example, the desire to help the victims of industrialization, which contemporary liberals would applaud, combined with the desire to restore morality to American life would translate into an imposition of middle-class American morality via legal social coercion in numerous areas (which many contemporary conservatives would support).
  - The prohibition amendment and laws against certain drugs were partially justified on the grounds that alcohol and drugs are immoral and create dependency that holds back the working class.

  - Social reform thus becomes social control as the government assumes functions previously performed by the church, family, and local community.

- The desire to help the victims of industrialization would also lead to a major movement to Americanize the new immigrants at the expense of their traditional cultures.

- Further, the Progressive emphasis on science, expertise, and professional standards actually hurt the poor by depriving them of the doctors, lawyers, and other professionals who—although they might have been ill-trained—had at least previously served them.

- Similarly, Progressive efforts to destroy political corruption deprived the new immigrants and other poor of the urban political machines that took care of them—in return, of course, for their votes.

- The fusion of science with preexisting racism would reinforce the desire to help the new immigrants by Americanizing them and destroying their native cultures. It would also lead to immigration restriction to prevent any more of these "inferior" peoples from competing with American labor.

- That fusion of science with racism would further lead to the rise of eugenics and, with it, calls for forced sterilization of "inferiors" to improve the genetic base of the population.
  - It is no accident that the great Progressive Woodrow Wilson would expand segregation in the federal government and praise D. W. Griffith's racist film *Birth of a Nation* as "history written with lightning."

  - This racism, along with the emphasis on imposing American middle-class standards of expertise and morality, would lead many Progressives to become avid imperialists. Indeed, most of the military interventions in Central America and the Caribbean occurred during the Progressive era.

- The Progressive emphasis on nationalism and centralization would reinforce, if not create, the suppression of civil liberties during World War I in the name of patriotism. The Espionage and Sedition acts of 1917 and 1918 virtually outlawed dissent against the war and criticism of the U.S. government.

The Legacy of Progressivism

- Much of the legislation introduced in the Progressive era failed, and many of the movement's goals were not accomplished.

- Big business today is in many ways more centralized and destructive of competition than it was 100 years ago.

- Big government has also, in many ways, failed to do what it promised to do, and it appears today to many Americans as worse than the problems it originally grew to address.

- Nevertheless, Progressivism created much of the broad value structure we live with today, whether liberal or conservative, regarding such issues as efficiency, expertise, morality, and government control, as well as the inculcation of such values through our education system. In that sense, most if not all of us, liberal and conservative, remain linked to Progressive ideas.

Suggested Reading

Blum, *Woodrow Wilson and the Politics of Morality.*

Cooper, *Woodrow Wilson: A Biography.*

Fink, ed., *Major Problems in the Gilded Age and the Progressive Era.*

Questions to Consider

1. In what ways do we still live within the value structure of the Progressive era?

2. Do contemporary liberals and conservatives truly divide over how powerful the national government should be or instead over the specific issues in which government should play a strong role?

Early Progressives Were Not Liberals
Lecture 14—Transcript

Many Americans, whether liberal or conservative, trace contemporary Liberalism back to the late 19th- and early 20th-century reform movement known as "Progressivism." Progressivism was a movement that began in the cities and that came to dominate both political parties and national politics during the first two decades of the 20th century. Indeed, at least two American presidents—Theodore Roosevelt and Woodrow Wilson—openly identified themselves as Progressives, and their programs with the Progressive cause.

Yet a close examination shows that the Progressives held many views totally repugnant to contemporary Liberals. As with other historical myths that we've looked at, there is a kernel of truth in the supposed connection between Progressivism and contemporary Liberalism. But it has been grossly overstated, and it distorts the history and meaning of Progressivism. It also distorts the meaning of contemporary Liberalism, and contemporary Conservatism for that matter.

Part of the problem is that our definitions of Liberalism and Conservatism have changed rather dramatically over the past century, and they have done so more than once. But the problem is also due to a misunderstanding regarding who the Progressives were and just what they stood for. This lecture will attempt to address that misunderstanding by analyzing the Progressives and their Progressive movement. After doing so, it will then explore the ways in which Progressivism is related to contemporary Liberalism, and the ways in which it is not.

The confusion over Progressivism is quite understandable. It was never a unified movement; it contained many different groups with many different goals. That fact is clearly illustrated by both the legislation that was passed during the Progressive Era and the four Constitutional Amendments that were passed during this time period. These Constitutional Amendments— numbers 16, 17, 18, and 19—established the income tax, direct election of senators, prohibition on the manufacture and sale of alcohol, and the vote for women. What in the world, one might ask, do those four have in common?

The situation is similar in regard to Progressive legislation. Major Progressive bills included establishment of the first income tax, bills to regular the railroad, antitrust legislation, the Pure Food and Drug Act, the creation of the Federal Reserve System, major attacks on civil liberties during and after World War I, and immigration restriction. Again, one might ask, what in the world do these have in common?

The Progressive Era would also see the creation of numerous professional organizations with enforced professional standards for doctors, for lawyers, for others. It would also see the rise of social work, social workers, and settlement houses to help the immigrants and the poor. It would also see the rise of a national birth control movement during this time; a further deterioration in the condition of African Americans; a major movement in the churches known as the "Social Gospel" movement promoting Progressive reform; and a racist eugenics movement that sought to sterilize those it labeled "inferior." Once again, what in the world do these have in common?

The movement also elected two of our best-known presidents, Theodore Roosevelt and Woodrow Wilson; but they came from different political parties and they had strikingly different personalities. They ran against each other in 1912 on two progressive platforms, but diametrically opposed platforms, and they came to hate each other. The Progressive movement also included people famous in other areas of American life, but with little if anything in common: You had philosophers such as William James and John Dewey, the father of our modern educational system; you had social workers such as Jane Adams, who was also a famous peace activist. At the same time, you had Army officers, such as General Leonard Wood, who helped bring Progressive efficiency to the Army and who wanted to inculcate Army values into the civilian population; you had ministers, such as Walter Rauschenbusch and Washington Gladden, who were leaders in the Social Gospel movement; you had jurists, such as Oliver Wendell Holmes and Louis Brandeis, highly influential Supreme Court justices, who came from different generations; you had exposé journalists, called muckrakers by Theodore Roosevelt, such as Lincoln Steffens and Ida Tarbell; and you had novelists such as Stephen Crane, Theodore Dreiser, Frank Norris, Jack London, and Upton Sinclair. You had imperialists, such as Theodore

Roosevelt, and anti-imperialists, such as Robert La Follette. Roosevelt was also an avid internationalist, where La Follette is known as an isolationist.

Nor is that the end of the contradictions and the confusion. Progressive programs included many ideas from the 1892 Populist Platform cited in a previous lecture, but most Progressive leaders had been anti-Populist in the 1890s. Most Progressives wanted to regulate big business, but numerous business leaders were part of the movement. Many immigrants supported the movement, even though many of its leaders were anti-immigrant. Many African American supported the movement even though many of the movement's leaders were highly racist. Many women supported the movement even though many of its leaders were proponents of legislation to "protect" women because of their alleged inferiority.

Historians have for many decades explored Progressivism and tried to understand these contradictions and this movement. Perhaps it is best described, in the words of one historian, Robert Wiebe, as a "search for order"; an attempt to redefine American politics and American society in light of the enormous, the revolutionary changes that had been created by the Industrial Revolution and the ensuing urbanization of the country. In this regard, a new class of urban, white collar professionals created by the Industrial Revolution and urbanization—accountants, clerks, midlevel managers—would join with the older urban, professional middle class of doctors, lawyers, and businessmen to be two of the driving forces in the movement, though far from the only ones.

The essential Progressive program focused on a series of general goals: One was to end the abuses of power and the corruption that had come to dominate American economic and political life. Progressives wanted to replace corrupted institutions with reformed ones that would restore power to the people via such measures as the initiative, so that the people could initiative legislation rather than the corrupt state legislatures; the referendum, where people could vote directly on the legislation; and the recall, whereby corrupt officials could be thrown out of office before the end of their turn. Progressives also favored direct election of senators instead of via corrupt state legislatures, the secret ballot, and extension of the franchise to many previously denied it.

Progressives also wanted to restore morality to American politics and American life: honesty in business, honesty in government, and honesty in production (witness the Pure Food and Drug Act). Progressives wanted to help the victims of industrialization: children and women forced to work, the new immigrants, and others. Progressives wanted to use scientific and efficiency principles and expertise from both the academic world and the business world to minimize disorder and establish cooperation. In Progressive minds, expertise and morality were fused; they were not contradictory, they were complimentary. As Woodrow Wilson once said to the experts that joined him going to the Paris Peace Conference—a group known as the Inquiry—"Tell me what is right and I will fight for it"; the experts would know what was right, what was morally right as well as what was factually right.

Also, Progressives wanted to professionalize and regularize aspects of American life by establishing clear standards for doctors, lawyers, and other professionals. Finally, Progressives wanted to restore a sense of discipline, virtue, and service; to get people to look beyond their narrow self-interest and look instead to the good of others and to the good of the country as a whole. The thought was best expressed by the philosopher William James in his essay "The Moral Equivalent of War." War, he believed, was hideous; but it did get people to think not first of themselves but of the soldier next to them, beyond their own self-interest. If we could get the civilian population to think the way soldiers do, James said, it would be a great advance. General Leonard Wood felt similarly: He called for inculcating military virtues into civilian life.

For Progressives, the key tool to do all of this was positive government action. This is the key shift in what we might call the "liberal perspective," and the one very clear link—in fact, some would say the only clear link—between the Progressives and contemporary Liberals: a belief that government is not the problem, but the solution to the problems that plagued American life at this time.

Traditional 18th- and 19th-century Liberalism feared government power; it saw government power as the key source of tyranny throughout history and it had sought to limit government power in whatever ways it could. Witness, in this regard, the policies that we have previously discussed of Thomas Jefferson and Andrew Jackson. But Progressives turned this traditional Liberalism on its head by arguing that the large, monopolistic corporations and the corrupt urban political machines had become the key problems, and that positive government action was now imperative to control big business, to reform the political and economic systems, and thereby to restore and save the American Dream.

There is no central theorist for the movement, but one of the most important Progressive thinkers was an individual named Herbert Croly who wrote a book entitled *The Promise of American Life*. What Croly essentially did was to attack Adam Smith's "hidden hand"; that laissez-faire would result in everything being rosy. The marketplace, he argued, was no longer self-regulating, and it was not leading automatically to better things in the economic sphere, or in any other sphere. The belief that it was, Croly maintained, was actually helping to destroy the American Dream. What was needed to restore "the promise of American life" was greater government power, nationalization and centralization; or, as one cliché to summarize the Progressive movement put it: use Hamiltonian means for Jeffersonian ends.

While Progressives tended to agree on these general goals and the positive use of government, they disagreed over just how government should be used. For example, should it be used in terms of regulating big business to break down large monopolistic corporations, to smash big business; or should it instead merely seek to regulate them? This fact can be most clearly seen in the competing Progressive platforms of Theodore Roosevelt and Woodrow Wilson in the presidential election of 1912. Wilson's New Freedom sought to use the government to break up big business in order to restore competition. Roosevelt's New Nationalism argued that this was both impossible and counterproductive. Instead, government should seek to control and legitimize big business. Government should also play the key role as arbitrator in differences between business and labor. Far from accidentally, this indirect attack on laissez-faire also led the New Nationalists to propose legislation to help the victims of industrialization, since these people in effect recognized that laissez-faire was not working and that some people would need government help.

Those who opposed the Progressive call for positive government action would henceforth be considered Conservatives; but in actuality, they were retaining one of the major principles of 18th- and 19th-century Liberalism: fear of government power. In that belief, these American Conservatives were diametrically opposed to traditional European Conservatives, who favored strong government power; indeed some favored absolute government power. It is important to realize in this regard that American Conservatives and Liberals both base their belief systems on John Locke's concept of the social contract, as was discussed in an earlier lecture; so do those who consider themselves neither Conservatives nor Liberals but Moderates. None of them follow the concepts of Thomas Hobbes and other European Conservative thinkers that underlay the very different European definition of Conservatism.

Hobbes had maintained that the natural, original state of human life was, in his words, "solitary, poor, nasty, brutish, and short," and that the only way to organize a society so as to overcome this was to give total power and obedience to a monarch or to a small aristocratic group empowered to decide every issue. While some American Conservatives just might agree with Hobbes's pessimistic view of human nature, they do not agree with his proposed solution of absolute obedience to a powerful, centralized, and authoritarian government. Instead they argue, as did 18th- and 19th-century Liberals, that strong centralized government—not big business—remains the greatest threat to freedom. This fear of big government has led to the crack that an American Conservative is actually a worshipper of dead Liberals. If that is true, does that make a Liberal a worshipper of dead Conservatives?

It is also important to note that while the logic of Progressive thought does lead to many programs contemporary Liberals could support, it also led to many programs that are anathema to contemporary Liberalism. Let me name but a few of these: A desire to help the victims of industrialization, which contemporary Liberals would applaud, combined with the desire to restore morality to American life, translate during this time period into an imposition of middle class American morality via legal social coercion in numerous areas. Some have argued that it is something contemporary Conservatives might support; another link of Conservatives to the Progressive movement. The prohibition amendment, as well as laws against certain drugs that were passed during this time period, were partially justified on the grounds that alcohol and drugs are immoral and that they create dependency that holds back the working class. In this mode of thinking, social reform becomes social control as the government assumes functions previously performed by the church, by the family, and by the local community.

The desire to help the victims of industrialization would also lead to a major movement to Americanize the new immigrants at the expense of their traditional cultures. Destroying traditional cultures may seem to us as anything but helpful to new immigrants, but that is because our values in this regard have changed so dramatically over the last century. Today, our belief in this regard is aptly summarized by Star Trek's "prime directive": not to upset or alter the cultures of other life forms with whom the Enterprise comes into contact. But the belief then was that the best thing you could do for the new immigrants was to make them think and behave just like middle class white Americans.

Furthermore, the Progressive emphasis on science, on expertise, and on professional standards actually hurt the new immigrants and other poor by depriving them of the doctors and lawyers who had been willing to serve them; while those individuals might not have been very well-trained, at least they were willing to provide service to the poor. Similarly, Progressive efforts to destroy political corruption deprived the new immigrants and other poor of the urban political machines that took care of them—in return, of course, for their vote—and acceptance of the graft that went with these machines. Tammany Hall's George Washington Plunkitt had admitted years earlier to a reporter that he knew every man, woman, and child in his district; and when there was a fire or some other emergency, he didn't ask questions as reformers would and get them to fill out forms. Instead, he found them a place to live, got them clothing to replace what they had lost, and they gratefully repaid him with their vote.

The fusion of science with preexisting racism would reinforce the desire to help the new immigrants by Americanizing them and destroying their native cultures. It would also lead to immigration restriction to prevent any more of these "inferior" peoples from coming over and competing with American labor. That fusion of science with preexisting racism would also lead to the rise of a movement known as eugenics, and with it calls for forced sterilization of "inferiors" so as to improve the genetic base of the population. Indeed, this Progressive era might very well have been the height of "scientific" racist thought in this country. It would witness in this regard the publication of Madison Grant's notorious *Passing of the Great Race*, soon followed by Henry Ford's previously-cited anti-Semitic tracts. Nor is it accidental in this regard that the great Progressive Woodrow Wilson would expand segregation in the federal government, introducing it to several departments where it had not existed before; and that he would praise D.W. Griffith's racist film *Birth of a Nation* as "history written with lightning."

This racism, along with the emphasis on the imposition of American middle class standards of expertise and morality, would also lead many Progressives to become avid imperialists in the name of what Rudyard Kipling had popularized as the "White Man's Burden": the need to help these inferior peoples by ruling them. It is no accident in this regard that the Progressive Era coincides with the establishment—as discussed in the last lecture—of the informal as well as the formal American Empire. In fact, most of the military interventions in Central America and the Caribbean occurred during the Progressive Era, under both the Republican Theodore Roosevelt and the Democrat Woodrow Wilson.

The Progressive emphasis on nationalism and centralization would reinforce, if not create, the suppression of civil liberties during World War I in the name of patriotism. It was done via creation of the first American propaganda bureau—the Committee on Public Information—and the passage of the Espionage and Sedition Acts in 1917 and 1918. Those laws virtually outlawed dissent against the war and criticism of the United States government, and they would be supported by the Supreme Court. Indeed, Eugene Debs would be jailed again under these laws, this time for opposing the war.

In addition to all of these problems, much Progressive legislation simply failed. Big business today is in many ways more centralized and destructive of competition than it was 100 years ago. Big government has in many ways failed as well—failed to do what it promised—and to many today, whether rightly or wrongly, big government appears worse than the problems it originally grew to address. Fascinating is the fact that Progressive political reforms would coincide with a decline in the percentage of Americans who vote, not an increase as the Progressives had desired and expected.

Nevertheless, Progressivism created much of the broad value structure that we live with today, whether Liberal, Conservative, or in between, regarding such issues as efficiency, expertise, morality, and government control, as well as the inculcation of such values through our educational system. We still use the word "Progressive." In this regard, we are in a situation similar to the continued use of the word "Populism." Do contemporary people who use the label "Progressive" have anything in common with the original Progressive movement? The answer is probably similar: This is not a lecture on contemporary Progressivism; but as with Populism, there are links, but there are dramatic differences. What I think can be clearly stated is that most if not all of us—Liberals, Conservatives, Moderates, Progressives—remain linked to Progressive ideas, and Progressivism thus remains very relevant to contemporary American life; but it does not necessarily remain relevant in the ways that we think it does.

Woodrow Wilson and the Rating of Presidents
Lecture 15

Woodrow Wilson is one of the most controversial presidents in U.S. history. In most presidential polls, he is put in the great or near-great category, yet to his numerous detractors, both at the time and later, he is vastly overrated. Examining the reasons for this sharp difference of opinion provides an opportunity to explore the broader issue of presidential ratings in general and the standards by which past presidents are judged.

Wilson's Accomplishments

- Woodrow Wilson's high rating in presidential polls rests on what appears to be an extraordinary series of accomplishments during his eight years in office.

- During his first two years as president, Wilson's Progressive program included the first major downward revision of the tariff since before the Civil War, the establishment of the Federal Reserve System and the Federal Trade Commission, and the passage of the Clayton Antitrust Act to curb monopolistic business practices.

- In 1916, he obtained passage of a second round of Progressive legislation that included programs to provide farmers with credit, construct and improve rural roads, prohibit interstate shipping of goods made with child labor, establish an eight-hour day for railroad workers, and create a worker's compensation system for federal employees.

- In obtaining this impressive collection of Progressive legislation, Wilson became the first president to propose and receive from Congress a full program (his New Freedom program). He also exhibited exceptional political skill and, by 1916, had united Progressive forces from both parties to support him for reelection.

- In foreign affairs, Wilson's supporters argue, he kept the United States out of World War I for nearly three years. When finally forced by German actions to enter the war, he quickly became the moral leader of the Allied nations and the major force for reform of the entire international system.
  - That reform program, as enunciated in his Fourteen Points address and other major speeches, focused on establishing a new world order based on the creation of a League of Nations and the principle of collective security.

  - Wilson obtained his League of Nations and much of the rest of his international program during intense negotiations with Allied leaders in Paris. But he failed to obtain Senate ratification of the Treaty of Versailles because of Republican obstructionists and because of a major stroke that prevented him from mobilizing the American people in favor of the treaty and membership in the League.

- Despite this final failure, Wilson's supporters argue that his record of achievements is extraordinary. He brought the Progressive movement to its zenith and helped to redefine the role and power of the presidency, the federal government as a whole, and the United States in the world arena.

Criticisms of Wilson

- Wilson's critics see a very different record and reach different conclusions. Although he carried 40 of 48 states in 1912 and won a massive victory in the electoral college, he was a minority president who obtained only 42 percent of the popular vote.

- Soon after he took office, Wilson abandoned portions of his New Freedom reform program and, by 1916, had embraced the much broader but diametrically opposed New Nationalism reform program of Theodore Roosevelt. This program emphasized regulation, rather than destruction of the trusts, and economic and social welfare legislation, which Wilson had previously opposed.

- Wilson also refused to support women's suffrage and was responsible for bringing racial segregation to the federal government.

- In foreign affairs, critics note, this supposed anti-imperialist intervened militarily in Latin America more than his openly imperialist predecessors, Roosevelt and Taft, and his military intervention in Mexico almost resulted in a war with that nation.

- His pro-Allied sympathies and actions made a mockery of American neutrality in World War I. By allowing extensive war trade and loans to the Allies, Wilson effectively made the United States an unofficial belligerent that Germany was more than willing to attack in 1917.

Library of Congress, Prints and Photographs Division.

Woodrow Wilson receives a relatively high ranking in most presidential polls, a somewhat puzzling result given the failures that seem to balance out his successes.

- Once in the war, Wilson's administration amassed almost dictatorial powers. It established a propaganda bureau and virtually outlawed dissent with the Espionage and Sedition acts, initiating a period of government repression and some of the worst violations of civil liberties in U.S. history.

- Wilson also participated in the Allied military intervention that attempted but failed to overthrow the Bolshevik regime in Russia and refused to recognize that government. These moves embittered relations between the two nations for decades and were an important factor in the development of the Cold War.

- At the same time, his administration attacked domestic and immigrant Leftists and, soon after the war, launched what became known as the first Red Scare.

- After World War I, Wilson's critics continue, he proved to be an inept negotiator at the peace conference and, in the end, abandoned many of the lofty principles he had previously championed.

- The primary cause of the Senate's refusal to ratify the Treaty of Versailles and join the League of Nations was Wilson's arrogant refusal to compromise with Senate Republicans. That refusal led to a second and bloodier world war only 20 years later.

Presidential Ratings

- Among the primary standards used in presidential rating polls are the consequences of presidential action. By that standard, Washington, Lincoln, and Franklin Roosevelt always rank as the top three: Washington for establishing the new government and setting key precedents, Lincoln for preventing the destruction of the country, and FDR for successfully leading the country through the worst domestic and international crises in its history.

- Similarly, the two presidents who preceded Lincoln, Franklin Pierce and James Buchanan, are usually placed at the bottom because their policies and incompetence resulted in the Civil War. In most polls Jefferson, Theodore Roosevelt, and Wilson are ranked just below Washington, Lincoln, and FDR.

- Wilson's high ranking is a bit puzzling in light of his numerous failures and their negative consequences.
  - But consequences do not constitute the only standard involved in rating presidents; assessments are often based on the values the assessors bring to their task.

○ Assessors who approve of the Progressive movement and an activist federal government in both domestic and international affairs tend to give Wilson positive assessments, while those who disagree with these positions tend to give lower assessments.

- Such value judgments play a major role in all presidential ratings. Presidents usually listed as the worst—Pierce, Buchanan, Ulysses Grant, and Warren Harding, for example—are put in that category for one of two reasons: incompetence or corruption. But those are not the only reasons to conclude that someone was a terrible president. What about hypocrisy, lying, breaking the law, or sheer stupidity?

- Similarly, those usually placed in the highest category—Washington, Lincoln, and FDR—are put in that category because of the enormous dangers the country faced during their tenures. But again, should this be the only category for determining a great presidency? What about political skill in office or, simply, lack of mistakes?

- Further, use of consequences as a standard requires treating the rankings of recent presidents with a grain of salt because we do not yet know the full consequences of their actions.

- It's also true that the consequences of presidential actions are sometimes both positive and negative, as can be seen in the record of James K. Polk or, in modern times, that of Richard Nixon.

- We should also recognize that presidential polls and ratings are affected by changing American values and perspectives over time. Andrew Jackson, for example, dropped from 6th place in a 1948 poll to 14th place in a more recent poll because of our changing views on just how "democratic" his presidency really was and the negative economic impact of his destruction of the second national bank.

- There is also often a sharp difference between the ratings of past presidents made by historians and those made by the general public. In a 2011 Gallup poll, Americans agreed with historians only on

Lincoln as one of the top three presidents. Instead of Washington and FDR, they put Ronald Reagan and Bill Clinton in that elite group!

- Of course, the public's views can change with the passage of time as much as historians' views. The public's rating of Truman went up in the 1970s and 1980s, at about the same time that it began to decline among historians, who argued that he deserved partial blame for both the Cold War and the rise of McCarthyism.

Wilson's Ratings

- Wilson's ratings have gone down somewhat since the 1960s as a result of our changing views on race relations, women's rights, civil liberties, and perhaps, the UN. He was number 4 in 1948, 7 in the 1990s, and a bit lower in the 21st century.

- Is he perhaps still overrated? As we have seen, both his achievements and his failures are consequential. Yet his supporters ask whether any of his predecessors or contemporaries could have done better given the significant problems he faced, both domestically and internationally.

- It's interesting to speculate what would have happened if Theodore Roosevelt had won the 1912 election instead of Wilson.
    - Whereas Wilson's New Freedom sought to return to a mid-19th-century world of competition, Roosevelt's New Nationalism realized that was impossible and was the first program to address 20th-century realities in terms of business regulation (rather than trust-busting) and social welfare legislation.

    - In foreign affairs, Roosevelt was one of the most successful diplomats in U.S. history, at least in regard to the great powers. He won the Nobel Peace Prize for mediating an end to the Russo-Japanese War and secretly mediated an end to the Moroccan crisis that could have easily led to the outbreak of World War I in 1905–1906.

o   Given that record, we must ask if World War I would have even broken out if Roosevelt had been elected in 1912. Certainly, he would have actively tried to prevent it, much more so than did Wilson, who was preoccupied at the time with the death of his first wife.

o   Had Roosevelt failed to halt the outbreak of war, he probably would have joined the conflict earlier than Wilson, and it's unlikely that his record in civil liberties would have been any better than Wilson's. But it's also unlikely that he would have attempted to replace the balance of power with collective security, a concept that has proven to be unworkable in the 20th and 21st centuries.

Suggested Reading

Blum, *Woodrow Wilson and the Politics of Morality.*

Cooper, *Woodrow Wilson: A Biography.*

Fink, ed., *Major Problems in the Gilded Age and the Progressive Era.*

Questions to Consider

1.   How do your values affect your ranking of Woodrow Wilson as president?

2.   How do your values affect your ranking of other presidents?

Woodrow Wilson and the Rating of Presidents
Lecture 15—Transcript

Woodrow Wilson is one of the most controversial presidents in all of U.S. history. In most presidential polls, he is put in either the great or the near-great category; yet to his numerous detractors, both at the time and later, he is vastly overrated. Examining the reasons for this sharp difference of opinion provides an opportunity to explore the broader issue of presidential ratings in general and the standards by which past presidents are judged.

Wilson's reputation and high rating in the polls rests upon what appear to be an extraordinary series of accomplishments during his eight years in office. A former professor of Political Science and then president of Princeton, Wilson possessed exceptional intelligence, knowledge, and rhetorical abilities. He used these to promote and obtain passage of his New Freedom Progressive program. This included during his first two years in office: the Underwood-Simmons Tariff, which was the first major downward revision of the tariff since before the Civil War; it also contained the first income tax in American history. Congress also passed the Federal Reserve Act establishing the Federal Reserve System. This was our first central banking structure since Andrew Jackson destroyed the Second National Bank of the United States in the 1830s. Congress also passed the Federal Trade Commission Act, which established the Federal Trade Commission, and the Clayton Antitrust Act to curb monopolistic business practices.

But that was not the end of it: Wilson then expanded his reform program so as to obtain passage in 1916 of a second round of Progressive legislation. You had the Federal Farm Loan Act and Warehouse Act to provide farmers with credits; the Highway Act to help construct and improve rural roads; the Owen-Keating Act prohibiting the interstate shipment of goods made with child labor. You also had the Adamson Act, establishing an eight-hour day for railroad workers; and the Kern-McGillicuddy Act, which created a workmen's compensation system for federal employees.

That's impressive; and in obtaining this collection of Progressive legislation, Wilson also became the first president to propose and obtain from Congress a full program. He was also the first president to address Congress personally and use his rhetorical abilities to get what he wanted since George Washington and John Adams; Thomas Jefferson had ended that practice. Wilson also exhibited exceptional political skill, both with the Congress and with the public; and by 1916 he had united Progressive forces from both parties to support him for reelection.

In foreign affairs, Wilson's supporters argue, he kept the United States out of World War I for nearly three years; and when forced by German actions to enter the war in the spring of 1917, he quickly became the moral leader of all the Allied nations and the major force for reform of the entire international system. That reform program, as enunciated in his "14 Points Address" and other major speeches, focused on creating a new world order to be based on the creation of a League of Nations and the principle of collective security. In the past, peace had been maintained by the balance of power; and that balance of power had failed numerous times, most obviously during World War I. Wilson argued that the world should now ditch the balance of power and replace it with an international institution (the League) and a system whereby all nations would unite to stop any aggressor state. This would be collective security.

Wilson obtained his League of Nations and much of the rest of his international program during his intense negotiations with Allied leaders in Paris. But he failed to obtain Senate ratification of the ensuing Treaty of Versailles. According to his supporters, that was because of Republican obstructionists and because of a major stroke that tragically prevented him from successfully mobilizing the American people in favor of the treaty and membership in the League. Wilson had undertaken a tour of the country to mobilize support and suffered the stroke in the midst of that tour, forcing him to cancel it, return home, and in effect no longer act as the president he previously had.

Despite this final failure, Wilson's supporters argue that his record of achievements is extraordinary. He brought the Progressive movement to its zenith; he helped to redefine the role and the power of the presidency and the Federal government as a whole; and he redefined the role of the United States in the world arena. Even his failure to obtain Senate agreement to join the League of Nations boosts his reputation, according to these supporters, by clearly illustrating that he was simply ahead of his time; for in 1945, the United States would join the successor to the League of Nations, the United Nations.

Wilson's critics see a very, very different record and reach very different conclusions. For a start, although Wilson carried 40 of 48 states in 1912 and won a massive victory in the Electoral College—he carried the Electoral College 435–96—the popular vote was another matter: Wilson was a minority president. He ran against Taft on the Republican Party and Theodore Roosevelt on the third party, known as the Bull Moose Party. When the vote was counted, Wilson had obtained only 42 percent of the popular vote. Wilson also ran in 1912 on a very limited New Freedom reform program, the critics argue; a program designed essentially and limited to destroy the trusts and restore competition. Yet soon after taking office, he abandoned portions of that program, and by 1916 he had embraced the much broader, yet diametrically opposed New Nationalism reform program of Theodore Roosevelt, with its emphasis not on destruction but regulation of big business and on economic and social welfare legislation. Wilson had opposed all of this in 1912. Why, the critics argued, did he do so; did he now change? Primarily to obtain the votes of Roosevelt's 1912 supporters and thereby to achieve reelection. Critics also note that Wilson refused to support women's suffrage and that he was responsible for bringing added racial segregation to the federal government.

In foreign affairs, critics note that this supposed anti-imperialist wound up intervening militarily in Latin America more than his openly imperialist predecessors combined. He sent troops into the Dominican Republic, into Haiti, and into Mexico. He maintained troops in Nicaragua that had been sent there by his predecessor, William Howard Taft. His military intervention in Mexico almost resulted in a war with that country.

What about World War I? Critics point out that Wilson was so pro-Allied in his sympathies and his actions that he made a mockery of American neutrality in World War I. He held Germany to much stricter standards than the Allies regarding violations of American neutral rights; in fact, those stricter standards led to the resignation in protest of his first Secretary of State, William Jennings Bryan. By allowing extensive war trade and loans to the Allies, Wilson effectively made the United States an unofficial belligerent whom Germany was more than willing to attack in 1917. Along with his diplomatic blundering and blindness, this behavior eventually forced Wilson into a war he did not want and one he both could and should have avoided. Once in the war, the critics continue, Wilson's administration amassed almost dictatorial powers. It also established America's first propaganda bureau—the Committee on Public Information—and virtually outlawed dissent with the Espionage and the Sedition Acts. These initiated a period of severe government repression and some of the worst violations of civil liberties in American history.

Wilson also participated in the Allied military intervention that attempted but failed to overthrow the Bolshevik government in Russia, and he refused to recognize that government for the duration of his term; in fact, the Bolshevik government would not be recognized until 1933. These moves embittered relations between Russia and the United States for decades, and they were an important factor in the development of the Cold War.

At the same time that all of this was going on, the critics note, the Wilson administration attacked domestic and immigrant Leftists, and soon after the war it launched what became known as the First Great Red Scare. Wilson's Attorney General, A. Mitchell Palmer, launched what are now recognized to be the totally illegal Palmer Raids: the arrests of numerous American citizens as well as immigrants, and the deportation of some of them. After World War I, the critics continue, Wilson also proved to be a very inept negotiator at the Paris Peace Conference, and in the end he abandoned many of the lofty principles he had previously championed. The primary cause of Senate refusal to ratify the League of Nations and Treaty of Versailles, these critics maintain, was Wilson's own arrogant refusal to compromise with Senate Republicans; a refusal that doomed the treaty and that one historian has labeled the "supreme infanticide." That refusal, along with the defective Treaty of Versailles for which he bore so much responsibility, led to a second and bloodier world war only 20 years later.

This is a record of overwhelming failure, despite all the lofty rhetoric. As one notable Progressive put it at that time, he gave us "nothing but words." Even those words are suspect, for in both domestic and foreign affairs, he championed 19th-century concepts that would be unworkable in the 20th century.

How does one deal with these diametrically opposed conclusions about Woodrow Wilson in assessing his presidency, and what can they tell us about presidential ratings and presidential polls in general? Such polls—usually of historians and political scientists—have taken place numerous times over the last 65 years. One of the primary standards used in such evaluations is, and should be, the consequences of presidential actions. By that standard, George Washington, Abraham Lincoln, and Franklin Roosevelt always rank as the top three presidents: Washington for establishing the new government and setting a host of key precedents; Lincoln for preventing the destruction of the country; and Roosevelt for successfully leading the United States through the worst domestic economic crisis and the worst international crisis in its history. Similarly, the two presidents who preceded Lincoln—Franklin Pierce and James Buchanan—are usually placed at the bottom in presidential ratings because of their policies and the fact that their incompetence resulted in the Civil War. So are Ulysses Grant and Warren G. Harding because of the massive corruption that occurred during their presidencies.

In most polls, Thomas Jefferson, Theodore Roosevelt, and Woodrow Wilson are ranked just below Washington, Lincoln, and Franklin Roosevelt; and then they are often followed by James K. Polk and James Monroe. Similarly, John Tyler, Millard Fillmore, Zachary Taylor, and Andrew Johnson are usually ranked at the bottom, either with or just a notch above Pierce, Buchanan, Grant, and Harding. The others who preceded Wilson fall somewhere in between in an "average" or "adequate" category.

Wilson's high ranking is a bit puzzling in light of his numerous failures and their negative consequences as well as his numerous successes. But consequences do not constitute the only standard involved in rating presidents. In the case of both Wilson and the others, assessments are often based on the values that the assessors bring to their task. For Wilson, whether or not one approves of the Progressive movement, and with it an activist presidency and an activist federal government, is critical in determining how one assesses his domestic record. If one is in favor of this, then the assessment will tend to be very positive. Similarly, whether or not one approves of an activist role for the United States in international affairs is critical in determining how one assesses Wilson's foreign policies. Again, if one favors a major role for the United States, the assessment of Wilson will be very high, both for entry into World War I and for his peacemaking efforts and the ensuing League of Nations. But in each case, the assessment will tend to be lower if one disagrees with the idea of an activist president and federal government, or an activist role for the United States in the world.

Such value judgments play a major role in all presidential ratings. Presidents usually listed as the worst—Franklin Pierce, James Buchanan, Ulysses Grant, Warren Harding, for example—are put in that category for one of two reasons: incompetence or corruption. But those are not the only reasons one could conclude that someone was a terrible president. What about hypocrisy? What about out and out lying? Or what about breaking the law? Finally, what about sheer stupidity? Similarly, those usually placed in the highest category—Washington, Lincoln, Franklin Roosevelt—are put in that category because of the enormous dangers the country faced during their tenures, dangers that they had to deal with: establishing a new government amidst a world war for George Washington; fighting a civil war for Lincoln; and dealing with both the Great Depression and World War II for Franklin Roosevelt. Again, however, should this be the only category for a great presidency? What about political skill in office? What about lack of mistakes? By that standard, I often quip, my choice for the greatest president in U.S. history is William Henry Harrison, primarily because he died before he could do anything wrong (he only served in office 32 days).

Furthermore, use of consequences as a standard requires treating with a grain of salt rankings of recent presidents, for we clearly do not yet know the full consequences of their actions. I received a telephone call from a journalist during the impeachment and trial of Bill Clinton asking me how Clinton's impeachment would look 10 years from now. My reply: That depends on what happens in the next 10 years. By the way, one of my colleagues and friends gave the same reply, but added a quip of his own: Historians don't predict the future, historians predict the past. Historians deal with the past, something that we have tried to emphasize in this course, and that the past is much more complex than it appears to be.

Sometimes the consequences of presidential actions are positive and negative. That is definitely true for Wilson, but he is far from the only president with a mixed record of consequences. James K. Polk, a relatively unknown president, unexpectedly showed up in a 1948 poll in the near-great category primarily because in his one term in office—he said in advance he would only serve a single term—he wanted to accomplish four major tasks, and he did: First, a downward revision of the tariff; next, a sub-Treasury plan to replace the Second National Bank; third, a settlement of the Oregon controversy with Great Britain whereby the United States obtained present-day Oregon and Washington in the Pacific Northwest; and finally, the waging of a successful and short war with Mexico by which the United States secured Texas and obtained both California and the present Southwestern states. But that war with Mexico guaranteed the enmity of Latin America against the "Yankee Colossus" to the North, and the acquisition of California and the Southwest led to a huge conflict over whether or not to allow slavery into these new territories. It thereby upset the sectional peace that had been maintained for so many years by the Missouri Compromise; and, of course, that led to the Civil War.

So should Polk be highly rated for massively expanding the size of this country as well as his other accomplishments, or should he be rated very low—perhaps even as low as Pierce and Buchanan—for the fact that this expansion played a major role in the coming of civil war? Similarly, how should one rate Richard Nixon given, for example, the positive consequences of his establishing relations with Communist China and his achievement of détente with the Soviet Union versus the very negative consequences of the criminal behavior that surrounded Watergate?

One also needs to recognize that presidential polls and ratings are affected by changing American values and perspectives over time. Our changing views on race relations, for example, have deeply affected our views of the causes of the Civil War and of the Reconstruction Era. No longer do we harshly condemn the radical Republicans and their program as was done 75 years ago; consequently, we no longer view Andrew Johnson, the president those Republicans impeached, as positively as we used to. Let me clarify: Johnson has never been in the top category, but in 1948, he was in the 19th position;

recently, he has moved all the way down to 41st place as one of the worst presidents in all of American history.

There is also a complementary tendency to revise our negative assessments of Johnson's successor, Ulysses Grant, who has recently gone up in some recent polls. Andrew Jackson dropped from 6th place in 1948 to 14th place in a more recent poll, probably because of our changing views on just how "democratic" his presidency really was, as well as the negative impact of his destruction of the Second National Bank, an impact that included the Panic and Depression of 1837.

Jumping ahead, in the 20th century, Dwight Eisenhower's rating as president went up rather dramatically by 1982 from where it had been in 1961. Why? There was release of additional documents, his diaries; but equally if not more important were the failures of his three more activist successors—Kennedy, Johnson, and Nixon—as well as belated recognition of Eisenhower's unique, indirect style of leadership.

Furthermore, there is often a sharp difference between the rating of a past president taken by historians and the rating by the general public. Harry Truman, for example, received a much higher rating from historians soon after his presidency ended than he did from the public in general. His successor, Eisenhower, at first received much higher ratings from the public than from the historians, and then the historians shifted. In a 2011 Gallup Poll, Americans agreed with the historians only on Lincoln as one of the top three. Instead of Washington and Franklin Roosevelt as the other two, they put Ronald Reagan and Bill Clinton in that elite group. Apparently, for the public, history consists only of an individual's lifetime.

Furthermore, public views can change with the passage of time as much as historians' views change. In an interesting irony, the public's rating of Harry Truman went way up in the 1970s and the 1980s at about the same time it began to decline amongst many historians. A group of historians began to argue that Truman deserved partial blame for both the Cold War and the Second Great Red Scare known as McCarthyism, even though McCarthyism would be directed against Truman. But, these critics argue, he had started it.

Try to keep all of this in mind as in the next two lectures we reexamine what I consider to be a few of our underrated and misunderstood presidents.

Finally, let us come back to Woodrow Wilson; what about his ratings? They have gone down somewhat since the 1960s; I would argue primarily as a result of our changing views on race relations, women's rights, and civil liberties, and perhaps of the U.N. In 1948, he ranked number 4; in the 1990s, he ranked number 7; and he is a bit lower in the 21st century; but he is still way up there. Is he perhaps still overrated? His achievements are indeed impressive and consequential, but as we have seen, so are his failures by their negative consequences and by many of our contemporary standards. Yet, his supporters ask, could any of his predecessors or contemporaries have done better given the new and enormous 20th-century problems that he faced, both domestically and internationally?

That, of course, is a "what if" question, a counterfactual; and in a sense it's unanswerable, since no one else was president from 1913–1921. But people love to ask, and I often wonder what would have happened if Theodore Roosevelt had won the 1912 election instead of Woodrow Wilson. Whereas Wilson's New Freedom sought to return to a mid-19th century world of competition, Roosevelt's New Nationalism realized that was impossible and his was the first program to address 20th-century realities in terms of business regulation rather than merely trust-busting and social welfare legislation. In foreign affairs, Theodore Roosevelt—at least in regard to his dealings with the great powers—was one of the most successful diplomats in all of U.S. history. He mediated an end to the Russo-Japanese War, for which he won the Nobel Peace Prize, and he secretly mediated an end to the Moroccan crisis that could have easily led to the outbreak of World War I in 1905–1906 (in fact, it almost did lead to the outbreak of war in those years).

Given that record, one must ask if World War I would have even broken out if Roosevelt had won in 1912. Certainly he would have actively tried to prevent it, much more actively than did Wilson who was preoccupied at that date with the death of his first wife. Had Theodore Roosevelt failed to halt the outbreak of war, he probably would have joined the war much earlier than Wilson, and I seriously doubt his record in civil liberties would have been any better than Wilson's; it could very well have been worse. But I also doubt he would have ever attempted to replace the balance of power with collective security; collective security was a concept that over and over again in the 20th and 21st centuries has proven to be unworkable. Given that fact, as well as the New Freedom's harkening back to a past era of competition, was Wilson indeed ahead of his time as his supporters often allege, or in reality, in many ways behind his time?

The Roaring Twenties Reconsidered
Lecture 16

The popular view of the 1920s is that the country was tired of Progressive reforms and overseas crusades. In 1920, it elected a president, Warren Harding, who verbalized this mood with his call for a return to "normalcy." The result would be a supposed return to the business values of the late 19th century and an isolationist foreign policy. But in reality, the 1920s set the stage for contemporary America far more than this decade looked back to the past.

An Economic Revolution

- Underlying all the changes that emerged in the 1920s is the economic revolution that took place at this time. This revolution was based on the continued consolidation and growing efficiency of business via "scientific management," as explained by Frederick W. Taylor and known as Taylorism. With this movement came the rise of a new class of business managers and an explosion in productivity.

- On the surface, the increase in per capita output and the emergence of giant national chains, such as A&P, the Woolworth Company, and Bank of America, may seem like a continuation of trends from the 1890s. But this business growth and concentration was accompanied by a major shift in American industry during this decade, from heavy industry to the production of new and cheap consumer items.

- Equally critical to the new economy was the automobile. Thanks to assembly-line techniques and scientific management, Henry Ford cut the price of automobiles by more than two-thirds and made them available to the middle and lower classes.
  - Ford paid his own workers the unheard-of sum of $5 a day so that they could buy the cars they made—in return for a ban on unions.

- Some consider this the start of welfare capitalism in industry to combat unionization, with the creation of pension funds, profit-sharing plans, and so on. This was hardly a return to late-19th-century conditions!

- As a result of Ford's innovations, auto production jumped from 4,000 in 1900 to 4.8 million in 1929, with auto ownership jumping from 8 to 23 million.

- Automobile production had a ripple effect on the entire economy, especially in such industries as steel, rubber, glass, and oil but also indirectly in the production of concrete, highway construction, and the emergence of roadside restaurants, gas stations, and motels.

- Along with this economic revolution came a phenomenal growth in advertising to convince people to buy cheap consumer products and automobiles.
  - Advertising was not new, but there was a massive expansion of the industry, along with a major shift, from informing the public of a product's existence to playing on psychological desires and needs, such as sex, acceptance, prestige, and popularity.

  - This advertising mania becomes known as "boosterism," a phenomenon epitomized by Bruce Barton's best-selling 1925 book, *The Man Nobody Knows*, which portrayed Jesus as the greatest advertising executive and businessman in history.

- The era also witnessed the rise of installment buying as a way for the middle and lower classes to afford all these new items.

A Cultural Revolution

- This economic boom would both feed and be fed by the continuing urbanization of the United States. In the 1920s, urban dwellers outnumbered rural dwellers for the first time. Helping to spread the new urban culture was the mass media that emerged during this era, most notably radio and motion pictures. These would also create new national heroes.

- Radio contributed to the rise of spectator sports as a big business, both professional and collegiate. Especially noteworthy in the professional realm was baseball, which became the national pastime and made heroes of Babe Ruth and other players.

- With the advent of sound, the movie industry exploded in the 1920s, with 100 million out of a population of 120 million attending at least one movie each week. Movies also played a major role in the expansion of American culture overseas and created their own national heroes in movie stars.

Government Actions in the 1920s

- The economic boom was fed by government assistance and other moves to help business and, thereby, create prosperity for all. As emphasized in a previous lecture, this was no "return" to a 19th-century laissez-faire approach, nor were the government's efforts to expand prosperity on a global scale isolationist.

- The 1920s witnessed a return to Republican dominance in national politics and the election of what are usually considered three highly conservative presidents whose administrations supposedly hearken back to the late 19th century: Warren Harding, Calvin Coolidge, and Herbert Hoover.

- Each of these administrations also retains a stigma in historical memory: Harding's for corruption, Coolidge's for not heeding warning signs about the state of the economy, and Hoover's for failure to act in the ensuing economic collapse. In reality, these reputations are not fully deserved, and they distort the records of all three.

- All three administrations believed in using the World War I experiences in government-business cooperation to foster even greater cooperation (rather than regulation) as a means to greater growth, efficiency, prosperity, and peace. Positive action in this regard included lowering taxes, raising protective tariffs, and providing federal aid for state roads and a plan for a national highway system.

- Government itself became more efficient via the Budget and Accounting Act, which established a director of the budget and enabled the executive to plan and produce a unified, coherent national budget.

- Progressivism was not dead in the 1920s either: Thirty-four states passed worker's compensation laws, and women obtained the right to vote in this decade. At the same time, the immigration restriction supported by Progressives achieved its most notable success with the passage of the National Origins Act of 1924, and scientific racism spread. The 1920s was also the decade of continued government assaults on American and immigrant Leftists, known as the first great Red Scare.

- Prohibition was also a Progressive reform. The Eighteenth Amendment to the Constitution passed in 1919, along with the

Prohibition represents just one of many Progressive reforms carried over into the 1920s.

Volstead Act, and went into effect the following year—with such well-known consequences as the rise of bootleg whiskey and organized crime.

- Hoover, who was a key figure before his own presidency as Harding's and Coolidge's secretary of commerce, had been a famous Wilsonian Progressive and, in many ways, remained one.
  - In the 1920s, Hoover actively used his commerce department to help American corporations find new and expanded overseas markets. Along with the state department, the commerce department also promoted overseas investment.

  - Most notable in this regard was the Dawes Plan, whereby the United States loaned money to Germany and negotiated a linked reparations repayment schedule with France and Britain, ending a major European crisis. This was hardly isolationism, despite the continued refusal of the United States to join the League of Nations.

- Similarly, the state department, under secretaries Charles Evans Hughes and Frank B. Kellogg, was active in promoting and signing a series of treaties to help preserve the peace and prosperity of the era. These included naval arms limitation agreements and the 1928 Kellogg-Briand Pact, outlawing war as an instrument of national policy.

Culture Clashes
- The 1920s saw major clashes between the newly emerging national urban culture and traditional American rural culture.
  - At its 1924 national convention, for example, the Democratic Party split badly between its northern urban and southern rural wings over who to nominate and such issues as Prohibition and condemnation of the revived Ku Klux Klan.

  - The conflict over the presidential candidate, pitting New York's "wet" Governor Al Smith against the "dry" Protestant William McAdoo, left the convention deadlocked for an incredible 102 ballots before a lackluster compromise candidate could be nominated on the 103rd.

- Equally if not more telling is the famous Scopes trial in Dayton, Tennessee, where the state had outlawed the teaching of evolution.
  o High school biology teacher John Scopes challenged the law, was arrested, and was convicted at the trial.

  o But Scopes was quickly forgotten in the duel that emerged between William Jennings Bryan, who stood as an expert Bible witness for the prosecution, and the prominent lawyer for the defense, Clarence Darrow. Darrow humiliated Bryan and his cause by mocking his literal interpretation of creation, but at least as telling was the rural-urban enmity that surfaced during the trial.

A Multifaceted Era
- Historians now recognize the 1920s as much more complex and multifaceted than the traditional popular image of the era.

- It was conservative in many ways, as in the passing of the 1921 Revenue Act that eliminated an excess-profits tax and dramatically lowered the income tax rate on the wealthy. But it can also be seen as both a continuation of portions of the Progressive era and the birth of the modern American economy and urban culture.

- We also see an active foreign policy in this era—despite the American refusal to join the League of Nations—befitting a nation with the largest economy in the world. At the same time, we see the continued development of a government-business partnership, both domestically and in foreign affairs, designed to achieve the twin goals of peace and prosperity.

- In most areas, the result was an incredibly peaceful and prosperous United States and world—probably the most peaceful and prosperous decade of the 20th century and the one in which the United States was more secure than in any other decade of the

20th century. But all of this depended on the continued health and growth of the American economy, which would collapse in late 1929, transforming both the United States and the world.

Suggested Reading

Allen, *Only Yesterday.*

Heilbroner, *The Worldly Philosophers.*

Wilson, *Herbert Hoover.*

Questions to Consider

1. Why did the 1920s gain a reputation for "normalcy" and conservatism, and what alternative words better describe the decade?

2. What ideas and policies from the 1920s do we still live with today?

The Roaring Twenties Reconsidered
Lecture 16—Transcript

The standard, popular view of the 1920s is that the country was tired of Progressive reforms and overseas crusades. It elected in 1920 a president, Warren G. Harding, who verbalized its desire for a return to the pre-Progressive era with his call for a return to "normalcy." The result would be a supposed return to the business values of the late 19th century as epitomized by President Calvin Coolidge's remark that "the chief business of Americans is business." Coolidge's becoming president on Harding's unexpected death in 1923 also epitomized the supposed return to the social values of the 19th century. He was sworn in by his father, a notary public, by kerosene lamplight at the family home in Plymouth Notch, Vermont, where he was visiting. This was supposedly also a decade of a return to an isolationist foreign policy as well as a focus on conformity, as epitomized in the popular novels of Sinclair Lewis. It was also a time period when Americans just wanted to have a good time; all of which would disgust the intellectuals and lead them to desert the United States for Paris as the "lost generation."

But in reality, the 1920s were far more complex than that, and more revolutionary. Indeed, in many ways, the 20s continued what had begun during the Progressive Era and set the stage for contemporary America far more than they looked back to any past era. Underlying all the changes of the 20s was the economic revolution that took place during the 1920s. That revolution was based on continued consolidation and the growing efficiency of business via "scientific management." This had been explained by Frederick W. Taylor and indeed was known as "Taylorism." With this came the rise of a new class of business managers, and an explosion in productivity as well as business consolidation. Per capita output went up 40 percent; production 46 percent. Giant national chains emerged in numerous fields, including food (A&P), clothes (Woolworth's), and banking (Bank of America). By 1930, 200 corporations owned 50 percent of the nation's corporate wealth.

What I just described may seem on the surface like a continuation of the trends from the 1890s; but in reality it is not, for this business growth and concentration was accompanied by a major shift in American industry during the 1920s: a shift from heavy industry to the production of new and cheap consumer items. This was largely made possible by the previously-cited earlier work of Thomas Edison and others with electricity generation in cities, both for factories and for urban homes. By the 1920s, that had developed sufficiently to make possible the development, sale, and use of a host of new electrical devices in the home: the vacuum cleaner, the toaster, the clothes washer, the refrigerator; the "mechanization of housework" was taking place, in the words of one historian.

Equally critical to the new economy was the automobile. The automobile was not a new invention in the 1920s; but by the 20s, Henry Ford had made it a consumer item available to the middle and lower classes by using assembly line techniques and scientific management to cut the price of an automobile by more than two-thirds: from $950 to $290. That made it affordable to most, including Ford's own workers, whom he paid the then-unheard-of sum of $5 a day so that they could buy the cars that they made; in return, however, he issued a total ban on unions, and would not tolerate them. Some consider what Ford did the start of what would be known eventually as0 "welfare capitalism" in industry, something that was put into effect to combat unionization; and you would have eventually the creation of pension funds, profit-sharing plans, etc. I would hardly call that a return to the conditions for workers of the late 19th century. As a result of Ford's innovations, automobile production skyrocketed from 4,000 in 1900 to 4.8 million in 1929. Auto ownership jumped from 8 million to 23 million.

Like electricity, the automobile would have a "ripple effect" on the entire economy, especially in such industries as steel, rubber, glass, oil, and electronics that were all involved in making cars. But there was also an indirect impact: highway constructions, concrete, roadside restaurants, gas stations, and the new "motor hotels," or motels. The automobile became the focal point of the entire economy, and it began to dramatically alter numerous aspects of American life, including—some have argued—sexual mores for youth. The back seat of the automobile, as one put it, became an American institution.

Along with this economic revolution came a phenomenal growth in advertising to convince people to buy all the cheap new consumer products that were now available, as well as the automobile. Again, advertising was not new, but there was a massive expansion of the industry along with a major shift from trying to inform the public of a product's existence and what it supposedly could do—truth in advertising was a flexible term at this time—but a shift from that to playing on psychological desires and needs such as acceptance, prestige, sex, and popularity. General Motors, for example, sought to compete with Ford by offering different brands of cars for different classes and different colors as opposed to Ford's single brand and single color. When asked about colors, Ford's crack was that his customers could buy a Ford in any color, as long as it was black.

This advertising mania became known as "Boosterism," and it was epitomized by Bruce Barton's bestselling 1925 book, *The Man Nobody Knows*. In it, Barton portrayed Jesus Christ as the greatest advertising executive and businessman in history. "He thought of his life as business," Barton wrote. "Every advertising man ought to study the parables of Jesus, schooling himself in their language and learning … [the] elements of their power." Why? Because, Barton wrote, he "picked up 12 men from the bottom ranks of business and forged them into an organization that conquered the world."

The 1920s also witnessed the rise of installment buying as a way the middle and lower classes could afford all these new items. The resulting economic boom would both feed and be fed by the continuing urbanization of the country. Indeed, it was in this decade that urban dwellers—and at this point, "urban" was defined as a city or town of 2,500 or more—came to outnumber rural dwellers. That would mean new and expanded markets for goods, and greater industrial concentration that was able to produce more, as well as a new and national urban culture that we still live with today. Helping to spread that new national urban culture would be the new mass media that emerged during this era, most notably radio and motion pictures. They would also create new national heroes.

Radio would aid in the rise of spectator sports as a big business, both professional and collegiate. Especially noteworthy in the professional realm is baseball, which had a major scandal in 1919—the Black Sox Scandal—but after the cleanup of that scandal, baseball became the national pastime, with such national heroes such as Babe Ruth. That is no accident: Baseball is a game made for radio, as I discovered a few years ago. Consequently, I now listen more frequently to baseball games than I watch them.

As for movies, aided by the advent of sound, the industry would explode in the 1920s, with 100 million people out of a total population of 120 million attending at least one movie each week; that's compared to 60 million who would go to church each week. The movies would also be shown overseas and they would play a major role in the expansion of American culture overseas and the overseas image of the United States. Movies, as with sports, would create their own national heroes, movie stars; one—if I can pronounce his name correctly—Rodolfo Alfonzo Rafaelo Pierre Filibert Guglielmi di Valentina d'Antognolla, better known, of course, as Rudolph Valentino, whose death at age 31 led to a mass hysteria at his funeral.

But the ultimate hero of the 1920s was Charles Lindbergh for his 33-hour solo flight across the Atlantic Ocean. Contrary to common belief, Lindbergh was not the first to fly across the Atlantic; it had been done in 1919 on a flight from Newfoundland to Ireland. Yet it is Lindbergh who became the hero, the ultimate symbol of the era, as man still the individual master of all these new machines.

Also contrary to popular belief, the economic boom did not occur in all areas of the economy. Agriculture, for example, suffered enormously during this decade as wartime overseas demand ceased and European agriculture recovered from World War I. The economic boom that did occur would also be fed by government assistance and other moves to help business and thereby create prosperity for all. Once again, as emphasized in a previous lecture, there was no return to a 19th-century laissez-faire attitude. The government would also help businesses to find new overseas markets during this time period to keep the prosperity going and to expand it globally as a way to preserve international peace. That was anything but "isolationist."

Let us take a look now at government actions—both domestic and overseas—during this era. The 1920s would witness a return to Republican dominance in national politics as the majority party; the Republicans had been the majority party really since William McKinley's election and the realignment of 1896. The only time they did not hold the White House and control the government was during the presidency of Woodrow Wilson; and Wilson, you will remember, won the first time with a minority of the vote because the Republican Party split. What you now got was a return to Republican majority rule, overseen by three presidents who are usually considered highly conservative; presidents whose administrations supposedly harkened back to the late 19th century: Warren G. Harding, Calvin Coolidge, and Herbert Hoover.

Each of these administrations also retains a stigma in historical memory: Harding's for corruption, Coolidge's for not heeding warning signs about the state of the economy, and Hoover's for failure to act in the ensuing economic collapse. But in reality these reputations are not fully deserved, and they distort the records of all three presidents. All three administrations believed in using the World War I experiences in government-business cooperation to foster even greater cooperation. That cooperation was admittedly to be an alternative to regulation; but it was still a very, very active role for the government. The aims: greater growth, greater efficiency, greater prosperity, and international peace on the grounds that a prosperous world would be a peaceful world and a peaceful world enabled you to have more prosperity.

Positive government action in this regard would include not only lower taxes, but also the very high Fordney McCumber Tariff and a Federal Highway Act and Bureau of Public Roads to provide federal aid for state roads and a plan for a national highway system now that you had all of these automobiles. Government itself would become more efficient during this time via the creation of the Budget and Accounting Act that established a Director of the Budget. That enabled the Executive Branch of government to plan and produce for the first time a unified, coherent national budget.

Progressivism was not dead, either. To cite but a few of the many examples of Progressivism in the 1920s: 34 states out of 48 would pass workmen's compensation laws during this time period. In the 1924 presidential election, a newly reformed Progressive Third Party nominated Wisconsin Progressive Robert La Follette for president; La Follette obtained 16 percent of the popular vote. Women would obtain the right to vote nationally, which had been a Progressive reform movement, and they did so with the passage of the

19th Amendment in 1920. Also on a national level, immigration restriction that had been championed by the Progressives achieved its most notable success with the passage in 1924 of the National Origins Act. That act totally excluded Asians and established very severe quotas on immigration that would henceforth be allowed from Eastern and Southern Europe; approximately two percent of the number of such people in the United States in 1890, which was before the great wave from Eastern and Southern Europe really peaked. This law would essentially stay in effect until the 1960s.

One might argue that Progressivism also continued via the related and continued, if not expanded, popularity of scientific racism, which in turn fed a continuation and expansion of the religious and racial intolerance that we had seen in the last years of the Progressive Era. This was the decade of Henry Ford's previously quoted anti-Semitic tracts. It was also the decade of the rise of a new Ku Klux Klan, which had somewhere between 3 and 5 million members, many of them now in the North as well as the South. This new, expanded Klan did not limit itself to attacks on blacks; it now also attacked Catholics, Jews, and immigrants. Forty thousand Klansmen would march in Washington in 1925. The continued "Great Migration" of Southern blacks into Northern cities would feed this emergence of the Klan as a Northern as well as a Southern phenomenon.

This was also the decade of continued government assaults on the American Left as well as Leftist immigrants, known from the Progressive Era as the first great "Red Scare." It had begun during World War I; it had continued immediately after the war with the notorious Palmer Raids of 1919–1920, engineered by President Wilson's Attorney General A. Mitchell Palmer. During those raids, more than 4,000 people were illegally arrested and detained for their political beliefs; 249 alien radicals were deported. This also continued throughout the 1920s, and was symbolized for many by the arrest, conviction, and execution in 1927 in Massachusetts of Nicola Sacco and Bartolomeo Vanzetti, two Italian immigrants and anarchists. They were charged with armed robbery and murder. Their numerous supporters, both in the United States and around the world, argued that they had not committed the crimes and that their guilt had not been proven at their trial. Instead, these people argued, Sacco and Vanzetti had been found guilty and had been executed for what they were: immigrants and radicals.

The 1920s was also the decade of Prohibition, another Progressive reform. The 18th amendment to the Constitution passed in 1919, and along with the Volstead Act—which defined anything as alcoholic that had one-half of one percent alcohol—went into effect in the following year, with such well-known consequences as the rise of bootleg whiskey and organized crime. But contrary to popular belief, Prohibition did lead to a significant decrease in alcohol consumption; it went down to one-third of the pre-World War I level and the lowest level in American history. It also led to the total demise of the saloon, which had been a key target of the temperance movement.

Interestingly, organized crime became a way for many in the new immigrant groups from Southern and Eastern Europe to rise out of poverty and for their families to enter the middle class and fulfill the American Dream as well as attain respectability and acceptance. Organized crime may have also been in one sense the only truly laissez-faire business at the time: The government did nothing to aid it, and some would argue the government did close to nothing to suppress it.

One other aspect of Progressivism in the 1920s needs to be mentioned here. Herbert Hoover, who was a key figure before his own presidency as Harding's and Coolidge's Secretary of Commerce, had been a famous Wilsonian Progressive; and as we will see, in many ways he remained one. He was also one of the great heroes of this era; an engineer and an efficiency expert who in World War I had used his expertise for the humanitarian goal of feeding the starving populations of Belgium and other European countries. In the 1920s, Hoover would actively use his Commerce Department to help American corporations find new and expanded overseas markets. Along with the State Department, the Commerce Department would also promote overseas investment.

One of the most notable such investments—and it was actually a lot more than an investment—was the Dawes Plan. In the Dawes Plan, the United States loaned private money to Germany and negotiated a linked reparations repayment schedule between German, France, and Britain. That ended a major European crisis over reparations payments. That, I would argue, was hardly isolationism, despite the continued American refusal to join the League of Nations. Similarly, the State Department under Secretaries of

State under Charles Evans Hughes and Frank B. Kellogg would be quite active in promoting and signing a series of treaties to help preserve the peace and prosperity of the era: You had naval arms limitation agreements, such as the 1921–1922 Washington Treaties, which included the four, five, and nine Power Pacts limiting the size of the world's navies and maintaining both the status quo in the Pacific and the open door for China. You also had the 1930 London Naval Arms Limitation Treaty, and the 1928 Kellogg-Briand Pact outlawing war as an instrument of national policy. Again, all of this was hardly isolationism.

The era would also witness major clashes between the newly emerging national urban culture and the traditional American rural culture. In its 1924 National Convention, for example, the Democratic Party would split so badly between its Northern urban and Southern rural wings over who to nominate, and over such issues as Prohibition and the Ku Klux Klan, as to virtually commit political suicide. Condemnation of the Klan failed to pass by one vote, 543–542. The conflict over the presidential candidate pitted New York's "wet" Governor Al Smith—a Catholic who opposed Prohibition—against the "dry" Protestant William McAdoo, who supported Prohibition. It left the convention deadlocked for an incredible 102 ballots before a lackluster compromise candidate, New York corporation lawyer John W. Davis, could be nominated on the 103rd ballot.

Equally if not more telling was the famous Scopes Trial in Dayton, Tennessee where the state had outlawed the teaching of evolution. High school biology teacher John Scopes challenged the law and was arrested. He would be convicted at the trial; but that was really not the main attraction. This was the first trial ever broadcast over radio, and the center of attention was the duel that emerged between William Jennings Bryan, who stood forth as an expert Bible witness for the prosecution, and the prominent lawyer for the defense Clarence Darrow. It was a duel in which Darrow humiliated Bryan and his cause by mocking Bryan's literal interpretation of creation, pointing out that if Joshua had indeed made the sun stand still, the Earth would have turned into a molten mess. He also forced Bryan to modify his literal interpretation by admitting that creation might have lasted millions of years rather than six days.

But at least as telling as all of that was a rural-urban exchange that took place during Darrow's interrogation of Bryan, when the courtroom audience applauded Bryan after he had made a statement. Darrow acidly commented, "Great applause from the bleachers." "From those you call the yokels," Bryan mockingly shot back. "That is the ignorance of Tennessee, the bigotry. … Those are the people who you insult." "You insult," Darrow responded, "every man of science and learning in the world because he does not believe in your fool religion!" The jury found Scopes guilty in less than 10 minutes, but his cause had won. Bryan was humiliated, and he died very soon after the trial.

Historians recognize the 1920s as much more complex and multifaceted than the traditional popular image of the era. It was conservative in many ways—the elimination of numerous taxes on the wealthy; the slashing of the federal budget—but in many ways we see in the 1920s both a continuation of portions of the Progressive Era and the birth of the modern American economy and urban culture. We also see a very active foreign policy, despite the refusal to join the League of Nations; and act of foreign policy befitting a nation with the largest economy in the world.

We also see the continued development of a government-business partnership, both domestically and in foreign affairs, designed to achieve the twin goals of peace and prosperity. In most areas, the result was an incredibly peaceful and prosperous United States and world; indeed, this was probably the most peaceful and prosperous decade of the 20th century and the one in which the United States was more secure than in any other decade of the 20th century despite the very low budgets and size for the armed forces.

But all of this depended on the continued health and growth of the American economy, a health and growth that collapsed in late 1929. That collapse would transform the United States and the world.

Hoover and the Great Depression Revisited
Lecture 17

Herbert Hoover is generally considered an abject failure as president for his refusal to deal aggressively with the Great Depression, yet he did more than any previous president to combat serious economic decline. In fact, he began many programs that would later be associated with the New Deal of Franklin Roosevelt, the man whose programs he would sharply attack. This lecture will take another look at Hoover to try to explain the reasons for the discrepancy between his record and his reputation.

Hoover's Pre-Presidential Career

- Herbert Hoover started his career as a mining engineer and developed a reputation as an effective and efficient administrator and humanitarian. He was considered to be a Progressive with great political possibilities—and both parties courted him. He chose to be a Republican and was a major figure in the administrations of Harding and Coolidge as secretary of commerce.

- In this position, Hoover exemplified the continued Progressivism and organizational revolution of the 1920s. He personified the new managers and social engineers who worshiped efficiency and business-government cooperation. In 1928, he optimistically predicted that the nation would soon see an end to poverty.

- Hoover easily defeated his Democratic opponent, Al Smith, in the 1928 election. But his prediction about ending poverty proved to be anything but accurate as the stock market, the American economy, and the global economy all collapsed from 1929 to 1932.

Causes of the Great Depression

- As numerous historians have noted, a mass production society requires mass consumption, and although the United States had become a consumer society by the late 1920s, its consumption was not adequate.

    o   One reason for underconsumption was the fact that the great prosperity of the 1920s was not shared by all; 40 to 60 percent of the population lived below the marginal subsistence level.

    o   Compounding this problem was an unsound corporate structure in which 200 of the 400,000 corporations in the nation owned 43 percent of the national wealth. That led to price rigidity despite a lack of consumer purchasing power and a "pyramid" structure that could collapse entirely via a chain reaction.

- The banking structure was equally unsound, with thousands of local, unstable, and unregulated banks. The Federal Reserve System, still in its infancy, was underutilized and had little or no control over many of these banks. The Fed's 1927 policies actually played a role in bringing about the collapse, and in the wake of the collapse, it made the situation worse by pursuing adverse policies.

- All of this was aggravated by unprecedented speculation in the stock market because of the lack of investment opportunities and the belief that the market would always go up.

- The international economic and financial structure was equally unstable as a result of World War I and its aftermath. Both the United States and other industrialized nations had instituted higher tariffs in the 1920s, but that led to a decline in international trade—which led to more economic strains, the withdrawal of foreign funds from the United States, and eventually, the withdrawal of U.S. funds from overseas.

- Installment buying and the creation of artificial demand via advertising masked these problems, postponing the day of reckoning and worsening the situation.

The Stock Market Boom
- Why did the stock market continue to boom with the economy already in serious trouble by 1928?

- With consumer demand saturated, corporate profits from the 1920s went into stock speculation rather than plant and machinery. And because there was less corporate demand for expansion loans, banks loaned more money for stock purchases.

- Much of this money went not into direct stock purchases but into call loans—loans that stock brokers make to customers at a high interest rate to enable customers to buy stock on margin (putting down only a percentage of the purchase price). This is actually a form of installment buying applied to the stock market.

- The Federal Reserve made matters worse by lowering the rediscount rate at which banks could borrow in 1927. With such easy credit, banks borrowed from the Fed at a low 3.5 percent rate and then reloaned the money to the call market for 10 percent or higher.

- The entire stock market boom had no economic foundation on which to rest; it was a bubble fueled by the belief that the market would go up forever, with previous shocks dismissed since they had stopped.

The Results of the Crash

- Panic in the market hit full blast during the last week of October 1929. Stocks would lose one-third of their value in three months. The crash didn't cause the Depression, but it made the situation substantially worse.

- The loss of stock money wiped out purchasing power and led to bank failures. No loans were available, and industries were forced to cut back on production, which meant layoffs, lower wages, and even less purchasing power.

- The banking system as a whole began to collapse in late 1930, with a total of 1,352 banks failing by the end of the year. That led to runs on other banks, requiring them to call in loans and sell assets to meet those runs. That, in turn, drove down the value of other assets and further contracted the money supply and tightened credit.

- In 1931, the European financial structure began to collapse, a result of the drying up of U.S. loans, which led to the drying up of German reparations to World War I Allies that had been linked to those loans.

- At first, the Federal Reserve did nothing to save the banks. Eventually, it raised the rediscount rate to stop the outflow of gold, which is exactly the opposite of what it should have done.

Library of Congress, Prints and Photographs Division.

Herbert Hoover, widely criticized for his failure to take action in the face of the Great Depression, actually did more than previous presidents had to combat economic decline.

Hoover Steps In

- Earlier financial collapses and economic depressions in U.S. history had been viewed as a normal part of the business cycle and part of the market's self-correcting mechanism via Adam Smith's "invisible hand." The traditional response of the government had been to do nothing and let the market correct itself, but Hoover did not accept this logic.

- Hoover came up with a program that reflected his belief in the so-called "associational society"—voluntary groups for rational, scientific planning, with government to stimulate and encourage such groups but not dictate to them. Hoover held a series of conferences with business and labor leaders to reach voluntary agreements to keep production and wages up.

- For agriculture, he used the just-passed Agricultural Marketing Act of 1929, establishing the Federal Farm Board, to promote agricultural cooperatives and stabilization corporations that agreed to limit production (with limited ability to buy surplus).

- Hoover also supported the Smoot-Hawley Tariff—the highest tariff in U.S. history—to eliminate external competition for agriculture, encourage business, and restore confidence.

- He agreed to a modest public works program to provide some jobs and encouraged state and local public works projects via the 1932 Emergency Relief and Construction Act.

- He supported voluntary programs to provide loans to endangered financial institutions, with sound banks providing funds to banks in trouble.

- When these programs failed to end the Depression, Hoover went even further, taking direct government action that marked a shift from his previous insistence on volunteerism. Measures included the Glass-Steagall Act (to address frozen assets), the Federal Home Loan Bank Act, and the institution of the Reconstruction Finance Corporation.

Hoover's Reputation

- Given these efforts, why does Hoover have such a "do-nothing" reputation? Part of the explanation can be found in Democratic campaign propaganda of the 1930s, and part of it is the fact that later New Deal measures that went further than Hoover made his efforts appear nearly nonexistent in comparison. In this regard, future events distort our understanding of what Hoover did during his presidency.

- Equally important was Hoover's own behavior from 1929 to 1932. Rather than a deeply respected efficiency expert, as he had seemed in good times, Hoover came across as cold during the Depression. He also consistently made optimistic statements that were at odds with reality, believing that he needed to restore confidence in what was basically a sound system.

- It's important to realize that Hoover had a tremendous fear of what would happen if government began to dictate policy. For this reason, he stuck with a voluntary, cooperative approach (at least at first), which failed because the agreements made could not be kept.

- In addition, and linked to this fear of the consequences of having the government dictate policy, Hoover adamantly refused to supply federal relief, believing it would destroy individual initiative and the American system. In this refusal, the great humanitarian came to be perceived as inhuman.

- To make matters worse, Hoover refused to take additional measures to provide federal aid to business. He rejected the so-called Swope Plan for an operation similar to what would become the New Deal's National Recovery Administration because of his fear of government control.

- If anything, Hoover became even more ideologically and personally rigid as a result of being forced into the drastic measures of 1931–1932. That rigidity can be seen in his continued support of Prohibition and his defense of the U.S. Army's attack on the marchers of the Bonus Army—World War I veterans who had come to Washington to demand early payment of the bonus granted them in the 1920s.

Perceptions Distorted by Future Events
- Our understanding of Herbert Hoover and his policies has been seriously distorted by a number of factors beyond the failure of his programs: the propaganda of his political opponents, later government measures that made his efforts appear almost nonexistent, and his own later attacks on those measures. In this regard, future events distorted our perceptions of what Hoover did from 1929–1933 and who he was.

- Equally important was Hoover's own behavior, most notably his ideological rigidity, which made him appear cold, heartless, and willing to save banks and big business but not the people.

- All of Hoover's intelligence, training, and experiences were, if anything, counterproductive. He is not alone in having had such an experience as president. Indeed, it is interesting to note that two of the brightest men elected president in the 20th century—both of whom were failures as presidents and were not reelected—were engineers: Hoover and Jimmy Carter. Intelligence and ability in the areas of engineering and administration, it appears, may not translate into success in the political realm.

Suggested Reading

Heilbroner, *The Worldly Philosophers*.

Wilson, *Herbert Hoover*.

Questions to Consider

1. How does the contemporary economic situation compare with what took place during the Great Depression? What similarities and differences do you note?

2. Given Hoover's failure as president despite his proven abilities, what personal characteristics are needed for success in the presidency?

Hoover and the Great Depression Revisited
Lecture 17—Transcript

Herbert Hoover is generally considered an abject failure as president for his refusal to deal aggressively with the Great Depression. In the process, he is often classed with his two Republican predecessors as a Conservative who did not believe that government should play a major role in the economy, or in anything else for that matter. As Franklin D. Roosevelt famously asserted in the 1936 presidential campaign, for 12 years the nation had been afflicted with "hear nothing, see-nothing, do-nothing government. The Nation looked to Government, but Government looked away." The Republican philosophy, Roosevelt sarcastically continued, was that Government was best that was "most indifferent."

Yet Hoover had previously been known as a major and highly successful Progressive figure; the "forgotten progressive" in the words of one of his biographers. Furthermore, he did more than any previous president to combat serious economic depression, and in doing so he began many programs that would later be associated with Franklin D. Roosevelt's New Deal; Roosevelt, the man who defeated him in the 1932 election and whose programs Hoover would sharply attack.

This lecture will take another look at Hoover and try to explain the reasons for this discrepancy between his record and his reputation.

Who was Herbert Hoover? He was a mining engineer who developed an extraordinary reputation as an effective and efficient administrator and humanitarian. During World War I, he organized Belgian food relief. He then served as head of the U.S. Food Administration once the United States entered the war. After the war, he accompanied Woodrow Wilson to Paris and organized major food relief programs for the peoples of Central and Eastern Europe. Throughout this time, he was considered a Progressive with great political possibilities; both parties courted him. He chose to be a Republican—he had been a Theodore Roosevelt Bull Moose supporter in 1912 before he joined the Wilson administration—and he was, as previously noted, a major figure in the administrations of Harding and Coolidge as Secretary of Commerce.

Again as noted in the last lecture, the 1920s were in some ways a continuation rather than a rejection of Progressivism. Hoover as Commerce Secretary became one of the great symbols of this; in many ways the perfect symbol of the organizational revolution of the 1920s. He was the personification of the new managers, specialists, and social engineers who worshipped efficiency and business-government cooperation; the men who were reorganizing American society. He also was optimistically predicting continued and never-ending prosperity. Indeed, in the 1928 election, Hoover famously stated that:

> We in America today are nearer to the final triumph over poverty than ever before in the history of any land. The poor house is vanishing from among us. We have not yet reached the goal, but given the chance to go forward with the policies of the last eight years, we shall very soon with the help of God be in sight of the day when poverty will be banished from this nation.

Hoover easily defeated his Democratic opponent Al Smith of New York in the 1928 election; but his prediction about ending poverty, of course, proved to be anything but accurate, as the stock market, the American economy, and the global economy all collapsed during his presidency.

The causes of this financial and economic collapse were numerous, complex, and still being debated; but in summary, the major factors were as follows: First, as numerous historians have noted, a mass production society required mass consumption; and while the United States had become a consumer society, its consumption was not adequate. This was true in both agriculture and industry, and it had been for many years. Again, as noted in the last lecture, agriculture was depressed throughout the 1920s. So were the coal and textile industries; and increased industrial mechanization had already led to serious unemployment. Whether you define the issue as overproduction or under-consumption, the result was a very serious economic problem.

One major reason was maldistribution of wealth. The great prosperity of the 1920s was not shared by all; indeed, anywhere from 40–60 percent of the population lived below the marginal subsistence level, then $2,000 per year. That translated into very limited purchasing power. Compounding this problem was an unsound corporate structure in which 200 out of 400,000 corporations owned 43 percent of the national wealth. That led to price rigidity despite lack of consumer purchasing power and a "pyramid" structure that could collapse entirely via a chain reaction.

The banking structure was equally unsound; it had been since the days of Andrew Jackson, with thousands of local, unsound, and unregulated banks. What about the Federal Reserve System? It was still in its infancy; it had only been established in 1914. It was still underutilized, and it had little or no control at this time over many banks. It did nothing to prevent an eventual collapse; in fact, as we will see, its 1927 policies played a role in that collapse. When it did finally act, the Fed pursued policies that in retrospect were the reverse of the policies it should have pursued. It thus made the problems worse. All of this was aggravated by unprecedented speculation in the stock market because of the lack of investment opportunities and because of the belief that the market would always go up.

The international economic and financial structure was equally unstable due to World War I and its aftermath. Both the United States and other industrialized nations had responded in the 1920s with higher tariffs; but higher tariffs in turn led to a decline in international trade. That led to more economic strains, the withdrawal of foreign funds from the United States, and eventually the withdrawal of U.S. funds from overseas. Installment buying and the creation of artificial demand via advertising only masked these problems; and in doing so, and thereby postponing the day of reckoning, installment buying and advertising made the situation worse.

While the economy was thus already in serious trouble by 1928, the stock market continued to boom. Obvious question: Why? With consumer demand saturated, corporate profits from the 1920s went into stock speculation rather than more plant and machinery. Since there was less corporate demand for loans for expansion, banks loaned more money for stock purchases. Much of this went not into direct stock purchases, but into call loans that stockbrokers made to customers at a high interest rate so as to enable people to buy stock on margin; to put down only a percentage of the money that was needed to purchase the stock. If you stop and think about it, it was actually a form of installment buying as applied to the stock market. Corporations did this, too; and you only needed anywhere from 10–50 percent down in this system.

People with money but already saturated with consumer goods and people without money who wanted to get in on the action could do so via this easy credit system; and the stock that you purchased on margin could then be used as collateral for more loans for more margin purchases on the market. For example, you could start off with $100, buy stock that costs $1,000; as that stock went up, sell it and use the proceeds to just keep on building this way. The Federal Reserve made matters worse by lowering the rediscount rate at which banks could borrow in 1927. With easy credit, the banks borrowed from the Fed at the 3.5 percent interest rate, but then re-lent the money they had borrowed to the call market for a 10 percent interest rate or higher.

This entire boom had utterly no economic foundation on which to rest. It was a speculative mania, a bubble, fueled by the belief that the market would go up forever. Previous shocks were dismissed since they had been temporary. As the historian David Kennedy has noted:

> Mere money was not at the root of the evil soon to befall Wall Street; men were—men and women whose lust for the fast buck had loosed all restraints of financial prudence or even common sense.

Full panic hit during the last week of October, first Black Thursday and then the incredible October 29. Stocks would lose one-third of their value in three months. Indeed, between September 3 and November 13, 1929, GE stock fell from approximately 396 to 168; General Motors from 72 ¾ to 36; Montgomery Ward from nearly 138 to less than 50; Union Carbide from nearly 139 to 59; U.S. Steel from nearly 262 to 150; Westinghouse fell from nearly 289 to less than 103; and Woolworth from about 100 to less than 53.

This did not cause the Depression; in effect, the Depression had previously begun. But it did make things substantially worse; how? The incredible loss of money wiped out purchasing power. The loss of stock money also led to bank failures; and a bank failure wipes out the savings of the people who had put their money into the bank, and thus hurts purchasing power even more.

There was, at this point, no Federal Deposit Insurance Corporation. If your bank went under, that was the end of your money. All of this forced industry to cut back on production, which meant layoffs, lower wages, and thus even less purchasing power for the nation as a whole. In addition, because of the bank failures, no loans were available; and loans were the needed lubrication for the entire economy to work.

The banking system as a whole then began to collapse in late 1930. Six hundred more banks failed in November and December of that year; the total of 1,352 by the end of the year. If you had money in a bank that had not failed, the immediate panic reaction was to pull your money out; and what occurred were runs on the other banks. Banks do not keep all their money on hand; they had to call in their loans and sell their assets in order to meet these runs. That in turn drove down the value of other assets and further contracted the money supply and tightened credit. The result: a vicious cycle that fed into other preexisting problems.

As if all that was not enough, in 1931 the European financial structure began to collapse. This was due to a drying up of American loans, which led to a drying up of German reparations to the World War I Allies that had been linked to those loans by the Dawes Plan. In addition, the French pressured to stop a German customs union with Austria, and that set off a panic in Vienna that then spread to Germany. Europeans—and the Americans as well—responded with high tariffs and capital export controls to prevent a gold drain; but that froze a large percentage of the world's financial assets and crippled international trade, which went down from $36 billion to $12 billion during the years 1929–1932. That in turn led to a new run on U.S. banks and more failures: In 1931, 2,294 failures; that was a record. The Federal Reserve at first did nothing to save the banks, and when it eventually acted, it raised the rediscount rate to stop the outflow of gold, which in retrospect was exactly the opposite of what it should have done once again. It had at first provided easy money when it should have been tight in 1927–1929, then it did nothing to save banks when it should have done something, and then it pursued a tight monetary policy in 1932 when it should have lowered the rediscount rate. You had the perfect storm.

What was Hoover's response going to be to this? Financial collapses and economic depressions were nothing new in U.S. history; previous ones had occurred in 1819, 1837, 1857, 1873, and 1893, to name but a few. These depressions had been viewed as a normal part of the business cycle and part of the market's self-correcting mechanism via Adam Smith's "invisible hand." The traditional response of government had been to do nothing and let the market correct itself. Contrary to popular opinion, Hoover did not accept this logic, and he refused to do so for a host of reasons: First, he was one of the world's most famous humanitarians. He would not let Europeans starve during World War I, and he was not about to let Americans starve under his presidency. He was also a famous Progressive who did not believe government was powerless and should do nothing. People no longer believed that government could or should do nothing either, and they no longer believed that a depression like this was normal; but what about all that talk that Hoover made in 1928 about wiping out poverty, many Americans asked? Surely he can and should do something? In addition—or connected with this—doing nothing could mean revolution; and indeed it did mean revolution in many countries, especially Germany, where the Nazis become the largest party because of the depression.

Hoover did come up with a program; it was a program that reflected his values, mostly notably his belief in the so-called "Associational Society": voluntary groups for rational, scientific planning. Government's role: Stimulate and encourage such groups but do not dictate to them. Hoover thus held a series of conferences with business and labor leaders to reach voluntary agreements to keep production up and wages up. For agriculture, he used the just-passed Agricultural Marketing Act of 1929, setting up the Federal Farm Board, to promote agricultural cooperatives and stabilization corporations that would agree to limit production. There was also some limited ability here to buy surplus. Hoover also agreed to a modest public works program to provide jobs; and he supported the Smoot-Hawley Tariff—the highest tariff in all of American history—to eliminate external competition for agriculture, to encourage business, and to restore confidence. Hoover would also encourage state and local public works projects via his 1932 Emergency Relief and Construction Act, which would provide $2 billion for public works and relief loans to the states. Nor was that the end of it: Hoover also supported voluntary programs to provide loans to endangered financial institutions, with sound banks to provide funds to the banks in trouble.

But these programs did not end the depression; the depression only got worse. With their failure, Hoover in 1932 went even further in an effort to save a financial structure about to collapse entirely. To deal with frozen assets, the Glass-Steagall Banking Act of 1932—not to be confused with the Glass-Steagall Banking Act under Roosevelt of 1933—allowed commercial paper to be accepted as collateral for Federal Reserve loans and notes. That also allowed for the release of gold and the expansion of the money supply. With the same goal, the Federal Home Loan Bank Act allowed home mortgage paper to be accepted as security for loans at new home loan banks. The Reconstruction Finance Corporation, modeled on the World War I War Finance Corporation to fund the construction of military plants, provided government funds for emergency loans to banks and large businesses. Congress provided the corporation with $500 million to start with and the authorization to borrow anywhere from $1–5 billion more.

This did mark a shift from Hoover's previous insistence on volunteerism to direct government action; direct government action would be a key component of Franklin Roosevelt's later New Deal measures as well. New Dealer Rexford Tugwell later stated in this regard that most of the New Deal policies were, as he said, "extrapolated from programs that Hoover started."

All of this was unprecedented. Obvious question: Why then, does Herbert Hoover gain such a bad, "do-nothing" reputation? There are numerous reasons: Partially it was the result of Democratic campaign propaganda in the 1930s. It was also the result of the fact that later New Deal measures went much further than Hoover and made his efforts appear nearly nonexistent in comparison. In this regard, future events would distort our understanding of what Hoover actually did during his presidency; and his own later strident attacks on the New Deal only exacerbated such perceptions.

But equally if not more important was Hoover's own behavior from 1929–1932. First, his public relations turned very bad as a result of his methods. In good times, Hoover had come across as a deeply respected efficiency expert; but now, in bad times, he came across simply as very, very cold. I think it is important to realize in this regard that despite being elected president in 1928, Herbert Hoover was not a professional politician. He was an engineer and an administrator; he had held no elected office since college. All of his positions had been appointed, not elected. As an engineer and an efficiency expert, he liked to cite statistics. That is fine during prosperity, not during depression. Hoover also consistently uttered optimistic statements that were simply at odds with reality. Why did he do so? He believed the system was basically sound and that he needed to restore confidence and maintain faith. But as a result, he seemed like a fool lost in his own world.

It is important to realize that Hoover was far from alone in a belief that the system was sound; it was a belief shared by numerous businessmen. Henry Ford would comment that the crash was just a "speculator's panic," and that the key remained production and "business leadership." He would also tell workers not to depend on employers but to find their own work and cultivate a plot of land; wonderful advice, given the situation. It is also important to realize that Hoover was an ideologue who insisted on working within clearly proscribed limits and who had a tremendous fear of what would happen if government ever began to dictate policy. He thus stuck at first with a voluntary, cooperative approach; and it failed because the system was not sound and the agreements made could not be kept. Furthermore, some of his actions to restore confidence, such as the Smoot-Hawley Tariff, only made recovery more difficult by shutting down international trade and finance.

In addition, and linked to this fear of the consequences of having the government dictate policy, Hoover adamantly refused to supply federal relief. He labeled it a "dole" that would destroy individual initiative and the American system. He thus vetoed the Garner-Wagner relief bill and insisted that the states must provide relief to prevent Federal tyranny. But the states had no funds to do so. "Well," Hoover said, "we can loan you the funds to do so." But that really was not going to do it; and in that refusal to provide federal relief, the great humanitarian came to be perceived as either inhuman or blind to reality, or perhaps both.

When Hoover's cooperative/associational approach failed, he fell back on the World War I model and "trickle down" theory, whereby he was willing to loan federal money to banks and big businesses through the Reconstruction

Finance Corporation and other units. Combined with his veto of federal relief, he looked like he was willing to save the banks but not the people from starving. In the words of historian David Kennedy, the "Great Humanitarian," the "Great Engineer" now appeared to be the "Great Scrooge."

To make matters worse, Hoover adamantly refused to go any further than he had to provide federal aid to business. He rejected the so-called Swope Plan for an operation similar to what would become the New Deal's National Recovery Administration because of his fear of government control. He also said no to corporate requests for cartel agreements; indeed, he even began to pursue antitrust prosecutions, which alienated business as well as everyone else. Hoover also followed his innovative 1932 acts with a counterproductive effort to rebalance the budget via tax increases as well as insistence on remaining on the gold standard and on international currency stabilization. If anything, he became even more ideologically and personally rigid as a result of being forced into the drastic measures of 1931–1932.

That rigidity can be seen in his continued support of Prohibition, a key experiment to him in moral values overcoming crass materialism, as well as being a Progressive measure and a way to counter the economic costs of drink, but one that has clearly failed by this time. Yet Hoover refused to admit this.

Even more illustrative of his growing rigidity was his reaction to the so-called Bonus Army: World War I veterans from the American Expeditionary Force (known as the AEF) who organized as the Bonus Expeditionary Force (the BEF). They marched on Washington, and they camped on Capitol Hill to demand early payment of the bonus granted them in the 1920s. When the Senate refused to agree, most of them accepted the offer of a free railroad ticket home, but 2,000 remained camped at Anacostia Flats. When conflict with the police in condemned buildings then occurred, Hoover on the recommendation of Secretary of War Patrick Hurley, called out the army on July 28. Army Chief of Staff General Douglas MacArthur, with his then-aides Dwight Eisenhower and George Patton, then exceeded his orders and attacked the veterans and their families with tanks, tear gas, machineguns and 1,000 troops. As an eyewitness put it, soldiers attacking former soldiers was "like sons attacking fathers." Hoover and Hurley then defended these actions by asserting that the Bonus marchers were subversives; an absurd charge, and a clear sign of Hoover's frustration and his losing touch with reality.

What can we conclude from all of this? First, our understanding of Hoover and his policies has been seriously distorted by a series of factors. These include not only the failure of his programs, but also the propaganda of his political opponents, later government measures that made his efforts appear nearly nonexistent, and his own later attacks on those measures. In this regard, future events distorted our perceptions of what Hoover actually did from 1929–1933 and who he was. But equally important was Hoover's own behavior, most notably his ideological rigidity, which made him appear cold, heartless, and willing to save the banks and big business but not the people. Ironically, his past image as a great humanitarian was thus not only shattered, but actually reversed. Furthermore, the shift in the economy from prosperity to depression, combined with his training and mentality as an engineer and reputation as an efficiency expert, turned his previously effective public relations into the exact opposite. Without extensive political experience, this highly intelligent super-administrator was not able to adjust and reverse the process.

In this regard, all of Hoover's intelligence, training, and experiences were, if anything, counterproductive. He is not alone in having had such an experience as president. Indeed, it is interesting to note in this regard that two of the brightest men elected president in the 20th century had been engineers, and both failed as president and were not reelected: Herbert Hoover and Jimmy Carter. Intelligence and ability in areas of engineering and administration, it appears, may not translate into success in the political realm.

What Did Roosevelt's New Deal Really Do?
Lecture 18

Franklin D. Roosevelt is simultaneously one of the most beloved and one of the most hated presidents in U.S. history. Despite what his critics say, Roosevelt and the New Deal did not destroy economic or political liberty in the United States, but it is equally true that the New Deal spawned many of the political and economic problems we now face. In this lecture, we will look at the New Deal in detail, noting a host of unintended consequences that resulted from its implementation.

Ending the Immediate Crisis
- Franklin Roosevelt was elected amid the greatest economic crisis in U.S. history. On inauguration day, March 4, 1933, the Great Depression had brought the economic and financial life of the country to a virtual standstill.

- The new president's first and most important goal was to end the financial crisis, primarily by psychological means that would restore people's confidence and prevent further runs on the banks. In this, he was quickly successful.

- On the day after his inauguration, Roosevelt used a World War I–era law to close all banks in the country that were still open in order to prevent more runs and a total financial collapse. He ingeniously labeled the measure a "bank holiday" and then disappeared with his staff to draft legislation that would provide for government inspection and assistance to reopen sound banks.

- On March 12, Roosevelt gave the first of his famous "fireside chats" over the radio; 60 million Americans heard him say that the banking system was sound and the banks would reopen on the following day. On March 13, people lined up at the banks, not to withdraw their funds but to make deposits! The immediate financial and psychological crises were over.

Relief, Recovery, and Reform

- Beyond ending the immediate crisis, Roosevelt and his advisers sought to achieve three fundamental goals—the "three Rs" of relief, recovery, and reform.

- To this end, Roosevelt proposed 15 major bills in the first few weeks of his administration, all of which Congress passed. These included the Agricultural Adjustment Act, the National Industrial Recovery Act, the Homeowners Loan Act, and others.

- In 1935–1936, Roosevelt and Congress went much further, passing the bills of the Second New Deal, including a massive public works program, the Social Security Act, the Wagner Labor Relations Act (establishing the National Labor Relations Board), higher taxes on the wealthy, rural electrification, and more federal control over banking and public utilities.

- These bills from both New Deals were only partially successful in achieving the three Rs.
  - In the First New Deal, the downward spiral was halted and recovery started, but the recovery stalled by 1934.

  - As a result of the Second New Deal measures, additional and major recovery took place, and the economy was nearing its 1929 levels by the end of Roosevelt's first term. But most of the gains were then wiped out by a major recession in 1937–1938.

  - The New Deal's relief bills succeeded in helping many of those who were suffering the most, but they were too modest to help all. And New Deal recovery policies simultaneously made the economic situation worse for many people.

Roosevelt's Thinking

- Roosevelt may well be the greatest politician the United States has ever produced, but for that very reason, he is extremely difficult to figure out. He was a master manipulator of people, with a front of jovial simplemindedness masking a complex and secretive interior.

- Ideas and consistency were not important to Roosevelt, and he was not a deep thinker. He also had a short attention span but a mind, according to one biographer, "like flypaper."

- He was willing to experiment and see what worked, but his experimentation had severe limits. He had no socialist or Marxian ideas and was actually a conservative man who wanted to preserve the essentials of the American system.

- Roosevelt's expertise was in getting ideas accepted by both Congress and the American people. In this, he was a political and a media genius, but his programs often made more political sense than economic sense.

- His advisers, known as the Brain Trust, disagreed sharply in their recommendations. All had roots in the Progressive era and believed government had the responsibility to ensure some sort of security for all, but there was no unity regarding the specific policies needed.

Roosevelt's New Deal was much more conservative than is generally recognized; indeed, its initial emphasis was on government planning in conjunction with big business.

- Contrary to popular mythology, most of the reformers associated with Roosevelt wanted a balanced budget and did not believe in massive deficit spending to create purchasing power, as recommended by the British economist John Maynard Keynes.

- The result of Roosevelt's thinking and style of government was a hodge-podge of legislation, all concerned with the three Rs but with different emphases at different times.

Limited Recovery and Opposition

- The recovery of the First New Deal was quite limited, primarily because of the competing nature of the spending programs and the continued fiscal conservatism of Roosevelt, his advisers, and Congress.

- The goal of the First New Deal remained a balanced budget, as seen in the early legislation to cut federal spending and increase revenues via a tax on beer and wine. Contrary to the myths, there was no great increase in government and deficit spending at this time.

- The relief measures were too limited to generate full employment and, thus, full recovery, and were often at cross-purposes with the recovery measures.

- Early failures made Roosevelt willing to experiment with more drastic measures in 1935–1936. At the same time, despite the pro-business orientation of some New Deal legislation, business turned against Roosevelt as the immediate crisis receded. He also came under attack from the Left and faced growing militancy among farmers, newly unionized industrial workers, and congressional Democrats.

- As if all that was not enough, in 1935, the Supreme Court declared both the National Industrial Recovery Act and the Agricultural Adjustment Act, the centerpieces of the First New Deal's recovery legislation, unconstitutional.

The Second New Deal

- Under the impact of these attacks and threats, Roosevelt swung to the Left in 1935–1936 and sided with both the anti–big business New Freedomites and the big spenders in the Brain Trust.

- The Second New Deal measures—particularly the heavy deficit spending and subsequent employment of millions of workers in work-relief projects—raised the economy nearly back to its 1929 levels and lowered unemployment to 14 percent.

- As with the First New Deal, however, these measures were much less radical than they appeared and negatively affected many Americans.

- Roosevelt made clear that he was not in favor of long-term relief, and he never called for an egalitarian society. One of his foremost biographers labeled him more a British-style classic conservative than a Progressive or liberal.

Major Recession, 1937–1938

- Contrary to the mythology, Roosevelt never accepted Keynesian concepts of deficit spending. He saw any deficit spending as a temporary expedient and remained firmly committed to the balanced budget.

- After his 1936 reelection, he incorrectly concluded that the Depression was over and tried to balance the budget by cutting government spending, with deep cuts in work-relief expenditures.

- At the same time, the new Social Security tax removed another $2 billion of potential spending money, with no benefits due until 1940. And the Federal Reserve, fearing inflation, contracted the money supply by increasing reserve requirements for member banks.

- The result was a major recession in 1937–1938 that wiped out many of the gains of Roosevelt's first term.

- In 1937, Roosevelt's ill-considered attempt to "pack" the Supreme Court broke his political hold over Congress and led to cries of dictatorship, in effect ending the New Deal after a final burst of legislation in 1938. Full recovery was not reached until 1941 and then largely under the impact of World War II.

The Real Results of the New Deal

- Clearly, the New Deal did not end the Great Depression; World War II did. Nor did it establish socialism, accept and institute massive deficit spending (that happened only during World War II), redistribute wealth, or change the basics of the American capitalist system. In retrospect, it was quite conservative in what it attempted to do.

- But that is only part of the story. It did not appear conservative at the time, and it had an enormous impact on almost all aspects of American life. Although some of these consequences were planned, many were examples of the historical law of unintended consequences.

- The New Deal stopped the downward economic spiral in the United States and achieved a good measure of recovery. As such, it may well have prevented a total collapse of the capitalist economic system and the American democratic political system. It also experimented and, in the process, created a new role for government in people's lives and the modern American government and economy—the so-called "welfare state."

- During the New Deal, power shifted from Wall Street to Washington, with the president becoming the nation's "chief economic engineer." Two of the negative results of this shift were a hodge-podge economic system and a growth in executive and federal power that has proven quite dangerous to the constitutional system of checks and balances.

- Although the New Deal did not redistribute wealth, it clearly brought previously "forgotten" groups into American politics and cultural life: labor, the elderly, the unemployed, and immigrant groups from eastern and southern Europe. Its pro-union stand broke with previous government policy and helped to create the largest middle class in history. Its impact on American agriculture, however, was mixed, as were its effects on African Americans and women.

- The New Deal helped to reassert an ethic of social consciousness in arts, letters, and society in general and pioneered government patronage of the arts. It also firmly established the Progressive concept of using experts in government and brought intellectuals back into government service.

- Politically, the New Deal made the Democrats the majority party of the country and created the Democratic coalition that would dominate U.S. politics for the next 40 to 50 years.

- This mixed bag of results should not blind us to all that the New Deal accomplished. In a nutshell, it gave us the American economic and political systems we still live with—and argue about—today, with all of their successes and problems.

Suggested Reading

Heilbroner, *The Worldly Philosophers*.

Kennedy, *Freedom from Fear*.

Sitkoff, ed., *Fifty Years Later*.

Questions to Consider

1. If the New Deal, in retrospect, was so conservative, why did conservatives condemn it and label it radical?

2. What personal characteristics led to Roosevelt's enormous popularity and success as a president, especially in comparison to his predecessor, Hoover?

What Did Roosevelt's New Deal Really Do?
Lecture 18—Transcript

During 1930s, Franklin D. Roosevelt was simultaneously one of the most beloved and one of the most hated presidents in U.S. history. In 1936, Roosevelt received the largest majority vote in the history of presidential politics; and to many he was one of the greatest presidents in all of American history for his New Deal Program to combat the Great Depression, as well as his leadership in World War II. To Roosevelt's numerous critics, however, he was a dangerous hypocrite with dictatorial tendencies whose New Deal program threatened the survival of economic and political liberty in the country.

With the advantage of all these years of hindsight—seven decades—it is now safe to say that Roosevelt and the New Deal did not destroy economic or political liberty in the United States. But it is equally true that the New Deal failed to end the Great Depression, and that it spawned many of the political and economic problems that we live with today. Yet both of those statements that I just made are only partially true; and each of them, if not qualified, provides a very distorted view of Franklin Roosevelt and the New Deal.

In this lecture, we will look at what the New Deal attempted to do and what it actually did; and once again we will see a host of unintended as well as some intended consequences. To do so we will first look at the crisis Roosevelt faced and briefly go through the major New Deal actions in that crisis. We will then assess Roosevelt's successes and failures, the reasons for those successes and failures, and the long-term consequences of the New Deal.

Let us begin with Roosevelt's basic goals and the facts. Roosevelt was elected and inaugurated amidst the greatest economic crisis in U.S. history. On Inauguration Day, March 4, 1933, the Great Depression had brought the economic and financial life of the country to a virtual standstill: A full 25 percent of workforce was unemployed. The *New York Times* Stock Index, which had been as high as 452 and then had fallen to 224 by the end of 1929, was now down to 58, with the Consumer Price Index having fallen from 53 to 38. U.S. Steel, which had gone from 250,000 employees to 18,000 employees, now had no full-time employees. The Gross National Product was now down to half its 1929 figure. One-third of all U.S. banks had already failed, and in February, 1933, the remainder began to fail. By Inauguration Day, 38 state governors had closed the banks so as to prevent a total financial collapse. Symbolically, the New York Stock Exchange and the Chicago Board of Trade both closed on what was a dark, gloomy Inauguration Day in Washington.

Roosevelt's first and most important goal was to end this financial crisis, and primarily by psychological means that would restore people's confidence and prevent further runs on the banks. In this, he was very successful; and quite quickly: The process began with his famous inaugural address, in which he insisted that there was nothing to fear but "fear itself." The address as a whole stunned a numbed nation and gave it what one biographer labeled "a huge shot of adrenaline."

> So, first of all, let me assert my firm belief that the only thing we have to fear is fear itself.

But saying there was nothing to fear was utter nonsense; there was plenty to fear. Yet what mattered on March 4 was not the content, but the tone; and the address hit a public nerve. The White House was flooded with mail of unprecedented volume and intensity: 450,000 letters arrived in the first week alone. That pace would not continue, but letters to Roosevelt would average 4,000–7,000 a week, and that would require an expansion of the White House mailroom staff from 1 to 70.

On the day after the inauguration, Sunday, March 5, Roosevelt used a World War I era law to shut all banks in the country still open in order to prevent even more runs and a total financial collapse on Monday. But he ingeniously labeled it a "bank holiday" and stopped all gold transactions, called Congress into special session—which was to begin on March 9—and then disappeared with his staff to draft legislation that would be presented to Congress. On March 8, he held his first press conference. When Congress convened the next day it was presented with an Emergency Banking Bill, largely written by and for bankers. It would provide for government inspection and assistance to reopen sound banks. It passed the House of Representatives unread in 38 minutes; it received Senate approval and presidential signature within eight hours. Roosevelt then presented and Congress quickly passed a bill to cut Federal spending in an effort to balance the budget by cutting veterans' benefits and Federal salaries. There was also a bill to allow the sale of and taxing of beer and wine now that the Prohibition Amendment had been repealed.

On March 12, FDR gave the first of his famous "fireside chats" over the radio. Sixty million Americans heard him say the banking system was sound and that the banks would reopen on the following day.

> The bank holiday, while resulting in many cases in great inconvenience, is affording us the opportunity to supply the currency necessary to meet the situation.

On that day, March 13, the banks opened to lines of people, not lined up to withdraw their funds, but to deposit more funds. The immediate financial and psychological crises were over.

But beyond ending the immediate crisis, Roosevelt and his advisers sought though their policies to achieve three fundamental goals, the so-called "3 Rs" (Relief, Recovery, and Reform): temporary relief for those suffering the most from the Depression until full recovery occurred; economic recovery in both agriculture and industry; and reform of the economic and financial system so a collapse like this could never occur again. To do this, Roosevelt would propose over the next few weeks 15 major bills, all of which Congress passed in the ensuing six weeks as part of the famous "100 Days." These included, to name a few of the most important and well-known, the Agricultural Adjustment Act, the National Industrial Recovery Act, the Homeowners Loan Act, and bills establishing the Civilian Conservation Corps, the Securities and Exchange Commission, the Federal Deposit Insurance Corporation, and the Tennessee Valley Authority.

Then in 1935–1936, Roosevelt and Congress went much further. The most famous of these so-called "Second New Deal" bills included a massive public works program that put millions unemployed to work, and with this the establishment of the Works Progress Administration under Harry

Hopkins that would wind up employing a total of eight million—about one-third of the jobless—for a total cost of about $11 billion; you also had the Social Security Act providing national old age insurance as well as care of the destitute and dependent and the beginnings of unemployment insurance; you had the Wagner Labor Relations Act that established the National Labor Relations Board and for the first time threw the weight of government behind the right of labor to collective bargaining; you had higher taxes on the wealthy; rural electrification; and more Federal control over the banking system and public utilities.

These bills from both the first and second New Deals were partially, but only partially, successful in achieving the goals of relief, recovery, and reform. In the First New Deal, the downward spiral was halted and recovery started, confidence was restored, starvation avoided, hope sustained, and suffering cushioned. There was also a modest recovery by 1934. But then recovery stalled, and it stalled far short of the economic figures of 1929. As a result of the Second New Deal measures, additional and major recovery did take place; indeed, the economy was nearing its 1929 levels by the end of Roosevelt's first term. But most of the gains were then wiped out by a major recession in 1937–1938. New Deal's relief bills did succeed in helping many of those suffering the most, but the bills were too modest to help all; and New Deal recovery policies simultaneously made the economic situation worse for many of these people (I'll talk a bit more about that later).

While the moves to reform the system did prevent another collapse—that is, until those moves were partially dismantled in the 1980s and 1990s—they did not prevent the major recession of 1937–1938. To understand fully why the New Deal was only partially successful, we must first take a closer look at Roosevelt himself and his advisers to see how they operated and what they believed.

Franklin Roosevelt may well have been the greatest politician this country has ever produced, but for that very reason he is extremely difficult to figure out. One can never take his public or even his private statements at face value. He was an evasive charmer, a master manipulator of people, with a front of jovial simplemindedness masking a very complex and secretive interior. He reserved his innermost thoughts to himself. Furthermore, ideas and consistency were not very important to him. He was not a deep thinker. Oliver Wendell Holmes once said he had a second class intellect but a first class temperament. He also had a very short attention span, but a mind like "flypaper," as one historian put it. Another has compared his mind to "a spacious cluttered warehouse, a teeming curiosity shop continuously restocked with randomly acquired intellectual oddments."

Roosevelt was willing to experiment and see what worked; but his experimentation had severe limits. He did not exist in an intellectual vacuum, and he was part of his era and his class. Consequently, he had no Socialist or Marxian ideas—nationalization of the banks in 1933, for example, was never considered an option—and he was actually a very conservative individual who wanted to preserve the essentials of the American system and believed the only way to do so was to change that system.

Roosevelt's expertise was not with ideas, but in getting ideas accepted by Congress and the American people. In this, he was a political genius and a media genius; but for that very reason as well as the others just cited, Roosevelt's program often made more political sense than it made economic sense. To make matters worse, his advisers—known as the Brain Trust—disagreed sharply in what they recommended to him. All of them had roots in the Progressive Era and believed that government had a responsibility to ensure some sort of security for all; but there was no unity beyond that regarding what specific policies needed to be enacted.

One group, the old Theodore Roosevelt Nationalists, accepted large corporations and the end of the free and open market. They wanted to establish some form of business-government cooperation that would both curb big business and restore it as well as agriculture, but within that group there was no agreement as to what or how to do this. You also had the old Woodrow Wilson New Freedomites, who wanted to discipline the financiers and break up Big Business to restore competition. Others had ideas that came from the Populists, such as a fear and hatred of Wall Street and a focus on helping and regulating agriculture. Urban social reformers, influenced by the old Social Gospel movement, favored aid to the aged and poor. Others with World War I experience would focus on central direction of the economy.

Contrary to popular mythology, most of these reformers also wanted a balanced budget and they did not believe in massive deficit spending to create purchasing power, something that was at that time being recommended by the British economist John Maynard Keynes. Further complicating the situation was Roosevelt's style of government, what we would today call the theory of competitive administration. Roosevelt staffed offices with people having opposing ideas, often within the same department. That can lead to great creativity when there is agreement on fundamentals, but as we have just seen there was not agreement on fundamentals and Roosevelt did not provide it. The result was often chaos and immobility.

The result of all of this would be a hodgepodge of legislation stemming from the ideas of all the different groups. All were concerned with the "Three R's" of Relief, Recovery and Reform, but with different emphases at different times. As the New Dealer Raymond Moley said, thinking there was a master plan was equal to believing that "the accumulation of stuffed snakes, baseball pictures, school flags, old tennis shoes, carpenter's tools, geometry books and chemistry sets in a boy's bedroom could have been put there by an interior decorator."

Roosevelt at first focused on restoring confidence and recovery; and while the emphasis was on recovery, there was "something for everyone" in the 15 bills of the First 100 Days. In the National Industrial Recovery Act, for example, there was one section for collective bargaining for labor and another section establishing work relief, even though the primary purpose of the bill was the recovery of business. But in general—and again contrary to the mythology—the emphasis in the First New Deal was very pro-big-business as per the New Nationalists and those with World War I ideas: government planning in conjunction with business. This was best seen in the National Recovery Administration, which actually encouraged price-fixing and the formation of cartels.

But the ensuing recovery was very limited; why? Two major reasons were the competing nature of the spending programs and, along with that, continued fiscal conservatism by the president, his advisers, and Congress. The goal remained a balanced budget, as seen in the New Deal's early legislation to cut federal spending and increase revenues via a tax on beer and wine; and contrary to the myths, there was no great increase in government and deficit spending at that time. Furthermore, the relief measures were too limited to generate full employment and thus full recovery. They were often at cross-purposes with the recovery measures. The Agricultural Adjustment Act, for example, focused on the destruction of crops to raise prices, but that had a very negative effect on tenant farmers.

The failures in the First New Deal made Roosevelt more willing to experiment with more drastic measures in 1935–1936. So did the fact that despite the conservative and pro-business orientation of the First New Deal, businessmen turned against Roosevelt as the immediate crisis receded; and by 1934, there were cries that the New Deal was going Communist. Obvious question: Why? Businessmen were appalled by the relief measures and the administrative chaos of the New Deal; and perhaps more importantly, they were appalled by what they perceived as a threat to their managerial power and a loss of status to the government that was implicit in such measures as the National Recovery Administration.

At the same time, Roosevelt came under attack from the Left and from a series of demagogues such as Huey Long of Louisiana, who threatened to challenge his reelection and claim that he was not doing enough. Roosevelt also faced a growing militancy from farmers, newly unionized industrial workers in the CIO who had more than tripled in numbers, and Congressional Democrats who had increased their numbers in the 1934 election and were pressing for much more than Roosevelt was willing to offer. As if all of that was not enough, the Supreme Court in 1935 declared both the National Industrial Recovery Act and the Agricultural Adjustment Act, which were the centerpieces of the First New Deal's recovery legislation, to be unconstitutional.

Under the impact of these attacks and threats, Roosevelt swung to the Left in 1935 and 1936 and sided with both the anti-big-business New Freedomites and the big spenders in the Brain Trust. These Second New Deal measures, particularly the heavy deficit spending—$4 billion in 1936—and the subsequent employment of millions of workers in work-relief projects, raised the economy nearly back to its 1929 levels and lowered unemployment to 14 percent.

But as with the First New Deal, these measures were much less radical than they appeared, and they negatively affected many Americans. For example, under Southern pressure, Roosevelt agreed that Social Security would not apply to farm laborers, domestic servants, or those working in establishments with fewer than 10 employees; that left out 9.4 million workers, disproportionately black. Furthermore, the new tax bills did not redistribute wealth, and parts of them were a sham and for show. For every dollar spent on unemployment relief and public works, another dollar was spent subsidizing banks and businesses.

Roosevelt also made clear that he was not in favor of long-term relief. He labeled it a "narcotic" that "induces a spiritual and moral disintegration fundamentally destructive of the national fibre"; and never did he call for an egalitarian society. One of his foremost biographers, James MacGregor Burns, has consequently labeled him more a British-style classic Conservative than a Progressive or a Liberal; and this is an aristocratic conservatism that focused on social responsibility, a respect for the limits of human knowledge and a respect for traditional forms of religious worship, a recognition of the importance of personal property, and perhaps most importantly an understanding that stability is not the equivalent of immobility.

Furthermore, and again contrary to mythology, Roosevelt never accepted Keynsian concepts of deficit spending. He saw any deficit spending as a very temporary expedient and he remained firmly committed to the balanced budget. Consequently, after his reelection in 1936, he concluded incorrectly that the Depression was over and it was time to rebalance the budget by cutting government spending, particularly deep cuts in the Works Progress Administration and the Public Works Administration's work relief expenditures. At the same time, the new Social Security tax actually removed another $2 billion of potential spending money; benefits would not begin until 1940. The Federal Reserve, fearing inflation, contracted the money supply by increasing reserve requirements for member banks. The result of all of this: a major recession in 1937–1938 that wiped out many of the gains of the first term. Industrial production dropped 33 percent, wages 35 percent, national income 13 percent, and unemployment increased by 4 million.

At the same time, Roosevelt's ill-considered attempt to pack the Supreme Court broke his political hold over Congress and led to cries of dictatorship. In effect, it ended the New Deal after one final burst of legislation in 1938. But full recovery was not reached until 1941, and then largely under the impact of World War II.

So what, then, did the New Deal actually do, and what did it not do? It clearly did not end the Great Depression; World War II did. Nor did it establish Socialism or even desire to do so. Nor did it accept and institute massive deficit spending; that happened only during World War II. There was no major redistribute wealth; no change in the basics of the American capitalist system. Indeed, in retrospect, it was quite conservative in what it attempted to do.

But that is only part of the story. It did not appear conservative at the time, and it had an enormous impact on almost all aspects of American life. The consequences were both positive and negative; and while some were planned, many were totally unplanned as the historical law of unintended consequences asserted itself once again. First of all, while the New Deal did not end the Great Depression, it did stop the downward spiral and did achieve a great deal of recovery, at least before the recession of 1937–1938. As such, it may well have prevented a total collapse of the capitalist economic system and the American democratic political system. Look in this regard at what happened in the rest of world with the appeal and rise of Fascism and Communism.

While the New Deal did not accept and institute massive deficit spending as a permanent and viable feature of the budget and the economy, or redistribute wealth, or challenge the basics of capitalism, it did experiment; and in the process, it created a new role for government in people's lives and the modern American government and economy, the so-called "welfare state." The welfare state was not socialism; the economy remained in private rather than government hands, with the partial exception of the Tennessee Valley Authority. But the New Deal did establish a new regulatory state to oversee the capitalist economy and prevent another Great Depression. It also established a safety net for individuals within the capitalist system. As Roosevelt stated in this regard:

Government has a final responsibility for the well-being of its citizenship. If private cooperative effort fails to provide work for willing hands and relief for the unfortunate, those suffering hardship through no fault of their own have the right to call upon the Government for aid; and a government worthy of its name must make fitting response.

That marked a fundamental shift in the role of government within this country. Historian David Kennedy sees coherence within the New Deal in this regard: the goal of security, stability. For good reason, Kennedy used one of Roosevelt's famous 1941 "Four Freedoms" as the title for his prizewinning book, which was a history of the United States from 1929 to 1945. The title: *Freedom from Fear*. In that "Freedom from Fear," the New Deal created a relatively riskless capitalism that kept it palatable to most Americans in their most difficult hours. The true legacy of the New Deal was thus not recovery, but reform.

The New Deal also led to a massive expansion of federal government, and with it a massive expansion of the power of the President. Power shifted from Wall Street to Washington, with the President becoming the nation's "chief economic engineer." But this had enormous negative as well as positive consequences. Two of the negative results were a hodgepodge economic system without coherency and a growth in executive and federal power that has proven quite dangerous to the Constitutional system of checks and balances. While New Deal did not redistribute wealth, it clearly brought previously forgotten groups into American politics and cultural life—labor, the elderly, the unemployed, and immigrant groups from Eastern and Southern Europe—on both symbolic and real levels.

The New Deal's pro-union stand also broke with previous government policy and helped to create the largest middle class in American history, as many industrial workers joined the middle class. The gains for labor were not just financial: Steel mills, which used to have 12-hour shifts seven days a week, shifted to five-day, 40-hour weeks with paid vacations and sabbaticals.

The New Deal's impact on agriculture was mixed. The aim to raise agricultural prices by cutting production succeeded to an extent, but this had a terrible impact on sharecroppers and tenant farmers in South—white as well as black—and it did not succeed in raising prices to the so-called "parity" level of the World War I years. In addition, New Deal measures, as well as the increased mechanization, wound up increasing consolidation in agriculture and led to agribusiness. Those who survived this consolidation become a vested interest group dependent on federal aid.

In this regard and in other ways, the New Deal also created what has been labeled the "broker state" or "interest group state" whereby groups would organize and pressure the government to get their piece of the pie. That in turn could be seen as a continuation of the organizational revolution from the Progressive Era and the 1920s. But groups that either could not or did not organize, such as migrant workers and tenant farmers, were left out in the cold.

African Americans were both helped and hurt by many New Deal measures. Agricultural policies hurt black tenant farmers and led to them being evicted from the land in favor of expanded mechanization, but other New Deal measures—such as support for organized labor—helped those who moved North and organized. Roosevelt refused to support civil rights for blacks, or even an anti-lynching bill, because he wanted the votes of Southern white legislators for his New Deal; but the "integrationist ethos" of many New Dealers and the rise of a new generation of black leaders set the foundation for the civil rights movement of the 1950s and 1960s, which then had a ripple effect on other minorities.

Women were similarly helped and hurt by the New Deal. On the positive side was their movement into the national political world, symbolized by the appointment of the first female cabinet member—Frances Perkins, as Secretary of Labor—and the incredible political activities of Eleanor Roosevelt, who redefined the role of First Lady. But from our 21st-century perspective, the New Deal also reinforced traditional roles and stereotypes of women, as illustrated by the assumption in the Social Security bill that women could not support themselves and the societal belief that any woman in the workforce was taking away a man's job.

The New Deal helped to reassert an ethic of social consciousness in the arts, letters, and society in general, and it pioneered in government patronage of the arts. It also firmly established the Progressive concept of using experts in government and brought intellectuals back into service. But that in turn precluded the intellectuals from fulfilling what some considered to be their proper role as social critics of the existing order.

Politically, the New Deal made the Democratic Party the majority party of the country and created the Democratic coalition that would dominate American politics for the next 40–50 years. But that coalition held within it seeds of its own destruction, something that had been predicted by Samuel Lubell as early as 1950. "Will," he asked, "groups that had made it during the New Deal agree to keep the door open for other groups, or will they turn in order to protect what they already have gained?"

Furthermore, the alienation of business not only led the Democratic Party to rely on labor unions for financial support but it also may have been a key reason for the limited nature of the economic recovery in the 1930s. Keynes had called for deficit spending to prime the pump in conjunction with moves to mollify business; but priming the pump, as well as other New Deal measures, alienated business, which made recovery totally dependent on deficit spending rather than partially dependent. Roosevelt never agreed that this was the case, and he never asked for enough deficit spending to compensate for the alienation of business and the ensuing lack of business confidence. Nor did he ever understand why business hated him. As Eleanor once told him in response to his puzzlement, "They are afraid of you."

All of these negative consequences should not blind us to all that the New Deal did accomplish. One historian who tried to summarize those accomplishments needed a sentence 24 lines long (240 words) just to begin the process. Perhaps in a nutshell, the New Deal gave us the American economic and political systems that we still live with—and that we still argue about—today, with all of its successes and all of its problems.

World War II Misconceptions and Myths
Lecture 19

World War II remains one of the most popular of all U.S. history subjects, but the version of the war that exists in our collective memory is filled with misconceptions and myths. Unfortunately, these myths have dominated our worldview ever since 1945 and have heavily influenced, often disastrously, our foreign and military policies. This lecture explains how some of these myths developed and challenges them with a comparison to the actual history of the war.

Myths about the Origins of World War II
- The standard approach to the origins of World War II holds that it was caused by dictators in Germany, Italy, and Japan who illegally seized power against the will of their peoples, sought to conquer the world, and combined into the Axis alliance for that purpose.

- They were aided in their efforts by the disastrous British and French policy of appeasement, a policy indirectly reinforced by American isolationism in the two decades between World War I and World War II.

- The Axis powers came close to total victory in 1940–1941 but were stopped by belated American recognition of the threat they posed and the ensuing decision to aid militarily those nations still fighting the Axis. That, in turn, led the Axis powers to make war on the United States via the Japanese sneak attack on the U.S. fleet at Pearl Harbor.

The Reality of the War's Origins
- The historical reality regarding the origins of the war is quite different, on at least seven major points.

- First of all, it is a misnomer even to think about a single war before December 1941. In effect, what began in the years 1931–1941 was a series of regional and largely unconnected wars in Asia and Europe that became partially fused in late 1941.

- Second, the Axis dictators did not seize power against the will of their peoples. Adolf Hitler, Benito Mussolini, and Tōjō Hideki all took power with the acquiescence and/or connivance of the existing powers in their countries.
  - o It's important to understand, in this regard, the enormous worldwide appeal during the interwar years of the ideology of fascism. This ideology held that true freedom lay in acting as part of a group, not individually, with a single dictatorial leader serving as the incarnation of the group's spirit.

  - o Fascism arose and gained enormous popularity during the interwar years as a result of World War I and the Great Depression, which was viewed as the failure of capitalism and democracy.

- Third, despite their common ideology, the Axis powers were united in name only. Their alliance was basically a diplomatic bluff designed to scare potential adversaries into inaction via the threat of having to fight all of them rather than just one.

- Fourth, as we've seen, the United States was not isolationist during this period. Despite its refusal to join the League of Nations in 1919–1920, it remained active in world affairs throughout the interwar years.

- Fifth, appeasement was not a new policy during the 1930s, nor a dirty word. It was, and still is, one of the oldest practices in the history of diplomacy. The British had practiced it vis-à-vis Germany during the 1920s and 1930s, as had the Americans.
  - o The problem in the 1930s was that Hitler was unappeasable. Successful appeasement is usually based on shared desires and values, something totally absent when Hitler dealt with the British.

- o Earlier appeasement, especially at Munich in 1938 with regard to Czechoslovakia, had helped Hitler by allowing him to begin the war enormously strengthened, but it also helped the British. It enabled them to be much better prepared from a military standpoint in 1939 than they had been at the time of Munich and to go to war with the full backing of the Commonwealth countries and the British public.

- Sixth, the Axis bid for total victory in 1940–1941 was halted not by American material aid but by the continued and successful resistance of the Chinese in Asia and of the British and Russians in Europe.

- Finally, the attack on Pearl Harbor was not brought on by U.S. aid to the Allied countries but by American economic sanctions against Japan in 1940–1941, combined with opportunities created by Hitler's European victories for the Japanese to pursue access to resources in Southeast Asia. The attack on Pearl Harbor was designed to remove the threat presented by the U.S. fleet to further Japanese conquests, and neither Hitler nor Roosevelt had anything to do with its conception or launch.

Myths about Fighting the War and "Losing" the Peace
- Our collective memory holds that the United States was primarily— and almost singlehandedly—responsible for total military victory over the Axis powers.
  - o We provided our allies with critical military supplies free of charge via the lend-lease program, while undertaking a massive military and economic mobilization that placed more than 15 million Americans in uniform and enabled us to equip them and our allies simultaneously.

  - o We then deployed our uniformed forces around the world, destroying the German and Italian armies in major battles in North Africa, Italy, and western Europe and the Japanese army and navy in the central and southwest Pacific theaters.

    o   At the same time, our air forces smashed German and Japanese war production and cities, culminating in the atomic bombs that destroyed Hiroshima and Nagasaki and ended the Pacific war.

- Our collective memory also holds that during the war, the American people realized we had made a terrible mistake by refusing to join the League of Nations at the end of World War I and that we had been granted a chance to correct this error by joining a new international collective security organization, the United Nations. This time, however, there would be no talk of disarmament.

- Roosevelt's great failure, Americans would soon argue, had been in not seeing a new Hitler in his Soviet wartime ally, Joseph Stalin, along with his naïve and futile attempt to appease Stalin, most notoriously at the 1945 Yalta Conference. There, Roosevelt supposedly gave away half the world to the Soviet dictator. The result of such naïveté and appeasement was the Cold War.

The American understanding of World War II is riddled with myths about the war's origins, our country's contributions, and our naïveté in negotiating the occupation of postwar Germany with Stalin.

The Reality of the Fighting and the Peace

- World War II was not won by the United States alone but by an Allied coalition whose other members contributed at least as much as our country.

  - The 15 million Americans in uniform constituted only 12 percent of the U.S. population and only 25 percent of the total Allied forces during the war. The United States did, however, produce more than 50 percent of the war material used to defeat the Axis powers.

  - At least as important as the U.S. contribution was the contribution of Great Britain and the Commonwealth countries, which played a major role in every victory claimed by the Americans in the North African, Mediterranean, and European theaters.

  - Although the British remain tremendously grateful for the American aid they received, it is important to note that the war would have ended in total German victory in 1940 without the British success in fighting alone in 1940–1941 and that, in British minds, we traded our weapons for British blood during that time.

  - It's also true that the Soviets' contribution to victory, and their ensuing casualties, dwarfed those of both the United States and Great Britain.

- As for Roosevelt's attempts to appease Stalin at Yalta, it's important to note that Yalta was a wartime conference, not a postwar peace conference.

  - Its accords were wartime agreements designed to maintain the alliance until the Axis had been totally defeated and to keep the alliance together in the postwar era so that the Germans could not rise again to start a third world war.

  - Roosevelt did not "give away" to Stalin any territory occupied by U.S. soldiers. Indeed, he struck some favorable bargains with the Soviet dictator, despite the relative weakness of his military hand.

Why Do We Sustain Our Myths?

- Many of our myths about World War II reinforce our preconceived ideological notions. Our faith in democratic elections, for example, is directly challenged by the fact that voters made the Nazis the largest party in Germany during the early 1930s. It's much easier to say that Hitler seized power than to admit this.

- Other myths reinforce our misconceptions about ourselves, such as the belief that we were ever truly isolationist or naïve.

- The overestimation of the American contribution to victory also reflects a traditional ethnocentrism shared by our allies, as well as a desire to downplay the critical Soviet contribution to victory. Admitting that the victory depended on alliance with a bloody dictator would challenge our view of the "Good War."

- In addition to these factors, conspiracy theories, such as those about Pearl Harbor, feed into what the historian Richard Hofstadter labeled the "paranoid style" in American politics. They also reflect an anachronistic projection of contemporary knowledge of events onto policymakers of the past who did not have such knowledge. The Yalta myths feed into this paranoid style and the anachronistic projection of later events, as well.

- In addition, there appears to be a natural tendency to make and misuse historical analogies to support preconceived notions and plans. In this regard, the myths and misconceptions about the war have proven useful in justifying American policies since the war.
  - o Almost every president since Franklin Roosevelt has used World War II myths in the collective memory to justify his own policies: Truman in Korea; Eisenhower, Kennedy, Johnson, and Nixon in Vietnam; Kennedy in Cuba; and both Bushes in Iraq.

o   Many if not most American policymakers believe the myths as much as the public does. But these events—in Korea, Vietnam, Cuba, and Iraq—had nothing to do with the reality of World War II, and relying on this historical analogy has consistently led to tragedy.

o   Indeed, those tragedies emphasize the fact that faulty perceptions of history are in some ways more important than what actually happened—because people act on the basis of their perceptions. And when perceptions differ so dramatically from historical reality, the results can indeed be tragic.

Suggested Reading

Adams, *The Best War Ever*.

Clausewitz, *On War*.

Kennedy, *Freedom from Fear*.

Weinberg, "Some Myths of World War II."

Questions to Consider

1.   Why are historical conspiracy theories so popular despite the fact that most of them cannot stand up to serious scrutiny?

2.   Exactly how have presidents during the last 65 years used World War II myths, misconceptions, and analogies to justify their policies?

World War II Misconceptions and Myths
Lecture 19—Transcript

World War II remains one of the most popular of all U.S. history subjects. Books and movies about it abound; new ones are constantly coming out; and college courses about the war consistently fill in record time. In our collective memory it is, to use the titles of two bestselling books, "The Good War" fought successfully by the "Greatest Generation."

Unfortunately, the version of the war existing within this collective memory is filled with misconceptions and myths, probably more misconceptions and myths than those existing for any other single event in U.S. history, save perhaps the Civil War. Those misconceptions and myths have ever since 1945 dominated our view of the world and heavily influenced—often disastrously—our foreign and military policies. This lecture will challenge some of those misconceptions and myths by comparing them to the actual history of the war as we now know it. It will also try to explain why these misconceptions and myths developed, and show the long-term and often pernicious effect they have had on American policies since 1945.

Let's begin with myths about the origins of the war. The standard approach to the origins of World War II holds that it was caused by power-mad dictators in Germany, Italy, and Japan who illegally seized power against the will of their peoples, sought to conquer the world, and combined into the Axis Alliance for that purpose. They were aided in their efforts by the disastrous British and French policy of appeasement, a policy indirectly reinforced by American isolationism in the two decades between World War I and World War II. All this appeasement actually did, according to this interpretation, was to whet the appetites of these dictators and allow them to begin the war enormously strengthened by their previous conquests.

They came very close to total victory in 1940–1941, and they were stopped by belated American recognition of the threat they posed and the ensuing American decision to aid militarily those nations still fighting the Axis: first Great Britain, then China, and the Soviet Union. That in turn led the Axis Powers to make war on the United States via the Japanese sneak attack on the U.S. fleet at Pearl Harbor; a day, in Roosevelt's words, which would "live in infamy." In many popular versions of the war, that attack, although launched by Japan, had actually been masterminded by Nazi Germany, though a minority has argued that it had been masterminded by FDR as a back door to war.

The historical reality regarding the origins of World War II is quite different on at least seven major points that I'll deal with here. First, it is a misnomer even to think about a single war before December, 1941. In effect, what began in the years 1931–1941 were a series of regional and largely unconnected wars in Asia and Europe that became partially fused in late 1941; but only partially: Russia and Japan, for example, remained at peace until August, 1945.

Secondly the dictators who ran the Axis Powers did not seize power against the will of their peoples. The Nazis, for example, were the largest party in Germany during the early 1930s, and Adolf Hitler had made crystal clear that if he was elected and made chancellor he would destroy the Weimar Republic. Furthermore, he, as well as Benito Mussolini in Italy and General Hideki Tojo in Japan, took power with the acquiescence and/or connivance of the existing powers-that-be in each of these three countries.

One must understand in this regard the enormous worldwide appeal during the interwar years of the ideology of Fascism, an ideology with deep roots in the 19th-century Romantic Movement. Fascism opposed capitalism and Communism; it also opposed democracy and individualism. It worshipped war, and it held that true freedom lay in acting as part of a group, not individually, with a single dictatorial leader serving as the incarnation of the group's spirit, or *Volkgeist* in German. This ideology arose and gained enormous popularity during the interwar years as a result of World War I and the Great Depression, which was viewed as the failure of capitalism and democracy. It also had enormous emotional appeal on its own, an appeal that Americans find difficult to comprehend. My students, when I describe that freedom is not individualism, being part of a group, they look at me as if I'm a bit nuts. But what I use as an analogy often is to ask them how they feel when they go to a huge rock concert; that surge of energy that comes with all those people around you and the feeling of being part of that mass. Then

I show them Leni Riefenstahl's *Triumph of the Will* where you see that mass in uniforms.

Third, and again in contrast to the popular version of the war, the historical reality is that despite their common ideology, the Axis powers were united in name only. They distrusted each other, they never coordinated their military activities, and they never informed of each other of their planned moves. Hitler, for example, never told the Japanese about either the Nazi-Soviet pact or his intention to invade Russia in 1941. Consequently, the Japanese, in April, 1941, signed a neutrality treaty with the Russians. Mussolini never told Hitler that he intended to invade Greece. The alliance was basically a diplomatic bluff designed to scare potential adversaries into inaction via the threat of having to fight all of them rather than just one.

Fourth, the United States was not isolationist during this time period, or, as we previously saw, at any other time period during its history. Despite its refusal to join the League, it remained quite active in world affairs throughout the interwar years. Indeed, its economic power and policies had undergirded the entire peace structure of the 1920s, and its isolationism in the 1930s as expressed in the Neutrality Acts was limited to a belief that entry into World War I had been an avoidable mistake not to be repeated should a second great war erupt in Europe.

Fifth, appeasement was not a new policy by any means during the 1930s, nor was it or is it a dirty word. The British had practiced appeasement vis-à-vis Germany during the 1920s as well as the 1930s, as had the United States; and it is one of the oldest principles and practices in the history of diplomacy. Indeed, it is one of the oldest practices between human beings as well. When was the last time, for example, that you appeased a friend or a family member, or they appeased you? The problem in the 1930s was that Hitler was unappeasable. Successful appeasement is usually based on some shared desires and values, something totally absent when Hitler dealt with the British. Indeed, British Prime Minister Neville Chamberlain was not a diplomat or soldier; he was a businessman before he became a politician who incorrectly believed that Hitler was a businessman too who shared his values. Needless to say, that was not the case. Furthermore, while appeasement did allow Hitler to begin the war enormously strengthened by the previous appeasement, especially at Munich in 1938 regarding Czechoslovakia, it also helped the British. It allowed them to be much better militarily prepared for war in 1939 than they had been at the time of the Munich Conference. They also went to war in 1939 with the full backing of the Commonwealth countries as well as the British public, which they would not have had 1938.

Sixth, the Axis bid for total victory in 1940 and 1941 was halted not by American material aid, but by the continued and successful resistance of the Chinese in Asia, and in Europe of first the British and then the Russians.

Finally, U.S. material aid to these countries did not lead to the Pearl Harbor attack. Rather, it was American economic sanctions against Japan in 1940–1941, combined with Japanese reliance on U.S. oil and steel that was now cut off plus the opportunities Hitler's European victories created for the Japanese to now obtain these resources in Southeast Asia. That is what led them to decide to conquer the European and American colonies in the area. The attack on Pearl Harbor was designed to remove the threat to the flank of their southward movement that was presented by the U.S. fleet, which Roosevelt had moved from its California base to Pearl Harbor as a deterrent against Japanese expansion. A deterrent, however, is also a target; and Hitler had utterly nothing to do with it.

Nor did Roosevelt: The "Back Door to War" thesis relies upon information not available to Roosevelt and his advisers. Proponents of the "Back Door to War" thesis, for example, say, "Ah, the United States had broken the Japanese codes; how could they not know the attack was coming?" The United States had broken the Japanese diplomatic code, not the highest naval code. The Americans knew war was coming, but they expected the attack to hit the Philippines, not Pearl Harbor, given where the Japanese troop ships were sailing. The Americans did not have a lack of information, they had too much information—what in the intelligence business is known as "noise"—and how do you separate the intelligence that can help you versus the intelligence that is not relevant? The critics also say, "Ah, the aircraft carriers were not in Pearl Harbor, the battleships were; and the battleships were dated." But that was not known on December 7, 1941; it was only with Pearl Harbor, followed by Coral Sea and Midway, that it was clear that the aircraft carrier had replaced the battleship.

Furthermore, any conspiracy like this would have had to involve the entire Cabinet, the Army and Navy Chief of Staff, the Secretaries of War and Navy; it would have also required Roosevelt to believe that Hitler would obey a treaty he had signed for the first time in his life, and indeed that he would go beyond the terms of the Tripartite Pact. The Tripartite Pact had established only a defensive alliance in the event that one of the three powers was attacked by a presently neutral power (meaning the United States). Why Hitler declared war on the United States anyway when he didn't have to has puzzled historians ever since; it has led to numerous hypotheses. All that is absolutely clear is that this move—Hitler's declaration of war on the United States—did link the existing regional wars that already existed, though not completely as previously noted.

Let's now turn our attention to numerous myths about fighting and winning the war, and losing the peace. Our collective memory holds that we were primarily—indeed, almost singlehandedly—responsible for the total military victory over the Axis Powers. We provided our allies with critically needed military supplies free of charge via the Lend-Lease Program. Simultaneously, we undertook a massive military as well as an economic mobilization that placed over 15 million Americans in uniform and enabled us to equip them and our allies simultaneously. We then deployed our uniformed forces around the world. We destroyed the German and Italian armies in major battles in North Africa, Sicily, Italy, and Western Europe. We then destroyed the Japanese Army and Navy in the central and southwest Pacific theaters in such major battles and campaigns as Midway, Guadalcanal, MacArthur's "leapfrogging" in New Guinea and the Philippines, and the Navy's Central Pacific advance and major naval victories over the Japanese Navy in the Philippine Sea and Leyte Gulf. Then, in 1945, you had Iwo Jima and Okinawa. At the same time, by this interpretation, our air forces destroyed German and Japanese war production and German and Japanese cities, culminating in the atomic bombs that destroyed Hiroshima and Nagasaki and ended the Pacific War.

Our collective memory also holds that during the war, we realized that we had made a terrible mistake at the end of World War I by refusing to join the League of Nations. We also realized that we had now been granted a second chance to correct this error and achieve Woodrow Wilson's dream by joining a new international collective security organization: the United Nations. But this time we would not be as naïve as Woodrow Wilson. This time there would be no talk of disarmament. Such talk only encouraged power-mad dictators. Instead, we would maintain our military strength. Munich and Pearl Harbor had been our lessons regarding the awful consequences of military unpreparedness as well as appeasement. As President Harry Truman stated in an October 27, 1945 Navy Day speech, this time there would be no full demobilization of the United States armed forces. Why? Because:

> We have learned the bitter lesson that the weakness of this Great Republic invites men of ill-will to shake the very foundations of civilization all over the world. ... We seek to use our military strength solely to preserve the peace of the world. For we know that this is the only sure way to make our own freedom secure.

Franklin D. Roosevelt's great failure, Americans would soon argue, had been his inability to see such a man of "ill-will"—a new Hitler—in his Soviet wartime ally Josef Stalin, along with his naïve and futile attempt to appease Stalin, most notoriously at the 1945 Yalta Conference where he supposedly gave away half of the world to the Soviet dictator for worthless promises of free elections in Europe that Stalin quickly broke, Soviet entry into the war against Japan that was totally unnecessary in light of the atomic bomb, and useless agreement to join what turned out to be the useless U.N. The result of such naïveté and appeasement was the Cold War.

That is the popular version. But what were the realities of fighting the war and "losing" the peace, as opposed to this collective memory of it? For a start, World War II was not won by the United States alone, but by an Allied coalition whose other members contributed at least as much as the United States. While the United States did put more than 15 million Americans into uniform, that constituted only 12 percent of its population. That was one of the lowest mobilization percentages for any major belligerent in the war; and American forces constituted only 25 percent of Allied forces during the war. The United States did, however, produce more than 50 percent—indeed, nearly two-thirds—of all the war material used by the Allies to defeat the Axis powers. It was able to do this both because of the size of its enormous economy and its protected geographic position behind two large oceans; the

United States was the only major belligerent in World War II not invaded or bombed.

At least as important as this U.S. contribution to the war was the contribution of Great Britain and the Commonwealth countries. They played a major role in every victory claimed by the Americans in the North African, Mediterranean, and European theaters, including Normandy, where they took and held three of the five total beaches. SHAEF, Eisenhower's headquarters, stands for "Supreme Headquarters, Allied Expeditionary Forces," not "Supreme Headquarters, American Expeditionary Forces." Indeed, while the British were and remain tremendously grateful for the American aid they received, it is important to note that the war would have ended in total German victory in the spring or summer 1940 without the British decision and success in fighting alone; indeed, in British minds we traded our weapons for British blood during that time period.

The British also found the Americans to be hypocritical and naïve. British wartime Foreign Secretary Anthony Eden once said, "Soviet policy is amoral; U.S. policy is exaggeratedly moral, at least where non-American interest are concerned." One British Foreign Office official referred in 1944 to U.S. foreign policy as "an unwieldy barge liable to wallow as a menace to navigation" without a British pilot. Future British Prime Minister Harold Macmillan told a subordinate in North Africa during the war that:

> We ... are Greeks in this [new] American empire. You will find the Americans much as the Greeks found the Romans—great big, vulgar, bustling people, more vigorous than we are and also more idle, with more unspoiled virtues but also more corrupt. We must run AFHQ [in Algiers] [Macmillan said] as the Greek slaves ran the operations of the Emperor Claudius.

As for the Soviets, their contribution to victory, and their ensuing casualties, dwarfed those of both the United States and Great Britain. U.S. combat deaths in World War II were 291,557; total deaths were approximately 405,000, combat deaths were 291,557. The Russians had at least that many dead in the single battle of Stalingrad. Total U.S. and British deaths combined were between 800,000 and 900,000; that compares to anything between 25 and 29 million for the Russians. For every American to die in the war, approximately 65 Russians died. In the process, they inflicted 93 percent of all German casualties prior to the D-Day invasion in June, 1944; and that invasion had previously been promised to them to relieve the German pressure in 1942 and again in 1943. It was not delivered until 1944, a two-year delay that they considered deliberate and designed to bleed them to death. Even after the Normandy invasion, the Russian contribution to victory far exceeded that of Britain and the United States combined. In their summer 1944 offensive that destroyed German Army Group Center, the Soviets inflicted 900,000 casualties on the Germans. That figure that exceeded by 200,000 the total number of German forces deployed against General Eisenhower at that time.

As for Roosevelt's supposed naïveté in dealing with Stalin, the Soviet leader did not consider him naïve at all. In June, 1944, he commented to the Yugoslav Communist leader Milovan Djilas that if you turned your back on him for a minute Churchill would steal a kopeck out of your coat pocket, but Roosevelt only "dips in his hand ... for bigger coins." More importantly, Yalta was a wartime conference, not a postwar peace conference. Its accords were wartime agreements designed to maintain the alliance until the Axis had been totally defeated and to keep the alliance together in the postwar era so that the Germans could not rise up yet again to start a third world war. The peace conference never took place, however, because of the Cold War, which is why we tend to think of Yalta as a peace conference.

In addition, Roosevelt did not give away at Yalta, or ever give away to Stalin, any territory occupied by U.S. soldiers. Indeed, at Yalta he struck some very favorable bargains with the Soviet dictator despite the relative weakness of his military hand. Please realize Yalta took place in early February, 1945. The Allies were just ending the Battle of the Bulge and really hadn't crossed into Germany yet at all. The Red Army, at the other hand, was within striking distance of Berlin. Despite these facts, Roosevelt obtained large German occupation zones for both the United States and Britain, and a zone for France, which Churchill wanted. He paid a modest territorial price in the Far East for still deeply-desired Soviet entry into the war against Japan given the casualties that the U.S. Army and Navy were suffering at that point. As for the atomic bomb, it did not exist at that time, and no one knew if it would ever exist. Furthermore, Stalin agreed to deal with Chiang Kai-shek's Nationalist government instead of Mao Tse-tung's Communists in China. Roosevelt also negotiated favorable compromises on the U.N. veto and General Assembly votes. The promised free elections in Poland and the rest of Europe were the best that could be obtained in light of the fact that the Red Army occupied Poland and the rest of Eastern Europe.

Was this appeasement, or was it hard bargaining and negotiation? If appeasement; didn't Stalin and Churchill practice it as well, as Allies usually do, in order to maintain the alliance and achieve their common goal of victory?

Given these facts about the war, an obvious question arises: Why do we maintain our myths and our misconceptions? The reasons are numerous. First of all, many of these myths and misconceptions reinforce our preconceived ideological notions. Our faith in democratic elections, for example, is directly challenged by the fact that voters made the Nazis the largest party in Germany during the early 1930s. It is much easier to say Hitler seized power than to admit this. Other myths and misconceptions reinforce beliefs about ourselves that are in turn misconceptions, such as the belief that we were ever truly isolationist, or naïve for that matter. The overestimation of the American contribution to victory does reflect traditional ethnocentrism shared by our allies. You go to England, you will see they won the war; you go to Russia, you will see they won the war. But it also reflects a desire to downplay the critical Soviet contribution to victory; that desire was quite strong during the Cold War that followed World War II. In addition, admitting that victory depended on alliance with a bloody dictator would challenge our view that this was "the Good War."

In addition to these factors, conspiracy theories, such as those about Pearl Harbor, feed into what the historian Richard Hofstadter aptly labeled "The Paranoid Style in American Politics." They also reflect, as we have seen, an anachronistic projection of contemporary knowledge of events onto policymakers of the past who did not have such knowledge. The Yalta myths also feed into this paranoid style, as well as the anachronistic projection of later military events—i.e., March, 1945–August, 1945—onto early February, 1945. No one knew in February that the German Army in the Ruhr would be encircled in March and that other German forces in the West would crumble in April, nor did anyone know that an atomic bomb would be successfully tested in July and used in August.

In addition, there also appears to be a natural tendency to make and misuse historical analogies to support preconceived notions and plans. In this regard, the myths and misconceptions about World War II have proven very useful in justifying American policies since World War II. Indeed, just about every president since Franklin Roosevelt—with the possible exception of Barack Obama—has used the World War II myths in the collective memory to justify his own policies, most notably but far from exclusively Truman in Korea; Eisenhower, Kennedy, Johnson and Nixon all in Vietnam; Kennedy again in Cuba; and both George Bushes in Iraq. These individuals were not necessarily lying; in all likelihood, they were not lying. Many if not most American policymakers believe the myths as much as the public does. But the events cited in Korea, Vietnam, Cuba, and Iraq by these presidents had utterly nothing to do with the reality of World War II, and relying on this historical analogy has consistently led us to tragedy.

Indeed, those tragedies emphasize the fact that faulty perceptions of history are in some ways more important that what actually happened, for people act on the basis of their perceptions. When perceptions differ so dramatically from historical reality, they can and do lead to tragedy, as we will see when we turn to the Cold War.

Was the Cold War Inevitable?
Lecture 20

W e shouldn't be surprised by the fact that some of the World War II myths discussed in the last lecture feed into myths about the Soviet-American conflict known as the Cold War. It's not true, however, that the Cold War could have been avoided if Roosevelt had not been naïve at Yalta or that the conflict was inevitable. In this lecture, we will explore how and why this conflict took place and lasted for as long as it did.

Conflicting Histories and Ideologies
- Russia and the United States always possessed diametrically opposed political systems: centralized autocratic tyranny versus decentralized democracy. Despite this difference, the two countries had been friendly throughout the late 18th century and most of the 19th century because their interests did not collide and because they shared a common enemy, Great Britain.

- Still, there were predictions in the 19th century that the two expansionist powers would eventually come into conflict, and these predictions became a reality at the end of the 19th century when the interests of the two nations collided in Manchuria.

- Ideology became much more of a factor in the conflict as a result of the 1917 Bolshevik Revolution, which established the communist government in Russia.
  - This took place at the very moment that Woodrow Wilson was restating and expanding the American mission to re-create the world in its own image.

  - The two nations thus had diametrically opposed and universalist ideologies, with each one claiming to negate the validity of the other.

Changes Wrought by World War II

- None of these differences prevented Russia and the United States from collaborating effectively as allies, along with Great Britain, during World War II. What changed in 1945 was the fact that they succeeded in defeating Nazi Germany and Japan. With their common enemies gone, there was nothing to offset their differing interests and ideologies.

- The world in which the two nations existed also changed dramatically after World War II. The Allied victory had created a massive and unprecedented global power vacuum at the same time that the United States and the Soviet Union became superpowers. As their differences became obvious after the Axis defeat, each began to see the other as its major adversary.

- Each also tended to view the other through the prism of the events they had just lived through and, thus, as potentially similar to the Nazi enemy they had just defeated. The historical lessons they took from that experience were never to "appease" and to negotiate only from positions of military strength.

- Further, each viewed its own ensuing actions as defensive reactions to the aggression of the other, thereby leading to a constant escalation of conflict.

Superpower Conflict, 1945–1946

- Given these factors, it is far from surprising that conflict between the two superpowers quickly erupted and escalated from 1945–1946.

- First came conflict over the boundaries and government of Poland, with cries on each side that the other was breaking the Yalta Accords. This was quickly followed by conflict over policies in occupied Germany.

- The American dropping of the atomic bomb without informing the Soviets heightened their suspicions and fears of the United States, as did the later discovery of communist spies in the wartime project to develop the bomb.

- The activities of local communist parties in Europe simultaneously heightened American suspicions and fears. Those parties had gained enormously in power and prestige because of their anti-Nazi resistance activities during the war, but Americans perceived them as stalking horses for the Soviets.

- In 1947, when Britain informed the United States that it could no longer afford to support the Greek government against communist guerrillas or Turkey against Soviet pressure, the United States—with the famous Truman Doctrine—replaced the British in both countries and announced a global policy to "support free peoples who are resisting attempted subjugation by armed minorities or by outside pressures."

The Marshall Plan and Containment
- With the failure of the foreign ministers conference in Moscow in 1947, Secretary of State George C. Marshall proposed the European recovery program that bears his name: the Marshall Plan.
  - The plan would include the economic rebuilding of Germany, which Stalin feared and opposed. Stalin interpreted the plan as designed to disrupt his empire in Eastern Europe.

  - Consequently, he refused to participate in the recovery program and forced his East European satellites to do the same.

- Later in 1947, in an effort to halt the rebuilding of Germany and the formation of a West German government, Stalin instituted a blockade of the western zones of Berlin. That move led to the Berlin airlift by the United States, escalated the formation of a West German government, and led to the formation of NATO by 1949.

- All of this was part of the new American policy enunciated in 1947 by State Department official George F. Kennan to contain Soviet expansionist tendencies, a policy that he asserted would lead either to a mellowing or a collapse of the Soviet system.

- Containment resulted in a major expansion of U.S. power as our nation moved into areas around the Soviet Empire. It also increased Soviet perceptions of American aggressiveness, necessitating a response. By 1948–1949, this "mirror image" effect brought the two superpowers to the edge of World War III.

- As we know, World War III did not occur, but by 1949, the two superpowers had, in effect, divided Europe into respective spheres of influence, spheres that each was willing to go to war to defend.

The Korean War

- In China, civil war between Chinese communists under Mao Zedong and nationalists under Chiang Kai-shek broke out soon after the Japanese defeat. In October 1949, Mao's forces won and Chiang fled to the island of Formosa.

  o Although his defeat had long been expected by experts in the State Department, it sent shock waves through the United States.

The victory of Mao Zedong's forces in 1949 shocked the American public and fanned the flames of anticommunist hysteria.

  o The "loss" of China took place at the same time as a series of spy cases and the detonation of the Soviets' first atomic bomb, all of which resulted in an anticommunist hysteria in the United States known today as McCarthyism.

  o In early 1950, Mao signed a treaty of alliance with Stalin.

- Meanwhile, the peninsula of Korea, previously part of the Japanese Empire, had been divided by Russian and American occupation forces after the Japanese surrender. The two superpowers had established rival governments in the North and South, but with Stalin's acquiescence, the North invaded the South on June 25, 1950.

- The Truman administration interpreted this as a Soviet move that could not be tolerated. Taking advantage of a Soviet boycott of the UN Security Council, the Americans obtained UN sanction for a military intervention to halt the North Koreans.

- The administration then decided to take advantage of the victory at Inch'ŏn to unify North and South Korea by force. General Douglas MacArthur's forces crossed the 38th parallel and moved toward the Chinese border on the Yalu River. That movement led to a massive military intervention by the Chinese communists. The conflict now threatened to turn into a full-scale world war.

- The Truman administration reverted to its previous aim of liberating only South Korea, and U.S./UN forces fought their way back up the peninsula. When MacArthur refused to accept this policy and pressed for an expanded war with China, he was dismissed. An armistice was signed in 1953.

- Also in 1953, Stalin died and was replaced by Nikita Khrushchev, who denounced Stalin and called for a more open society. For a brief moment, there appeared to be a possibility of a thaw in the Cold War, but instead, it intensified and expanded, becoming "hot" again in Vietnam.

Détente
- By the late 1960s and early 1970s, the bipolar world that had come into being in 1945 no longer existed. Instead, new centers of power had emerged, as Europe recovered from the war and China emerged as a major player—and as its major split with the Soviet Union became public and more intense.

- Sensing both the limits of American power in Vietnam and the possibilities inherent in this development, President Richard Nixon and his national security adviser, Henry Kissinger, pursued a triangular balance-of-power approach that led to a major lessening of global tensions.

- Despite predictions, the Cold War did not come to an end; instead, détente ended by the late 1970s, and a new "hot" war emerged when the Soviets invaded Afghanistan.

A New and Fierce Cold War

- In retrospect, the Soviet invasion of Afghanistan and the simultaneous Iranian Revolution constituted the wave of the future and threatened both superpowers, but they remained locked in their old conflict and did not see this. Both Jimmy Carter and Ronald Reagan reacted fiercely to the Soviet invasion of Afghanistan and supported the Islamic forces.

- A new and fierce Cold War thus began in the early 1980s—one we tend to forget because of what happened in the late 1980s, but one that nevertheless had many thinking that World War III was at hand once again.

- Again, World War III failed to materialize, primarily for two reasons. First, the old generation of Soviet leaders died and a new Soviet leader, Mikhail Gorbachev, instituted major reforms in both Soviet domestic and foreign policies. Second, Reagan embraced these reforms and, with Gorbachev, instituted a new era of Soviet-American cooperation.

- The Cold War finally did end between 1989 and 1991 when glasnost and perestroika led ultimately to the total collapse of the Soviet Empire in Eastern Europe, followed by the collapse of the Soviet Union itself.

Reexamining the Cold War

- In one sense, the Cold War was not a war at all but a state of abnormal bipolarity following World War II. Still, there were numerous bloody regional wars fought within the Cold War, including Korea, Vietnam, Afghanistan, and a series of civil and regional conflicts fought by proxies.

- As previously stated, conflict may have been inevitable when World War II ended, but the duration and intensity of the conflict was not. That intensity and duration resulted primarily from domestic and ideological factors in each country that, in retrospect, were almost totally at odds with international realities after 1949 or 1953.

Suggested Reading

Clausewitz, *On War.*

Gaddis, *Strategies of Containment.*

LaFeber, *America, Russia and the Cold War, 1945–2006.*

Leffler, *For the Soul of Mankind.*

Westad, *The Global Cold War.*

Questions to Consider

1. Why did the Cold War never erupt into a direct, global, and total Soviet-American war?

2. Why did most if not all of the major "thaws" in the Cold War take place under presidents who had strong anticommunist reputations?

Was the Cold War Inevitable?
Lecture 20—Transcript

World War II was followed immediately by the long Soviet-American conflict we know as the Cold War. Indeed, some people argue that it actually began even before World War II ended.

Given such an interpretation, it is far from surprising that some of the World War II myths discussed in the last lecture feed into a series of myths about the Cold War. For example, belief in the World War II Yalta myths—that Roosevelt gave away half of the world to Stalin at the Yalta Conference— can logically lead to a belief that the Cold War could have been avoided had Roosevelt not been so naive. But if one does not believe in the Yalta myths, one can reach an opposite conclusion that is equally incorrect: that the Cold War was inevitable. It was not; and in this lecture we will explore how and why the Cold War took place and lasted for so long. In the process, we will deal with additional myths about this long Soviet-American conflict.

Historians analyzing the origins of the Cold War usually cite divergent and conflicting histories, interests, ideologies, and personalities. Let us look at each of these briefly. History first: Russia and the United States had always possessed diametrically opposed political systems: centralized autocratic tyranny for Russia versus decentralized democracy for the United States. "Why?" is an interesting question. Perhaps geography: Russia, with a history of consistently being invaded across the open plains of Eastern Europe, may have needed centralized power to defend itself. The United States, protected by ocean moats, did not need centralized power.

Despite this difference, the two nations had been friends throughout the late 18th century and most of the 19th century. Why? Because their interests did not collide during this time period, and because they shared a common enemy: Great Britain. That was an enemy that sought to check the continental expansion of each of them—Russia in Eurasia, the United States in North America—and both the Russian and the United States governments operated on the basic principle in international relations that the enemy of my enemy is my friend.

Yet there were predictions in the 19th century that these two expansionist powers would eventually collide. Secretary of State William Henry Seward wrote in 1861 that:

> Russia like the United States is an improving and expanding empire. Its track is eastward while that of the United States is westward. The two nations, therefore, never come into rivalry or conflict. Each carries civilization to the new regions it enters and each finds itself occasionally resisted by states jealous of its prosperity, or alarmed by its aggrandizement. Russia and the United States may remain good friends [Seward concluded] until, each having made a circuit of half the globe in opposite directions, they shall meet and greet each other in the region where civilization first began.

Even earlier—25 years earlier, in fact—Alexis de Tocqueville had ended the first book of his famous *Democracy in America* with the following:

> There are now two great nations in the world which, starting from different points, seem to be advancing toward the same goals: the Russians and the Anglo-Americans. ... All other peoples seem to have nearly reached their natural limits and to need nothing but to preserve them; but these two are growing. ... Each seems called upon by some secret design of Providence one day to hold in its hands the destinies of half the world.

Seward's prediction of the friendship ending when the United States and Russia found their expansions colliding became a reality at the end of the 19th century, when their interests did collide in Manchuria; interestingly, at the same time the Russian government was cracking down on dissidents and Americans were becoming more aware of Czarist repression and condemning it.

Ideology became much more of a factor as a result of the 1917 Bolshevik Revolution, which established the Communist government in Russia that claimed its ideology of Communism was the wave of the future. This took place at the very moment Woodrow Wilson was restating and expanding the American mission to recreate the world in its own image. The two nations thus had diametrically opposed and Universalist ideologies, with each one claiming to negate the validity of the other. Not surprisingly, given that fact, the United States participated in Allied military interventions in Russia in 1918 at least partially designed to overthrow the Bolsheviks. It also refused to recognize the Communist government of Russia until 1933. Reinforcing the ideological conflict was the mentality of the Soviet leader Josef Stalin, a bloody tyrant who, many argue, possessed a paranoid personality that saw enemies everywhere and who in the 1930s had murdered all his potential rivals, as well as hundreds of thousands if not millions of others, through his brutal domestic policies.

Yet none of these differences prevented the two nations from collaborating effectively as allies, along with Great Britain, during World War II. What had changed by 1945 was the fact that they had succeeded in totally defeating Nazi Germany and Japan. With their common enemies gone, there was nothing to offset their old differing interests and ideologies. A related factor was that Roosevelt had died in April, 1945. His successor, Harry Truman, did not possess Roosevelt's skill at compromise, nor the respect that the Soviet dictator had had for Franklin Roosevelt. Given these facts, some postwar conflict between the two wartime allies was probably inevitable at end of war. But conflict, however serious, is not the same as 45 years of global hostility and the constant threat of World War III. Indeed, conflict between these two nations had existed since the 1890s and had not led to any Cold War before now.

What had changed from previous eras, and changed quite dramatically, was the world in which these two nations existed. World War II had created a massive and unprecedented global power vacuum. Germany, Italy, and Japan, all totally defeated, occupied, and no longer major powers. Nor was France a major power, or any of the other nations of Europe that had been conquered and occupied during the war by the Germans. Nor was China, which never really had been a great power during the war and that was now on the verge of civil war. Nor was Great Britain, who despite the Allied victory had been massively weakened by the war effort and who as a result would soon lose its overseas empire and its ranking as a great power. In effect, only the United States and the Soviet Union remained as great powers; and their power had grown so substantially during the war that they were, in effect, superpowers.

As their differences became obvious after the defeat of the Axis powers, each began to see the other as its major adversary and to view the entire world as a zero sum game in which a victory for one was a defeat for the other. Each also tended to view the other through the prism of the events they had just lived through, and thus as potentially similar to the Nazi enemy they had just beaten. The historical "lessons" they took from that World War II experience were never to appease and to negotiate only from positions of military strength. In addition, each viewed its own ensuing actions as defensive reactions to the aggressions of the other, thereby leading to a constant escalation of conflict. Yet they were also incapable of defeating each other militarily, even before the advent of nuclear weapons. In August, 1944, the Joint Chiefs of Staff had issued a study that pointed out that neither Russia nor the United States could defeat each other, and had pointed out that there would be after the war a shift in the global balance of power unprecedented since the time of Rome. Nuclear weapons only reinforced this perceived military stalemate.

Given all of these factors, it is far from surprising that conflict between the two powers quickly erupted and escalated from 1945–1946. First came conflict over the boundaries and government of Poland and the other countries of Eastern Europe that had been occupied by the Red Army; cries on each side that the other was breaking the Yalta Accords. Then quickly came conflict over policies in occupied Germany, with the Allied Council of Foreign Ministers unable to reach any agreement on a combined policy, or on a final peace treaty with Germany; there never was a final peace treaty with Germany. The dropping of an atomic bomb by the United States without informing the Soviets in advance of this weapon heightened Soviet suspicions and fears of the United States. Similarly, the later discovery of Communist spies in the wartime atomic bomb project increased American suspicions of the Soviets. The activities of local Communist parties in Europe only heightened American suspicions and fears.

Those Communist parties had gained enormously in power and prestige during the war because of their anti-Nazi resistance activities. But Americans perceived them as stalking horses for the Soviet Union. That was a perception strongly reinforced by the so-called "Fifth columns" of the fascist powers that they had witnessed before World War II in such countries as Spain and

Czechoslovakia. As those local Communist parties took power in Eastern Europe behind the Red Army, and looked like they could win elections and take power in Western Europe, American fears grew of a Russian "Red Fascist" takeover of all of Europe.

The ideological conflict between the two, which lay dormant during World War II, had reemerged in early 1946 with two major speeches: First, a major February speech by Stalin in which he revived talk of conflict with the capitalist countries as well as between the capitalist countries. That was soon followed in early March by a major speech by Winston Churchill in Fulton, Missouri, with President Truman sitting on the stage, during which Churchill warned that an "Iron Curtain" was descending across Eastern Europe.

> From Stettin in the Baltic to Trieste in the Adriatic an iron curtain has descended across the Continent.

Then a year later, in 1947, when Britain informed the United States that it could no longer afford to support the Greek government against Communist guerrillas, or Turkey against Soviet pressure, the United States—with the famous Truman Doctrine—replaced the British in both Greece and Turkey and announced a global policy to "support free peoples who are resisting attempted subjugation by armed minorities or by outside pressures." With the failure of the March–April, 1947 Foreign Ministers Conference in Moscow, new Secretary of State George C. Marshall proposed in early June the European Recovery Program that bears his name: the Marshall Plan.

The European Recovery Program would require and include the economic rebuilding of Germany, which Stalin feared and opposed. He was invited to join the European Recovery Program, but he interpreted it as designed to disrupt his empire in Eastern Europe. Consequently, he rejected participation, he forced his European satellites to do likewise, and he clamped down in the satellites where there was still a degree of freedom, most notably Hungary in late 1947 and then in early 1948 in Czechoslovakia via a coup. 1948 was the 10th anniversary of the Munich Conference; and what we saw here in the United States was the role of historical memory as a major war scare ensued.

Then, just four months later, in an effort to halt the rebuilding of the western zones of Germany and the formation of a West German government, Stalin also instituted a blockade of the western zones of Berlin; Berlin lay totally within the Soviet occupation zone for Germany as a whole. That led to the Berlin Airlift by the United States. It also would up escalating the formation of a West German Government rather than stopping it and the formation of the North Atlantic Treaty Organization by 1949 with the United States as a member; the first peacetime alliance in American history, unless you want to count the continuation of the War of Independence alliance with France after that war.

All of this was part of the new American policy enunciated in 1947 by State Department official George F. Kennan to contain Soviet expansionist tendencies. This policy, Kennan asserted, would lead either to a mellowing of the Soviet system or its total collapse. But containment also led to a major expansion of American power, as the United States moved into areas around the Soviet Empire, and thus Soviet perceptions of American aggressiveness necessitating a Soviet response. This "mirror image" effect by 1948–1949 led the two superpowers to the edge of World War III.

But World War III did not occur. Neither side wanted it, and in all likelihood neither side could win it. Indeed, by 1949, the two superpowers had in effect divided Europe into spheres of influence; spheres that each was willing to go to war to defend. Each side knew that about the other. As a result, and rather ironically, Europe began the longest period of peace in its modern history; a "long peace" that did not end until the Cold War did four-and-a-half decades later.

But if peace had resulted from this division of Europe, why did the Soviet-American conflict not end at this point? One key reason was that by this time it had expanded to the rest of the world because of the global power vacuum that I previously talked about. Indeed, in Asia it resulted in a "hot war" instead of just a cold one, by 1950. In China, civil war between the Chinese Communists under Mao Tse-tung and the Nationalists under Chiang Kai-shek broke out soon after Japanese defeat. In October, 1949, Mao's forces won and Chiang fled to the island of Formosa. Although his defeat had long been predicted and expected by experts in the State Department, it sent shockwaves through the United States because of the public's long-held perception of China as an American ward; and this "loss" of China became a highly-charged partisan issue that Republicans now used against the incumbent Democrats.

The loss of China also took place at the same time as a series of spy cases and Soviet detonation of its first atomic bomb, all of which resulted in an anti-Communist hysteria in the United States known today as McCarthyism. Then in early 1950, Mao went to Moscow and signed a treaty of alliance with Stalin. Meanwhile, the peninsula of Korea, previously part of the Japanese Empire, had been divided by Russian and American occupation forces, much as Germany had been divided by occupation forces. Russia and the United States had then each established a rival government, one in the North and one in the South. That division may have suited the two superpowers; it did not suit either Korean government. Both of them threatened to unify the peninsula by force. With Stalin's acquiescence —if not his blessing—the North then invaded the South on June 25, 1950.

The Truman Administration interpreted this as a Soviet move that could not be tolerated. In a telling analogy showing the impact of World War II thinking, Truman asserted that it was Nazi Germany's 1936 forcible military occupation of the demilitarized Rhineland all over again. Taking advantage of a Soviet boycott of the United Nations Security Council due to its refusal to replace Nationalist China with Communist China, the United States obtained U.N. sanction for a military intervention to halt the North Koreans. Led by General Douglas MacArthur, U.S. and UN forces first halted the North Koreans and then routed them via a surprise amphibious landing at the port of Inchon. The Administration then decided to take advantage of this victory to unify North and South Korea by force, with MacArthur's forces crossing the 38th parallel dividing line and moving north toward the Chinese border on the Yalu River. That led to a massive military intervention by the Chinese Communists, who viewed this U.S. military movement as a mortal threat. The result was a much-expanded war that now threatened to turn into a full-scale global world war.

The Truman Administration now reverted to its previous aim of liberating only South Korea, and U.S. and U.N. forces fought their way back up the peninsula. When MacArthur refused to accept this policy and pressed for an expanded war with China, he was dismissed with the concurrence of the Joint Chiefs of Staff. As Joint Chiefs General Omar Bradley put it, to expand this war would be "the wrong war [in] the wrong place at the wrong time [against] the wrong enemy."

An armistice was signed in 1953. That same year witnessed major changes in leadership on both sides, as Dwight Eisenhower became president and Stalin died and was replaced by Nikita Khrushchev. Khrushchev denounced Stalin and called for a more open society; and for a brief moment, there appeared to be a possibility of a thaw in, and perhaps an end to, the Cold War.

But instead, the Cold War intensified and expanded into new areas. Partially this was because the pace of decolonization increased during the 1950s and 1960s, thereby opening new areas for superpower competition. But equally if not more important, the patterns of thought and behavior that had already been established could not suddenly be reversed. Indeed, Republicans had come to power condemning the Democrats as being "soft on Communism" and could not now reverse themselves; and the anti-Communist hysteria was at its height. Indeed, both American political parties had learned by now that to be "soft" on Communism was to court defeat and disaster.

Meanwhile, in the Soviet Union, anti-American propaganda continued while Khrushchev halted reforms and used brute force when it became clear—as witnessed in Hungary in 1956—that those reforms could lead to the demise of the Soviet Empire. The Cold War thus continued and expanded across the entire globe, and it became "hot" again in Vietnam, which will be the subject of the next lecture.

But it remained "cold" in terms of direct Soviet-American military confrontation; with massive numbers of nuclear weapons on each side creating a "balance of terror" that maintained the peace, albeit always at the verge of a miscalculated nuclear holocaust. By the late 1960s and early 1970s, however, the bipolar world that had come into existence in 1945 no longer existed. Instead, new centers of power had emerged as Europe recovered from World War II and China emerged as a major player, and as

China's major split with the Soviet Union became public and more intense, leading to armed border clashes by 1969.

Sensing both the limits of American power in Vietnam and the possibilities inherent in the Sino-Soviet split, U.S. President Richard Nixon and his National Security Adviser Henry Kissinger pursued a triangular balance of power approach that led to a major lessening of global tensions. As a former hard Cold Warrior, Nixon was able to use his reputation to "sell" this policy of détente to the American people. As the cliché asserted, "Only Nixon could go to China." Predictions arose that the Cold War might finally be coming to an end. But it did not come to an end. Instead, the Nixon/Kissinger détente ended by the late 1970s, and a new "hot" war emerged as the Soviet Union invaded Afghanistan to prevent the collapse of its puppet government there and a victory by Islamic fundamentalist.

In retrospect, this event in Afghanistan and the simultaneous Iranian Islamic Revolution constituted the wave and face of the future, and it threatened both superpowers; but they remained locked in their old conflict and did not see this. Instead, both Democrat Jimmy Carter and his Republican successor Ronald Reagan reacted strongly to the Soviet invasion of Afghanistan and supported the Islamic forces. Reagan also attacked the entire notion of détente; and a new and fierce Cold War thus began. It was a new and fierce Cold War that we tend to forget because of what happened in the late 1980s, but it was one that nevertheless had many people thinking they were once again on the brink of World War III. The Soviets shot down a South Korean airliner bound from Alaska to Seoul, South Korea; the nuclear arms race accelerated; and some people talked about actually winning a nuclear war.

World War III, of course, did not occur, and for two basic reasons: First, the old generation of Soviet leaders died and a new, young Soviet leader from a younger generation, Mikhail Gorbachev, instituted major reforms in Soviet domestic and foreign policy; those reforms summarized by the terms "glasnost" and "perestroika." Secondly, rejecting the advice of his hard-line advisers, Reagan embraced the reforms and with Gorbachev instituted a new era of Soviet-American cooperation. The Cold War finally did end between 1989 and 1991 when glasnost and perestroika led not only to reform and a lessening of Soviet-American tensions, but to the total collapse of first the Soviet Empire in Eastern Europe and then the Soviet Union itself.

What, then, was the Cold War, and why did it last so long? It was in one sense not a war at all, but a state of abnormal bipolarity following World War II that could have, but never did, result in World War III because neither side thought it could militarily defeat the other. Yet there were numerous bloody regional wars fought within the Cold War, including Korea, Vietnam, Afghanistan, and a series of civil and regional conflicts fought by proxies. As previously stated, conflict may have been inevitable when World War II ended, but the duration and intensity of this conflict was not.

That intensity and duration resulted primarily from domestic and ideological factors in each country that in retrospect were almost totally at odds with the international realities after 1949 or at the latest after 1953. Without those domestic and ideological factors, the Soviets and the Americans could and should have ended the Cold War either with the European stalemate of 1949 or the Korean armistice and death of Stalin by 1953. But ideological and partisan hysteria prevented that, on both sides. So did the fact that thousands of American soldiers had lost their lives to international Communism in Korea. After that, no American politician dared act in a way that could lead to accusations that he was "soft on Communism." Similarly, Khrushchev and his successors halted reforms when it became clear from events in Poland, Hungary, and Czechoslovakia that those reforms could lead to the end of the Soviet Empire. They also severely limited their contacts and relations with the United States for fear of the impact on their people. Instead, they continued their propaganda against "American capitalism and imperialism."

But ironically, monolithic international Communism never really existed; witness the Russian-Yugoslav split by 1947, the Sino-Soviet split a few years later, and many others. In fact, one could say the real conflict was never really about ideology at all—though many thought it was—rather, what you had here was a global power conflict between Russia and the United States in a uniquely bipolar world that followed World War II. The real threat for the United States in this regard was never Communism per se but Soviet power and its ability to expand into the global power vacuum that existed at the end of the war. The early Cold Warriors clearly recognized this, as well as the limits of American power, and the dangers of creating a garrison state in the process of combating the Soviets. Marshall, Kennan, and Eisenhower all realized this and warned about it. As Kennan put it, the "greatest danger that can befall us in coping with the problem of Soviet communism is that we shall allow ourselves to become like those with whom we are coping." Eisenhower, in 1961, warned Americans of the "Military-Industrial Complex."

Containment was thus originally designed as a non-military and limited economic policy for Europe. But such limited concepts of containment changed in 1950–1951 as the Cold War became global and hot in Korea, leading to the globalization and militarization of containment despite the continued objections and warnings by these individuals and others. Although the Republicans in 1952 attacked containment as defeatist and promised a more aggressive policy of "liberation," containment remained the American policy under Eisenhower, and then under Kennedy, Johnson, Nixon, Ford, Carter, Reagan, and Bush; albeit, as the historian John Gaddis has pointed out, with different strategies and different emphases in each administration. In this regard, and again contrary to more recent mythology, Ronald Reagan did not "win" the Cold War or abandon containment. He maintained containment, albeit with different emphases. If containment did succeed in winning the Cold War, the credit belongs to all administrations from Truman though Reagan and Bush. All of them desired to end the Cold War; none of them proved able to do so until the late 1980s.

Was the conflict inevitable? Some Russian-American conflict was probably inevitable after World War II, but not the 45-year global conflict that left hundreds of thousands dead around the world and left the entire planet on the brink of World War III and nuclear annihilation. Indeed, as one of my students once wrote in response to an essay question regarding whether an earlier war (1812) was inevitable, he answered it was not because no event in history is inevitable even though it may appear that way in hindsight. Even that economic determinist Karl Marx asserted that "man makes his own history," though often not out of cloth of his own choosing.

The Real Blunders of the Vietnam War
Lecture 21

The Vietnam War was one of the most unsuccessful and internally divisive conflicts in U.S. history. Indeed, the reasons for our failure in that war continue to divide Americans today. But none of the scapegoats usually put forth—Lyndon Johnson, the military's counterproductive strategy, the domestic antiwar movement—addresses the central reasons for the American failure in Vietnam, which lie in the realm of faulty perceptions—of both the nature of the conflict and of Vietnam itself.

The Course of American Involvement

- American involvement in Vietnam began in 1950—if not earlier—and lasted until 1975. Throughout this period, the United States viewed Vietnam as part of its larger Cold War conflict with the Soviet Union.

  o This American perspective was partially explained by the fact that the insurgencies against French colonial rule and the South Vietnamese government were led by Vietnamese communists under Ho Chi Minh.

  o In addition, rebuilding France as a bulwark against communist expansion in Europe and helping to maintain French control of Indochina were key components of America's Cold War policy of containment.

- The United States followed a policy of benevolent neutrality toward France in the early stages of its war with Ho and then active support of the French from 1950–1954, by which time our nation was paying for approximately 70 percent of the French war effort.

- That effort ended in failure, however, and in 1954, France decided to sue for peace. The result was the Geneva Conference of 1954; the withdrawal of the French; and the creation of the independent states of Cambodia, Laos, and a temporarily divided Vietnam in what had been French Indochina.

- At that point, the United States shifted its support to the anticommunist entity below the 17th parallel known unofficially as South Vietnam. All U.S. efforts were now directed at defending South Vietnam militarily against the actions of both communist guerrillas in the South and the North Vietnamese army.

- The effort was at first limited to economic and military aid, along with military advisers, but when that failed, the number of military advisers was increased dramatically. And when that effort failed, President Lyndon Johnson began a sustained bombing campaign against North Vietnam and sent major U.S. military forces into the South.

- Those forces failed to achieve more than a military stalemate. That fact and the damage being done by the war—both domestically and internationally—led Johnson's successor, Richard Nixon, to scale down U.S. military forces and sign a peace accord with the North. Simultaneously, he tried to build up the effectiveness of the South Vietnamese army, a process known as "Vietnamization."

- This was done at the same time that Nixon was creating the policy of détente with the Soviet Union, which led to the belief that the Soviets would hold back the communists in Vietnam while Nixon completed Vietnamization and the American military withdrawal. The Soviets failed to do so, however; Vietnamization also failed, and North Vietnam was able to conquer the South in 1975.

- The key problems with the American approach were threefold: (1) The South Vietnamese government was never a viable entity; (2) the Vietnam War was much more than a Cold War conflict; and (3) the war was not a Cold War conflict at all to the Vietnamese fighting in it.

Decolonization after World War II

- The Cold War was but one of two major international events to take place in the aftermath of World War II. The other was the decolonization of Asia, Africa, and the Middle East, as nationalist movements in these areas succeeded in throwing out the European colonial powers that had previously ruled them.

- Nationalist sentiments had been strong in the French colony of Indochina since its creation in the 1880s. At the end of World War I, Vietnamese nationalist Ho Chi Minh, having been rejected by President Wilson, pled the case for his country's independence to the Bolsheviks, who were more than willing to provide support.

- During World War II, the United States had supported decolonization, and after the war, Ho had worked with American agents to launch guerrilla attacks against the Japanese, who had seized control from a French puppet government in 1945. After the Japanese surrender, Ho announced the independence of Vietnam from France.

- But by 1945, both Roosevelt and his successor, Truman, were having second thoughts about decolonization. As the Cold War increased in intensity from 1946–1949, so did U.S. support for our nation's European allies with colonial empires.

- The final blows to any American support for Ho, or even neutrality during his ensuing war with the French, were the 1949 communist victory in China and the Korean War that began in 1950. From that point onward, the United States was determined to contain communism in Asia.

The Geneva Conference and Its Aftermath

- American support for the French in the early 1950s failed to change the outcome in Vietnam. At the 1954 Geneva Conference, the French agreed to recognize Vietnamese independence, as well the independence of Laos and Cambodia. Vietnam itself was temporarily divided at the 17th parallel.

- The United States refused to sign the Geneva Accords, though it did state that it would not disturb them by force. Privately, it labeled them a disaster that would lead to the communization of all Southeast Asia.

- To prevent this from happening, the United States found an anticommunist Vietnamese nationalist, Ngo Dinh Diem, to wrest control of the French puppet government in South Vietnam. The Americans hoped that Diem could establish an anticommunist alternative to Ho.

Increasing U.S. Commitments
- South Vietnam appeared to be a success in nation-building, but beneath the surface, Diem's government was in serious trouble, leading the United States into deeper commitments. By 1959, Ho's communist government in the North had decided to support the insurgency brewing in the South.

- The Kennedy administration sent in military forces to stop the communists with the goal of "winning hearts and minds." But by 1963, that effort had failed, and the United States sanctioned a military coup that overthrew and assassinated Diem.

- Ensuing military coups added to the instability of the government and the failure in the war against the communists. By 1964–1965, the communists were on the verge of winning.

- President Johnson then escalated American involvement via selective bombing of North Vietnam, followed by a sustained bombing campaign against the North and the decision to send combat troops into the South in 1965.

Escalation, De-escalation, and the End
- By 1968, American forces in Vietnam numbered more than 500,000. The Americans had succeeded in preventing the communists from winning but not in defeating them.

- In addition to misunderstanding the nature of the war, the United States had grossly miscalculated the enemy's will—perhaps because it tended to view that enemy in Cold War terms, as puppets of the Soviet Union rather than fierce nationalists.

- To make matters worse, the war was tearing America apart and weakening U.S. military containment of the Soviet Union elsewhere. The war had also prompted severe questioning of American policy by our European allies and increased the prestige and influence of the Soviets in the Third World.

- In 1968, Nixon realized the failure of the Americanization of the war and the damage it was doing both domestically and internationally, but like his predecessors, he would not accept defeat.

- Instead, Nixon began the process of Vietnamization and the de-escalation of the American presence in South Vietnam but combined with an expansion of the air war against the North. He also believed that with détente, the Soviets would lessen their military support of the North and apply diplomatic pressure.

- All of Nixon's efforts failed as badly as those of his predecessors. At the peace talks in Paris, he managed to obtain a return of U.S. POWs, an armistice in place, and the ability to remove the last U.S. combat forces from Vietnam, but no lessening of communist pressure.

- The South Vietnamese government continued to be weak, corrupt, totally reliant on U.S. aid, and unable to win nationalist support from the population. It thus collapsed in the face of the North Vietnamese offensive of 1975. As a result of the Watergate break-in and a host of related illegal activities, the Nixon presidency had also collapsed by this time.

The True Causes of American Failure
- There were many additional reasons for the American failure in Vietnam, but the basic problem that underlay all the others was the

insistence on viewing the war in Cold War terms rather than Third World nationalist terms.

- Along with this went a related ignorance of Vietnamese history and culture, itself at least partially the result of the Cold War. That ignorance resulted in the underestimation of both the willingness of Hanoi to face American firepower and the difficulty of creating an effective government in the South.

- Given that Washington viewed Vietnam as part of the global Cold War, it did not ever make Vietnam its top priority. In effect, every administration put into Vietnam only what was necessary to avoid defeat during its watch, not enough to win. This decision was also motivated by domestic factors, most notably a desire not to be charged with being "soft on communism" or having "lost" Indochina.

By early 1968, American forces in Vietnam numbered more than 500,000, but those forces failed to achieve more than a military stalemate.

Consequences of the War

- Ironically, the negative domestic consequences of the American failure in Vietnam far outnumbered the international ones. It did not lead to the communization of all of Southeast Asia or seriously affect the global balance of power between the United States and the Soviet Union.

- It did, however, rip the United States apart internally, destroy two presidencies, and end the bipartisan consensus in foreign affairs that had existed since World War II. It also shattered the faith of many Americans in their government and, indeed, their country.

- Decades after the Vietnam War and the Cold War ended, we still live with these negative consequences and their aftermath. Ever since the war ended, Americans have either sought to ignore it or to draw analogies between it and more recent military interventions. But the truth is that every event in history is unique. History does not repeat itself, and every analogy is, thus, inherently flawed.

- Although history does not repeat itself, patterns of human behavior do. With Vietnam, perhaps the most important lessons are in that realm, in particular, in the tragedies of faulty perceptions that result from historical and cultural ignorance.

Suggested Reading

Clausewitz, *On War.*

Herring, *America's Longest War.*

McMahon, ed., *Major Problems in the History of the Vietnam War.*

Questions to Consider

1. What additional errors did the United States make in Vietnam?

2. Why were American policymakers and strategists so ignorant of the history and culture of Southeast Asia and, indeed, of Asia in general?

The Real Blunders of the Vietnam War
Lecture 21—Transcript

The Vietnam War, aptly labeled by historian George Herring as "America's Longest War," was also one of the most unsuccessful and internally divisive conflicts in American history. Indeed, the reasons for our failure in that war continue to divide Americans today. Many blame President Johnson and his advisers in particular for attempting to micromanage the war and for placing impossible limits on what the armed forces were allowed to do. In the famous words of actor Sylvester Stallone as he went back to Vietnam in one of his *Rambo* movies: "Do we get to win this time?" Others blame the armed forces themselves for using a counterproductive military strategy. Still others blame the domestic antiwar movement and/or the press.

While each of these factors may or may not contain a kernel of truth, none of them—individually or together—deal with the central reasons for the American failure in Vietnam. If anything, they distract attention from those central reasons. The fundamental reasons for the American failure in Vietnam lie in the realm of political failures and faulty perceptions, both of the nature of the conflict and of Vietnam itself.

From the beginning of the American involvement in Vietnam—which began not in 1965 (a common assumption) but in 1950, if not earlier—right down to North Vietnam's military conquest of South Vietnam and the departure of the last Americans in 1975, throughout this time period the United States viewed Vietnam as part of its larger Cold War conflict with the Soviet Union. That was primarily because the insurgency against French colonial rule from 1945–1954, and then against the South Vietnamese government, was led by Vietnamese Communists under Ho Chi Minh. It was also due to the fact that rebuilding France as a bulwark against Communist expansion in Europe was a key component of America's Cold War policy of containment; and you do not rebuild French power by supporting a revolt in the French Empire.

Consequently, the United States followed a policy of benevolent neutrality toward France in the early stages of its war with Ho, and then active support of the French from 1950–1954. Key National Security Council documents at that time defined helping to maintain French control of Indochina as a key part of what Secretary of State Dean Acheson defined in early 1950 as the American "Defense Perimeter" in Asia and the Pacific against further Communist expansion.

The outbreak of the Korean War in June, 1950 strongly reinforced that decision. Consequently, the United States began to support the French in Indochina financially and in terms of military supplies. By 1954, it was paying for approximately 70 percent of the French war effort. But that war effort ended in failure; a failure symbolized by the Communist capture of the key French fortress at Dien Bien Phu in 1954 and France's decision to sue for peace.

The result of this was the Geneva Conference of 1954, the withdrawal of the French, and the creation of independent states of Cambodia, Laos, and a temporarily divided Vietnam in what had been French Indochina. At that point, the United States shifted its support to the anti-Communist entity below the 17th parallel officially known as the Republic of Vietnam and unofficially as South Vietnam in an effort to contain the Communist victory north of the 17th parallel that was the dividing line between the two Vietnams. All American efforts from that point on were directed at defending South Vietnam militarily against the attempt by both Communist guerrillas in the South and the North Vietnamese Army to conquer the South. These efforts started under South Vietnamese President Ngo Dinh Diem, and then, after his assassination by the South Vietnamese military in 1963, under a series of military governments.

The effort was at first limited to economic and military aid along with military advisers, but when that failed the number of military advisers was increased dramatically under President John Kennedy. It had been 900 under President Eisenhower in early 1961; by the time of Kennedy's death in November, 1963, it was up to nearly 17,000. When that effort failed to halt the Communists, President Lyndon Johnson began a sustained bombing campaign against North Vietnam and sent major U.S. military forces into the South. By early 1968, those forces numbered over 500,000 and they had largely Americanized the war.

Those forces failed to achieve more than a military stalemate. That fact, and damage being done by the war both domestically and internationally in terms of America's global Cold War policy and commitments, led Johnson's successor Richard Nixon to scale down U.S. military forces and sign a peace accord with the North. Simultaneously, Nixon tried to build up the effectiveness of the South Vietnamese Army, a process known as "Vietnamization." This was done at the same time Nixon was creating the policy of détente with the Soviet Union, which led him and his advisers to believe that the Soviets would hold back the Communists in Vietnam while he completed this process and the American military withdrawal. The Soviets did not do so, Vietnamization failed, and the North Vietnamese Army was able to conquer the South in 1975.

The key problems with the whole American approach to the war were threefold: First, the South Vietnamese government was never a viable entity; second, the Vietnam War was much more than a Cold War conflict; and third, in some ways it was not a Cold War conflict at all to the Vietnamese fighting in it.

The Cold War was but one of two major international events to take place once World War II ended; the other was the decolonization of Asia, Africa, and the Middle East as nationalist movements in these areas succeeded in throwing out the European colonial powers that had previously ruled them. But those powers had been seriously weakened by World War II. Many of these nationalist movements had begun long before the 1940s. In Vietnam, they had existed ever since the French had created the colony of Indochina in the 1880s. The French had forcefully suppressed early rebellions against their rule, but not the nationalist sentiments that had always been strong. Indeed, the Vietnamese had previously fought against Chinese imperialism for a thousand years.

At end of World War I, one of these Vietnamese nationalists then living in Paris—who would later take the name Ho Chi Minh—tried to see President Wilson at the Paris Peace Conference to plead his case for Vietnamese independence. He failed in this effort, at which point he went to Moscow, where the new Bolshevik Government was more than willing to support any efforts that would weaken the capitalist European powers then attempting to overthrow them. Ho thus was a Communist and a Nationalist; a fact Americans would have a difficult time understanding and accepting during the Cold War. We still do, for reasons to be discussed later in this lecture.

During World War II, the United States had supported decolonization of Indochina, with Roosevelt explicit and emphatic in his condemnation of all colonialism and French Indochina his prime example of the worst aspects of colonialism. "After 100 years of French rule in Indochina," he said at one point, "the inhabitants were worse off than they were before." In Indochina, Ho and his Viet Minh organization worked with American agents of the Office of Strategic Services—the World War II predecessor to the CIA—to launch guerrilla attacks against the Japanese, who had seized control from a French puppet government in 1945. Ho and the Americans worked well together, and after the Japanese surrendered Ho announced the independence of Vietnam from France with words taken directly from the 1776 American Declaration of Independence from England.

By 1945, however, both Roosevelt and his successor Harry Truman were having second thoughts about decolonization; and as the Cold War developed and increased in intensity from 1946–1949, so did American support for its European allies with colonial empires. The final blows to any American support for Ho, or even neutrality during his ensuing war with the French, were the 1949 Communist victory in China and the 1950 Korean War. From that point onward, the United States was determined to contain Communism in Asia.

It was also determined to rebuild Japan as its major ally in the area and as a counterweight to Communist China. Vietnam was seen as critical to this effort, at least partially because of its geographic proximity to the resource-rich Dutch East Indies (soon to become Indonesia) and British Malaya. In an extraordinary irony, the United States was now in effect fighting to obtain for Japan the economic component of the Greater East Asia Co-Prosperity Sphere that it had fought to deny Japan during World War II. Please note in this regard that Japanese military movements into French Indochina led to the American freezing of Japanese assets in 1941 that in turn led to Pearl Harbor.

As previously noted, American support for the French in the early 1950s failed to change the outcome of this war in Vietnam. The United States did consider but eventually rejected a military intervention to save Dien Bien Phu. The Army Chief of Staff General Matthew Ridgway was particularly strong in his dissent against this idea. The French at the 1954 Geneva Conference agreed to recognize Vietnamese independence, as well the independence of Laos and Cambodia. Vietnam itself was temporarily divided at the 17th parallel, with French forces to withdraw south of that line and Vietminh forces north of that line. Unification elections were to be held in two years.

The United States refused to sign the Geneva Accords. It did state that it would not disturb them by force, but privately it labeled them a "disaster" that would lead to the communization of all of Southeast Asia. President Eisenhower publicly voiced this fear in his famous reference to a row of dominoes falling after the first one had fallen, an analogy that would become known as the Domino Theory. To prevent this from happening, the United States searched for and found an anti-Communist Vietnamese nationalist in Diem, who was then living in the exile in the United States; and the Americans hoped that Diem could establish an anti-Communist alternative to Ho in the South. In the South at that point was a French puppet government known as the Republic of Vietnam with its headquarters in Saigon. If Diem could establish a successful government in the South, it would prevent any further expansion of Communism into Southeast Asia. It would also prevent Democrats at home from claiming that Republicans had "lost" Indochina, much as the Republicans had previously accused the Democrats of having "lost" China.

Diem succeeded in wresting control of this South Vietnamese puppet government from Emperor Bao Dai—who had been both the Japanese and a French puppet—and with it Diem obtained temporary control of the area below the 17th parallel. By the Geneva Accords of 1954, that area was to remain separated from the North until unification elections in 1956. Taking advantage of this time period, the United States poured aid into South Vietnam, created the South East Asia Treaty Organization to defend the area, and supported Diem's refusal to hold elections in 1956; Eisenhower and others noting that had they been held, the North would have won. In effect, the United States had decided not so much to defend South Vietnam as to create it as a non-Communist alternative to the North and as part of the global effort to contain Communism. "Nation building" as a major U.S. policy did not begin in the 21st century, but in the mid-20th century.

On the surface, South Vietnam appeared to be a brilliant success in nation-building; indeed, it became a showcase of what American aid could do. But beneath the surface, Diem's government was always in serious trouble; and that trouble led the United States into deeper and deeper commitments to salvage what is had helped to create. Within a few years, Diem had alienated much of the population in the South. He was a centralizer and a Catholic in an area historically decentralized and Buddhist. As he moved to eliminate his political opponents, they fled to the old Vietminh cadres, they formed the National Liberation Front, and they conducted guerrilla warfare against Diem. By 1959, Ho's Communist government in the North, unwilling to accept the cancellation of elections and permanent division of the country, had decided to support this insurgency with military aid and forces.

The new Kennedy administration strongly believed in the doctrine of counterinsurgency as a way to counter Communist guerrillas globally. It therefore decided to send in the newly-created Special Forces, or Green Berets, as well as other military forces to stop the Communists by "winning the hearts and minds" of the South Vietnamese people. By 1963, that effort had failed miserably, and the United States then sanctioned a military coup that overthrew and assassinated Diem. But that only made the situation worse, with ensuing military coup after military coup just adding to the instability of the government and failure in the war against the Communists. Indeed, by 1964–1965, the Communists were about to win. That was one of the two major reasons Kennedy's successor Lyndon Johnson decided to escalate the American involvement via the bombing of North Vietnam in retaliation for two supposed attacks on U.S. warships in the Tonkin Gulf. That event we will examine in greater detail in the next lecture.

The second major reason for Johnson's escalation was politics. 1964 was a presidential election year, and Johnson wished to neutralize the issue of Vietnam in his campaign against Republican Barry Goldwater. The bombing and the Tonkin Gulf Resolution served this latter purpose very well, and

Johnson swept to a stunning victory over Goldwater in the November, 1964 elections.

But it had much less impact on the Vietnamese Communists, who were not scared off by Johnson's actions and who continued their successful military campaigns. Consequently, Johnson decided in April, 1965 both to launch a sustained bombing campaign against the North instead of merely retaliatory bombing and to send combat troops into the South, officially to defend U.S. airbases but in reality to conduct combat operations against the Communists as well. By June, 1965, the armed forces had made clear that they would need hundreds of thousands of troops and a new strategy: "search and destroy." Johnson agreed, once again both to stop a Communist victory and for domestic political reasons, this time to obtain passage of his "Great Society" bills as well as head off any Republican charge of being "soft on Communism" and "losing Vietnam."

By 1968, American forces numbered over 500,000. They had succeeded in preventing the Communists from winning, but not in defeating them. To do that, it became clear after the Communist Tet Offensive of early 1968, would require hundreds of thousands of more troops and placing the United States on a war footing with no end in sight and no guarantee of eventual victory. In addition to misunderstanding the nature of the war, the United States had grossly miscalculated the enemy's will, perhaps because it tended to view the enemy in Cold War terms as merely puppets of the Soviet Union rather than as fierce nationalists.

To make matters worse, the war was by this time ripping the country apart and severely weakening United States global military containment of the Soviet Union everywhere else. Vietnam by this point contained a very high percentage of American ground, naval, and air forces, including 40 percent of all U.S. combat-ready divisions, one-half of U.S. tactical airpower, and one-third of its naval strength, meaning those forces were not available to be used anywhere else in the world.

The war was also leading to a severe questioning of American policy by its European allies, with the possibility of losing those allies. It was also leading to increased prestige and influence for the Soviets in the entire Third World, which for obvious reasons viewed the American war effort as neocolonial rather than anti-Communist.

The war destroyed the presidency of Lyndon Johnson, who in the spring of 1968 decided not to run for reelection. His successor Richard Nixon realized the failure of the Johnson's Americanization of the war and the damage it was doing both domestically and internationally, but like his predecessors— and for the same reasons—he would not accept defeat. Instead, he began the process of "Vietnamization" and the de-escalation of the American military presence in South Vietnam, but combined with an expansion of the air war against the North to force it to agree to American terms at the Paris peace talks. He also believed that with détente, the Soviets would lessen their military support of the North and apply diplomatic pressure.

All of this failed as badly as the efforts of his predecessors. Nixon did obtain with the Paris Peace Accords a return of American prisoners of war, an armistice in place, and the ability to remove the last U.S. combat forces from Vietnam; but no lessening of Communist pressure. North Vietnam used the Sino-Soviet split to get aid from both China and Russia. The Soviets, in addition, refused to see détente as including Vietnam; and the South Vietnamese government continued to be weak, corrupt, and totally reliant on American aid, and unable to win nationalist support from the population. It thus collapsed with incredible rapidity in the face of a North Vietnamese offensive in 1975.

So did the Nixon presidency by this time. Nixon resigned under threat of impeachment and conviction for his role in the Watergate break-in to Democratic National Headquarters during the 1972 election campaign and the ensuing cover up. On the surface, this was a purely domestic issue; it had nothing to do with the Vietnam War. But beneath the surface it had a great deal to do with the Vietnam War. The Watergate break-in and a host of related illegal activities had involved members of the Committee for the Reelection of the President (with the acronym CREEP), former CIA operatives, and members of a group known as the Plumbers. The Plumbers had been formed to stop leaks of classified information having to do with Nixon's foreign policy in general and Vietnam in particular; leaks such as

Daniel Ellsberg's release of the classified Pentagon Papers on the history of the Vietnam War.

While the administration sought to stop future leaks by charging Ellsberg with a crime and prosecuting him in the courts, the Plumbers broke the law by breaking into the office of Ellsberg's psychiatrist in an attempt to find incriminating evidence against him. This effort soon broadened into a host of illegal operations against the entire anti-Vietnam War movement, and eventually against any opposition to Nixon, including the Democratic Party. Thus, the break-in to Democratic Headquarters in the Watergate building was part and parcel of a much larger issue. The Watergate break-in was just the tip of the Watergate iceberg.

Indirectly, then, the Vietnam War destroyed two presidencies: that of Nixon as well as that of Johnson. The links are not obvious on the surface, but they are definitely connected; and one task of the skeptic is to look for and find such historical connections that may not be apparent.

Why did the Americans fail? There were, of course, many additional reasons to those analyzed here for the American failure. To name but a few: Johnson's incremental bombing campaign against the North faced a lack of effective targets and totally failed to intimidate the North Vietnamese. It was also based on the very questionable doctrine that strategic bombing could force an enemy to surrender. Furthermore, the Army's "search and destroy" strategy also led to massive civilian casualties and destroyed the very society the United States was trying to create. Indeed, some have argued that the United States never really had a clear strategy.

Many others could be listed and analyzed; but the basic problem that underlay all the others was the insistence on viewing the war in Cold War terms rather than Third World Nationalist terms. Along with this went a related ignorance of Vietnamese history and culture. That ignorance actually was at least partially the result of the Cold War, for during the McCarthy era in the 1950s many if not most of our few Asian experts had been purged from the State Department for their policies and their prophecies regarding China. That ignorance of Vietnamese history and culture resulted in a subsequent underestimation of both the willingness of Hanoi to face American firepower and suffer massive casualties and the difficulty of creating an effective South Vietnamese government.

Furthermore, since Washington viewed Vietnam as part of the global Cold War, it did not—indeed it could not—ever make Vietnam its top priority. In effect, every administration put into Vietnam only what was necessary to avoid defeat during its watch, not enough to win. As one high-ranking Defense Department official—Assistant Secretary of Defense John McNaughton—would admit in 1965, a full 70 percent of the reason for the bombing of the North was "to avoid a humiliating defeat." Even the more than 500,000 troops that Johnson sent were not enough. Given Hanoi's ability to send 200,000 soldiers a year into the South, and the length and size of the enormous American logistical tail, closer to 2 million soldiers would have been needed; and that was utterly impossible given America's global commitments and priorities. In addition, those troops would probably have been needed for a decade or more given the Asian as opposed to the Western concept of time. As Chinese Communist leader Chou En-Lai supposedly said when asked for his views on the significance of the 18th-century French Revolution, "it is too soon to say." Vietnamese Nationalists viewed their struggle through the lens of nearly a century of struggle against the French and a thousand years against the Chinese.

This decision by each administration only to do what was necessary to avoid defeat during its watch was also motivated by domestic factors, most notably a desire not to be charged by your political opponents with being "soft on Communism" or having "lost" Indochina. Ironically, or perhaps appropriately, in light of these facts, the American failure in Vietnam had far more negative domestic consequences than international ones. Contrary to domino theory, it did not lead to the Communization of all of Southeast Asia; and the nations in which Communists did triumph soon went to war with each other: Vietnam invaded Cambodia, China invaded Vietnam, while China and Russia almost went to the verge of total war. Does that sound like monolithic Communism?

Nor did the American failure in Vietnam seriously affect the global balance of power between the United States and the Soviet Union; but it massively affected the United States domestically, ripping the country apart, destroying two presidencies, and ending the bipartisan consensus in foreign affairs that had existed since World War II. It also led for the first time to a shattering of the faith of many Americans in their government, and indeed their country. Decades after the Vietnam War and the Cold War ended, we still live with these negative consequences and their aftermath.

Ever since the war ended, Americans have either sought to ignore it or else to draw analogies between the Vietnam War and more recent military interventions. The problem with such analogies is that one tends to look for events in the past that will support one's preexisting position on any contemporary issue and to ignore contrary historical analogies even though they might be more appropriate. There is also a related tendency to look for analogies to events in one's own lifetime only rather than the distant past. Illustrating both points was the proper analogy and search for historical lessons for the Cold War and Vietnam. Was it the 1930s, as most Americans thought? Or were the events and lessons of the long Peloponnesian War between Athens and Sparta 2,500 years earlier more appropriate?

In addition to this, every event in history is unique. History does not repeat itself, and every analogy is thus inherently flawed. A colleague of mine, when asked about analogies during the 1980s between El Salvador and Vietnam, said there were none. How do you compare what occurred in Southeast Asia with what was occurring in Central America? But we apparently insist upon drawing historical analogies anyway; and if we are ignorant of history, we will draw them only from what we have experienced in our own lifetimes. A deep knowledge of history can avoid that, and with it perhaps some of the worst pitfalls of historical analogies.

While history does not repeat itself, patterns of human behavior do. For Vietnam, perhaps the most important lessons are in that realm; in particular, the tragedies of faulty perceptions that result from historical and cultural ignorance.

Myths about American Wars
Lecture 22

In the last lecture, we examined some of the major misunderstandings associated with the Vietnam War. But Vietnam is far from the only American war that is misunderstood. Indeed, numerous misunderstandings and myths exist about most American wars: the idea that America has a tradition of defense by citizen-soldiers, that we go to war only for defensive reasons, and that we always "win the war but lose the peace." In this lecture, we will dispel such myths by examining the history and results of some of our wars.

The Defensive War

- Many if not most of our wars have been wars of choice. Indeed, only in the two world wars were we actually forced to declare war by the actions of our enemies.

- In the 19th century, both the 1846–1848 war with Mexico and the 1898 war with Spain were wars by choice—the first to acquire California and New Mexico and the second to force the Spanish out of Cuba. Similarly, in the 20th century, we chose to go to war in Korea in 1950 and in Vietnam in the 1960s as part of the Cold War.

- In a somewhat gray area is the War of 1812. Madison and the Congress went to war in desperation because of the failure of their previous measures of economic retaliation designed to force the British to cease violating American neutral rights on the high seas.

- In the Civil War, the South chose to secede and fight for independence, while the North chose war to prevent that. Similarly, Americans chose to fight against what they saw as British violations of their rights in 1775, while Britain chose to crush their rebellion by force.

- Even in the two world wars, our enemies argued that our previous non-neutral acts had made us an unofficial belligerent and forced them to attack us.

Incorrect and Manipulated Evidence for War

- The fact that America went to war against Iraq in 2003 on the basis of faulty or manipulated intelligence regarding "weapons of mass destruction" is viewed incorrectly as an anomaly in American history. In reality, numerous past presidents have presented incorrect information—sometimes knowingly and sometimes unknowingly—in order to obtain congressional and public approval of war.

The faulty basis for America's war on Iraq is not an anomaly in our history; presidents from Madison, to FDR, to Johnson, to Bush have relied on faulty intelligence to launch military actions.

- In 1846, President James K. Polk sent an army under General Zachary Taylor into disputed territory along the Rio Grande River, and when that army clashed with the Mexican army, he asked Congress for war on the grounds that "American blood" had been shed on "American soil." In reality, Polk may have sent Taylor's army into the territory to provoke a war in order to obtain California.

- In September of 1941, President Franklin Roosevelt claimed that the U.S. destroyer *Greer* had been "wantonly attacked" by a German submarine in the Atlantic and launched an unofficial naval war against Germany in response. In reality, however, the *Greer* had been trailing the German submarine and radioing its position back to a British fleet, which had responded with air attacks. The submarine had fired on the *Greer* in self-defense.

- More common historically than such blatant manipulation of the facts has been the presentation of evidence that was believed at the time but that later research showed to be incorrect. Such was the case in the declaration of both the War of 1812 and the Spanish-American War.

Dispensing with Contrary Evidence
- In a separate category are war-causing events that were believed at the time because the administration wanted to believe them and, consequently, ignored contrary evidence.

- In order to obtain passage of the Gulf of Tonkin Resolution, President Lyndon Johnson and Defense Secretary Robert McNamara claimed, in August 1964, that two attacks had taken place against U.S. destroyers by North Vietnamese torpedo boats in the Gulf of Tonkin.
  - o The resolution authorized the president to use force to prevent future attacks and would later be used by Johnson to justify his Americanization of the Vietnam War.

  - o Johnson's original aim in getting the resolution passed, however, had been to "send a message" to the North Vietnamese regarding American unity and seriousness of purpose and to neutralize the issue of Vietnam in the 1964 presidential election campaign.

  - o The administration had, in fact, prepared the resolution months earlier and simply waited for an "episode" to justify presenting it. It thus chose to ignore evidence that the second attack may not have occurred, as well as its own actions that probably led to the first attack.

- Nearly 40 years later, the Bush administration relied on faulty intelligence to claim that Saddam Hussein possessed weapons of mass destruction and ignored contrary evidence, in all likelihood because it had already decided to go to war and had convinced itself that the Iraqi dictator possessed such weapons.

Winning the War and Losing the Peace

- The belief that Americans always "win the war but lose the peace" because of our political naïveté is also incorrect. In point of fact, the reverse has often been the case.

- Militarily, the United States did not win the War of 1812, and politically, it did not lose the peace. In fact, U.S. military forces were consistently defeated by the British, and only last-minute defenses prevented total American defeat. Yet American diplomats at Ghent proved superior to British diplomats and obtained a highly favorable peace treaty.

- In 1846–1848, the United States both won the war with Mexico and achieved the original territorial aims of President Polk. In fact, one reason Polk accepted the final treaty was that despite its military victories, his small army in Mexico City was in danger of being cut off and having to deal with guerrilla warfare.

- The United States also won both the war and the peace in the 1898 war with Spain. Indeed, our nation acquired an overseas empire that territorially went beyond what we had actually conquered during the war.

- In World War II, the United States played a role in Allied victory, but its participation in the war was brief and it was not primarily responsible for victory. Still, the limited role played by our forces was sufficient to enable President Woodrow Wilson to claim a dominant role at the Paris Peace Conference.

- Similarly, the United States did not win World War II all by itself, nor did it "lose the peace."

- There was, in fact, never a peace to lose because the Cold War precluded the negotiation of any peace treaty—or even the calling of a peace conference.

- The claim that we lost the peace at the wartime Yalta Conference, where a naïve Roosevelt gave away half the world to Stalin, incorrectly assumes that Roosevelt possessed half the world to give away, which he did not.

- Further, despite its limited contribution to military victory, the United States emerged from the war as by far the most powerful nation in the world.

- Militarily, the Korean War was a stalemate. Nevertheless, the United States succeeded in attaining its original political goal: the halting of North Korean aggression and the maintenance of the preexisting South Korea.

- In Vietnam, the United States clearly lost the war yet achieved, in the Paris Peace Accords, what Nixon and Kissinger had desired regarding a "decent interval" for Vietnamization and the removal of U.S. forces from what had clearly become a military quagmire.

- In the first Persian Gulf War, the United States succeeded both militarily and in its stated political goal of halting Iraq's aggression against Kuwait.

- And, of course, with the 1991 demise of the Soviet Union, the United States "won" the Cold War without ever having defeated a Soviet army.

Roots of the Myths
- To a large extent, our myths about war are the result of our bitterness and disappointment regarding its results, especially the results of the two world wars. That disappointment was linked to our unrealistic expectations regarding the ability of total military victory in a coalition war to translate into the total re-creation of

international relations in the image we desired. Victory in the two world wars did not—and could not—accomplish that.

- The two world wars, and the nature of American democracy, also helped to create a mythical belief that the only wars worth fighting are total wars for total victory and a total re-creation of the world. None of that is true.

- These myths are also part of our national mythology about ourselves—that we are a peace-loving people who go to war only when left with no choice; who are then militarily victorious against evil enemies because of our goodness, our military prowess, and divine protection; but who are foiled and defeated in the peace because as a peace-loving people we are naïve about war and peacemaking.

- That national mythology is, in turn, based on a belief that war is evil and should be undertaken only when we are attacked and there is no choice. Many of us believe that, but that does not mean that what we should do—avoid war unless we are attacked—is what we actually have done in our history.

- The mythology also stems from the fact that we confuse success in battle with success in war.
  - o Our failure to understand the difference between war and battle was boldly illustrated after the Vietnam War by the American who commented to his Vietnamese counterpart that throughout the war, we never lost a battle. The statement may have been correct, but it was also irrelevant.

  - o George Washington came to understand this idea during the Revolutionary War, as he achieved the political goal of independence despite the fact that his army lost most of its battles. The few that it won, as shown in an earlier lecture, were enough because of their political consequences.

o   We have forgotten that lesson from our 18th-century past. Perhaps that is because as our power has grown, so has our arrogance and our blindness to our own history.

Suggested Reading

Buhite, ed., *Call to Arms.*

Clausewitz, *On War.*

Paterson, et al., *American Foreign Relations.*

Questions to Consider

1.   Why does total victory on the battlefield usually not result in obtaining stated political goals?

2.   Why do Americans insist that war should be total when most of its wars have not been total?

Myths about American Wars
Lecture 22—Transcript

In last lecture, we examined some of the major misunderstandings associated with the Vietnam War. But Vietnam is far from the only American war that is misunderstood. Indeed, numerous misunderstandings exist about most American wars. So do numerous myths.

One major myth concerns our tradition of "citizen soldiers" to fight our wars, a tradition that began in the Colonial Era with every able bodied male colonist supposedly ready to grab his trusty musket off the mantelpiece of his home and go out to successfully defend his community, be it against Indians, or the French, or the Spanish, or during the Revolutionary War against the British.

As with most myths, this one contains an element of truth; indeed, much more than simply an element. During the 17th century, colonists had to rely upon themselves for defense and they thus created in the New World from English tradition the militia system, in which every able bodied adult male in the community was a member and liable for military training on "muster days" as well as military service when called up. Militia was heavily involved in the Revolutionary War, and the militia system was enshrined in federal law after the Revolutionary War with the Militia Act of 1792. That remained the basic military legislation for the country until the early 20th century.

But in reality, the muster days during the Colonial Era were more social events than occasions for military training, and the militia proved to be an unreliable as well as untrained body. Their members came and went as they pleased, and their elected or politically-appointed officers were anything but competent. There were also numerous exemptions from military service, and the system was in a state of serious decay, if not outright collapse, by the time of the Revolutionary War.

The war did witness a major revival of the militia system, but its members for the most part remained unreliable and unable to stand up to British regulars, especially a British bayonet charge. Washington consequently placed little faith in the militia and instead focused during the war on the creation and the rigorous training of his Continental Army to fight the British regulars. Militia did play a crucial role in numerous battles and in winning the war, but only when properly led and primarily in conjunction with the Continental Army.

Had Washington been able to have his way, little reliance would have been placed on militia after the war. But realizing that would be politically impossible—as well as ideologically and practically impossible— Washington called for a system whereby the central government would control the militia and impose uniformity on it in terms of arms, organization, and training. But that proved to be equally impossible. Consequently, a dual defense system emerged under the Constitution. It consisted of a small professional army and the state militia, with authority over state militia split between the national and state governments.

But with the passage of the Militia Act of 1792, what that actually translated into was no centralized control and no uniformity. All males aged 18–45 were required by this act to enroll in the militia, but there was no federal control over training, arms, or officer selection. Primary reliance was thus placed not on the militia but on a small professional army, augmented by volunteers in times of war—as well as a draft during the Civil War—and on special, elite volunteer militia units that had begun to form in the Colonial Era. These gradually evolved during the late 19th century into the present-day National Guard.

Militia units were used during the 19th century, usually with disappointing results. They did very poorly during the War of 1812, and their lawless behavior during the war with Mexico was so outrageous that the Mexicans labeled them "Bandits vomited from hell." Regular officers concurred, and there was little love lost between militia and the regular army. Indeed, regular army reformers consistently called for either an end to the militia system or strong federal control over it.

The National Guard did come under greater federal control during the 20th century, but during the two world wars and the Cold War, primary reliance for manpower was placed upon a national draft. A system of universal military training was proposed, but it never passed. Consequently, we retain today the dual system of a regular army and elite volunteer militia units, but that is not the citizen-soldier concept of universal military obligation and service. That, as well as the belief that untrained or poorly trained citizens can defeat regulars, is part of our national mythology.

Another major myth is that we and our leaders only go to war for defensive reasons and when forced by aggressors to do so. In this regard, many view the decision by President George W. Bush to go to war against Iraq in 2003 as an anomaly; a break from past American history and traditions. It was not. The fact that we went to war in Iraq on the basis of faulty or manipulated intelligence regarding "weapons of mass destruction" is also viewed incorrectly as an anomaly in American history. In reality, numerous past presidents have presented incorrect information—sometimes knowingly, sometimes unknowingly—in order to obtain Congressional and public approval of war. Similarly incorrect is the belief that we Americans always "win the war but lose the peace" because of our political naiveté. In point of fact, the reverse has often been the case.

This rest of this lecture will attempt to dispel such myths by examining presidential behavior prior to America's major wars, as well as the military history of those wars and the political results.

Let's look first at the issue of "defensive" wars versus "wars by choice." Historically, many if not most of our wars have been wars by choice. Point in fact, only in World War I and World War II were wars in which we were actually forced to declare war by the previous actions of our enemies. In the 19th century, both the 1846–1848 war with Mexico and the 1898 war with Spain were wars by choice; the first to acquire California and New Mexico, as well as a favorable boundary for Texas, and the second to force the Spanish out of Cuba. Similarly, in the 20th century, we chose to go to war in Korea and in Vietnam in the 1960s as part of the Cold War. In a somewhat gray area is the War of 1812, as President Madison and the Congress went to war in desperation because of the failure of their previous measures of economic coercion designed to force the British to cease violating American neutral rights on the high seas. What about the Civil War? The South chose to secede and to fight for independence, while the North chose war in order to prevent this. Similarly, Americans chose to fight against what they saw as

British violations of their rights in 1775, while Britain chose to crush their rebellion by force.

Even in the two world wars, our enemies argued that our previous non-neutral acts had made us an unofficial belligerent and forced them to attack us. In 1917, it was our booming trade in war material and our loans to the Allied powers that led the Germans to announce unrestricted submarine warfare against our shipping, as well as everybody else's. In 1941, it was our freezing of Japanese assets, which in effect embargoed the oil and steel that Japan relied upon, and that is what led Tokyo to try to obtain those resources by force in the Southeast Asia and to attack the only military force capable of stopping them: the U.S. fleet at Pearl Harbor. Similarly, the decision via the Lend-Lease Act of 1941 to give war material free of charge first to Britain and eventually the Soviet Union, and then to use the U.S. Navy to help convoy that war material across the Atlantic, made the United States an unofficial belligerent in the war against Germany. In all of these wars, we argued that our enemies left us no choice but to go to war. But because we made such a claim does not mean that it was true.

What about incorrect and/or manipulated evidence for going to war? In 1846, President James K. Polk manipulated both the evidence and the way it was presented so as to leave the Congress with no choice save to declare war. First, he sent an army under General Zachary Taylor into disputed territory along the Rio Grande River, and when Taylor's army clashed with the Mexican Army Polk asked Congress for war on the grounds that "American blood" had been shed upon "American soil." But it was disputed soil, not American soil, as a one-term Illinois Congressman named Abraham Lincoln and others would point out. Indeed, Lincoln would get the nickname "Spotty" for asking Polk to identify the spot on which American blood had been shed upon American soil. In addition to this, Polk may very well have sent Taylor's army into the disputed territory to provoke a war, as he was determined to obtain California and his efforts to do so by diplomatic negotiation had failed. In addition to all this, Congressional Democrats attached the war resolution as a rider to a military appropriations bill for the Army, and a portion of that Army was then engaged in hostilities. That made it nearly impossible to vote against the measure.

Jumping to World War II: In September, 1941, President Franklin D. Roosevelt claimed that the U.S. destroyer *Greer* had been "wantonly attacked" by a German submarine in the Atlantic. He responded as Commander-in-Chief with an order for U.S. warships to "shoot on sight" when they spotted German submarines. That began an undeclared naval war with Nazi Germany, one that became official when Hitler declared war on the United States soon after Pearl Harbor. But in reality, the *Greer* had been trailing the German submarine and radioing its position back to a British fleet that had responded with air attacks against the sub. The submarine had fired on the *Greer* in self-defense.

More common historically than such blatant manipulation of the facts has been the presentation of evidence that was believed at the time but that later research showed to be incorrect. One of the major factors that President James Madison cited in asking Congress for a declaration of war in June, 1812 were the British Orders-in-Council that Madison claimed violated American neutral rights. Actually, those Orders-in-Council had already been rescinded, but neither Madison nor the Congress knew that in June of 1812 because the news could not travel to America that rapidly; the only way was sailing ship, and the news arrived after war had already been declared war.

In 1898, one of the major reasons Congress declared war on Spain was the sinking of the U.S. battleship *Maine* in Havana harbor; a sinking that two Navy boards of inquiry concluded had been caused by an external mine, and that the public believed obviously had been planted there by the Spanish. But no evidence was ever presented that the Spanish had been responsible for the mine; and in the 1970s, a detailed Navy study concluded that the previous boards of inquiry had been incorrect and that in all likelihood the *Maine* had been destroyed by an internal explosion caused by spontaneous combustion in a coal bunker that then ignited a powder magazine and blew up the entire ship.

In a separate category are war-causing events that were believed at the time because the administration wanted to believe them and consequently ignored contrary evidence. In August, 1964, President Lyndon Johnson and Defense Secretary Robert McNamara claimed that two attacks had taken place against American destroyers in the Gulf of Tonkin by North Vietnamese torpedo boats. They did this in order to obtain passage of the Tonkin Gulf Resolution authorizing the president to use force to prevent future attacks. Johnson would later use that resolution to justify his ensuing Americanization of the Vietnam War.

That had not been his aim in August of 1964. Rather, his aim had been to "send a message" to North Vietnam regarding American unity and seriousness of purpose, and—as I previously noted—to neutralize the issue of Vietnam in the 1964 presidential election campaign. For those reasons, the administration had prepared this resolution months earlier and was simply waiting for an "episode" to justify presenting it. It thus chose to ignore contrary evidence arriving that the second attack may never have taken place—the first attack clearly did, but that the second attack had never taken place—that the blips on U.S. sonar were actually caused by the wakes of the ships as they took evasive action that was not needed (the second supposed attack took place at night). The administration also chose to ignore its own actions that had probably led to the first attack; in particular, DeSoto intelligence-gathering missions with warships running into North Vietnamese territorial waters and then racing out, and Oplan 34A operations against the North Vietnamese coast by South Vietnamese commandos who were transported in American naval vessels.

Similarly, the Bush Administration nearly 40 years later relied on faulty intelligence to claim that Saddam Hussein possessed weapons of mass destruction and it ignored contrary evidence, in all likelihood because it had already decided to go to war and had convinced itself that the Iraqi dictator did possess such weapons.

What about the cliché that the United States always wins the wars and loses the peace? Historically, the reverse has been the case more often. Militarily, the United States did not win the War of 1812, and politically it did not lose the peace. To the contrary: Its military forces were consistently defeated by the British in 1812 and in 1813; and in 1814, the British invaded and burned Washington. Only the last-minute turning back of a British assault on Baltimore and the turning back of a British invasion down the Champlain Valley at the Battle of Plattsburgh Bay prevented total defeat. Yet American diplomats at Ghent in Belgium proved superior to British diplomats and obtained a highly favorable peace treaty, one that ended previous British talk of obtaining American territory in the war and creating a separate Indian nation to block further American expansion. The peace treaty also implicitly accepted American sovereignty much more strongly than had the peace treaty of 1783 that had ended the Revolutionary War. As for the neutral rights issues that had led the United States into a declaration of war, they were rendered immaterial because of the simultaneous end of the Napoleonic Wars.

What about the war with Mexico, 1846–1848? Here, we won both the war and the peace, at least the peace President Polk had wanted when the war started. But as the war went on, Polk and many Americans thought more and more about acquiring all of Mexico; just annexing the entire country. Polk then accepted a more limited treaty that obtained his original territorial desires (California, New Mexico and the Rio Grande boundary. One reason he did so, and indeed one reason his peace envoy (Nicholas Trist) disobeyed orders—Polk had ordered him home—and negotiated this peace treaty was because despite its military victories, the small army in Mexico City faced the risk of being cut off and having to deal with guerrilla warfare. The head of that army, General Winfield Scott, asked Trist to stay and to sign the peace treaty.

What about the 1898 war with Spain? Here, we also won the war and the peace. Indeed, we acquired an overseas empire that territorially went beyond what we had actually conquered during the war.

As for World War I, contrary to popular belief, while the United States did play an important role in the eventual Allied victory, its participation in the war was brief—officially less than two years, in reality less than one on the actual battlefields—and the United States was not primarily responsible for the Allied victory. Indeed, the initial collapse of the German Army and the Central Powers as a whole took place in areas far removed from American forces. Yet the very limited role played by those forces was sufficient to enable President Woodrow Wilson to claim a dominant role at the Paris Peace Conference. Indeed, his only very firm instruction to General John J. Pershing was to keep the American army separate—not to allow it to be amalgamated into French and British forces—so that he would have a strong bargaining position at the Paris Peace Conference. Wilson did not get everything he wanted at Paris, but the compromises in the Treaty of Versailles reflected most of what he had wanted, most notably the League of Nations. That the League failed to keep the peace is not relevant; that is a separate issue.

Similarly, and as discussed in a previous lecture, the United States did not win World War II all by itself. It provided only 25 percent of the Allied armed forces during that war. Nor did it lose the peace. First of all, there never was a peace to lose, as the Cold War precluded the negotiation of any peace treaty, or even the calling of a peace conference. As for the claim that we nevertheless lost the peace to Josef Stalin during the wartime Yalta Conference, a conference in which a supposedly naïve Roosevelt gave away half of the world to Stalin, that very statement incorrectly assumes that Roosevelt possessed that half of the world to give away. As previously explained, he did not. Furthermore, despite its limited contribution to military victory, the United States emerged from World War II as by far the most powerful nation in the world, and indeed the most powerful nation the world has ever seen. British historian A.J.P. Taylor once quipped that Roosevelt was the most successful—indeed in some ways the only successful—World War II leader. He made the United States the greatest power in the world, Taylor noted, at a cost much lower than that of any other major belligerent.

What about the Korean War? Militarily that was a stalemate. Nevertheless, the United States did succeed in obtaining its original political goal; it did not succeed in obtaining the later one of liberating and unifying all of Korea, but it did succeed in the original goal: the halting of North Korean aggression and the maintenance of the preexisting South Korea.

In Vietnam, the United States clearly lost the war, even though it may never have lost a battle; yet it achieved in the Paris Peace Accords what Nixon and Kissinger had desired regarding a "decent interval" for Vietnamization and the removal of American forces from what had clearly become a military quagmire.

What about the first Iraq War? Here the United States succeeded both militarily and in its stated political goal of halting Iraq's aggression against

Kuwait. Overthrowing Saddam Hussein was not in the original American, or the U.N., sanctions to go to war in Iraq.

Of course, with the 1991 demise of the Soviet Union, the United States "won" the Cold War without ever having defeated a Soviet army.

Why then, in light of all these facts, do we continue to believe that we do not start wars, that we only go to war in response to attacks upon us and on the basis of solid evidence, and that we always win the wars but lose the peace? To a large extent, these myths are the result of our bitterness and disappointment regarding the results of the wars we fought, especially the two world wars. That bitterness and disappointment was linked to our very unrealistic expectations regarding the ability of total military victory in a coalition war to translate into the total recreation of international relations in the image that we desired and that President Wilson and President Roosevelt enunciated. It did not; it could not accomplish that.

The two world wars and the nature of American democracy also helped to create a mythical belief that the only wars worth fighting are total wars for total victory and a total recreation of the world. None of that is true. The American belief that it is led State Department official George Kennan, who left the State Department and became a famous historian, more than 60 years ago in a lecture to compare the United States to a prehistoric dinosaur with a body the size of a large room and a brain the size of a pin. You virtually have to whack its tail off, Kennan noted, to wake it up and make it aware that its interests are being threatened; but once awake, it responds with such fury over having been disturbed and a response that has no limit that it winds up destroying not only whoever has disturbed it its own habitat.

These myths are also part of our national mythology about ourselves: That we are a peace-loving people who only go to war when left with no choice, who are then militarily victorious against evil enemies because of our goodness as well as our military prowess and divine protection, but we are then foiled and defeated in the peacemaking because as a peace-loving people we are naïve about war and peacemaking.

This national mythology is in turn based on a belief that war is evil and therefore should be undertaken only when we are attacked and there is no choice. That may be true. I definitely believe that it is true, on moral grounds but on practical grounds as well; for war is almost always a great gamble whose outcome cannot be accurately predicted. But that does not mean that what we should do—avoid war unless we are attacked and there is no choice—is what we have actually done in our history.

The mythology is also due to the fact that we tend to confuse success in battle with success in war. One of the most misnamed books of the late 20th century was a history of the German General Staff entitled *A Genius for War*. As numerous critics pointed out, it should have been entitled *A Genius for Battle*, as starting and losing two world wars does not illustrate a genius for war. A the Prussian military officer and theorist, Carl von Clausewitz, knew this, emphasized in his classic study *On War* almost 200 years ago that wars are fought for political goals and make sense only within that political context. Indeed, he argued, political goals should to a great extent determine the military strategy that is used so that strategy does not inadvertently negate the very reasons one went to war. War, Clausewitz pointed out, has a tendency to go to the absolute, which was mindless violence. Real war was fought for political goals, but war did have that tendency to the absolute unless it was controlled.

Our failure to understand this and to understand the difference between war and battle was boldly illustrated after the Vietnam War by the American who commented to his Vietnamese counterpart that throughout the war, "we never lost a battle." That may be correct, the Vietnamese responded, but "it is also irrelevant." George Washington came to understand that during the War for Independence, as he achieved the political goal of independence despite the fact that his army lost most of its battles and won very few. But those few, as shown in an earlier lecture, were enough due to their political consequences.

We have forgotten that lesson from our 18th-century past. Perhaps that is because as our power has grown, so has our hubris—our pride, our arrogance—and our ensuing blindness to our own history.

Who Matters in American History?
Lecture 23

Most Americans think they know the names of the great political figures in American history: Washington, Jefferson, Lincoln, and so on. Yet there are numerous other figures whose contributions were just as important, but who are far less familiar to us. In this lecture, we'll examine a few such individuals and try to understand why, despite their accomplishments, they are less familiar than other figures. Our analysis will also enable us to explore who in history we choose to remember and why.

John Adams

- John Adams was probably the most important and respected of all the Revolutionary leaders from New England. He played a major role in both Continental Congresses; he nominated George Washington to command the Continental Army; he helped draft the Declaration of Independence; and he drafted the instructions that would result in the wartime treaty of alliance with France.

- He also obtained a critical Dutch loan while a diplomat in Europe during the war, played a major role in the peace negotiations that ended the war, and became the first official U.S. representative to Great Britain after the war.

- When he took office as president, Adams inherited a diplomatic crisis with France, as well as a growing partisan rift at home, with the opposition led by Thomas Jefferson.

- The crisis with France erupted into an undeclared naval war in 1798 that the Hamiltonian wing of Adams's own Federalist Party wanted to turn into a full-scale declared war. Such a war, when combined with the recently passed Alien and Sedition Acts virtually outlawing dissent, would have guaranteed his reelection, but Adams refused to agree. He never filled the ranks of the special army Congress had agreed to create, and when France proposed negotiations to end the conflict, he quickly agreed.

- He also fired the Hamiltonian members of his cabinet when he discovered that they were subverting his plans to negotiate an end to the war. As a result, he obtained peace with France but at the cost of splitting his Federalist Party and, thus, dooming his own reelection. Adams realized the political cost of his behavior but considered it the most meritorious act of his life.

- As the only one of the five Founding Fathers elected president but not reelected for a second term, Adams became the forgotten one. Recent biographers have done their best to give Adams his due, but he nevertheless remains relatively unknown to the public.

John Quincy Adams

- At Adams's death in 1826, his son, John Quincy, was in the midst of his own largely forgotten presidency. Yet like his father, the younger Adams had had a brilliant career before he became president, primarily as a diplomat. He had helped negotiate the Treaty of Ghent, ending the War of 1812; had served as ambassador to the Netherlands, Prussia, Russia, and Great Britain; and had been James Monroe's secretary of state.

- In these roles, Adams had been responsible for some of the most important treaties and announcements in the history of U.S. foreign relations: the agreement to limit naval forces on the Great Lakes, which was the basis of the peaceful border between Canada and the United States; joint Anglo-American occupation of the Oregon Territory; and the acquisition of Spanish Florida.

- As noted in an earlier lecture, the 1824 presidential election boiled down to a choice in the House of Representatives between Adams and Andrew Jackson.

- o Speaker of the House Henry Clay encouraged his supporters to vote for Adams, even though Jackson had more electoral and popular votes.

- o When Adams won, he appointed Clay secretary of state; Jackson cried that the appointment was a "corrupt bargain" and immediately began a campaign to win the election of 1828 and subvert Adams's presidency.

- Unlike his father, Adams did not allow his failure to win a second term as president end his political career. He won election to the House of Representatives from his home district and became a fierce opponent of slavery and its expansion. He also opposed the annexation of Texas and the war with Mexico.

George C. Marshall

- In 1939, Franklin Roosevelt appointed George C. Marshall army chief of staff over 33 senior officers. He held that post from the day Hitler invaded Poland to begin World War II to the end of the war, and during that time, he created the largest American armed force in U.S. history.

- In the process, he won the respect and admiration of Congress, the American people, America's wartime allies, and his colleagues on the U.S. Joint Chiefs of Staff and the Anglo-American Combined Chiefs of Staff. Churchill called him the "true organizer" of Allied victory.

- Marshall was the obvious choice to command Operation

Unlike the elder or younger Adams, General George C. Marshall never became president—but only because he chose not to run.

Overlord, the 1944 invasion of France. But questions arose as to whether he could be spared from Washington; he was, in effect, running the global U.S. war effort from that city.

- Marshall refused to request the command, telling Roosevelt that he had to do what was best for the country, not for himself. Roosevelt then chose Marshall's protégé, Dwight D. Eisenhower. As we know, the success of the operation guaranteed Eisenhower both historical immortality and the presidency.

- In early 1947, President Truman appointed Marshall secretary of state. In the two years he served, he established the containment policy of the Cold War and, as part of it, the European Recovery Program that bears his name and for which he received the Nobel Peace Prize in 1953: the Marshall Plan. He also established a bipartisan foreign policy with a Republican Congress that lasted for 20 years.

- In September 1950, at nearly 70 years of age, Marshall agreed to become secretary of defense in order to rebuild the U.S. army for the Korean War. He played a key role in the 1951 relief of General Douglas MacArthur in what many historians consider the greatest threat to civilian control of the military in U.S. history.

- When Marshall died in 1959, he remained one of the most respected men in the country, yet his reputation faded as the generation that knew him passed away.

The Reasons for Obscurity

- One common factor that may account for the relative obscurity of John Adams, his son, and George Marshall today is their refusal to allow personal political ambition to control their behavior or violate their sense of what was right. Another factor may have been their utter honesty and refusal to compromise that honesty for political gain, along with their knowledge of history and ability to take the "long view" regarding what was truly important.

o For Adams, what was important was peace with France in 1800 more so than reelection. For his son, it was first the geographic expansion of his country without war, followed by the crusade against slavery. And for Marshall, it was the preservation of a truly democratic society in the midst of a global war.

o A fourth factor that may account for the relative obscurity of these three was the strong belief each had in the concept of selfless public service, a belief that may have precluded them from actively seeking the publicity and popularity necessary for lasting fame.

• Who matters most to us from a given past era may vary depending on what we wish to know about that era. Certain figures who are not well known to the public may be very important to historians who specialize in particular aspects of U.S. history.

• Beyond that, many figures who are known primarily to historians come from relatively recent fields of historical study that developed during the 1960s and 1970s as part of the "new" social history. This social historical approach examined groups that had been left out of the traditional "grand narrative" of U.S. history, a narrative that had focused on white, male political leaders. In the process, the new historians transformed and continue to transform the study of U.S. history.

• These historians also played a major role in the destruction of the traditional grand narrative, because minorities and women have histories of their own that do not appear to fit the political history of white men in that narrative—or do they?

o One could argue, for example, that the 20th-century theologian Reinhold Niebuhr was at least as important in the emergence of the United States as a superpower as Franklin Roosevelt and Harry Truman—for his religious concepts regarding the nature of power and the need to grasp it to do good and the simultaneous recognition of human limits and the corrupting nature of power.

o One could similarly argue that the revivalist preacher Charles G. Finney, active during the Second Great Awakening, was at least as important as any of the presidents of his era in that the link he preached between religious conversion and political reform had enormous political and societal consequences, including the antislavery crusade that led to the Civil War.

o Shifting to economics, one could maintain that Eli Whitney was more important than any political figures in "causing" the Civil War, not only for his well-known invention of the cotton gin and its enormous impact on Southern slavery but also for his impact on Northern industry via his pioneering work to mass produce muskets for the U.S. Army using interchangeable parts.

o Similarly, one could claim that industrial and financial leaders from the late 19th century through the 20th were more important in America's rise to superpower status than any generals, admirals, or presidents. The foundation of U.S. military power in the 20th century was its economic power that these men had helped to create.

o One could also claim that pioneers in the struggle for minority rights and women's rights from the pre–Civil War years through the 20th century were more important than the presidents, legislators, and judges responsible for government actions in these realms. These leaders changed the consciousness of the public, mobilized people, and thereby pressured politicians into action.

• Our old grand narrative is dated and fractured, but a new one may be actually forming right now—one that synthesizes all of the "new" histories with the old one to give us a much fuller, more informative, and more useful picture of our past.

Suggested Reading

Dangerfield, *The Era of Good Feelings.*

McCullough, *John Adams.*

Pogue, *George C. Marshall.*

Stoler, *George C. Marshall: Soldier-Statesman of the American Century.*

Questions to Consider

1. What other major American figures are lesser known than they should be and why?

2. What qualities lead to historical fame in this country, and are they appropriate?

Who Matters in American History?
Lecture 23—Transcript

Most Americans think they know the names of the great political figures in American history, names such as Washington, Jefferson, Jackson, Lincoln, Wilson, Theodore Roosevelt, Franklin Roosevelt, Harry Truman. There are, however, numerous other political figures whose contributions were just as important, but who, while far from being totally unknown, are far less familiar to most Americans. For events covered in the last few lectures, for example, what about Harry Hopkins, Franklin Roosevelt's right-hand man and virtual alter ego during World War II? Or George Kennan, the head of the State Department Policy Planning Staff, who in 1947 authored the Cold War policy of containment and co-authored the Marshall Plan? Or Matthew Ridgway, the Army Chief of Staff who played such a critical role in preventing American military intervention in Vietnam in 1954? There are also lesser-known historical figures in realms outside of politics who, one might argue, are at least as important as any political figures.

In this lecture we will examine the numerous accomplishments of a few such political and nonpolitical individuals and try to understand why, despite those accomplishments, they are less familiar than other figures. Such an analysis will also enable us to explore who in history we choose to remember, and why.

Let's do politics first. In that political realm, I have chosen one statesman from the 18th century, one from the 19th, and one from the 20th century: John Adams, his son John Quincy, and George Catlett Marshall. Although two were presidents and the third was one of our greatest soldiers and statesmen, and although each was very well known in his time, they are relatively unknown today, especially in comparison to their peers: Washington, Jefferson, Jackson, Franklin Roosevelt, Truman, and Eisenhower.

After looking at these three, we will then look at some nonpolitical figures in American history and try to figure out why they too are lesser-known than our major political figures. In the process, we will also explore the so-called traditional "Grand Narrative" of American history, and how it is under assault, yet perhaps in the midst of enormous change and expansion. But first let us first look at the three lesser-known political figures: Adams, Quincy Adams, and Marshall.

John Adams first. Adams was probably the most important and respected of all the Revolutionary leaders from New England. He played a major role in both Continental Congresses, he nominated George Washington to command the Continental Army, he helped draft the Declaration of Independence, and he drafted the instructions that would result in the wartime treaty of alliance with France. He also obtained a critical Dutch loan while a diplomat in Europe during the war, he played a major role in the peace negotiations that ended the war, and he became the first official U.S. representative to Great Britain after the war. He was also a major political theorist, he wrote the Massachusetts Constitution, and perhaps surprisingly, he defended the British soldiers put on trial as a result of the Boston Massacre.

During the Revolution, he had nominated George Washington to command the Continental Army in order to commit the Southern colonies to a conflict that then centered on Boston. Similarly, he was elected as our first vice president, partially to provide a sectional balance to Washington, the Virginian, in the new government. He was the obvious choice to succeed Washington as president, but he inherited a diplomatic crisis with France as well as a growing partisan rift at home, with the opposition led by none other than his vice president and old friend Thomas Jefferson.

The crisis with France erupted into an undeclared naval war in 1798 that the Hamiltonian wing of his own Federalist Party wanted to turn into a full-scale declared war. Such a war, when combined with the recently passed Alien and Sedition Acts, which virtually outlawed dissent, would have guaranteed Adams's reelection (though it also could have led to a civil war). But Adams refused to agree. He never filled the ranks of the special army Congress had agreed to create, and when France proposed negotiations to end the conflict he quickly agreed. He also fired the Hamiltonian members of his Cabinet when he discovered that they were subverting his plans to negotiate an end to rather than an expansion of the war. As a result of his moves, he was able to obtain peace with France, but at the cost of splitting his Federalist Party and thus dooming his own reelection attempt against Jefferson.

Adams realized the political cost of his behavior, but considered it the most "meritorious actions of [his] life":

> I will defend my missions to France, [he wrote] as long as I have an eye to direct my hand, or a finger to hold my pen. They are the most disinterested and meritorious actions of my life. I reflect upon them with so much satisfaction, that I desire no other inscription over my gravestone than: "Here lies John Adams, who took upon himself the responsibility of the peace with France in the year 1800."

But the cost was not limited to the election of 1800. As the only one of the five Founding Fathers elected president but not reelected for a second term, he became the forgotten one. Fittingly, he died on July 4, 1826, the 50th anniversary of the Declaration of Independence, as did Thomas Jefferson, his old friend who had become his political enemy but with whom he had eventually reconciled. His final words: "Thomas Jefferson still lives!" Jefferson, however, had died just a few hours earlier. Equally fitting, Adams once summarized and explained his own career by explaining to his wife Abigail that, as he put it, "I must study politics and war that my sons may have the liberty to study mathematics and philosophy … navigation, commerce, and agriculture, in order to give their children a right to study painting, poetry, music, … and porcelain."

David McCullough, Joseph Ellis, and others have over the past few decades done their best to give Adams his due, and he is now better known than he previously had been. Nevertheless, he remains relatively unknown to the public, especially in comparison to his peers: Washington, Jefferson, Hamilton, and Madison.

At Adams's death in 1826, his son, John Quincy Adams, was in the midst of his own largely-forgotten presidency. Yet, like his father, he had had a brilliant career before he became president, primarily as a diplomat. He had helped to negotiate the Treaty of Ghent that had ended the War of 1812. He had also served as Minister (really ambassador) to the Netherlands, to Prussia, to Russia, and to Great Britain. He had then been appointed by James Monroe as Secretary of State. In these roles, Adams had been responsible for some of the most important treaties and announcements in the history of U.S. foreign relations: the Rush-Bagot agreement to limit naval forces on the Great Lakes, which was the first naval arms limitation agreement in modern history and the start of what would eventually become the famous undefended Canadian-American border; the boundary convention of 1818 that established a boundary with Canada all the way to the Rocky Mountains as well as joint Anglo-American occupation of the Oregon Territory and thus a U.S. claim to the Pacific coast; the Adams-Onis Transcontinental Treaty of 1819, by which the United States acquired Spanish Florida and a clear continental boundary with the Spanish Empire all the way to the West coast—that also established an American claim to the Pacific coast, and it is a treaty that ranks in importance with the Louisiana Purchase of 1803; finally, the famous Monroe Doctrine that Adams, rather than Monroe, actually authored.

Perhaps one reason Adams remains relatively unknown is that all these diplomatic achievements remain relatively unknown. Adams became president in 1825, but he did so via a unique route that would plague and doom his presidency. Since none of the numerous candidates for president had received a majority of the votes in the Electoral College—or in the popular vote, for that matter—the election was decided by the House of Representatives with each state casting one vote. As noted in a previous lecture, the choice boiled down to Adams or Andrew Jackson. Eliminated from the race by his low vote total, Speaker of the House Henry Clay of Kentucky encouraged his supporters to vote for Adams, even though Jackson had more electoral votes and more popular votes. Clay's support ensured Adams's election, whereupon he appointed Clay Secretary of State, the position traditionally seen and used as the stepping stone to the presidency. Jackson and his supporters screamed "corrupt bargain"—which it was not—but they immediately began a campaign to win the election of 1828, and in the process subvert Adams's entire presidency. In this they were successful, and Adams was defeated in his 1828 reelection bid.

Unlike his father, however, Adams did not allow this defeat to end his political career. He agreed to run for and won election to the House of Representatives from his home district, commenting that being so elected by your neighbors was an honor higher than the presidency. In the House of Representatives, he became a fierce opponent of slavery and its expansion. He also acted to subvert the "gag rule" that had barred antislavery petitions from Congress; and he defended the right of slaves who had taken over their slave ship the *Amistad* to have their freedom. He also opposed of the annexation of Texas and the war with Mexico. In the process, he developed his nickname "Old Man Eloquent." In 1848, he suffered a massive stroke while speaking out against that war, and he was carried out of the House chamber and died two days later.

Unlike the two Adams's, George Catlett Marshall was never elected president, but only because he chose not to run. In 1939, Franklin Roosevelt appointed him Army Chief of Staff over 33 senior officers. He held that post from the day Hitler invaded Poland to begin World War II, September 1, 1939, to the end of that war. During that time, he created a huge and highly successful Army and Air Force of over eight-and-a-quarter million men, by far the largest Army in U.S. history. In the process, he won the respect and the admiration of Congress, the American people, America's wartime allies, and his colleagues on both the U.S. Joint Chiefs of Staff and the Anglo-American Combined Chiefs of Staff, where he quickly emerged as the "first among equals." Churchill called him the "true organizer" of Allied victory.

Marshall was the obvious choice to command Operation Overlord, the 1944 invasion of France and the largest amphibious operation in history. But questions arose as to whether he could be spared from Washington, for he was, in effect, running the global U.S. war effort. Nevertheless, the command was his for the asking. But he refused to ask. When Roosevelt asked, "Do you want the command?" Marshall responded that Roosevelt as president he had to do what was best for the country, not what was best for George C. Marshall. Roosevelt then chose Marshall's protégé, Dwight D. Eisenhower, for the command, commenting to Marshall that he "could not sleep at night with you out of the country." The Overlord command and his success at it guaranteed Eisenhower historical immortality and the presidency in 1952.

"You have never thought of yourself," Secretary of War Henry Stimson told Marshall on V-E Day in May of 1945, and he continued: "… there is no one for whom I have such deep respect and, I think, greater affection. I have seen a great many soldiers in my [day]," Stimson movingly concluded, "and you, Sir, are the finest soldier I have ever known." Stimson was far from alone in that judgment. In late 1945, President Harry Truman, who considered

Marshall "the greatest living American," appointed him special emissary to China in a hopeless effort to avert a civil war. Then in early 1947, he appointed Marshall Secretary of State. Marshall proved to be one of the great secretaries of state, even though he served only two years. He established the containment policy in the Cold War, and as part of it the European Recovery Program that bears his name as the Marshall Plan. For that, he received the Nobel Peace Prize in 1953, the first professional soldier ever to win that prestigious award. Marshall also established a bipartisan foreign policy with a Republican Congress and a Democratic president that lasted for 20 years.

Nor was that the end of it. In September of 1950, at the age of nearly 70, he agreed to become Secretary of Defense in order to rebuild the U.S. army for the Korean War. He also ended the inter-service feuding that had erupted into the so-called "revolt of the Admirals" a year earlier, and he reestablished good civil-military relations with the State Department, which had become badly frayed. He also played a key role in the 1951 relief of General Douglas MacArthur in what many consider the greatest threat to civilian control of the military in U.S. history.

Throughout this extraordinary career, Marshall utterly refused to run for political office, or even to vote. When asked for his "political faith," he would respond, "My father was a Democrat, my mother a Republican, and I am an Episcopalian." Nevertheless, he came under savage political attack in 1950 and 1951 by Joseph McCarthy and his supporters for the "loss of China" and MacArthur's relief. In the words of another senator, William Jenner, Marshall was "a living lie" and a "front man for traitors." When Marshall died in 1959, he nevertheless remained one of the most respected men in the country. But his reputation faded as the generation that knew him passed away. When I ask students today if they know who George Marshall was, most say no; and the few who respond in the affirmative can only say— indeed ask me—"He had something to do with the Marshall Plan, didn't he?"

Why, then, are these great statesmen lesser known than many of their peers? For Adams, a major reason is that he followed George Washington into the presidency; and to say Washington was a tough act to follow is a major understatement. He was also an argumentative and often disagreeable person, and a one-term president defeated for reelection by none other than the author of the Declaration of Independence, his former friend Thomas Jefferson. He could have defeated Jefferson and had a second term by turning the quasi-war against France into a full-fledged war, but he refused to do so because it violated his principles, which he would not do, especially for political gain. As with his defense of British soldiers on trial for the Boston Massacre, he was indeed, as per the title of one biography, "Honest John Adams."

His son John Quincy possessed a similar if not even more difficult personality. "I am a man of reserved, cold, austere, and forbidding manners," he wrote; "my political adversaries say a gloomy misanthropist, and my personal enemies, an unsocial savage." One historian, George Dangerfield, has concluded that Adams was "peculiarly fitted" for public service "except in one [respect]." As Dangerfield wrote, Adams "was almost totally deficient in the art of getting on with other people." Adams also followed into the presidency the last of the Founding Fathers, James Monroe; he was a one-term president, and was defeated for reelection by the immensely popular and studied Andrew Jackson. Quincy Adams was also the only president to be selected by the House of Representatives, and under circumstances that led many Americans at the time to question whether he ever should have become president. In addition, much of his prior brilliant success as a diplomat and Secretary of State was hidden from the public view, and it remains hidden to this very day.

Marshall also possessed what many have described as a forbidding personality. Nevertheless, he could have easily been elected president after World War II had he agreed to run, for he was clearly the most respected man in the country for his wartime work. But he refused to do so, much as he had refused to ask Roosevelt for the Overlord command. As a result, he never achieved battlefield fame. That honor, and with it the presidency and historical immortality, went to his protégé Eisenhower. The name of the European Recovery Program in his honor is what he is most remembered for by those who recognize his name at all, but it is merely the tip of an iceberg of accomplishments.

One common factor that may account for the relative obscurity of these three individuals today, despite their enormous accomplishments during the eras in which they lived, is their refusal to allow personal political ambition to control their behavior or to violate their sense of what was right. Another may have been their utter honesty and refusal to compromise that honesty for political gain. Honest John Adams. Marshall had a reputation of never lying to Congress. A third factor may have been their knowledge of history and their subsequent ability to take the "long view" regarding what was truly important. For Adams, that was peace with France in 1800 over reelection. For his son, John Quincy Adams, it was first, the geographic expansion of his country without war, and then the crusade against slavery and for civil liberties. For Marshall it was the preservation of a truly democratic society in the midst of a global war.

That is perhaps best illustrated by his refusal to lie to Congress, but by his charge in early 1943 to General John Hilldring, the officer he had appointed to head a new civil affairs division in the army general staff that was to train military governors for occupied enemy territory. Marshall's charge to Hilldring was never to forget that he was being handed what he called "a sacred trust": the fact that the American people trusted their army officers. Hilldring could destroy that trust overnight, Marshall warned; it "could happen" if he did not understand this. "This is my principal charge to you," Marshall said, "this is the thing I never want you to forget in the dust of battle and when the pressures will be on you."

A fourth factor that may account for the relative obscurity of all three was the strong belief each had in the concept of selfless public service. That belief may have precluded them from actively seeking the publicity and popularity necessary for lasting fame.

But let us expand our analysis further to explore not only why we tend to remember certain political figures and not others, but also why we tend to remember political figures at all as opposed to figures whose accomplishments lay outside the political realm. What about great religious leaders and theologians, like Jonathan Edwards, Charles G. Finney, and Reinhold Niebuhr? What about economic and technological leaders from Eli Whitney to Steve Jobs? What about black civil rights leaders from Frederick Douglass to Martin Luther King, Jr. and James Farmer? What about feminist leaders from Lucretia Mott and Elizabeth Cady Stanton through Betty

Friedan (the author of *The Feminine Mystique*) and Gloria Steinem? In this regard, who matters most to us from a given past era may vary depending upon what we wish to know about that era. These figures who I've named are very well-known to historians who specialize in U.S. religious, economic, civil rights, or women's history, as opposed to political history.

But beyond that rather obvious fact, many of the figures I cited come from relatively recent fields of historical study that developed during and after the 1960s and 1970s as part of the "new" social history: a history of groups that had been left out of the traditional "grand narrative" of the United States—a narrative that had focused on white, male political leaders. In the process, these new historians transformed and continue to transform the study of U.S. history.

These historians also played a major role in the destruction of the traditional "grand narrative" of U.S. history, for minorities and women have histories of their own that do not appear to fit the political history of white men in that narrative. Or don't they? One could argue, for example, that the 20th-century theologian Reinhold Niebuhr was at least as important in the emergence of the United States as a superpower as Franklin D. Roosevelt and Harry Truman, essentially for his religious concepts regarding the nature of power and the need to grasp it to do good, while simultaneously recognizing human limits and the corrupting nature of power. Niebuhr attacked isolationism in the 1930s as immoral in the face of Nazism. He also attacked it after World War II in the face of Communism. He argued that isolationism was an attempt to maintain moral purity—which he considered impossible for a Christian—by refusing to accept the responsibilities of power.

Niebuhr also attacked American efforts in the Cold War to remake the war in its own image. He considered this an example of arrogance and the corrupting influence of power, and he pressed for a recognition of human limits. Or, as he phrased it in his famous prayer:

> God, grant me the serenity to accept the things I cannot change;
> The courage to change the things I can;
> And the wisdom to know the difference.

George F. Kennan, who worked under Marshall as head of the Policy Planning Staff in the State Department, and who authored the U.S. Cold War policy of containment, referred to Niebuhr as "the father of us all," and he even invited Niebuhr into meetings of the Policy Planning Staff.

One could similarly argue that the Second Great Awakening revivalist preacher Charles G. Finney was at least as important, if not more important, than any of the presidents of his era. Why? Because of the link he preached between religious conversion and political reform, and the enormous political as well as societal consequences that that had, including—but by no means limited to—the antislavery crusade that led to the Civil War. In the First Great Awakening, the minister Jonathan Edwards: One could argue that he and his colleagues were more important than any of the Revolutionary-era political leaders because their work for the first time created a common bond between the 13 colonies, and led many to question established authorities for the first time.

Shifting to economics, one could maintain that Eli Whitney was more important than any political figures in "causing" the Civil War, not only for his well-known invention of cotton gin, which had an enormous impact on Southern slavery, but also for his equally enormous impact on Northern industry via his pioneering work in the early 19th century to mass produce muskets for the U.S. Army via interchangeable parts. Whitney is far less well-known for that, but it is, one might argue, just as important as the cotton gin. Similarly, one could claim that industrial and financial leaders from the late 19th century through the entire 20th century were more important in America's rise to superpower status than any generals, or admirals, or presidents; for the foundation of U.S. military power in the 20th century was its economic power that these men had helped to create.

One could also claim that pioneers in the struggle for minority rights and women's rights from the pre–Civil War years through the entire 20th century were more important than the presidents, legislators, and judges responsible for government actions in these realms. Why? Because they changed people's consciousnesses; they mobilized people, and they thereby pressured politicians into action.

While our grand narrative—our old grand narrative—is thus dated and fractured, a new one may not only be possible, but actually forming right now; one that synthesizes all of the new histories with the old one to give us a much fuller, more informative, and more useful picture of our past.

History Did Not Begin with Us
Lecture 24

Many of us have the tendency to believe that history either began or was dramatically altered during our lifetimes. Many have argued, for example, that the personal computer has brought unprecedented change to our lives. In this final lecture, we will explore the historical realities that challenge several incorrect or questionable beliefs and look at why so many Americans tend to believe them.

Antiwar Movements

- Contrary to popular belief, Vietnam was not the first American war opposed by many Americans. Indeed, even the War for Independence was, in all likelihood, not supported by a majority of American colonists.

  o The quasi-war with France in 1798–1800 was vehemently opposed by Jefferson's Democratic-Republicans and nearly brought on a civil war. The War of 1812 was opposed by an entire section of the nation (New England) and the Federalists. Major sectional and partisan opposition also existed to the 1846–1848 war with Mexico, as well as the Civil War.

  o There was no opposition to speak of during the brief 1898 war with Spain but plenty of opposition to McKinley's ensuing decision to acquire an overseas colonial empire as a result of the war. Even more opposition arose to the ensuing war with the Filipinos.

  o Major opposition also existed with regard to American entry into World War I, even though the war vote passed the Senate and House by overwhelming majorities.

  o Although there was virtually no opposition to U.S. entry into World War II after the Pearl Harbor attack and Nazi declaration of war, there had been plenty of opposition to Roosevelt's pre–Pearl Harbor policies, most notably aid to Britain.

o   Opposition also existed to major U.S. policies in the early days of the Cold War. Even during the supposedly placid 1950s, major antinuclear and pacifist movements existed.

o   Republicans attacked President Truman during the Korean War for executive war-making without congressional consent and his limited-war strategy, with backing instead for MacArthur's calls for an expanded war against China.

o   Interestingly, similar dissent occurred during the Vietnam War, with those calling for escalation and expansion of the war outnumbering those who favored de-escalation or withdrawal before 1968.

•   Why has this long history of major antiwar movements been forgotten by most Americans?
   o   The history was partially buried in the outpouring of patriotism after the Pearl Harbor attack and by the bipartisan foreign policy during the early years of the Cold War. Related was the anticommunist hysteria during the 1950s that stifled dissent.

   o   In addition, all these previous antiwar movements failed, including—contrary to mythology—the Vietnam antiwar movement, and we tend to study successes rather than failures.

   o   The government also actively suppressed many of these antiwar movements—especially those during the Civil War and World War I.

   o   Further, the bipartisan foreign policy and anticommunist hysteria of the 1950s created an environment in which "consensus school historians" tended to emphasize the lack of conflict in American history rather than the conflicts.

The Civil Rights Movement

- The civil rights movement has an equally long history. For African Americans, it began with the antislavery movement that started in the mid- to late 18th century and accelerated in the 1830s. Simultaneously, free blacks and their white supporters fought against segregation laws in the northern states.

- Booker T. Washington gave up on such rights in his Atlanta Compromise of 1895, but he did so only temporarily in order to obtain white support for improving the economic condition of African Americans. He was almost immediately challenged by other black leaders, such as W. E. B. Du Bois.

- Du Bois would help to found the NAACP in the early 20th century, and that organization would begin to challenge southern segregation laws and other denials of black civil rights throughout the first half of the 20th century.

- Why was most of this history forgotten by many Americans before the 1960s?
  - The plight of free blacks and their efforts to obtain civil rights before the Civil War tended to be forgotten amid the much larger and more basic struggle against slavery.

  - The movement for black civil rights after the Civil War failed, despite the passage of constitutional amendments guaranteeing rights for blacks during the Reconstruction era.

  - Further, white America as a whole was racist and did not support equal rights for blacks either before the Civil War or in the century following it. Consequently, there was little interest in the history of the struggle for black civil rights outside the African American community.

  - Finally, the consensus historians of the early Cold War years tended to downplay if not ignore this struggle, much as they ignored previous antiwar movements.

The Women's Movement

- The women's movement also has a lengthy history in this country. As noted in a previous lecture, it began with the prominence of women within the abolitionist movement of the 1830s.

- During the Reconstruction era, the women's movement pressed for inclusion in the Fourteenth and Fifteenth Amendments guaranteeing rights for black males, but those efforts were unsuccessful. Women finally gained the right to vote in 1920.

- Women also achieved symbolic moves toward equality with Franklin Roosevelt's appointment of the first female cabinet member and the political redefinition of the role of first lady by Eleanor Roosevelt during the 1930s.

- During World War II, the Women's Auxiliary Corps was established in the army under a female colonel, and women obtained jobs in a host of occupations previously closed to them.

- Why was this history lost in the years following World War II?
  - The situation in World War II was generally perceived as a temporary aberration caused by the exigencies of war and the removal of millions of men from the workforce for military duty.

  - After the war, working women were perceived as taking jobs away from men; the same attitude had been expressed during the Great Depression.

  - The combination of the Great Depression and World War II had led many women to postpone having children; that situation ended with the end of the war, leading to the postwar baby boom and the reassertion of women's "traditional" roles as mother and housekeeper. In this reassertion, the history of the earlier women's rights movement seemed largely irrelevant.

The Rediscovery of Histories
- Each of these three histories was rediscovered during the 1960s and 1970s as members of the three movements searched for a usable past.
    - At numerous teach-ins during the 1960s, professors and students challenged the myth of past wartime consensus (and, with it, the implicit attacks on their patriotism) by highlighting previous antiwar movements.
    - Civil rights activists and feminists similarly challenged prevailing racial and gender stereotypes and the idea that blacks and women had docilely accepted their inferior status in the past.

    - These rediscoveries led a new generation of scholars to explore these histories in great depth and produce a rich literature about them, which has since altered our views of American history and affected the ensuing development of the antiwar, civil rights, and women's movements.

- History is not an objective and unchanging discipline that simply studies the facts of a dead past. Rather, it is a subjective and constantly evolving study of a living past that is heavily influenced by the questions each generation asks of it in light of contemporary concerns. As a result, history tells us much about ourselves in the present, as well as the past being studied.

The Personal Computer: Unprecedented Change?
- Consider our current belief that the personal computer is the most important invention in history, that it has ushered in a new era in history, and that the pace of change is accelerating at an unprecedented rate and influencing every aspect of our lives.

- A careful examination of American history reveals a series of fundamental technological changes long before the computer, each one considered at the time the most important and consequential in history: the steamboat and canal boom of the early to mid-19th century, the development of railroads, mass production, the telegraph, the internal combustion engine, the automobile, the airplane, and nuclear weapons and power.

- Is the computer any different than these innovations, or is it just another major change—and perhaps one not nearly as significant and life-altering as these earlier ones?

An 80-Year Lifespan

- Imagine a man born on a Midwestern farm in 1835 or 1840 who lived

Many believe that the personal computer has accelerated the pace of change in our world, but the belief that change is accelerating at an unprecedented rate is itself far from new.

into his mid- to late 80s. In the course of his lifetime, he might have experienced the railroad for the first time; participated in the industrial revolution; acquired a telephone, an automobile, a toaster, a vacuum cleaner, and a radio; seen the success of the Wright brothers; and witnessed the "war to end all wars."

- Are we really experiencing technological changes more rapid, dramatic, and life-transforming than this individual did? Or is the belief that we are a distortion caused by our ignorance of history or by "tunnel vision"—whereby the past in front of us as we enter a tunnel appears longer (and more important) than the rest of the tunnel?

The Spiral of History

- History does not repeat itself save, perhaps, in terms of the emotions—love, anger, fear—that drive human beings to behave in certain ways. Each event and era in history is unique, as is each new interpretation of the past that arises within each era.

- We should think of history neither as a straight line or a circle but as a spiral. In this view, we are separate from all past events but also linked to them in a multidimensional time stream of which we are a part. Being linked, we see that history did not begin with us and will not end with us either.

- In this course, we've learned to be skeptical, to challenge historical myths, and to search for the truth behind those myths. It's also important for us to realize that the search for truth is quite different from the claim to have found it; as we've seen repeatedly, historical truth changes over time as new events lead to new questions and new interpretations of the past.

Suggested Reading

Franklin and Higginbotham, *From Slavery to Freedom.*

Morison, Merk, and Freidel, *Dissent in Three American Wars.*

Questions to Consider

1. Why do we prefer to study successes rather than failures in history, even though failures can often teach us much more?

2. What other aspects of U.S. history have been "lost" and rediscovered, and why?

History Did Not Begin with Us
Lecture 24—Transcript

There's an apparent tendency to believe that history either began or was dramatically altered during our lifetimes. A few examples: Many believe the Vietnam War spawned the first major antiwar movement in U.S. history during the 1960s and that it established the precedent for opposition to U.S. wars since then. Many also believe that the 1960s gave birth to the Civil Rights Movement; and similarly that the Women's Movement began in the 1970s. More recently, many have argued that the personal computer is the most important invention in U.S. history, if not in world history, and that with it we have entered an utterly new era. More broadly, many argue that the pace of change is accelerating at an unprecedented rate and is influencing every aspect of our lives, and not always for the better.

Some of these statements are simply incorrect. The Antiwar and Civil Rights Movements did not begin during the 1960s, nor did the Women's Movement begin in the 1970s; and the validity of the other statements regarding the computer and the pace of change are subject to severe questioning given a careful reading of U.S. history. In this final lecture, we shall explore the historical realities that challenge these incorrect or questionable beliefs, as well as why so many Americans tend to believe them.

Let's look at the antiwar movement first. Contrary to popular belief, Vietnam was not the first American War opposed by many Americans. The Revolution and War for Independence were in all likelihood not supported by a majority of the colonists. There were no public opinion polls at the time, but John Adams claimed that one-third favored the revolution, one-third opposed it, and one-third were neutral. In the 1798–1800 Quasi War with France, one of the two major political parties—Jefferson's Democratic-Republicans—opposed the war, and they responded to wartime attacks on their civil liberties (the Alien and the Sedition Acts) with the doctrine of nullification in their Virginia and Kentucky Resolutions. The result was nearly a civil war.

The War of 1812 was opposed by an entire section of the nation (New England) and the other major political party (the Federalists). The war vote in June, 1812 revealed a badly divided nation: 79–49 in the House, 19–13 in the Senate, with all Federalists and most of New England voting no. New England states also refused to allow their militias to participate in attempted invasions of Canada during the war and they continued their wholesale smuggling across the Canadian border that had been in effect since Jefferson's embargo in 1806 and 1807. There was even talk of secession, and at the Hartford Convention in late 1814 the Federalists proposed a series of states-rights-oriented Constitutional Amendments designed to limit the power of both the South and the national government.

Major sectional and partisan opposition also existed to the 1846–1848 war with Mexico. Many Northerners and many Whigs condemned the war as one of aggression designed to expand slavery. Indeed, by 1848, the Whigs were threatening to cut off funds for continuation of the war, which may have been a factor in President James K. Polk's decision to accept a peace treaty that acquired California and New Mexico rather than all of Mexico. As noted in a previous lecture, a one-term Whig Congressman from Illinois named Abraham Lincoln obtained the nickname "Spotty" for challenging Polk to identify the spot where American blood had supposedly been shed upon American soil.

Mythology to the contrary, major opposition to the Civil War existed in both North and South. Lincoln was a minority president; he had won less than 40 percent of the popular vote, and there was major opposition to his policies in the North as well as the South. Indeed, Lincoln's administration became notorious for its violations of the civil liberties of those opponents during the war—that included the arrest and deportation of a pro-Southern former Congressman in Ohio—and Lincoln came very close to being defeated for reelection in 1864 by one of his former generals, George McClellan, who ran as a Democrat, the party that included a large number of peace supporters. The South also badly divided into pro- and antislavery factions, as well as secession versus union factions. West Virginia seceded from Virginia over this.

There was no opposition to speak of during the brief 1898 war with Spain, but there was plenty of opposition to President McKinley's ensuing decision to acquire an overseas empire—a colonial empire—as a result of that war. The Treaty of Paris ending the war and formalizing the acquisition of that empire faced major opposition in the Senate and in the public. You had the formation of the bipartisan Anti-Imperialist League and acidic criticisms from such notable Americans as Mark Twain. The Senate accepted the treaty, but only by a vote of 57—27, barely the two-thirds needed for ratification.

Even more opposition arose to the ensuing war with the Filipinos who desired independence rather than merely to trade one colonial master for another. There were revelations of American torture of the Filipino guerillas leading to Congressional investigation and denunciations of the army and the administration.

Major opposition also existed in regard to American entry into World War I in 1917, even though the war vote passed the Senate and House by the overwhelming majorities of 82–6 and 373–50. In 1935, Marine Major General Smedley Butler, who had participated in military actions in the Philippines, in China, in numerous Central America and Caribbean countries, as well as France during World War I, proclaimed that during his 33-plus years in active military service he had spent "most of my time as a high class muscle man for Big Business, for Wall Street and the bankers. In short, I was a racketeer, a gangster for capitalism."

While there was virtually no opposition to our entry into World War II after the Pearl Harbor attack and the Nazi declaration of war, there had been plenty of opposition to Roosevelt's pre-Pearl Harbor policies, most notably aid to Britain; policies that his numerous anti-interventionist critics claimed would lead the United States into an unnecessary war.

Opposition also existed to major U.S. policies in the early days of the Cold War, with former Vice President Henry Wallace and the Progressive Party challenging Truman in the 1948 election. Even during the supposedly placid 1950s, major antinuclear and pacifist movements existed.

There was also opposition to the Korean War, though not antiwar opposition per se; rather, there were Republican attacks on President Truman for executive war making without the consent of Congress and on his limited war strategy. Instead, many Republicans backed General MacArthur's calls for an expanded war against China. Interestingly, similar dissent occurred during the Vietnam War, with those calling for escalation and expansion of the war outnumbering those who favored de-escalation and/or withdrawal before 1968. That history has in turn been relatively ignored in the new historical emphasis on antiwar movements.

Why was this long history of major antiwar movements forgotten by most Americans? Partially it got buried in an outpouring of patriotism after the Pearl Harbor attack and by the bipartisan foreign policy during the early years of the Cold War. Related to this was the anti-Communist hysteria during the 1950s that stifled dissent. Furthermore, all these previous antiwar movements failed—including, contrary to mythology, the Vietnam antiwar movement, save perhaps in the sense of avoiding even more escalation—and we tend to spend more time studying successes than failures.

In terms of specific wars, many of the Loyalists during the Revolutionary War fled the country and resettled in England or Canada. In doing so, they deprived the United States of the people who would have written the antiwar history of that conflict. Federalist demands and threats at the 1814 Hartford Convention became public news after the arrival of the peace treaty that ended the war and Andrew Jackson's smashing victory at New Orleans, and it led to the demise of the Federalists as a national party soon thereafter. That served as a warning to future politicians never to risk open dissent against the war.

As discussed in a previous lecture, some presidents manipulated the facts so as to minimize antiwar dissent and force dissenters to vote for war. James K. Polk, for example, had his supporters attach the war vote as a rider to an appropriations bill for the army, then under attack by Mexico along the Rio Grande. How are you going to oppose that?

The government also actively suppressed many of these antiwar movements, especially those during the Civil War and World War I; and in suppressing them, it wound up also suppressing their history. The bipartisan foreign policy and anti-Communist hysteria of the 1950s created an environment in which "consensus school historians" such as Louis Hartz and Daniel Boorstin tended to emphasize the lack of conflict in American history rather than the conflicts.

The Civil Rights Movement had an equally long history. For African Americans, it began with the antislavery movement itself that started in the mid-to-late 18th century and accelerated in the 1830s. Simultaneously, free blacks fought against segregation laws in the northern states; so did black leaders like Frederick Douglass and their white supporters before the Civil War, during the Civil War, and after the Civil War. Black leader Booker T. Washington did give up on such rights in his famous "Atlanta Compromise" of 1895, but he did so only temporarily in order to obtain white support for improving the economic condition of African Americans; and he was almost immediately challenged by other black leaders, such as W.E.B. DuBois.

Indeed, DuBois would help to found the NAACP in the early 20th century, and that organization would begin to challenge Southern segregation laws and other denials of black civil rights throughout the first half of the 20th century. This effort would culminate legally in the famous 1954 Supreme Court Case of *Brown v the Board of Education* of Topeka, Kansas, a case in which the court by a 9–0 vote declared segregation unconstitutional. But there had been many previous years of litigation and court decisions leading up to this moment. The equally important Court insistence that desegregation occur "with all deliberate speed" occurred only a year later. So did the critical Montgomery Bus Boycott, which brought to public attention a young black minister named Martin Luther King, Jr.

Why was most of this history forgotten by so many Americans before the 1960s? The plight of free blacks and their efforts to obtain their civil rights before the Civil War tended to be forgotten amidst the much larger and more basic struggle at that time against slavery. The movement for black civil rights after the Civil War failed, despite the passage of the 13th, 14th, and 15th Amendments to the Constitution during the Reconstruction era; and as was stated in regard to the antiwar movement, we tend to spend more time studying successes than failures. In addition, white America as a whole was racist and did not support equal rights for blacks, either before the Civil War or in the century following it. Indeed, segregation laws and other denials of black civil rights occurred in the North as well as the South before the Civil War, and de facto segregation existed in the North throughout the 20th century. Consequently, there was little interest in the history of the struggle for black civil rights outside of the African American community. Finally, the consensus historians of the early Cold War years tended to downplay if not ignore this struggle, much as they had ignored previous antiwar movements.

The Women's Movement also has a lengthy history in this country. As noted in a previous lecture, it began within the abolitionist movement of the 1830s over the issue of women speaking in public at antislavery rallies and serving in leadership positions. That led to the 1848 Seneca Falls Convention and the birth of the movement for equal rights for women, a movement spearheaded by Elizabeth Cady Stanton, Lucretia Mott, and Susan B. Anthony. The key issue during this time was the right to control their own property and wages, and the right to vote. That struggle would last more than 70 years. During the Reconstruction Era, the Women's Movement pressed for inclusion in the 14th and 15th Amendments that guaranteed black males their rights, but effort was unsuccessful; and throughout the late 19th and early 20th centuries, women pressed to obtain the right to vote. They were finally successful with the passage in 1920 of the 19th Amendment to the Constitution. They also achieved symbolic moves towards equality with the Franklin Roosevelt's appointment of the first female Cabinet member—Frances Perkins as Secretary of Labor—and the political redefinition of the role of First Lady by Eleanor Roosevelt during the 1930s. During World War II, the Women's Auxiliary Corps was established in the Army under a female colonel, Oveta Culp Hobby, and women obtained jobs in a host of occupations previously closed to them and symbolized by Rosie the Riveter.

Why, then, was this history lost in the years following World War II? The situation that women found themselves in during World War II was generally perceived in the country as a temporary aberration caused by the exigencies of war and the temporary removal of millions of men from the workforce for military duty. During the Depression and New Deal, working women were perceived—as they would be again after the war—as taking jobs away from men. In addition to that, the combination of the Great Depression and World War II had led many women to postpone having children; a postponement that ended with the end of World War II and led to the postwar baby boom, and with that baby boom a reassertion of women's "traditional" roles as mother and housekeeper. That reassertion of traditional roles in turn made the previous history of the early Women's Rights Movement appear largely irrelevant.

Why were these three histories rediscovered in the 1960s and 1970s? As with most movements, members of these three movements in the 1960s and 70s searched for a usable past, and they found it in these previous histories. At numerous teach-ins during the 1960s, professors and students challenged the myth of past wartime consensus—and with that myth, implicit attacks on their patriotism—by bringing up these previous antiwar movements as well as challenging the government's version of the history of the Vietnam War. Civil rights activists similarly challenged prevailing racial stereotypes and values: stereotypes of docile and inferior blacks who had always accepted inferior status. Feminists challenged prevailing gender stereotypes and values and the idea that women had in the past docilely accepted their inferior status. That in turn led a new generation of scholars to explore these histories in great depth and to produce a rich literature about them. That in turn has altered our views of American history. It also affected the ensuing development of the antiwar, civil rights and women's movements; movements that are now aware of their past history.

So what we see once again, both in the burying of the history of previous movements and in their rediscovery and expansion, is how the present influences our knowledge and views of the past. The search for what has been labeled a "usable past" often results in a powerful beam lighting up previously neglected history, and in such a way as to alter our view of the past. Women's history, for example, did not even exist as a field of study in the 1960s. That does not mean women did not have a history; of course they did. But it took the modern Women's Movement to rediscover and expand that history.

History in this regard is not an objective and unchanging discipline that studies simply the facts about a dead past. Instead, it is a subjective and constantly evolving study of an alive and constantly changing past that is heavily influenced by the questions each generation asks of it in light of contemporary concerns. As a result, history tells us much about ourselves in the present as well as the past that is being studied.

What about our present belief that the personal computer is the most important invention in U.S. history, if not in world history; that it has ushered in a new era in history; and that the pace of change is accelerating at an unprecedented rate and influencing every aspect of our lives, and not always for the better? Is that true? Ironically, the belief that change is accelerating at an unprecedented rate is itself far from new. Alvin Toffler, in his 1970 book *Future Shock*, propounded such a view many years before the personal computer revolution. In addition, a careful examination of American history reveals a series fundamental technological changes long before the computer, each one considered at the time the most important and consequential in history.

Each of these did produce profound changes in American life, and each was touted at the time as the most important and profound, as well as ushering in change so rapid as to be overwhelming. First, the steamboat in 1807 and the canal boom—3,300 miles of canals by the 1840s—that tremendously sped up transportation and communication. Before this, transportation had been limited by the course of a river, its current, and the inability to move upstream save by rowing or poling. The trip from Pittsburgh to New Orleans, for example, had previously taken one month to get downstream and four months to get back. What did canals do? The 363-mile-long Erie Canal, built between 1817 and 1825, cut the cost of sending a ton of produce from Buffalo to New York City from 20 days to 6, and the cost from $100 a ton to $5 a ton, or from 20–30 cents per ton per mile to 2–3 cents per mile. It also created a direct water route from the Midwest and from the Midwest to New England and northeastern ports with access to European markets. In short, it opened the Midwest to settlement and economic development; and as all of this flowed into New York City, it made New York City the largest city in the United States.

Then came the railroad, the first major improvement in land transportation since the invention of the wheel. Ralph Waldo Emerson, taking his first ride on a train, commented: "distance is annihilated." Railroad construction began in the U.S. in the 1830s and it then exploded: By 1840, there were 3,300 miles of track; by 1850, 8,879; by 1860, 30,000 miles. Beyond transportation and communication, the railroad deeply affected our agriculture, our industry, our westward expansion, our politics, our warfare, our culture, even our language—words such as "sidetracked," "full head of steam," "uncoupled," "railroaded"—and the railroad was perceived as altering everything and creating a new age. Indeed, it even led to the creation of our time zones, which previously had not existed.

The same can be said about mass production, from the first assemblyline factories that begin to replace cottage or household manufacturing, with power-driven machines replacing hand-operated tools. At about the same time came the staggering, almost instant communication of the telegraph, 1844, in Samuel Morse's famous first words tapped out on that instrument, "What Hath God Wrought." Then came the internal combustion engine and the automobile, which had equally if not more profound consequences in each of these areas, as has been previously explored; consequences that, in effect, remade the nation. Then came the airplane, which first revolutionized warfare, and then domestic and international travel and trade. Then nuclear weapons and power, which transformed warfare, technology, values, and culture in ways we are still trying to understand.

So is the computer any different, or is it just another major change, and perhaps one not nearly as significant and altering as these earlier ones? Imagine for a moment a man who had been born on a Midwestern farm between 1835 and 1840 and who lived into his mid-to-late 80s. Think about the incredibly dramatic and life-altering changes he experienced. As a child or teenager, he would have seen and perhaps experienced his first railroad, and would have been staggered by its speed much as Emerson was. He might have also visited the local telegraph office and been astounded by this near-instant communication. As a young man in his 20s, he would have fought in the Civil War and thereby experienced what many historians consider the first modern and total war. As a young married man, he then would have experienced the industrial revolution, first on his own farm in terms of mechanization and transportation, and then in all likelihood in the city into which he moved; perhaps Chicago, which had hardly existed when he was born. Whether out of choice or necessity given the plight of American farmers at that time, he would probably become an urban dweller. That industrial revolution and the move to the city would dramatically transform virtually every aspect of his life.

By the end of the century or the beginning of the next, he and his children would probably be using a telephone and have seen an automobile; by the

1920s, they would have been able to purchase one. That would transform his life and the life of his family even further. So would a host of new devices that could purchased and run by electricity in his home. Of course, that included the radio by which he now received his news and entertainment. He would also see with the Wright Brothers success, and be staggered by, the airplane; the fulfillment of a dream as old as human history: the ability to fly like a bird. He would have also seen—and perhaps his grandchildren would have fought in—the largest and most costly war in human history; what they thought and hoped would be "the war to end all wars," World War I.

Are we really experiencing technological changes more rapid, dramatic, and life-transforming than this individual did? Or is the belief that we are a distortion or a conceit caused by our ignorance of history, or by the syndrome known as "tunnel vision" whereby the past right in front of us as we enter a tunnel appears longer and more important than the bulk of the tunnel, in this case the entire past before we were born? This is a common human trait that can be overcome only by a knowledge of history, and an understanding of its complexities that this course has hopefully provided.

Does all of this mean I and other historians think history does repeat itself after all, and that the present offers nothing new? Not at all. History does not repeat itself, save perhaps in terms of the emotions that drive human beings to behave in certain ways—love, anger, fear—and thus there is repetition in terms of patterns of human behavior. But history never repeats itself in terms of events. Each event is unique, as is each era in human history, and as is each new interpretation of the past that arises within each era. Historical interpretation is always linked to specific eras.

Always try, as we did especially in the lecture on the causes of the Civil War, to think of history as neither a single straight line or as a circle—the two most common methods of viewing the past—but instead as a spiral. Remember that I suggested visualizing such a spiral with a classroom blackboard as the event and time as three-dimensional and running to the back of the room and beyond. Via this analogy, we are separate from all past events and thus unique; but we are also linked to them in a multidimensional time stream of which we are a part. Being linked, we simultaneously see that history did not begin with us and will not end with us either.

This course has discussed only some of the many myths that abound in U.S. history. I hope you have gained facts and insights you did not have before, and that it has encouraged you to be a skeptic yourself, to challenge other historical myths, and to search for the truth behind those myths. But the search for the truth is quite different from the claim to have found it. "Keep the company of those who seek the truth," Czech President Vaclav Havel once said; "run from those who have found it." That is appropriate advice for all people, but especially for those who study history; for as we've seen repeatedly—though perhaps most clearly in the lecture on the causes of the Civil War—historical truth changes over time as new events lead to new questions and new interpretations of the past. History is an interpretive discipline in which we try to understand not only the past but also the present by looking into the past. But as the present changes with the passage of time, our concerns change, and with them what is considered the "truth" about history.

My interpretations in this course are as time-bound as any others we have discussed; so if you take a skeptic's approach to history yourself, you may very well challenge some of the interpretations I have presented in my effort to counter some of the myths of U.S. history. If you do not, in all likelihood your children, grandchildren and their teachers almost certainly will. There is always new and different light to cast on the past.

Bibliography

Adams, Michael C. C. *The Best War Ever: America and World War II.* Baltimore: The Johns Hopkins University Press, 1994. Adams identifies and attacks many myths regarding the United States and World War II.

Allen, Frederick Lewis. *Only Yesterday: An Informal History of the 1920s.* New York: Harper Collins, 2000. First published in 1931, this popular history helped to establish the standard interpretation of the 1920s.

Bailyn, Bernard. *The Ideological Origins of the American Revolution.* Cambridge: Harvard University Press, 1967, 1992. This pathbreaking book played a major role in refocusing historical study of the Revolution back to ideas. It won both the Pulitzer and the Bancroft prizes and was republished in an enlarged edition in 1992.

Beisner, Robert. *From the Old Diplomacy to the New, 1865–1900.* 2nd ed. Arlington Heights, IL: Harlan Davidson, 1986. This is a brief and useful introduction to the events and historical interpretations of late-19th-century American foreign relations.

Blum, John M. *Woodrow Wilson and the Politics of Morality.* Boston: Little, Brown, 1956. This brief but insightful biography is highly critical of Wilson.

Buhite, Russell D., ed. *Call to Arms: Presidential Speeches, Messages and Declarations of War.* Lanham, MD: Rowman and Littlefield, 2003. This valuable collection provides a fascinating and informative view of the official reasons U.S. presidents from John Adams to George W. Bush have given for both requesting congressional declarations of war and justifying specific military actions.

Chernow, Ron. *Alexander Hamilton.* New York: Penguin, 2004. A recent full-length biography.

————. *Washington: A Life.* New York: Penguin, 2010. A recent and highly regarded full biography.

Clausewitz, Carl von. *On War*, edited and translated by Michael Howard and Peter Paret. Princeton, NJ: Princeton University Press, 1976. Although written in the early 19th century by a Prussian military officer and not revised before his untimely death, this volume is generally considered the most insightful, important, and influential analysis of the nature of war ever written. One of its emphases is the relationship of war to political goals. This particular edition contains three outstanding introductory essays by the editors and Bernard Brodie on the genesis, influence, and continued relevance of the work.

Cooper, John M. *Woodrow Wilson: A Biography.* New York: Alfred A. Knopf, 2009. The most recent and best full biography of Wilson available. It strongly defends Wilson.

Dangerfield, George. *The Era of Good Feelings.* Chicago: Ivan R. Dee, 1989. First published in 1952, this prize-winning history of the years between the Jefferson and Jackson presidencies provides extensive and excellent information on John Quincy Adams as diplomat and president.

Ellis, Joseph J. *American Sphinx: The Character of Thomas Jefferson.* New York: Random House, 1996. Winner of the National Book Award, this volume focuses on Jefferson's contradictions and inconsistencies.

———. *Founding Brothers: The Revolutionary Generation.* New York: Random House, 2000. This Pulitzer Prize–winning volume offers insightful analyses of Hamilton and Jefferson, as well as five other major political figures of this era and a good introduction to their conflicts.

———. *His Excellency: George Washington.* New York: Random House (Knopf), 2004. This brief biography focuses on Washington's character and personality, as well as his numerous accomplishments.

Fink, Leon, ed. *Major Problems in the Gilded Age and the Progressive Era.* 2nd ed. Boston: Cengage, 2001. This collection of primary and secondary sources provides a useful introduction to these two eras and their numerous historical interpretations.

Bibliography

Franklin, John Hope, and Evelyn Brooks Higginbotham. *From Slavery to Freedom: A History of African Americans.* 9th ed. New York: McGraw-Hill, 2010. First published in 1947 and written by the recently deceased Franklin, one of the most revered and honored figures in the historical profession, this has long been the preeminent text for African American history.

Gaddis, John L. *Strategies of Containment: A Critical Appraisal of American National Security Policy during the Cold War.* Rev. and exp. ed. New York: Oxford University Press, 2005. Cold War senior scholar Gaddis explores the different types of containment that the United States used throughout the Cold War.

Goodwyn, Lawrence. *The Populist Moment: A Short History of the Agrarian Revolt in America.* New York: Oxford University Press, 1978. This major and overall positive reinterpretation of the Populists is a condensation of Goodwyn's longer *Democratic Promise: The Populist Moment in America* (New York: Oxford University Press, 1976).

Hamilton, Alexander, James Madison, and John Jay. *The Federalist Papers.* New York: Bantam Books, 1982. First published in 1787–1788 as part of an effort to convince New Yorkers to vote in favor of the Constitution, these 85 essays are pivotal to understanding that document and are considered by many to be the most important works of political theory in U.S. history. Numerous editions are available. This particular one is inexpensive and contains an introduction and commentary by Garry Wills.

Heilbroner, Robert L. *The Worldly Philosophers: The Lives, Times and Ideas of the Great Economic Thinkers.* Rev. 7th ed. New York: Touchstone/Simon and Schuster, 1999. First published in 1953, this best-selling classic provides an excellent introduction to the most important economic theorists and their ideas from the 18th through the 20th centuries.

Herring, George C. *America's Longest War: The United States and Vietnam, 1950–1975.* 4th ed. Boston: McGraw-Hill, 2002. This remains one of the best and most comprehensive histories of the Vietnam War.

Hofstadter, Richard. *The Age of Reform: From Bryan to F.D.R.* New York: Alfred A. Knopf, 1955. An influential historian of the 1950s and 1960s, Hofstadter, in this Pulitzer Prize–winning volume and other works, such as *The Paranoid Style in American Politics* (New York: Alfred A. Knopf, 1965), sharply criticizes and attacks the Populists as irrational reactionaries rather than true reformers.

Howe, Daniel W. *What Hath God Wrought: The Transformation of America, 1815–1848.* New York: Oxford University Press, 2007. This Pulitzer Prize–winning book offers comprehensive coverage of all aspects of American life during the years 1815–1848.

Kennedy, David. *Freedom from Fear: The American People in Depression and War, 1929–1945.* New York: Oxford University Press, 1999. In this Pulitzer Prize–winning volume, Kennedy provides a superbly researched and written account of the Great Depression, the New Deal, and World War II. The work is also available in two separate volumes, one on the New Deal and one on World War II.

LaFeber, Walter. *America, Russia and the Cold War, 1945–2006.* 10th ed. New York: McGraw-Hill, 2006. First published in 1966 and now in its 10th revised edition, this volume, by one of the foremost U.S. diplomatic historians, provides an excellent introduction to the entire Cold War. It has long been a standard text in college courses.

Leffler, Melvyn P. *For the Soul of Mankind: The United States, the Soviet Union, and the Cold War.* New York: Hill and Wang, 2007. In this work, senior Cold War scholar Leffler offers a wide-ranging analysis of Cold War origins, why the conflict lasted so long, and how and why it finally came to an end.

McCullough, David. *John Adams.* New York: Simon and Schuster, 2001. This Pulitzer Prize–winning and popular biography helped to restore Adams as one of the major figures of the Revolutionary era.

McMahon, Robert, ed. *Major Problems in the History of the Vietnam War: Documents and Essays.* 4th ed. Boston: Cengage, 2010. This volume presents key primary and secondary sources on the most debated and important aspects of the Vietnam War.

McPherson, James M. *Battle Cry of Freedom: The Civil War Era.* New York: Oxford University Press, 1988. This Pulitzer Prize–winning work remains the basic single volume on the causes and conduct of the Civil War.

—. *Tried by War: Abraham Lincoln as Commander in Chief.* New York: Penguin, 2008. This volume examines the process by which Lincoln came to understand the relationship of battles to politics, as well as the appropriate grand strategy for the Union, and his emergence as what the author considers the nation's greatest commander in chief.

Meacham, Jon. *American Lion: Andrew Jackson in the White House.* New York: Random House, 2008. Winner of the Pulitzer Prize, this recent biography focuses on Jackson's personal life, as well as his numerous and controversial actions as president.

Middlekauff, Robert. *The Glorious Cause: The American Revolution, 1763–1789.* Rev. and exp. ed. New York: Oxford University Press, 2007. A Pulitzer Prize finalist, this critically acclaimed work provides a recent and highly readable analysis of the Revolutionary era from the end of the French and Indian War through ratification of the Constitution.

Morgan, Edmund S. *The Puritan Dilemma: The Story of John Winthrop.* Boston: Little, Brown, 1958. Despite its age, this brief volume remains an excellent introduction not only to the first governor of the Massachusetts Bay colony but also to Puritan religious beliefs and conflicts.

Morison, Samuel E., Frederick Merk, and Frank Freidel. *Dissent in Three American Wars.* Cambridge, MA: Harvard University Press, 1970. Written in the midst of the Vietnam War, this volume by three eminent historians explores antiwar movements during the War of 1812 and the 1846–1848 war with Mexico, as well as opposition to the war against Philippine insurgents that followed the 1898 war with Spain and acquisition of the archipelago. It offers a classic case of rediscovered history in the search for a "usable past."

Paterson, Thomas G., et al. *American Foreign Relations: A History*. 7th ed., 2 vols. Boston: Wadsworth/Cengage, 2010. This excellent textbook contains up-to-date and useful analyses of both the actual and the official reasons for American wars and military actions throughout U.S. history.

Perman, Michael, and Amy M. Taylor, eds. *Major Problems in the Civil War and Reconstruction*. 3rd ed. Boston: Wadsworth/Cengage, 2011. This collection of primary and secondary sources provides a useful introduction to the numerous interpretations regarding the Civil War and Reconstruction.

Pogue, Forrest C. *George C. Marshall*. 4 vols. New York: The Viking Press, 1963–1987. The official biography of Marshall, as well as the most accurate and comprehensive.

Reardon, Carol. *Pickett's Charge in History and Memory*. Chapel Hill: University of North Carolina Press, 1999. Reardon traces and analyzes the history of this battle and the historical memories of it. The two are related but, as she emphasizes, very different.

Salvatore, Nick. *Eugene V. Debs: Citizen and Socialist*. 2nd ed. Urbana and Chicago: University of Illinois Press, 1984. An award-winning biography of one of the major American labor leaders and Socialist Party political figures of the late 19th and early 20th centuries.

Sitkoff, Harvard, ed. *Fifty Years Later: The New Deal Evaluated*. Philadelphia: Temple University Press, 1985. The nine essays in this volume provide excellent assessments by different historians of the impact of the New Deal on different aspects of American life. The essays are revised and expanded versions of papers originally presented at a 1983 symposium at the University of New Hampshire.

Stampp, Kenneth M., ed. *Causes of the Civil War*. 3rd rev. ed. New York: Touchstone/Simon and Schuster, 1991. This collection of both primary and secondary sources provides a useful introduction to the numerous interpretations of the war's causes.

Stephanson, Anders. *Manifest Destiny: American Expansionism and the Empire of Right.* New York: Hill and Wang, 1995. This brief volume analyzes the role of exceptionalism as a driving force in the history of American expansionism.

Stoler, Mark A. *George C. Marshall: Soldier-Statesman of the American Century.* Boston: Twayne, 1989. This brief biography offers an introduction to both Marshall and the rise of the United States as a world power during his lifetime. For greater detail on Marshall, see Pogue's four-volume biography cited above.

Tocqueville, Alexis de. *Democracy in America*, translated and edited with an introduction by Harvey C. Mansfield and Delba Winthrop. Chicago: University of Chicago Press, 2002. Originally published in French and in two volumes in 1835 and 1840, this classic work is based on the author's nine-month sojourn in the United States during 1833. It is generally considered one of the most important and insightful texts on the United States during this period and in general.

Tyler, Alice Felt. *Freedom's Ferment: Phases of American Social History to 1860.* Minneapolis: University of Minnesota Press, 1944. Despite its age, this volume remains important for its comprehensive and valuable coverage of American religion, communal experiments, and reform movements during the first half of the 19th century.

Ward, John W. *Andrew Jackson: Symbol for an Age.* New York: Oxford University Press, 1962. The author analyzes how and why Jackson became a symbol of his time and its values.

Weinberg, Gerhard L. "Some Myths of World War II." *Journal of Military History* 75, no. 3 (July 2011): 701–718. Written by the dean of World War II scholars, this essay identifies and attacks a series of World War II myths. Weinberg identifies and attacks even more of them in his monumental *A World at Arms: A Global History of World War II* (New York: Cambridge University Press, 1994).

Westad, Orde Arne. *The Global Cold War: Third World Interventions and the Making of Our Time.* New York: Cambridge University Press, 2007. This award-winning book focuses on the globalization of the Cold War and its impact on the Third World.

Wilentz, Sean. *Andrew Jackson.* New York: Henry Holt, 2005. In this brief volume, the author portrays Jackson as a product of his time and a Democrat, despite behavior that is not considered democratic today.

Williams, William A. *The Tragedy of American Diplomacy.* 2nd rev. and enlarged ed. New York: Dell Publishing Co., 1972, Norton reprint, 1988. First published in 1959, this highly influential reinterpretation emphasizes the economic and informally imperial nature of 20th-century American diplomacy stemming from the Open Door Notes of 1899–1900.

Wills, Garry. *Cincinnatus: George Washington and the Enlightenment.* New York: Doubleday, 1984. Wills places Washington's character and values within the context and values of his time, as exemplified in his resignation as commander in chief of the Continental Army, his role at the Constitutional Convention, and his decision to retire after two terms as president.

Wilson, Joan Hoff. *Herbert Hoover: Forgotten Progressive.* Boston: Little, Brown, 1975. This volume provides a brief reinterpretation of Hoover as a Progressive.

Wood, Gordon S. *The Creation of the American Republic, 1776–1787.* Chapel Hill: University of North Carolina Press, 1969. This major and highly regarded interpretive work focuses on the beliefs and ideas that led many of the Revolutionary generation to favor establishing a strong central government as the only way to preserve American liberty.

Woodward, C. Vann. *Tom Watson: Agrarian Rebel.* New York: Macmillan Publishing Company, 1938. This classic biography of one of the major Populist figures in the South was written by one of the most influential U.S. historians of the 20th century.